First World War
and Army of Occupation
War Diary
France, Belgium and Germany

46 DIVISION
Divisional Troops
Monmouthshire Regiment (Territorial Force)
1st Battalion Pioneers
1 September 1915 - 22 July 1919

WO95/2679/1

The Naval & Military Press Ltd
www.nmarchive.com
Published in association with The National Archives

Published by

The Naval & Military Press Ltd

Unit 10 Ridgewood Industrial Park,

Uckfield, East Sussex,

TN22 5QE England

Tel: +44 (0) 1825 749494

www.naval-military-press.com

www.nmarchive.com

This diary has been reprinted in facsimile from the original. Any imperfections are inevitably reproduced and the quality may fall short of modern type and cartographic standards.

© Crown Copyright
Images reproduced by permission of The National Archives, London, England, 2015.

Contents

Document type	Place/Title	Date From	Date To
Heading	WO95/2679/1 1 Battalion Monmouthshire Regiment		
Heading	46th Division. 1st Monmouths Vol V Sept 15		
Heading	War Diary 1/1th Moumouthshire Regt. From 1st September 1915 to 30th September 1915		
War Diary	Locre	01/09/1915	03/09/1915
War Diary	Reninghelst	04/09/1915	06/09/1915
War Diary	Headqrs at Reninghelst	07/09/1915	07/09/1915
War Diary	3 Companies an Dugouts In Ypres Salient	08/09/1915	08/09/1915
War Diary	1. Co. at rest at Headqrs.	09/09/1915	13/09/1915
War Diary	Headqrs near Reninghelst	14/09/1915	14/09/1915
War Diary	3 Compaines in Dugouts In Ypres Salient.	15/09/1915	15/09/1915
War Diary	1. Co. at test at Headqrs.	16/09/1915	20/09/1915
War Diary	Battn Headqrs Reninghelst map reference G29. C 8.8. (Sheet 28. NW Belgium)	21/09/1915	30/09/1915
Miscellaneous	1st Batt Monmouthshire Regt.	02/09/1915	02/09/1915
Miscellaneous	Extract from 84th Infantry Brigade Routine Orders dated 2nd Sept 1915	02/09/1915	02/09/1915
Miscellaneous	1st Batt Monmouthshire Regt. Appendix I		
Miscellaneous	Perforated Sheet giving detail of personnel and horses wanting to complete, shown on Army Form B.213		
Miscellaneous	Field Return	19/04/1915	19/04/1915
Miscellaneous	Field Return	12/04/1915	12/04/1915
Miscellaneous	Perforated Sheet giving detail of personnel and horses wanting to complete, shown on Army Form B.213		
Miscellaneous	Field Return	05/09/1915	05/09/1915
Miscellaneous	Perforated Sheet giving detail of personnel and horses wanting to complete, shown on Army Form B.213	05/09/1915	05/09/1915
Miscellaneous	Field Return	26/09/1915	26/09/1915
Miscellaneous	Perforated Sheet giving detail of personnel and horses wanting to complete, shown on Army Form B.213	26/09/1915	26/09/1915
Heading	46th Division. 1/1 Monmouths Shire Rgt. Oct & Nov & Dec Vol VI-VII		
War Diary	Reninghelst	01/10/1915	02/10/1915
War Diary	Bas Rieux	03/10/1915	06/10/1915
War Diary	Fourquerail	07/10/1915	12/10/1915
War Diary	Vermelles	12/10/1915	22/10/1915
War Diary	St. Saveur	23/10/1915	25/10/1915
War Diary	Drouvin	25/10/1915	03/11/1915
War Diary	Les 8 Maisons	04/11/1915	03/12/1915
War Diary	Caudescure	04/12/1915	09/12/1915
Miscellaneous	1/1st Monmouth Regt		
War Diary	Les & Maisons	01/12/1915	03/12/1915
War Diary	Caudescure	04/12/1915	18/12/1915
War Diary	Haverskerque	19/12/1915	24/12/1915
War Diary	In Train	25/12/1915	26/12/1915
War Diary	Marseilles	27/12/1915	31/12/1915
Heading	1/1st Bn Monmiounthshire Regt. T.F. War Diary For January & February 1916		
War Diary	Marseilles	01/01/1916	06/01/1916
War Diary	S/s Anchises	07/01/1916	07/01/1916

Diagram etc	Map. After 1.125,000 Sheet North 17-96/1-IV		
War Diary	S/s Anchises At Sea	08/01/1916	12/01/1916
War Diary	Alexandria	13/01/1916	13/01/1916
War Diary	Serapeum	14/01/1916	14/01/1916
War Diary	Shallufa	15/01/1916	30/01/1916
War Diary	Alexandria	31/01/1916	05/02/1916
War Diary	Atsea S/S Megantic	06/02/1916	07/02/1916
War Diary	Marseilles	08/02/1916	11/02/1916
War Diary	Brucamps	11/02/1916	28/02/1916
War Diary	Candas	29/02/1916	29/02/1916
Heading	War Diary of 1/1st. Bn Monmouthshire Regt. T.F. For Month Of March 1916		
War Diary	Candas	01/03/1916	05/03/1916
War Diary	Etree Wamin	06/03/1916	08/03/1916
War Diary	Maizieres	09/03/1916	10/03/1916
War Diary	Ecoivres	11/03/1916	11/03/1916
War Diary	Neuville St Vaast	12/03/1916	31/03/1916
Heading	War Diary of 1/1st Batt The Monmouthshire Regt. T.F. from 1st April 1916 To 30th April 1916		
War Diary	Neuville St. Vaast	01/04/1916	21/04/1916
War Diary	ACQ	22/04/1916	22/04/1916
War Diary	Tilloy-Les-Nermaville	23/04/1916	28/04/1916
War Diary	Agnieres	29/04/1916	30/04/1916
Heading	War Diary of 1/1st Batt The Monmouthshire Regt T.F. from 1st May 1916 To 31st May 1916 Vol 12		
War Diary	Agnieres	01/05/1916	04/05/1916
War Diary	Maizieres	05/05/1916	05/05/1916
War Diary	Maizieres Beaudricourt	06/05/1916	06/05/1916
War Diary	Pommier	07/05/1916	31/05/1916
Miscellaneous	Appendix No. 1. Wire received from General Officers Commanding, 46th Division.		
Heading	War Diary of 1/1st Battalion The Monmouthshire Regt. from 1st june 1916 to 30th june 1916 vol 13		
War Diary	Pommier	01/06/1916	09/06/1916
War Diary	HQ Pommier Coys At Fonqueviller	10/06/1916	12/06/1916
War Diary	H.Q. at Pommier. Companies At Fonquevillers	13/06/1916	20/06/1916
War Diary	M.O. Pommier Coys At Fonquevillers	20/06/1916	22/06/1916
War Diary	Pas Huts	23/06/1916	24/06/1916
War Diary	Pas	24/06/1916	29/06/1916
War Diary	Fonquevillers	30/06/1916	30/06/1916
War Diary	Pommier	15/06/1916	15/06/1916
War Diary	Pas	25/06/1916	25/06/1916
Miscellaneous	46th Division. T.M.N. 800/8	05/08/1916	05/08/1916
Heading	War Diary of 1/1st Batt. The Monmouthshire Regiment From 1st July To 31st July 1916 Inclusive Vol 14		
War Diary	Fonquevillers	01/07/1916	01/07/1916
War Diary	Pommier	02/07/1916	02/07/1916
War Diary	La Cauchie	03/07/1916	03/07/1916
War Diary	Berles-Au-Bois D. Coy At Lacauchie	04/07/1916	23/07/1916
War Diary	La Cauchie	24/07/1916	24/07/1916
War Diary	Berles-Au-Bois	25/07/1916	26/07/1916
War Diary	Lacauchie	24/07/1916	24/07/1916
War Diary	Berles-Au-Bois	26/07/1916	31/07/1916
War Diary	Berles-Au-Bois	05/07/1916	05/07/1916
War Diary	Lacauchie	24/07/1916	24/07/1916

Heading	War Diary 1st. Batt. The Monmouthshire Regt. T.F. 1st August 1916 To 31st August 1916 Vol 15		
War Diary	Berles-Au-Bois	01/08/1916	31/08/1916
Heading	War Diary for September 1916 of 1/1st Bn. Monmouth Rgt.		
Miscellaneous	46th Division.	04/10/1916	04/10/1916
Heading	War Diary 1/1st Batt The Monmouthshire Regiment T.F. 1st September 1916 To 30th September 1916 Vol 16		
War Diary	Berles-Au-Bois	01/09/1916	30/09/1916
Heading	War Diary 1st Monmouthshire Regiment. T.F. 1st October 1916 To 31st October 1916 Vol 17		
War Diary	Berles Au-Bois	01/10/1916	31/10/1916
Heading	1st Monmouthshire Regiment T.F. November 1st 1916 To November 30th 1916 Vol 18		
War Diary	Berles Au-Bois	01/11/1916	09/11/1916
War Diary	Humbercourt	10/11/1916	10/11/1916
War Diary	Caours	11/11/1916	23/11/1916
War Diary	Mezerolles	24/11/1916	25/11/1916
War Diary	Lucheux	26/11/1916	30/11/1916
War Diary	Appendix I Speech By Gen. Sir. E. Allenby K.C.B. G.O.C. 3rd Army To The Officers Of The Battalion.		
Heading	1st Monmouthshire Regiment T.F. December 1st 1916 To December 31st 1916 Vol 19		
War Diary	Lucheux	01/12/1916	05/12/1916
War Diary	Souastre	06/12/1916	31/12/1916
War Diary	Appendix I		
Heading	1st Batt. Monmouthshire Regiment T.F. January 1st 1917 To January 31st 1917 Vol 20		
War Diary	Souastre	01/01/1917	31/01/1917
Heading	1st Batt. Monmouthshire Regiment T.F. February 1st 1917 To February 28th 1917 Vol 21		
War Diary	Souastre	01/02/1917	19/02/1917
War Diary	Fosseux	20/02/1917	21/02/1917
War Diary	Arras	22/02/1917	28/02/1917
Heading	1st Monmouthshire Regiment T.F. March 1st 1917 To March 31st 1917 Vol 22		
War Diary	Bienvillers	01/03/1917	11/03/1917
War Diary	Hebutern	11/03/1917	21/03/1917
War Diary	Couin	22/03/1917	23/03/1917
War Diary	Bertrancourt	24/03/1917	24/03/1917
War Diary	Lealvillers	25/03/1917	25/03/1917
War Diary	Villers-Bocage	26/03/1917	26/03/1917
War Diary	Ferriers	27/03/1917	29/03/1917
War Diary	Ecquedecques	30/03/1917	31/03/1917
War Diary	Complementary Letter Received From G.O.C. 46th Division.		
Heading	1st Batt Monmouthshire Regiment T.F. April 1st 1917 To April 30th 1917 Vol 23		
War Diary	Ecquedecques	01/04/1917	13/04/1917
War Diary	Houdain	14/04/1917	14/04/1917
War Diary	Ecoivres	15/04/1917	15/04/1917
War Diary	St. Aubin	16/04/1917	20/04/1917
War Diary	Boyeffles Bovigny	21/04/1917	30/04/1917
Heading	1st Batt The Monmouthshire Regiment. T.F. May 1st 1917 To May 31st 1917 Vol 24		

War Diary	Bouvigny-Boyeffles	01/05/1917	31/05/1917
Heading	War Diary 1st Batt. Monmouthshire Regiment T.F. June 1st 1917 To June 31st 1917 Vol 25		
War Diary	Bouvigny Boyeffles	01/06/1917	30/06/1917
Miscellaneous	Appendix 2. Copy of memo received from G.O.C. 46th Division. on June. 11st 1917	11/06/1917	11/06/1917
Miscellaneous	Appendix I Copy of. memo received from Major E.A. Lewis D.S.O. Commanding Divisional Signal Company.	10/06/1917	10/06/1917
Map	Lens (2)		
Map	First Army Front 3		
Map	Lens (2)		
Map	La Folie		
Heading	1st Battalion The Monmouthshire Regiment. T.F. July 1st 1917 To July 31st 1917 Vol 26		
War Diary		01/07/1917	01/07/1917
War Diary	Fosse 10	02/07/1917	06/07/1917
War Diary	Ourton	06/07/1917	16/07/1917
War Diary	Mazingarbe	17/07/1917	31/07/1917
Heading	O/C 1st Monmouths Appendix I		
War Diary	Summary of Events for July 1917		
Heading	1st Battalion The Monmouthshire Regiment. T.F. August 1st 1917 To August 31st 1917 Vol 27		
Miscellaneous	Appendix I, O/C 1st Monmouthshire Regt.	11/08/1917	11/08/1917
War Diary	Mazingarbe	01/08/1917	30/08/1917
War Diary	Sailly	30/08/1917	31/08/1917
Heading	1st Battalion The Monmouthshire Regiment T.F. September 1st 1917 To September 30th 1917 Vol 28		
War Diary	Sailly-Laborse	01/09/1917	30/09/1917
Miscellaneous	Summary Of Events For August 1917		
Miscellaneous	Summary Of Events For September 1917		
Heading	1st Battalion The Monmouthshire Regiment T.F. October 1st 1917 To October 31st 1917 Vol 29		
War Diary	Sailly Laborse	01/10/1917	31/10/1917
Heading	1st Battalion The Monmouthshire Regiment T.F. November 1st 1917 To November 30th 1917 Vol 30		
War Diary	Sailly-Laborse	01/11/1917	30/11/1917
Heading	1st Batt The Monmouthshire Regt. T.F. December 1st To December 31st 1917 Vol 31		
War Diary	Sailly Labourse	01/12/1917	31/12/1917
Heading	1st Batt The Monmouthshire Regt. T.F. January 1st 1918 To January 31st 1918 Vol 32		
War Diary	Sailly Labourse	01/01/1918	23/01/1918
War Diary	Bethune	23/01/1918	24/01/1918
War Diary	Bellerive	25/01/1918	31/01/1918
Miscellaneous	Battalion 23/1/1918 O/C 1st Monmouthshire Regt.	23/01/1918	23/01/1918
Heading	1st Batt The Monmouthshire Regiment T.F. February 1st 1918 To February 28th 1918 Vol 33		
War Diary	Hinges	01/02/1918	09/02/1918
War Diary	Labeuvriere	10/02/1918	14/02/1918
War Diary	Bethune	15/02/1918	26/02/1918
War Diary	Lapugnoy	27/02/1918	28/02/1918
Miscellaneous	Appendix I.		
Heading	1st Batt The Monmouthshire Regt. T.F. March 1st 1918 To March 31st 1918. Vol 34		
War Diary	Lapugnoy	01/03/1918	06/03/1918

War Diary	Beuvry	07/03/1918	12/03/1918
War Diary	Sailly-Labourse	13/03/1918	27/03/1918
War Diary	Noeux-Les-Mines.	27/03/1918	29/03/1918
War Diary	Bully-Grenay	30/03/1918	31/03/1918
Miscellaneous	Appendix I		
Heading	46th Divisional Pioneers 1st Battalion Monmouthshire Regiment (Pioneers) April 1918		
Heading	1st Batt The Monmouthshire Regt. T.F. April 1st 1918 To April 30th 1918 Vol 35		
War Diary	Maroc	08/04/1918	11/04/1918
War Diary	Maroc	01/04/1918	12/04/1918
War Diary	Hersin	13/04/1918	13/04/1918
War Diary	Bruay	14/04/1918	23/04/1918
War Diary	Bethune	24/04/1918	30/04/1918
Heading	1st Batt The Monmouthshire Regt. T.F. May 1st 1918 to May 31st 1918 Vol 36		
War Diary	Bethune	01/05/1918	31/05/1918
Heading	1st Batt The Monmouthshire Regt. T.F. June 1st 1918 To June 30th 1918 Vol 37		
War Diary	Bethune	01/06/1918	30/06/1918
Heading	1st Batt. The Monmouthshire Regt. T.F. July 1st 1918 To July 31st 1918 Vol 38		
War Diary	Bethune	01/07/1918	31/07/1918
Heading	1st Batt The Monmouthshire Regt. T.F. August 1st 1918 To August 31st 1918 Vol 39		
War Diary	Bethune	01/08/1918	31/08/1918
Heading	War Diary 1/1st Batt The Monmouthshire Regt. T.F. 1st September 1918 To 30th September 1918 Vol 40		
War Diary	Bethune	01/09/1918	11/09/1918
War Diary	Lapugnoy	12/09/1918	12/09/1918
War Diary	Lahoussoye	13/09/1918	18/09/1918
War Diary	Sheet France 629. (Q 33C)	19/09/1918	20/09/1918
War Diary	(Q33c) Sheet France 62C	20/09/1918	21/09/1918
War Diary	Vendelles	22/09/1918	28/09/1918
War Diary	G.32.d.45.80	29/09/1918	29/09/1918
War Diary	G.33.6.05.80	29/09/1918	30/09/1918
Miscellaneous	Account Of The Part Taken By The 1/1st Batt Monmouthshire Regiment. In the Battles Of Bellenglise, Ramicourt, & Sequehart.	27/09/1918	27/09/1918
Heading	War Diary 1/1st Batt The Monmouthshire Regt T.F. 1st October 1918 To 31st October 1918 Vol 41		
War Diary	G27d 1.6	01/10/1918	03/10/1918
War Diary	G 16 C Railway Cutting	04/10/1918	04/10/1918
War Diary	Nauroy G 17	05/10/1918	05/10/1918
War Diary	G 20 B 6.5	06/10/1916	07/10/1916
War Diary	H.33d 3.7	08/10/1918	10/10/1918
War Diary	Mericourt	11/10/1918	13/10/1918
War Diary	Fresnoy Le Grand	14/10/1918	31/10/1918
Heading	1/1st Batt The Monmouthshire Regt T.F. Nov 1st 1918 To Nov 30th 1918 Vol 42		
War Diary	Bohain	01/11/1918	03/11/1918
War Diary	L'Arbre De Guise	04/11/1918	05/11/1918
War Diary	La Groise	06/11/1916	06/11/1916
War Diary	Prisches	07/11/1918	08/11/1918
War Diary	Cartigny	09/11/1918	12/11/1918
War Diary	Avesnes	13/11/1918	13/11/1918

War Diary	Bousies	14/11/1918	30/11/1918
Heading	1/1st Batt The Monmouthshire Regt. T.F. 1st December To 31st December 1918 Vol 43		
War Diary	Bousies	01/12/1918	31/12/1918
Miscellaneous	General Review Of Situation Of The Battalion On 31/12/18	31/12/1918	31/12/1918
War Diary	Bousies	01/01/1919	20/02/1919
War Diary	Montay	21/02/1919	28/02/1919
Miscellaneous	46th. Div. Packet.	05/04/1919	05/04/1919
War Diary	Montay	01/03/1919	04/03/1919
War Diary	Troisvilles	05/03/1919	31/03/1919
Heading	1/1 Monmouthshire Rgt Vol 47 War Diary For April 1919 1/1st Bn The Monmouthshire Regt T.F. Vol 47		
War Diary	Troisvilles	01/04/1919	30/04/1919
Miscellaneous	46th Divisional Packet.	04/06/1919	04/06/1919
War Diary	Troisvilles	01/05/1919	31/05/1919
Miscellaneous	46th Div. Packet.	21/07/1919	21/07/1919
Miscellaneous	46th Divisional Packet	02/07/1919	02/07/1919
War Diary	Troisvilles	01/06/1919	25/06/1919
War Diary	Caudry	26/06/1919	22/07/1919

WO/45/2679/1

1 Battaglia Manorthisima Raparea

121/6930.

P/446

46th Division

1st Monmouths

Vol X

Sep 15

Confidential

War Diary

of

1/1st Monmouthshire Regt.

From 1st September 1915 to 30th September 1915

Army Form C. 2118.

WAR DIARY
or
INTELLIGENCE SUMMARY.
(Erase heading not required.)

Instructions regarding War Diaries and Intelligence Summaries are contained in F.S. Regs., Part II and the Staff Manual respectively. Title pages will be prepared in manuscript.

Hour, Date, Place	Summary of Events and Information	Remarks and references to Appendices
1915 Sept. 1st LOCRE	C.O. & Cantor B. Co. visited A.Co. in SP 8 & SP 9. A good bit of shelling during the day.	
Sept 2nd	Orders received that the Battn would be transferred from the 28th Divn to the 46th Divn & then to take place tomorrow. General Bulfin gave 28th Divn in which the officers in afternoon to say goodbye to the Battn. A battn parade was ordered but cancelled owing to wet weather. Gunning SP 8 & SP 9 returned in evening. Heavy shelling during day. Casualties. 1 man killed SP 8. All detached details rejoined Battn during night preparatory to moving.	Appendix I (a) General Bulfin's words to officers AH I (b) Extract from 20th Sept 1915 on Sept [unclear] Sept.
Sept 3rd	Move to REMING HERST. The II Corps commander [unclear] in Chester Ferguson stopped us on road & thanked C.O. & Regiment for work done. The regiment is billeted in a farm [unclear].	NOTE Appendix I (C) words of Genl Sir Charles Ferguson

WAR DIARY or INTELLIGENCE SUMMARY.

(Erase heading not required.)

Army Form C. 2118.

Hour, Date, Place	Summary of Events and Information	Remarks and references to Appendices
1915 Sept 4th RENINGHELST	Very wet weather. Batt'n billeted at POPERINGHE. C.O. & Capt. Williams & Capt. PRYCE DAVIES (46th Div'n Staff) reconnoitred country to be worked on by Batt'n. This is in YPRES Salient & in heavily shelled area.	
Sept 5th RENINGHELST	Capt. Williams & 3 Co. Officers went over ground to be worked in by night. B & D Companies moved up at night to 40 yrds C. Co. located as follows (Reference Sheet 28. 1/20000) B & D BEDFORD House. H.26.a C. TRANSPORT FARM. H.21.a.7.0 The work to be done is work incs[?]ting "Defended Localities" in construction of wire [?].	
Sept 6th "	Remainder of C. Co. & woods [?] under 2/Lt DAVIDSON to CHATEAU in H.30. C.O. & other officers visited companies. (Casualties of day m.t. [?] being [?] w?t.	

WAR DIARY or INTELLIGENCE SUMMARY

Army Form C. 2118.

(Erase heading not required.)

Instructions regarding War Diaries and Intelligence Summaries are contained in F.S. Regs., Part II and the Staff Manual respectively. Title pages will be prepared in manuscript.

Hour, Date, Place	Summary of Events and Information	Remarks and references to Appendices
HeadQrs at REMINGHURST 1915 Sept. 7th	The Adjutant & Lieut Thompson went up to Companies in the Ypres Salient	
3 Companies in trenches in YPRES Salient 8th	C.O. & 2/Lieut Hackett visited Companies. Lieut Thompson took over command of "B" Co. Draft of 51 men arrived 10.30 p.m. - mostly wounded men from 3rd line.	
1 Co. at rest at headqrs. 9th	Capt [?Anthony] & Capt Fitz Evans visited companies. The men at BEDFORD House had to stop work today in early morning owing to shelling. C.O. inspected draft. Adms also inspected draft in the afternoon.	
" 10th	New draft went to trenches. Casualties 2 wounded (shell) BEDFORD House.	
" 11th	A.C.O. relieved C. Co. C.O. visited Companies	
" 12th	Our machine guns detailed for training purposes to act under the 3 Brigades of the Division. C.O. & Adjutant visited companies. Draw I being trained under 2/Lt GORDON-LLOYD & 2/Lt DAVIES	

WAR DIARY
or
INTELLIGENCE SUMMARY.
(Erase heading not required.)

Army Form C. 2118.

Instructions regarding War Diaries and Intelligence Summaries are contained in F.S. Regs., Part II. and the Staff Manual respectively. Title pages will be prepared in manuscript.

Hour, Date, Place	Summary of Events and Information	Remarks and references to Appendices
1915		
Sept. 14. Hdqrs near REXINGHELST. 3 Companies in Dug- 15". outs in YPRES Salient 1 Co at rear of HEADqrs. 16"	Casualties. 1 man accidentally injured. C Co relieved B Co in dugouts nil	
17"	B. C. breastwd. Site at back of Headqrs. billet for 30 y/hr range proved by C.R.E.	
18"	Transport went to YPRES for bricks etc to make standing for horses. A quantity of Pioneer equipment was drawn today. Casualties. 1 wounded. (Lt.G.m Lee Tm)	
19"	B. Company relieved D. Company	
20	Our companies are working on new dugouts in front (nie at HILL 60. The dugouts in Railway cutting have been destroyed by an intense bombardment — 380 shells falling in 40 minutes in a small area.	

WAR DIARY or INTELLIGENCE SUMMARY

Army Form C. 2118

Place	Date	Hour	Summary of Events and Information	Remarks and references to Appendices
HeadQrs at RENINGHELST	1915 Sept 21		Nil - casualties. 1 wounded. A.Co.	
	22		2/Lt JORDAN - LLOYD + M gun detachment relieved. Transport-party all people of KRUISTRAAT have been packing up going away.	
	23		b. Co. relieved A. Co.	
	24		C.O. inspected M. guns & Pioneer transport. 2 m guns under 2/Lt JORDAN-LLOYD taken up to firing line Bridiul	Ref. Map. Sheet 28 N.W. Belgium
	25		Our m guns took part in "v" attack at HOOGE today-firing 2000 rounds indirect fire from behind Trench, on 6 cross roads & 2600 yards range. One gun was seen out of action owing to lock becoming defective & mostly amount of misfires, returns, one gun only. The Battn thanked 1st good work of m guns. casualties. 1 wounded.	
	26		Nil	
	27		A.Co. relieved C.Co. Since 25th inst Companies have been working on back positions	
	28		Belgian workmen (30) began work on mv nas partly constructed 30 yards range. Orders received to concentrate Battn at Battn Headqrs by 6 pm 29 inst. Company have withdrawn from BEDFORD House & TRANSPORT FARM during night & put into trams near Headqrs. last company reporting in about 11 am.	
	29	9.15 pm	Stores Stores + clothing issued to Companies - who also took over their Pioneer equipment. Casualties: 2 men accidentally Killed: The over-weight roofs of a large dug out, combined with effects rain falling in m. 2 Headqrs orderly room vicinities in field near Headqrs. Both due to suffocation.	

1 Company at HEAD of BETHUNEHEZST
2 Companies in Dugouts, BEDFORD House, YPRES SALIENT
1 Company " " TRANSPORT FARM

Army Form C. 2118

WAR DIARY
or
INTELLIGENCE SUMMARY
(Erase heading not required.)

Place	Date	Hour	Summary of Events and Information	Remarks and references to Appendices
Batm Hearan REININGHELST map reference G29.c.8.8. (sheet 28 NW Belgium)	1915 Sept 30	2.30 pm	Batln paraded in full outside HQ Batn.	
		4.45 pm	Funeral of 2 riflemen accidentally killed 29/9/15. Buried REININGHELST Church. German aeroplanes active in evening	
			Copies of weekly {illegible} attached to the diary	
			Diminishing {illegible}	

Instructions regarding War Diaries and Intelligence Summaries are contained in F.S. Regs., Part II. and the Staff Manual respectively. Title Pages will be prepared in manuscript.

"War Diary   1st Batt Monmouthshire Regt.
Appendix 1.(a)
        "Words of General BULFIN G.O.C. 28th Division to
            Officers Sept 2nd 1915.

I have called you together to express to you
my regret at your departure from this Division.
The Battalion leaves behind it nothing but praise,
& I wish to thank the men, for the splendid
work they have done. You have had a rough
time & you have made a name to be proud
of, & I hope you will continue to make
history for the Battn in your new Division
as you have made it in this one. Whenever
you might leave your new Division, I am
certain they will part with you with almost
as much regret as I do. I wish you all
good luck, God Speed & a safe return to
England. I ask you to convey to your
men all that I have said to you. I shall
be on the road tomorrow to have a last
look at the Battalion.

                                                            BmN

War Diary.   1st Batt. Monmouthshire Regt.
Appendix I (b)
              Extract from 84th Infantry Brigade Routine
                    Orders, dated 2nd Sept 1915.

"Valedictory   On leaving the 84th Brigade the G.O.C. desires to express to the Officers, N.C.Os & men of the 1st Monmouthshire Regt. his deep regret that the Battalion, after being in his command for 7 months is being transferred to the 46th Division. During this time all ranks are to be congratulated upon the cheerfulness & energy which they have devoted to their work in and out of the trenches, & especially upon their splendid and distinguished conduct the field. The Battn has established a reputation of which the County of Monmouthshire may justly feel proud. The G.O.C. wishes the Battn the best of good luck and a continued brilliant career in its new Brigade.

                                                        Cmd.

"War Diary.   1st Batt. Monmouthshire Regt.
   Appendix I (c)
"Words of 2nd Corps Commander, General Sir Charles Ferguson.

   Sir Charles Ferguson rode for some distance with the C.O. and said "Major Evill & thank you and your Battn. for all you have done. I am very sorry you are going and I wish you were coming back".

                                        OMW.

(Copy)

Perforated Sheet giving detail of personnel and horses wanting to complete, shown on Army Form B. 213.

Number of Report _____

Detail of Wanting to Complete	Drivers					Gunners	Smith Gunners	Range Takers	Farriers				Wheelers			Saddlers or Harness Makers	Blacksmiths	Bricklayers and Masons	Carpenters and Joiners	Fitters & Turners (R.E.)		Fitters				Electricians			Signalmen	Engine Drivers		Air Line Men	Permanent Line Men	Operators, Telegraph	Cablemen	Brigade Section Pioneers	General-duty Pioneers	Signallers	Instrument Repairers	Motor Cyclists	Motor Cyclist Artificers	Telephonists	Clerks	Machine Gunners	Armament Artificers			Storemen	Privates	W.O's. and N.C.O's. (by ranks) not included in trade columns	TOTAL, wanting to agree with complete		Horses			
	R.A.	R.E.	A.S.C.	Lorry	Steam				Sergeants	Corporals	Shoeing, or Shoeing and Carriage Smiths	Cold Shoers	R.A.	H.T.	M.T.					Wood	Iron	R.A.	Wireless	Plumbers	Ordinary	W.T.		Loco.	Field														Fitters	Range Finders	Armourers				Officers	Other Ranks	Riding	Draught	Heavy Draught	Pack
CAVALRY																																																		4	53	4			
R.A.																																																						
R.E.																																																						
INFANTRY									1	8																																					334			71			
R.A.M.C.																																																						
A.O.C.																																																						
A.V.C.																																																						

Remarks:—

(Sd) E H Gull Lt-Col   Signature of Commander.

1/1st Monmouthshire Regiment   Unit.

_____   Formation to which attached.

19th Sept. 1915.   Date of Despatch.

Army Form B. 213.

FIELD RETURN. (Copy)

No. of Report _____

(To be furnished by all arms, services, and departments (except A.S.C. units) to the A. G.'s Office at the Base in accordance with Field Service Regulations, Part II.)

RETURN showing numbers RATIONED by, and Transport on charge of, 1st Monmouthshire Regt at _____ Date 19 Sept 15.

DETAIL	Personnel			Animals							Guns, carriages, and limbers and transport vehicles										REMARKS
	Officers	Other ranks	Natives	Horses Riding	Horses Draught	Horses Heavy Draught	Pack	Mules Large	Mules Small	Camels	Oxen	Guns, carriages and limbers, showing description	Ammunition wagons and limbers	Machine guns	Aircraft, showing description	Horsed 4 Wheeled	Horsed 2 Wheeled	Motor Cars	Tractors	Lorries / Trucks / Trailers (Mechanical)	Motor Bicycles	Bicycles	
Effective Strength of Unit	26	447		8	37	8	9							4		16	3					8	1 Details 1 Offr. 8th Bty Mmy Co / 6 Offrs. 4th Div R.E. Coys / 6.0 Randm / 1 O.R. 8th Bty Mmy Co / 1 " 46 Div Train / 2 " do Ordnce / 2 Signallrs 137th Bde / 2 " 139th " / 2 " 46th Divisn Hdars / 1 Offr + 20 R.E.
Details, by Arms attached to unit as in War Establishment:—																							
To A.M.C.	1	2																					
Interpreter		1																					
A.S.C.		6																					
Total	27	456		8	37	8	9							4		16	3					8	
War Establishment	30	800		12	35	8	9							4		16	3					9	
Wanting to complete	4	353		4	—	—	1							1		—	—					1	
Surplus				x2																			
(Detail of Personnel and Horses below)																							
*Attached (not to include the details shown above)																							
Civilians:— Employed with the Unit Accompanying the Unit																							
TOTAL RATIONED ...	19	426		8	37	8	9																

* In the case of field ambulances, hospitals or depots, the number of patients are to be included here, the names being shown in A. F. A. 36.

Sgd. C. A. Earll Lt Col. Signature of Commander.
Sept 19/15 Date of Despatch.

x One of the surplus draught horses is used for Officers' Mess Wagon, being four wheeled instead of two.

FIELD RETURN.

No. of Report _____ (Copy)

Army Form B. 213.

(To be furnished by all arms, services, and departments (except A.S.C. units) to the A. G.'s Office at the Base in accordance with Field Service Regulations, Part II.)

RETURN showing numbers RATIONED by, and Transport on charge of, 1st Monmouthshire Regt 1F at _____ 1st Sept '15 Date.

Detail	Personnel			Animals						Guns, carriages, and limbers and transport vehicles			Horsed		Mechanical					Remarks
	Officers	Other ranks	Natives	Horses Riding	Horses Draught	Horses Heavy Draught	Horses Pack	Mules Large	Mules Small	Camels	Oxen	Guns, carriages and limbers, showing description	Ammunition wagons and limbers	Machine guns	Aircraft, showing description	4 Wheeled	2 Wheeled	Motor Cars	Tractors	Lorries, showing description	Trucks, showing description	Trailers	Motor Bicycles	Bicycles	
Effective Strength of Unit	21	159		8	32	8	9							4		14	3							9	Details:
Details, by Arms attached to unit as in War Establishment:— 1st Mon R 19 756 A.S.C. 6	1 3 6																								
Total	27	459		8	32	8	9							4		14	3							9	
War Establishment	30	800		8	32	9	9							4		14	3								
Wanting to complete	4	347		½	2	1								4		2									
Surplus																									
*Attached (not to include the details shown above)																									
Civilians:— Employed with the Unit Accompanying the Unit																									
Total Rationed	26			8	32	8	9																		

* In the case of field ambulances, hospitals or depots, the number of patients are to be included here, the names being shown in A. F. A. 36.

_____ Signature of Commander.

12th Sept 1915 Date of Despatch.

Perforated Sheet giving detail of personnel and horses wanting to complete, shown on Army Form B. 213.

Number of Report _____

Detail of Wanting Complete	Drivers						Gunners	Smith Gunners	Range Takers	Farriers			Shoeing, or Shoeing and Carriage Smiths	Cold Shoers	Wheelers			Saddlers or Harness Makers	Blacksmiths	Bricklayers and Masons	Carpenters and Joiners	Fitters & Turners (R. E.)		Fitters			Electricians			Signalmen	Engine Drivers		Air Line Men	Permanent Line Men	Operators, Telegraph	Cablemen	Brigade Section Pioneers	General-duty Pioneers	Signallers	Instrument Repairers	Motor Cyclists	Motor Cyclist Artificers	Telephonists	Clerks	Machine Gunners	Armament Artificers			Armourers	Storemen	Privates	W.O's. and N.C.O's. (by ranks) not included in trade columns	TOTAL, wanting to arrive with to complete		Horses			
	R.A.	R.E.	A.S.C.	Car	Lorry	Steam				Serjeants	Corporals				R.A.	H.T.	M.T.					Wood	Iron	R.A.	Wireless		Plumbers	Ordinary	W.T.		Loco.	Field														Fitters	Range Finders						Officers	Other Ranks	Riding	Draught	Heavy Draught	Pack
CAVALRY																																																							
R.A.																																																							
R.E.																																																							
INFANTRY										12	16																																							319	5	4	347	31		
R.A.M.C.																																																							
A.O.C.																																																							
A.V.C.																																																							

Remarks :—

Signature of Commander. Major
1st Batt. The Warwickshire Regt. A.I.F. Unit.
Formation to which attached.
10/12 Sept 1915 Date of Despatch.

FIELD RETURN.

Army Form B. 213.
Army Form B. 213.
(Army Regulations, Part II.)

No. of Report _____

(To be furnished by all arms, services, and departments (except A.S.C. units) to the A. G.'s Office at the Base in accordance with Field Service Regulations, Part II.)

RETURN showing numbers RATIONED by, and Transport on charge of, 1st Mon. Regt. at _____ Sept 5th '15 Date.

(Copy)

Detail	Personnel			Animals							Guns, carriages, and limbers and transport vehicles									Remarks
	Officers	Other ranks	Natives	Horses			Mules		Camels	Oxen	Guns, carriages and limbers, showing description	Ammunition wagons and limbers	Machine guns	Aircraft, showing description	Horsed		Mechanical			
				Riding	Draught	Heavy Draught	Pack	Large	Small							4 Wheeled	2 Wheeled	Motor Cars	Tractors	Lorries, showing description	Trucks, showing description	Trailers	Motor Bicycles	Bicycles	
Effective Strength of Unit	26	412		8	32	8	9									14	3							9	1 Officer attached 2nd M Bgde Prisoner's Escort. 1 Officer at Park. 20 other ranks with 2nd Bgde H.Q. ...
Details, by arms attached to unit as in War Establishment: — R.A.M.C.	1	2																							
A.S.C.		6																							
Instructor		1																							
Total	27	421		8	32	8	9									14	3							9	
War Establishment	30	800		12	34	9	9									16	3								
Wanting to complete (Detail of Personnel and Horses below)	4	388		4	2	1	1									2									
Surplus																									
*Attached (not to include the details shown above)																									
Civilians: — Employed with the Unit Accompanying the Unit																									
Total Rationed ...	25	412		8	32	8	9																		

* In the case of field ambulances, hospitals or depots, the number of patients are to be included here, the names being shown in A. F. A. 36.

_____ Signature of Commander.

31st Sept '15 Date of Despatch.

Perforated Sheet giving detail of personnel and horses wanting to complete, shown on Army Form B. 213.

Number of Report _____

Detail of Wanting to Complete			CAVALRY	R.A.	R.E.	INFANTRY	R.A.M.C.	A.O.C.	A.V.C.
Drivers	R.A.								
	R.E.								
	A.S.C.								
	Car								
	Lorry								
	Steam								
Gunners									
Smith Gunners									
Range Takers									
Farriers	Sergeants					1/16			
	Corporals								
	Shoeing, or Shoeing and Carriage Smiths								
	Cold Shoers								
Wheelers	R.A.								
	H.T.								
	M.T.								
Saddlers or Harness Makers									
Blacksmiths									
Bricklayers and Masons									
Carpenters and Joiners									
Fitters & Turners (R.E.)	Wood								
	Iron								
Fitters	R.A.								
	Wireless								
	Plumbers								
Electricians	Ordinary								
	W.T.								
Signalmen									
Engine Drivers	Loco.								
	Field								
Air Line Men									
Permanent Line Men									
Operators, Telegraph									
Cablemen									
Brigade Section Pioneers									
General-duty Pioneers									
Signallers									
Instrument Repairers									
Motor Cyclists									
Motor Cyclist Artificers									
Telephonists									
Clerks									
Machine Gunners									
Fitters									
Armament Artificers	Range Finders								
Armourers									
Storemen									
Privates					358				
W.O.'s and N.C.O.'s. (by ranks) not included in trade columns									
TOTAL wanting to agree with complete	Officers								
	Other Ranks								
Horses	Riding								
	Draught				121				
	Heavy Draught								
	Pack								

Remarks:—

Signature of Commander. _Major_ 1st Man Regt I.F.

Formation to which attached. _1st Man_

Unit.

Date of Despatch. _Sept 5th '15_

[P.T.O.

Copy

FIELD RETURN.

Army Form B. 213.

No. of Report _____

(To be furnished by all arms, services, and departments (except A.S.C. units) to the A. G.'s Office at the Base in accordance with Field Service Regulations, Part II.)

RETURN showing numbers RATIONED by, and Transport on charge of, 1/4th Monmouth Regt. at _____ Date 26th Sept/15.

DETAIL	Personnel			Animals								Guns, carriages, and limbers and transport vehicles						Mechanical				REMARKS
	Officers	Other ranks	Natives	Horses Riding	Horses Draught	Horses Heavy Draught	Mules Pack	Mules Large	Mules Small	Camels	Oxen	Guns, carriages and limbers, showing description	Ammunition wagons and limbers	Machine guns	Aircraft, showing description	Horsed 4 Wheeled	Horsed 2 Wheeled	Motor Cars	Tractors	Lorries, showing description	Trucks, showing description	Trailers	Motor Bicycles	Bicycles	
Effective Strength of Unit	26	435		12	53	9	14							4		23	3							8	Details:- 8 H.Q. Divisional Off 1. H.Q. Div. R.E. 4. Deserter 1 Leave 9 Signallers detached 2 Div. Order too 1 do train 6 / 25
Details, by Arms attached to unit as in War Establish-ment:—																									
R.A.M.C.	1	2																							
Interpreter	1																								
R.S.E. attached		6																							
Total	27	444		12	53	9	14							4		23	3							8	
War Establishment	30	809		12	60	9	14							4		23	3							9	
Wanting to complete	4	365			8									1										1	
Surplus																									
(Detail of Personnel and Horses below)																									
*Attached (not to include the details shown above)																									
Civilians:— Employed with the Unit Accompanying the Unit																									
TOTAL RATIONED ...	27	443		12	53	9	14																		

* In the case of field ambulances, hospitals or depots, the number of patients are to be included here, the names being shown in A. F. A. 36.

X two extra Light Draught horse in excess of establishment required, as 4 wheeled Wagon is being used in possession instead of a 2 Wheeled Officers Mess Cart.

(Sd) E.C.F. Ewell Lt. Col. Signature of Commander.

26th Sept/15. Date of Despatch.

Perforated Sheet giving detail of personnel and horses wanting to complete, shown on Army Form B. 213.

Number of Report _____

Detail of Wanting to Complete	Drivers						Farriers				Wheelers								Fitters & Turners (R.E.)		Fitters			Electricians		Engine Drivers										Armament Artificers							W.O's. and N.C.O's. (by ranks) not included in trade columns	TOTAL wanting to complete to agree with		Horses			
	R.A.	R.E.	A.S.C.	Car	Lorry	Steam	Gunners	Smith Gunners	Range Takers	Sergeants	Corporals	Shoeing, or Shoeing and Carriage Smiths	Cold Shoers	R.A.	H.T.	M.T.	Saddlers or Harness Makers	Blacksmiths	Bricklayers and Masons	Carpenters and Joiners	Wood	Iron	R.A.	Wireless	Plumbers	Ordinary	W.T.	Loco.	Field	Air Line Men	Permanent Line Men	Operators, Telegraph	Cablemen	Brigade Section Pioneers	General-duty Pioneers	Signallers	Instrument Repairers	Motor Cyclists	Motor Cyclist Artificers	Telephonists	Clerks	Machine Gunners	Fitters	Range Finders	Armourers	Storemen	Privates		Officers	Other Ranks	Riding	Draught	Heavy Draught	Pack
CAVALRY																																																						
R.A.																																																						
R.E.																																																						
INFANTRY									2	20																																					327		4	356		8		
R.A.M.C.																																																						
A.O.C.																																																						
A.V.C.																																																						

Remarks :—

(Sd) C.A. Bill Lt Col Signature of Commander.
1/1st Monmouthshire Regt Unit.
_____ Formation to which attached.
26th Sept 1915 Date of Despatch.

[P.T.O.

46th Durham

1/ Mommonia China Bgr.
Oct + Nov + Dec
Nov - VII
VI - VII

WAR DIARY
or
INTELLIGENCE SUMMARY
(Erase heading not required.)

1/1ˢᵗ Monmouthshire Regt. Army Form C. 2118

Place	Date	Hour	Summary of Events and Information	Remarks and references to Appendices
RENINGHELST	1915 Oct 1ˢᵗ		Orders to prepare to move.	MOVE
	Oct 2		Battⁿ moved to BAS RIEUX map reference V.13.c (sheet 36a). B+C companies under Major O.N. WILLIAMS marched at 12.30. Entrained ABEELE station 4.34 pm. Arrived FOURQUEVRAIL station about 6.15 pm map reference E.13.A (sheet 36b) marched to BAS RIEUX arriving 10.30 pm. A+D companies under C.O. entrained 6.30 pm. m grays the Tm entrained GODEWAERSVELD TRANSPORT bus SAA map reference E.17 + E.24 (sheet 36a) also carts marched. Patrol night of Oct 2/3 near VIEUX BERQUIN.	
BAS RIEUX	Oct 3		A+D companies arrived BAS RIEUX 2.30 am bringing blankets in hand waggon, m gun teams arrived during night Oct 2/3. Total approximate distance marched by Battⁿ from RENINGHELST 14 mile no men falling out. weather fine. Billets very good. TRANSPORT (less SAA carts) arrived 4.30 pm.	
BAS RIEUX	Oct 4		SAA carts arrived 11 am having been moved by night under RFA. Battⁿ had short route march in afternoon.	
" "	Oct 5		Company parades. Battⁿ warned to move.	
" "	Oct 6	10.30 am	marched at to N.E of FOURQUEVRAIL reference E.14.A.7.6 (sheet 36 BETHUNE) arrived 2.30 pm. New billeting area allotted. Tms found to be occupied by NOTTS + DERBY Regt. As this regiment had had a rough time - having spent night in streets of BETHUNE - m did not turn out, but billeted very "close" inadres. weather fine.	MOVE
FOURQUEVRAIL	Oct 7		Company parades - chiefly musketry. C.O. was informed that men were required to take part in our assault on HOHENZOLLERN REDOUBT. Brigade Officers. Major BURNE + various Company Officers taken up to VERMELLES in motor lorry to reconnoitre trenches to view of the position. Company parades at billets.	

WAR DIARY
or
INTELLIGENCE SUMMARY

Army Form C. 2118

Place	Date	Hour	Summary of Events and Information	Remarks and references to Appendices
FOUQUEREUIL	1915 Oct 9th		Company parades at billets. Arrangements being carried out between Brigade, Brigades themselves.	
"	10th		Lt. Col. Webb went up to trench to supervise a carrying party from 139th Bde. of R.E. Stores. Party did not turn up. 2Lts Rawson, Darby, Peek visited trenches to become acquainted with communications etc. Evening Officers held meeting of officers in manager after church parade. Church parades held for all denominations. Corps Officer address Bn. 9th at 2-30 p.m. on parade ground. The 11th Corps Commander addressed all four army Commanders & senior officers of the 46th Div. at Divl HQrs. at 5-15 p.m.	
"	11th		Companies occupied in bombing practice. C.O. attended conference of Headquarters 138th Infantry Brigade. Lieut Parkes detailed in charge of 125 bombers attached to his Battalion from 139th Inf. Brigade.	
"	12th		Two Battalions paraded and marched with 46. 138th Brigade in rear of 4th Lincolns during at 2 p.m. via HESDIGNEUL VERQUIN to SAILLY-LABOURSE where bivouac arrived about 6 p.m. where tea was provided & rations issued. 9 U.C. 46th Div. saw to & allow march by at SAILLY. Marched saw at 8 p.m. and marched to BREWERY VERMELLES where ballow picked up R.E. STORES & water. Great number of troops on the road and some confusion. C.O. reported to Brigade HQrs.	

WAR DIARY or INTELLIGENCE SUMMARY

Army Form C. 2118

Place	Date	Hour	Summary of Events and Information	Remarks and references to Appendices
VERMELLES	1915 Oct 13th		Communication trenches were very crowded and the Battalion did not reach the Reserve trenches of the 2nd Bn Irish Guards until 5.30 am on the 13th inst. A party of officers had reconnoitred the trenches the same day. 2nd Lieut Burot during the afternoon in his trench & Lieut J Lieut Stephens 13 men wounded & others. Our guides were therefore short. The trenches occupied were very narrow and the men were very cramped there being no shelter for them though 14 Officers & 358 O.Ranks.	
do	13th		The Battalion was ordered to side slip to the left to make room for more troops, who were taken out of the front trenches in order to thin the line as gas was to be used. This necessitated moving the men again & making them still more cramped. This was done at 9.30am & at 12 noon a heavy bombardment was started which lasted until 2pm at which hour the assault was delivered. The 5th Lincs & the 1st Leicesters leading; to be followed by the 4th Lincs & Leics the 1st Monmouths who were to follow in reserve also the positions after secured. "A" & "C" Companies were ordered to lead on the left & right respectively. Their advance was most gallantly led & executed. Both Companies rushing to the assault from the support trench & passing over our trenches with great dash. Owing to the rapidity of their advance they both arrived in the Redan B98 close behind the first two Battalions & helped to secure it. The attacked bombers	

WAR DIARY
or
INTELLIGENCE SUMMARY
(Erase heading not required.)

Army Form C. 2118

Instructions regarding War Diaries and Intelligence Summaries are contained in F. S. Regs., Part II. and the Staff Manual respectively. Title Pages will be prepared in manuscript.

Place	Date	Hour	Summary of Events and Information	Remarks and references to Appendices
VERMELLES	1915 Oct 13th contd		followed, led by the C.O. 1 B & D Companies followed and 2 the Machine Guns. There was much confusion in the Redoubt owing to the congestion of troops, the attack having been held up beyond. Immediate steps were taken to consolidate the Western face of the Redoubt while A & C Companies faced the Eastern face. Guns were posted on the flanks & parties of bombers told off. At 3 p.m. the Germans counter-attacked with bombs, but this attack was beaten off. He was an attempted retirement of troops, but this was stopped at the Western face, & the ground held. At 5.30 another counter attack was delivered and another attempt at retirement of our troops which was partially arrested at the Western face. A shortage of bombs made it obviously impossible but the counter attack was again beaten. Work of consolidation was proceeded with. Half Western face parapet reversed. The C.O. 1st R. Fusiliers left the Redoubt in charge of C.O. 1st Munsters at this point. The night was very cold and the men were very fatigued indeed. At dawn no advance in advance of the Western face for observation purposes. The flanks of the Redoubt could not be joined owing to lack of bombers. Parties and a message was sent to the	

1875 Wt. W593/826 1,000,000 4/15 J.B.C. & A. A.D.S.S./Forms/C. 2118.

WAR DIARY or INTELLIGENCE SUMMARY

Army Form C. 2118

Place	Date	Hour	Summary of Events and Information	Remarks and references to Appendices
VERMELLES	1915 Oct 13th		ran to this effect. Further supplies of bombs arrived, but bombers were very scarce indeed. At 4 am a heavy attack was made on both flanks by the enemy, accompanied by rifle fire and rifle grenades. The position was very critical for some time, but the arrival of the 8th Sherwoods on the right saved the situation, and the attack was beaten off. At 6 am the men who had been in the Redoubt for 24 hours were relieved, and the 8 command was handed over to Lt. Col. SH of the Leicesters, and the 1st Lincolns withdrew. The Officers in the Redoubt also came out. There were Lt. Col. O. C. H. Ewell, Captains R. F. L. Thomas & Hartopp, Lieut. L. Jardine, Lloyd & Sgt. E. G. Liddall. The Battalion were mustered in the Reserve trenches awaiting orders, still under a heavy artillery fire. At 4 pm orders were received from the Brigade to withdraw to the Lowas line trenches, near VERMELLES, where the men were billeted for the night. Casualties 4 Officers killed, 4 wounded, 2 suffering from gas poison, 3 missing. Other ranks 151.
	14th		An uneventful night occurred. All ranks were able to rest by day. Two salvage parties of 1 Officer and 25 men each were found to sap the Communication trenches & collect clothing & equipment. Two Officers were detached to act as O.C. burying parties found by the 5th Lincolns.
	15th		

Army Form C. 2118

WAR DIARY
or
INTELLIGENCE SUMMARY
(Erase heading not required.)

Instructions regarding War Diaries and Intelligence Summaries are contained in F. S. Regs., Part II. and the Staff Manual respectively. Title Pages will be prepared in manuscript.

Place	Date	Hour	Summary of Events and Information	Remarks and references to Appendices
	1915 Oct 15		Off 4 hrs orders were received to march to VERMELLES, in lieu the Regt was to remain in our former Billets to the original billets in FOUQUEREUIL.	
	" 16th		Batta blow parade at 2.30 pm for roll call.	
	" 17th		Church parades for all denominations held in morning. Kits of men inspected by officers after.	
	" 18th		Batta inspected by G.O.C. 46th Division. Major General the Hon E.J. Montagu Stuart Wortley. C.B. C.M.G. M.V.O. at 10 am on Battn Parade ground. Total on parade 6 Officers, + 184 other ranks. After inspection the Battn the G.O.C. addressed it as follows:- He thanked the Battn for its good work at the recent attack and record a letter which he had sent to the Mon Div Force Recig, so that they should know at home about the work of the Battalion. He regretted the losses sustained.	
	" 19th		Coy being starting bathing in tubs purchased for the purpose. There being no bathing facilities at all in this district.	
	" 20th		Notice received at 2 pm to move billets to ST SAUVEUR, near CHOQUES. Battn moved off at 3.20 pm.	
	" 21st		Company drill. Billets inspected. Fatigues detailed to form more room.	
	" 22nd		Battn went for route march in morning. Two Battal Urdes, for arrangements	

1875 Wt. W503/826 1,000,000 4/15 J.B.C. & A. A.D.S.S./Forms/C. 2118.

Army Form C. 2118

WAR DIARY
or
INTELLIGENCE SUMMARY
(Erase heading not required.)

Instructions regarding War Diaries and Intelligence Summaries are contained in F. S. Regs., Part II. and the Staff Manual respectively. Title Pages will be prepared in manuscript.

Place	Date	Hour	Summary of Events and Information	Remarks and references to Appendices
ST. SAVEUR	1915 Oct 23		Three Officers arrived Capt. F.J. TROMP 2/Lieut. I.E. EVANS, & 2/Lt. EVANS. Church parade 9.30am for all, other than R.C's. 2 Officers arrived them 2/Lt. BLOW, & 2/Lt. SELINE.	
	" 24			
DROUVIN	" 25		Battalion ordered to move to DROUVIN about 5 miles away. Left Column Cross to by 5pm.	
	" 26		Regt warned that an inspection of 11th Corps would take place on October 24th or 28th. This Unit was ordered to find 250 men & 6 Officers. This was subsequently reduced to 4 Officers & 120 men. Parade 10.30am. So far we knew.	
	" 27		The 120 men selected and 4 Officers paraded for a preliminary inspection at 2.30 pm.	
	" 28		Representative regt of the 11th Corps inspected by H.M. KING GEORGE V. This Unit found 120 men & 4 Officers. The Officers on parade being Capt. R.C.L. Thomas in Command of Company. "" K.C. Raikes 2nd in do do do Lieut. H.C.R. Thompson Commdg No 1 Platoon 2/"" E.J.G. Lt E. Weedall " No 2 do	
	" 29		Company parades.	
	" 30		Parties sent off on fatigues, one to VERQUIN to make horse lines, another to Loose No 6 to load slag on to our 8 Wagons. The slag is to be used for making paths round billets.	

1875 Wt. W593/826 1,000,000 4/15 J.B.C. & A. A.D.S.S./Forms/C. 2118.

WAR DIARY
or
INTELLIGENCE SUMMARY
(Erase heading not required.)

Army Form C. 2118

Place	Date	Hour	Summary of Events and Information	Remarks and references to Appendices
DROUVIN	1915 Oct 31		Church parade were cancelled owing to the weather. Fatigues other than urgent fatigues done today, by special order of G.O.C. Division. Men had baths.	
	Nov 1		Went on fatigues as on Oct 30 but were withdrawn owing to rain & only work under cover was carried out. Wire received from 6th Division to say No 838 Pte J. Dryford awarded the D.C.M. for his conduct on Oct 13. 1915.	
	Nov 2		Fatigue work carried out & parties sent as yesterday. 2nd Lieuts L.J. Beynon and R. Rutherford arrived.	
	Nov 3		Fatigue work as yesterday, work stopped at 1 p.m. as orders received to move tomorrow. 2nd Lieut W.H. Freeton & draft of 60, OR arrived.	
LES 8 MAISONS	Nov 4		Battalion paraded at 7.45 a.m. & marched to LES 8 MAISONS arrived about 12 noon. Troops refreshed. R.29. R4.8. Bethune bombed trap.	MOVE
	Nov 5		Battalion engaged in clearing billets etc which were left in very dirty condition.	
	Nov 6		Billeting improvements & parades in eden O.C. Coys.	
	Nov 7 Nov 8		Billeting improvements & parade in order O.C. Coys. Coy parade in morning. Coy. Lunes bathed at LA GORGUE in afternoon. C.O. inspected CORPSE ST. Communication trench & reported to Division in afternoon.	
	Nov 9		C + D Coys continued the work of cleaning up CORPSE STREET C.T. and laying down gratings.	

WAR DIARY or INTELLIGENCE SUMMARY

Army Form C. 2118

(Erase heading not required.)

Instructions regarding War Diaries and Intelligence Summaries are contained in F. S. Regs., Part II. and the Staff Manual respectively. Title Pages will be prepared in manuscript.

Place	Date	Hour	Summary of Events and Information	Remarks and references to Appendices
LES 3 MAISONS	1915 Nov 10		A & B Companies continued above work. C & D carried on with improvements & general repairs under O C Companies. Lieut BURNICK RAME reported for duty as M.O.	
	Nov 11		C & D Companies worked on COPSE ST. C.T. A & B Coys held in reserve etc.	
	Nov 12		A & B Boys worked at COPSE ST. C & D in camp. Lieut BURNYEAT reported for duty from NORTHUMBRIAN FIELD CO. R.E. CAPT. FORREST, RAME, left for ETAPLES.	
	Nov 13		C & D Coys carried on work at COPSE ST C.T. Very high wind caused escape of hay used as brush store dump near trench. Snow slightly improved. A & B Boys engaged in camp on billet improvement. Rame Barracks etc.	
	Nov 14		Two Coys worked as usual on COPSE ST. C.T. Church parade & billet improvement in reserve. See Lt FISHER reported for duty.	
	Nov 15		Two Coys worked on C.T. Two carried on under company commander. Recd. promul. to Lotus Bur. etc	
	Nov 16		Two companies on C.T. Two at home. 2nd Lt F.BELL reported for duty.	
	Nov 17		Two companies worked on C.T. Two Coys worked on billet improvements.	
	Nov 18		Coy Lt.t. Attach of M.O.R. arrived from base. Lt E.J.JENKINS reported for duty.	
	Nov 19		Work as yesterday. A & B Boys bathed at VIEILLE CHAPELLE	
	Nov 20		Work as yesterday. C & D Boys bathed.	
	Nov 21		Work as yesterday. Church parade for all denominations in morning for the 2 Coys working on trench. 2nd Lt A.H. WELBY PUGIN reported for duty.	

Army Form C. 2118

WAR DIARY
or
INTELLIGENCE SUMMARY
(Erase heading not required.)

Instructions regarding War Diaries and Intelligence Summaries are contained in F.S. Regs., Part II. and the Staff Manual respectively. Title Pages will be prepared in manuscript.

Place	Date	Hour	Summary of Events and Information	Remarks and references to Appendices
LES 8 MAISONS	1915 Nov 22		2 Companies at work on C.T. & 1 Coy sent to construct a bomb store at ST VAAST CROSS RD.	
	Nov 23		2 Companies (C&B) on bofore St Renal & D Coy at work on bomb stores	
	Nov 24		As yesterday but A&C Coys on trench & B on bombstores	
	Nov 25		A & B at work on trench	
	Nov 26		B&C Coys on trench, A on bombstore. draft of 9 men arrival from base hospital &C. CAPT. A.C. RENWICK returned to Field Ambulance.	
	Nov 27		A&C Coys on trench & D on bombstore. A night working party of 25 men and 1 officer found for R.E's. Clear drains for RUE DU BOIS.	
	Nov 28		Voluntary Church Services, all denomination. morning work as usual on trench A & B Coys	F.I. Drury Major.
	Nov 29		C&D trench working parties. One ac party found to work on drains at factory corner of RUE DU BOIS.	
	Nov 30		A&C on trench, B Coy on drains at factory corner.	OC 1st Monmouth Rgt.
	DEC 1		Continued to proceed with drains at factory corner as find as found. Continuous work started thereon. 3 shifts of 8 hrs each. B Coy on trench. 100 men went on furlough to Uk from 3.00pm. school of instruction on Tuesday, Wednesday 3 shifts worked on drains. Draft of 10 others, arrival from Base	
	DEC 2		B shifts on drains & digging, but were received of opposing neighbourhood. Ordered to move	
	DEC 3		Paraded at 9.15 am and marched to CAUDESCURE	
CAUDESCURE	DEC 4		MOVE	
	DEC 5		Bath parade 9.30 am for inspection by G.O.C. owing to message not being received, cancelling the parade. Parade dismissed at 1pm.	
	DEC 6		All furloughs & collected. Companies at disposal of O.C. Coys	
	DEC 7		Coys at disposal of O.C. Coys. Draft of men arrival from Base	
	DEC 8		Coys at disposal of O.C. Coys on nothing. 60 inspected baths at 2pm	
	DEC 9		Coys at disposal of O.C. Coys for physical and P.C, clear order drill cleaning &c.	Act. Lt. Commanding Regt.

Monmouth Ken

WAR DIARY or INTELLIGENCE SUMMARY

Army Form C. 2118

Place	Date	Hour	Summary of Events and Information	Remarks and references to Appendices
LES 6 MAISONS	DEC 1		Ordered to proceed with drawn at factory corner as fatigue party. continuous work started thereon 3 shifts of 8 hrs each 15 boys on French.	
	DEC 2		100 men sent on fatigue to 46th Divisional School of Instruction as yesterday 3 shifts worked on drain. Draft of 10 others arrived from Base.	
	DEC 3		3 shifts arranged for drawn but were received stopping night work. Ordered to move billets tomorrow.	
CAUDESCURE	DEC 4		Paraded at 9.15 am and marched to CAUDESCURE.	MOVE.
	DEC 5		Battn. parade 9.30 a.m. for inspection by G.O.C. owing to message not being received co. calling the parade. Parade dismissed at 1 p.m.	
	DEC 6		All fire coats &c. collected. Companies at disposal O.C's Coys.	
	DEC 7		Coys at disposal of O.C. Coys. Draft of nine men arrived from Base.	
	DEC 8		Coys at disposal of O.C Coys in morning. G.O. inspected battn at 2 p.m.	
	DEC 9		Coys at disposal of O.C. Coys for Physical drill, close order drill, saluting &c.	

WAR DIARY or INTELLIGENCE SUMMARY

Army Form C. 2118

Place	Date	Hour	Summary of Events and Information	Remarks and references to Appendices
CAUDESCURE	DEC 10		Coys at disposal of O.C. Coys for Physical drill, close order drill, saluting &c.	
	DEC 11		Do. Section made up to strength of 32.	
	DEC 12		Coys at disposal of O.C. Coys for Physical drill, close order drill & saluting &c. 2 lynx pairs of new order drill are now engaging those men at the front to be sent under those conditions.	
	DEC 13		Coys at disposal of O.C. Coys as on 12th. Bath parade at 2 p.m. for route march.	
	DEC 14		Coys at disposal of O.C. Coys for Physical drill, close order drill, saluting &c. Drill to follow Syll. Details would be at A Coy for drill purpose, then will be issued to each Coy in turn.	
	DEC 15		DO.	
	DEC 16		Coys out for route marches in morning. 3 Officers sent to reconnoitre LILLERS & BURGETTE station in view of a possible entrainment there.	
	DEC 17		Coys at disposal of O.C. Coys in morning for close order drill &c. Bath parade at 2 p.m. for route march.	
	DEC 18		Orders received to change billets tomorrow. Coys at disposal of Coy Officers for Physical training & usual routine.	
HAVERSKERQUE	DEC 19		Bath paraded at 9.15 a.m. and marched behind 138th Brigade to HAVERSKERQUE and occupied billets in and around the village. At CAUDESCURE between 6 a.m. & 8 a.m. asphyxiating gas was distinctly smelt from direction of wind on others & was probably delivered by Germans just south of YPRES but no information received throughout day & considered the Bilan in ordered in afternoon by G.O.	MOVE
	DEC 20		Coys at disposal of O.C. Coys. Billets inspected by G.O. 1/3 B.C.L.I. instructed on bombing in afternoon by Lt. Rutherford	

Army Form C. 2118

WAR DIARY
or
INTELLIGENCE SUMMARY
(Erase heading not required.)

Instructions regarding War Diaries and Intelligence Summaries are contained in F. S. Regs., Part II. and the Staff Manual respectively. Title Pages will be prepared in manuscript.

Place	Date	Hour	Summary of Events and Information	Remarks and references to Appendices
HAVERSKERQUE	DEC 21		Coys at disposal of O.C. Coys. Suspected gas attack on 19th confirmed by report in English papers of a German gas attack N.W. of YPRES which completely failed. The gas was blown back roughly 18-20 miles and although high wind along enough to make our eyes water & made uncomfortable to breathe.	
	DEC 22		Coys at disposal of O.C. Coys. Rained nearly all day.	
	DEC 23		Orders received to entrain at KILLERS on the 25th inst. Coys at disposal of O.C. Coys during morning. Battalion Parade 2.30 p.m.	
	DEC 24		Battalion parade at 11 a.m. when L.O. inspected & made Christmas dinner enquiries today owing to move the following advances at rations were issued being substituted for by the residents of Haspres & Haverskerque. Christmas puddings, nuts, oranges, apples, cake, dates, butter, and Christmas puddings from the Daily News. G.O.C. Div. visited Companies.	MOVE
IN TRAIN	DEC 25		Battalion paraded at 6.39 a.m. & marched to KILLERS station and entrained. All vehicles were taken but no animals. These were left behind with the transport personnel and attached to the H.Q. 6th Divisional Bag Train. Strength entraining 23 Officers 336 Other Ranks 31 vehicles. Personnel left with A.S.C. 20 Officers 66 Other Ranks.	
	DEC 26		In train all day. Ration of 1 hour morning & evening.	
MARSEILLES	DEC 27		Arrived MARSEILLES 1/p.m. detrained and marched to CAMP BORELY. Arrived at CAMP BORELY	
	DEC 28		Coys at disposal of O.C. Coys for inspections	
	DEC 29		Battalion parade at 10 a.m. for route march. Battalion inspected by G.O.C. 46th Division at 10 a.m.	
	DEC 30		C.O. inspected baths by companies. Berga Band rendered music & Buglers	
	DEC 31		Kept on camp duty from H.q.m.	

A.Smith

1/1st Bn Monmouthshire Regt 44

Confidential

War Diary
for
December 1915, January & February 1916.

Vide VII / VIII / IX

M W Thomas Cap^n & Adj^t
for Lieut Colonel
Comdg 1/1st Monmouthshire Regt T.F.

Army Form C. 2118

WAR DIARY
or
INTELLIGENCE SUMMARY
(Erase heading not required.)

Instructions regarding War Diaries and Intelligence Summaries are contained in F. S. Regs., Part II. and the Staff Manual respectively. Title Pages will be prepared in manuscript.

Place	Date	Hour	Summary of Events and Information	Remarks and references to Appendices
MARSEILLES	JAN 1		1916 Boys at disposal of O.C. boys for cleaning up and fitting equipment	
	2		Church parade for all denominations in morning. Vaccination of men started. Also a part of 'B' boy completed. O.C. boys and G.R. betting palades in afternoon.	
	3		Baths at 13 RUE DE LA REPUBLIQUE placed at disposal of regt. All companies bathed. Orders received at 8 a.m. to entrain with all vehicles on S.S. BELTANA with all vehicles on morning of January 5th	
	4		Orders re embarked cancelled at 10.30 am. C.O. inspected battalion at 10 a.m. Route march from 11-12.30. 'B' boy vaccinated	
	5		Battalion route march in morning. The following officers N.C.Os and men of the Regt were returned by Biplanes dated 30.11.15. for gasland and Distinguishing conduct in the field Lieut (temp Capt) T. A. Bourne Capt W.d. Hepburn P.S.O. A.Q.M. R.J. Clarkson 10669 Sgt S.G. Crump (killed in action) 1570 Pte W. Shaw	
	6		Orders received to embark on 7th on S.S."ANCHISES" Draft of 126 O.R. arrived from base	
SS ANCHISES	7		Battalion again inspected by G.O.C. 46th Division at 10.30 a.m. Battalion fell in on main road and marched to embark on "ANCHISES" who agreed on station quay as was done to embarked on "ANCHISES" Battalion paraded at 8 am, marched to docks and embarked on S.S. ANCHISES. Strength embarking 22 Officers 1130 Other ranks. Attached officer - R.t. O.R. Langford handed to Officer Commanding Before sailing of MARSEILLES 20 Officers 512 other ranks	MOVE

1875   Wt. W593/826 1,000,000 4/15 J.B.C. & A.   A.D.S.S./Forms/C. 2118.

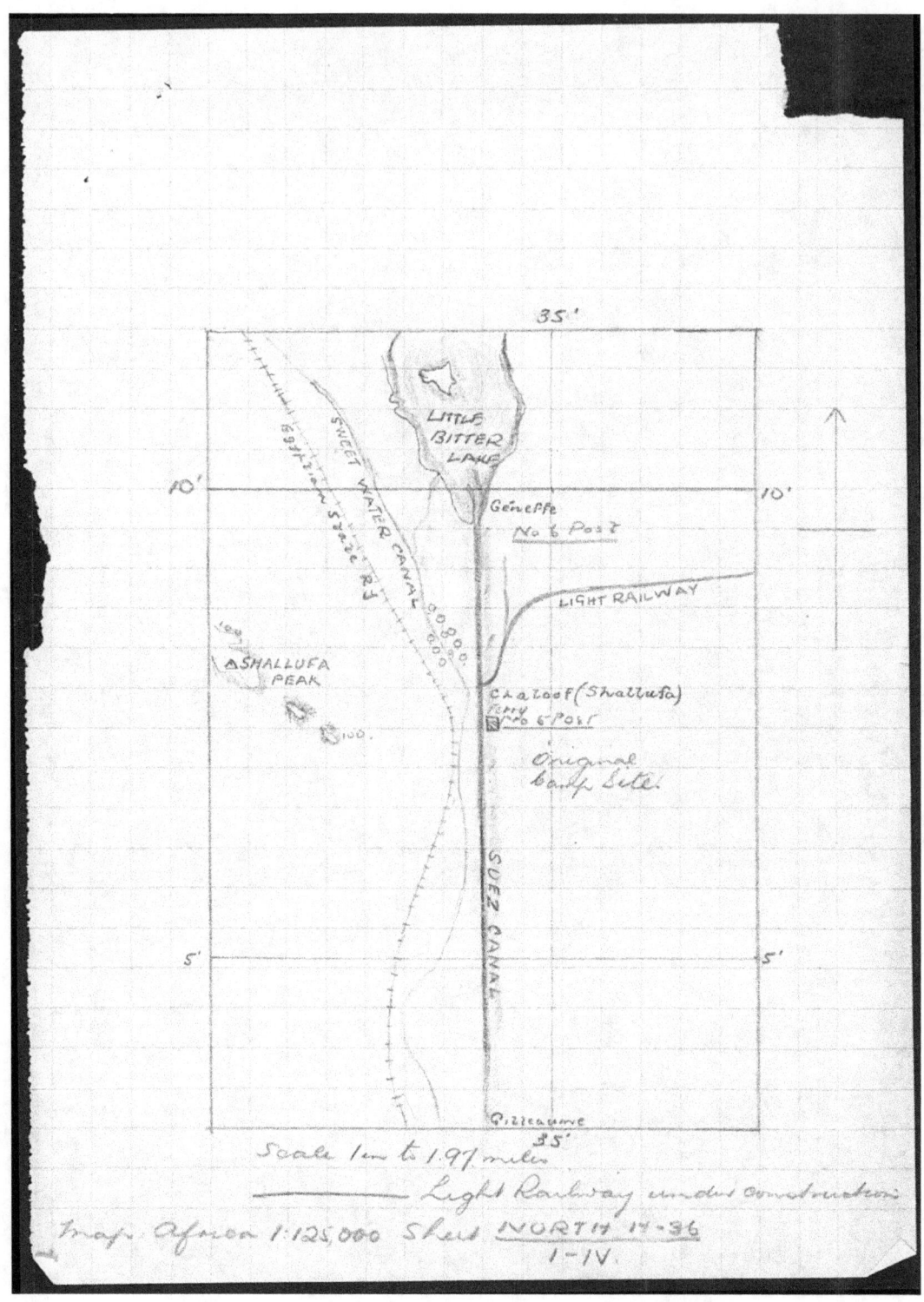

WAR DIARY or INTELLIGENCE SUMMARY

Army Form C. 2118

(Erase heading not required.)

Place	Date	Hour	Summary of Events and Information	Remarks and references to Appendices
ST AVENUES AT SEA	Jan 8		Started at 7.30 a.m. Officers went on board last night. H.S. lines. Divisional Hdqrs 138th Bde & Light Armoured Bad. Embarked on duty for guidance.	
	Jan 9		Daily Routine – the Colonels of Rose bay Light & 9 p.m. Physical training on top deck – 2 lamps per day at gun – 11 a.m. at the barbers alarm stip to inspection. Company officer along Kingstown K well caught out with Regiment placed on duty. Lunch along at 2 p.m. everything worked without the slightest confusion Dispatch boat ACORN signalled at 7 p.m. and accompanied as an escort. Enemy submarine reported in vicinity.	
	Jan 10		Saw boat rigged upon deck. All men of regiment bathed. Boy physical training parade were held either before or after bathing in the afternoon.	
	Jan 11		Preliminary orders in orders embarked issued as the ship will probably reach ALEXANDRIA tomorrow. Boy physical drill parade.	DISEMBARKED & ENTRAINED
ALEXANDRIA	Jan 13		Arrived off ALEXANDRIA at 7 p.m. tied up alongside at 11 a.m. but did not disembark until 5.30 p.m. when entrained for SHALLUFA leaving at 7 p.m. Troops rations were drawn on the quay. Very cold with sand storm.	
SERAPEUM	Jan 14		Per to arrive at SHALLUFA at 8 a.m. but owing to a delay on our train caused by an engine of another train getting off the rails stopped at SERAPEUM at 4 a.m. and stayed there the rest of the day.	
SHALLUFA	Jan 15		Started from SERAPEUM at 5 a.m. and arrived at SHALLUFA where the regiment detrained and ferried across the Canal to a Divisional Camp situated opposite Shallufa Station immediately under the brow of sand caused by the Canal excavations but on the further side of the mound from the Canal. Tents were drawn in the afternoon. All baggage had to be carried by hand to and from the ferry boat.	

Army Form C. 2118

WAR DIARY
or
INTELLIGENCE SUMMARY
(Erase heading not required.)

Instructions regarding War Diaries and Intelligence Summaries are contained in F. S. Regs., Part II. and the Staff Manual respectively. Title Pages will be prepared in manuscript.

Place	Date	Hour	Summary of Events and Information	Remarks and references to Appendices
SHALLUFA	Jan 16		Church parade at 9 a.m after which battalion started to dig a line of trench to protect the camp in case of a sudden attack, the trench is situated about 750 yds east of the Canal. Orders received to relieve 1/5 South Staffs in No 5 Post a defence work allotted to our battalion. The 2nd Dorsets to now in the 9th Army Corps commanded by Lieut-General Hon. Sir J. H. G. BYNG., K.C.M.G., C.B., M.V.O.	MOVE
	Jan 17		Battalion paraded at 10 a.m and moved into No 5 Post. A Company under Lt BURNYEAT marched to GENEFFE and relieved the Coy of the Sth Staffs acting as garrison. Remainder of day spent in carrying baggage from Canal to No 5 Post. Machine Guns & Signalling stations made up to establishment.	
	Jan 18		Owing to large number of progress and guards which have to be found there are available for duty the very small numbers over 120 O.R. being on guard nightly. Coys detailed to clean up No 5 Post.	
	Jan 19		Continued bathed in Canal. C.O. & Major Dunmop marched to 6 Post	
	Jan 20		Corps Commander marched SHALLUFA No 5 Post and inspected its supply arrangements. C.O. & Adj: visited No 6 Post who reported that a police boat fired on a party of Arabs the previous night, who did not halt when challenged by the about 12 mile north of No 6 Post. The ground was inspected by the C.O. but the only bare foot tracks were those of 2 men who swam approached across there from one of the regiment.	
	Jan 21		Pontoon Bridge which is during across the canal daily from 6 am - 9 am placed under the supervision of this regiment. G.O.C. Division arrived at SHALLUFA	

Army Form C. 2118

WAR DIARY
or
INTELLIGENCE SUMMARY
(Erase heading not required.)

Instructions regarding War Diaries and Intelligence Summaries are contained in F.S. Regs., Part II. and the Staff Manual respectively. Title Pages will be prepared in manuscript.

Place	Date	Hour	Summary of Events and Information	Remarks and references to Appendices
SHALLUFA	Jan 22		Surprise alarm at 7.30 a.m. - all battalion were manned under 10 minutes. No 6 post visited by G.O. Alarm again sounded at 5.20 p.m.	
	Jan 23		Guards & piquets found as usual. South Piquet visited by G.O. in evening when turn to changing the position.	
	Jan 24		B Coy relieved A at GENEFFE (No 6 Post). C.O. & Adjt visited No 6 post in the afternoon.	
	Jan 25		Night march by comp & plats carried out by officers. Working party on subs. leading to piquets partly reconnaitering & partly new work. North piquet inspected by C.O. at 11 p.m.	
	Jan 26		No 5 Post. The position held by the regiment visited by Major General Sir A.J. MURRAY, KCB, KCMG, CVO, DSO, C. in C. Expeditionary Force, on a tour of inspection, which also included the new railway line & pipe. The C. in C. inspected the regimental QM Stores & rations which were being issued. 1/6 S.STAFFS REGT with section of RE's went out into desert to No 3 POST (Valley) about 1 mile out to commence construction of the post and adjoining first line trenches. Camels were used for transport, all told numbering 292, with 2 days rations & water were carried.	
	Jan 27		O.C. Coy inspected No 6 Post. Unofficial rumour that the 46 Div both being allowed on 3 days leave to CAIRO.	

Army Form C. 2118

WAR DIARY
or
INTELLIGENCE SUMMARY
(Erase heading not required.)

Instructions regarding War Diaries and Intelligence Summaries are contained in F.S. Regs., Part II. and the Staff Manual respectively. Title Pages will be prepared in manuscript.

Place	Date	Hour	Summary of Events and Information	Remarks and references to Appendices
SHALLUFA	Jan 27		Lt. I.E. EVANS, Lt. C. KIRBY & Lt. Qmr R.H.MARTIN went on leave until evening of 29th	
	Jan 28		Regular guards found as usual very heavy rain with short intervals all day	
	Jan 29		½ Batt. paraded at 8 a.m. marched out 2 miles to a rifle range to fire a grouping course 5 rounds. Only 5 details had fired when orders were received to return to Camp as division was entraining. Orders received for Battalion to entrain at SHALLUFA STATION at 1.45 p.m tomorrow	
	Jan 30		Handed over No 5 Post to 42nd Division. No 6 Post relieved by 9th MANCHESTERS. Pontoon bridge fired upon (owing to 10 p.m went completed in 1 hour. Third bridge in 130 yards long with one piece omitted in the centre) Battalion paraded 10.30 a.m. was ferried across the Canal to the Station. Entrained at 1.30 p.m. Strength 22 Off. 404 Other Ranks	ENTRAIN-MENT.
ALEXANDRIA	Jan 31		Arrived ALEXANDRIA 2.30 a.m and detrained marched to SIDI BISHR CAMP a distance of 6 miles where the regiment bivouacked for remainder of night no tents being pitched. At 9 a.m tents were drawn & pitched on the ground on which the battle of ABOUKIR was fought. The 3 officers who left on January 27th for leave returned, the following went. Lt. Col. C.A. EVILL, Capt & Adjt. R.C.L. THOMAS. Capt M.C.R. THOMPSON, Capt K.C. RAIKES Capt S.R. MARTIN. Lt. W.L. ROBERTS.	

WAR DIARY
or
INTELLIGENCE SUMMARY

(Erase heading not required.)

Army Form C. 2118

Instructions regarding War Diaries and Intelligence Summaries are contained in F. S. Regs., Part II. and the Staff Manual respectively. Title Pages will be prepared in manuscript.

Place	Date	Hour	Summary of Events and Information	Remarks and references to Appendices
ALEXANDRIA	Feb 1		Batt: parade 7.80 a.m. for Physical Drill & from 9.30 a.m - 12 p.m for Company Drill. Bathing parade in afternoon under Company arrangements.	
	Feb 2		As yesterday, only no bathing parade held. The following officers reported for duty from the 3rd line 2/Lts. W Q GOLDSWORTHY, H E D HARRIES & A C CORRY-SMITH. Orders received to embark tomorrow at 9 a.m. The 6 officers who left for leave on Jan 31st returned.	
	Feb 3		Battalion paraded 6.30 a.m and marched from Camp to SIDI BISHR Station where train cars were provided to take the Regiment to docks. Embarked at 9 a.m on S.S. MEGANTIC Strength embarking 12 officers 391 Other Ranks. 13 Officers with servants were left to come on S.S TRANSYLVANIA which sails tomorrow. Other Units on board are 4th & 5th Lincolns, 46th Divisional & 138th Brigade Head Quarters, and unattached officers going to England on leave. All men are in bunks. W.Os & N.C.Os in 2nd Class Cabins.	
	Feb 4		Everyone on the ship paraded 6.15 a.m when boats were allotted. Boat deck allotted to this regiment. Sailed at 10.30 a.m.	
	Feb 5		Daily routine is like on voyage out except that no alarm afternoon given. Coy Physical Training parade.	

Army Form C. 2118

WAR DIARY
or
INTELLIGENCE SUMMARY
(Erase heading not required.)

Instructions regarding War Diaries and Intelligence Summaries are contained in F. S. Regs., Part II. and the Staff Manual respectively. Title Pages will be prepared in manuscript.

Place	Date	Hour	Summary of Events and Information	Remarks and references to Appendices
AT SEA ST MEGANTIC	Feb 6		As yesterday. Physical training morning & afternoon	
	Feb 7		12 baths allotted to regiment everyone was bathed. An epidemic of sickness throughout the men, pains in stomach & violent sickness caused probably by food poisoning. 60 men of this regiment paraded sick but other regiments had many more, the St Lincolns 300.	
MARSEILLES	Feb 8		Arrived MARSEILLES at 10 a.m. Orders received to disembark tomorrow.	DISEMBARKED ENTRAINED
	Feb 9		Regt disembarked at 4.30 p.m & marched to ARENC Station entraining at 6 p.m with 3 Cos of this & 4 Lincoln Regt. The train being under the command of O.C 4 Lincoln Regt.	
	Feb 10		In train all day, tea being provided in morning and evening by French Railway Authorities.	
	Feb 11		Arrived at 8 p.m at PONT REMY Station near ABBEVILLE where the regiment detrained and marched to BRUCAMPS to billets a distance of 10 miles, each man carried in addition to his rifle & equipment a rolled blanket, only 3 men fell out. The march took 4 hrs to complete	DISENTRAINED
BRUCAMPS	Feb 12		Coys at disposal of O.C. Coys for inspections &c	
	Feb 13		6 Officers & 14 Other Ranks left by motor lorry for RAINCHEVAL to take over billets of 16th Royal Irish Rifles & work by hand. Regiment arrived at RAINCHEVAL by motor lorry in morning motor lorries being supplied. Were received at 6 p.m cancelling move.	
	Feb 14		Company parade 2.30 p.m for route march. 2/Lt T.G.FRY reported for duty from 3rd Line. Baths - bayonet fighting &c in morning	

Army Form C. 2118

WAR DIARY
or
INTELLIGENCE SUMMARY

(Erase heading not required.)

Instructions regarding War Diaries and Intelligence Summaries are contained in F. S. Regs., Part II. and the Staff Manual respectively. Title Pages will be prepared in manuscript.

Place	Date	Hour	Summary of Events and Information	Remarks and references to Appendices
BRUCAMPS	Feb 15		Coys at disposal of O.C. Coys for instructions re orders received to proceed tomorrow to proceed tomorrow to BEAUVAL & on the day following to FORCEVILLE by march route. These orders were subsequently cancelled. C.O. addressed Coys in afternoon on occasion of Regt. having completed one year's war service in this country & on leaving the regiment to take up a position of Commandant of the "Divisional Cleaning School	
	Feb 16		Move to BEAUVAL cancelled. Coys at disposal of O.C. Coys medically inspected	
	Feb 17		Companies at disposal of O.C. Coys. Authority received to reduce regimental reserve of S.A.A. by one limbered wagon & to carry 768 rounds of grenades (No 5) in the spare limber. 1 officer & 5 men detailed per company to be instructed in bombing and 6 men per company to be instructed in Lewis Gun, 4 of which were issued to this unit on Feb 14th. 60 mules arrived from the A.S.C. these with 9 heavy draft horses & 17 pack horses & mules previously drawn on the 15th – complete establishment of transport	
	Feb 18		As yesterday	
	Feb 19		As yesterday. All companies medically inspected. Winter clothing issued to the Batt. Two cooks to	
	Feb 20		Coys at disposal of O.C. Companies. All officers demonstrated in use & action of LEWIS GUN	

WAR DIARY
or
INTELLIGENCE SUMMARY

(Erase heading not required.)

Army Form C. 2118

Place	Date	Hour	Summary of Events and Information	Remarks and references to Appendices
BRUCAMPS	Feb 21		Billeting Party sent to FRANKVILLE. Orders at disposal of O.C. Coys. Wire received 10.30 a.m. cancelling move to FRANKVILLE, the original move to FRANSU being altered to FRANKVILLE at 10 a.m. 1 man accidentally wounded by bomb.	
	" 22		Companies at disposal of O.C. Companies. Parties instructed in Bombing.	
	" 23		A & B Companies marched to LONGVILLERS to commence work on house occupied by the 3rd South Midland Field Ambulance. Operation orders received ordering attachment of the regiment to 137th Brigade from the 25th inst.	
	" 24		137th Bde orders received to march to BEAUVAL on 26th instant, the distance is approximately 16 miles. Companies at disposal of O.C. Coys.	
	" 25		Heavy snow fell all day. Coys at disposal of O.C. Coys.	
	" 26		Coys paraded at 7.15 a.m. for Batt. parade at 7.45 a.m. as Batt. was ordered to march to BEAUVAL. This move was cancelled at 7.30 a.m. Roads covered with snow 6 inches deep. Coys paraded at 8.30 a.m. for work on clearing snow from roads.	
	" 27 28		Coys at disposal of O.C. Coys. Coys at disposal of O.C. Coys for drill, musketry re orders received to prepare to move early tomorrow.	
CANDAS	" 29		Battalion paraded at 8.45 a.m. and marched to CANDAS about 12 miles distance.	MOVE

46

Vol X

Confidential
War Diary
of
1/1st Bn Monmouthshire Regt. T.F.
for
Month of March 1916

R A Stoner
Capt & Adjt.
for O.C. 1/1st Mon Regt. T.F.

Army Form C. 2118

WAR DIARY
or
INTELLIGENCE SUMMARY
(Erase heading not required.)

Instructions regarding War Diaries and Intelligence Summaries are contained in F. S. Regs., Part II. and the Staff Manual respectively. Title Pages will be prepared in manuscript.

Place	Date	Hour	Summary of Events and Information	Remarks and references to Appendices
CANDAS	Mar 1		Companies at disposal of O.C. Companies.	
	" 2		Companies at disposal of O.C. Companies for bathing of men and washing of underclothing	
	" 3		Battalion Parade for Route March. Washing grooming in afternoon	
	" 4		Battalion paraded 9 a.m. with shovels marched to MONTRELET & FIEFFES to fill in trenches dug by troops for practice purposes	
	" 5		Work on filling in trenches continued as yesterday. Boys returned at 1 p.m. as Batn. moves early tomorrow.	
ETREE WAMIN	" 6		Batn. paraded at 6.45 a.m. and marched to ETREE-WAMIN a distance of 15 miles. No one fell out. Arrived in billets at 1 p.m.	MOVE
	" 7		Battalion attached to 137th Brigade for tactical purposes as from today and until further orders	
			C.O. Major Dumpf, Adjutant, & L.G. Lusby (MGO) left by bus at 1 a.m. with a scouting party of officers from the 137th Bde & inspect trenches to be taken over tho' begun in to take over the village of NEUVILLE ST VAAST which is at present held by the French	
	" 8		Companies at disposal of O.C. boys.	
MAIZIERES	" 9		Battalion paraded 10.30 am and marched to MAIZIERES about 4 miles and billeted there	MOVE
	" 10		Advance party of 2 officers and 4 N.C.O.s per company marched to ECOIVRES. This party is to go into NEUVILLE ST VAAST tomorrow morning to reconnoitre the trenches	
			Four officers O/Rks BLOW, SELINE, HARRIS and FRY temporarily attached to 6th North Stafford Regt to gain experience in front line work	

WAR DIARY
or
INTELLIGENCE SUMMARY
(Erase heading not required.)

Army Form C. 2118

Place	Date	Hour	Summary of Events and Information	Remarks and references to Appendices
ECOIVRES	7-4-11		Battalion paraded at 8.30 a.m and marched to ECOIVRES distance about 12½ miles. A hot dinner was ready at 12 noon when tea was issued. Battalion billeted in huts at ECOIVRES for the night	MOVE
NEUVILLE ST VAAST	" 12		Battalion paraded 6.30 a.m. and marched to NEUVILLE ST VAAST and relieved 326 t Regiment French Army, commanded by Col. PERROCHAT (who had held position with his regiment for 8 months) at 11 p.m. The Lewis Guns were sent up on the evening of the 11th and were placed in position this morning. Batt. marched up 18 Officers and 404 other ranks. Companies were met at cross roads LA TARGETTE by company guides and were billetted in dugouts and large dug outs i.e. were carved by the evacuation of hand chalk glow. Dust down are very deep, the one at the RIETZ cross roads having 67 steps.	MOVE
	" 13		C.O visited all companies and with O.C boys visited the position of officers allotted to them to repair and hold in case of attack. A plan of NEUVILLE ST VAAST is given on adjoining page 2/21 & 2. Began appointed TOWN MAJOR of NEUVILLE ST VAAST	
	" 14		Every thing quiet the road to BETHUNE was shelled North of LA TARGETTE CLUB ROADS. Positions further reconnoitred by C.O Major Dury & Captns by night & day	
	" 15		Every quiet nothing of note except on a mouse by night. R.H. Moore reported for duty from 3rd Line. At 9 pm message received from 137. Bale that German message had been deciphered that a mine was to be exploded at 10 pm. Bays were warned but work was carried on as usual under control was placed under immediate control that everyone	

WAR DIARY or INTELLIGENCE SUMMARY

Army Form C. 2118

(Erase heading not required.)

Instructions regarding War Diaries and Intelligence Summaries are contained in F.S. Regs., Part II. and the Staff Manual respectively. Title Pages will be prepared in manuscript.

Place	Date	Hour	Summary of Events and Information	Remarks and references to Appendices
NEUVILLE ST VAAST	March 16		Enemy quiet all day until evening (They) when man about of village was shelled with Shrapnel & M.G. offensive probably caused by noise of our transport bringing up to last night at this time. No casualties. 25 shells burst in village. 2nd Lt. E.S. RICHARDS reported for duty from the 3rd line.	
	17		Enemy quiet all day working parties carried on with work on cellars & pit 6th defences. Our artillery opened from 8-9pm from 9.30-10.30 pm. Enemy retaliated slightly shelling main road through village. 42 shells fell in village.	
	18		Patrols again instructed by C.O. At 1 & 9pm. Bump Forking of any casualties to report. 10 shells fell in village.	
	19		At 10 am our heavy artillery fired about 25 rounds at the cross roads in BROWN N° 136. Blowing front the entrance to the PORTIQUE H. Work appeared good. Paralled from 12-12.30 noon & 1pm & 1.30 pm the enemy bombarded copse 6 in vicinity of RIET2 Cross Roads with shrapnel, 10 cm high explosive shells about 250 shells fell. Our damage was one or two of the "chevaux de frise" in advance of the BRITISH generally not actually working.	
	20		Co-operated defences with O.C. Bombing Asylum. Working parties found as usual at 5pm. No reports of offensive out of Asylum and no Gas. We informed offr. com. 137th Brigade. DUMPS 25/26. 25 shells fell in village.	
	21		Continued work on NEUVILLE defences. CO. C 46th DIVISION visited NEUVILLE at 11.30 a.m. & inspected position of defences. We expressed himself satisfied with the way work had been carried out. 10 shells fell in village.	

1875 Wt. W593/826 1,000,000 4/15 J.B.C. & A. A.D.S.S./Forms/C.2118.

Army Form C. 2118

WAR DIARY
or
INTELLIGENCE SUMMARY
(Erase heading not required.)

Instructions regarding War Diaries and Intelligence Summaries are contained in F.S. Regs., Part II. and the Staff Manual respectively. Title Pages will be prepared in manuscript.

Place	Date	Hour	Summary of Events and Information	Remarks and references to Appendices
NEUVILLE ST VAAST	Mar 22		B Company relieved by A Coy. The arrangement to now has a Company here 16 days in and then goes back to ECOIVRES 6 days rest, wash and bath. Owing to the extreme defensive work was much interfered with at night 20 shells fell in village	
	-23		The defences of NEUVILLE ST VAAST inspected by General the EALLENBY, K.C.B. Commanding 3rd Army. He was accompanied by Lt. Gen the Hon. J. BYNG, Commander of 17th Corps. Owing to muddy weather working parties were all to carry on by day. 10 shells fell in village	
	-24		Sharp fall of snow in the night which melted during the course of the day. This advice all men did not muster owing to thumbs[?] fait en, in places. The snow interfered with working parties.
2d Lt VACHELL returned to duty as Lieutenant from England. Also RSM HUMPHRIES who left the regiment in Oct 1915 & who has been employed at G.H.Q. during interval to date. 10 shells fell in village	
	-25		Enemy quiet all day. At 2.20 a.m on the 26th the enemy expoloded a mine of the left of the 51st Division (the division on our right) every heavy bombing & machine gun fire followed. This regt stood to arms, the alarm was out out at 12.30 A.m. The battalion chambered at 3.45 am. All companies however at their accustomed posts without confusion REM2 Eress Roads bombarded from 4 to 6 p.m. 225 shells fell in village	
	-26		Enemy very quiet all day. On a relief (46.51.) Division fired two Shellers at 6 p.m at dump at VIMY. Germans replied with 6 H.E Shrapnel on road by PORTIQUE at 6.5 p.m and again at 9.30 p.m	
	-27		Enemy quiet, the enemy has diminished noticeably lately but an occasional shell at the corner done by Church Corner.	

Army Form C. 2118

WAR DIARY
or
INTELLIGENCE SUMMARY
(Erase heading not required.)

Instructions regarding War Diaries and Intelligence Summaries are contained in F. S. Regs., Part II. and the Staff Manual respectively. Title Pages will be prepared in manuscript.

Place	Date	Hour	Summary of Events and Information	Remarks and references to Appendices
NEUVILLE ST VAAST	7.4.27 (contd)		Every quiet. Draft of 93 N.C.O's & men arrived from Base, 88 from 3rd Line & 5 from Base Details. Details of draft 7 N.C.O's & 86 men. Of these 88 & 3rd Line N.C.O's & men:— 9 N.C.O's & men have served with B.E.F before 3 N.C.O's & men are Signallers 3 men have had training in Stokes Gun 1 man has had Grenade training 1 man has had Transport training	
	"28		25 Shells fell in village. Working parties as usual. C Company relieved by B by Evg & out all day.	
	"29		Every quiet thro day. Operation orders received that a counter attack to take L37 by no later 6.50 p.m to try to explode the German mine under R.4. Alarm posts were manned at 6.30 p.m & the counter attack was to turn the explosion & was followed by heavy artillery fire, a barrage being placed behind the German lines. & they our guns & to several points thro the directed through by artillery observer. At 8.30 p.m was received from 1st South Staffords Bn. that two of their platoons had been sent up to reinforce "B" Coy. & had been moved up to PUITS 26 & large car on main road. No reinforcements to pass up along the front of Parallel VIII without orders from "B" Coy. at 9.15 p.m. a second alarm was sounded by the Staffords & our machine guns opened fire then 2.4 in & 9.30 a.m the enemy bombarded Parallel VIII with shrapnel with RIETZ CROSS ROADS – LATARGETTE CROSS ROADS with heavy shells. 100 shells fell in village. 2/Lts E S RICHARDS & A C CORRY-SMYTH advised to keep in with shrapnel & from which repairing	

1875 Wt. W593/826 1,000,000 4/15 J.B.C. & A. A.D.S.S./Forms/C. 2118.

Army Form C. 2118

WAR DIARY
or
INTELLIGENCE SUMMARY
(Erase heading not required.)

Place	Date	Hour	Summary of Events and Information	Remarks and references to Appendices
NEUVILLE ST VAAST	7 Nov 30		Working parties as usual. Carrying parties found for the Brigade, 2 officers & 100 other ranks. From report received it thought that the enemy's mine was not destroyed by our camouflet last night, 100 shell fell in village.	
		3.45	At 3.45 am a mine was exploded by the 51st Division on our right by MOULIN ROUGE. At 7h— another mine was exploded near the above place. After both explosions there was an exchange of artillery trench mortar, machine gun, and rifle fire also bombs.	

D. J. Drury
Major Commanding
1/1st Monmouthshire Regiment T.F.

46

Vol 11

Confidential

War Diary

of

1/1st Batt the Monmouthshire Regt., T.F.

from 1st April 1916 to 30th April 1916

WAR DIARY
or
INTELLIGENCE SUMMARY

Army Form C. 2118

Place	Date	Hour	Summary of Events and Information	Remarks and references to Appendices
NEUVILLE ST. VAAST	4/1		Work commenced on BOYAU ROY, an old communication trench running up through the centre of the village. Major Front relieved Major of Highnett from 21.30 of EVILL who has gone to 46th Divisional Bomb. at Bombardant. 25 Shell fell in village	
	" 2		Lt. Gen. the Hon J. BYNG. 17th Corps commander visited NEUVILLE ST VAAST. Working parties found. Firing ceased day for communication trench in village. At 6.15 p.m. the enemy exploded a mine of BH No. 2 trench. They overpowered by 6 S. STAFFS who occupied the crater. They overran our line from 2 of the line. The regt. stood to from 6.45 p.m. to 9.45 p.m. but beyond furnishing carrying parties for Bombs, an abbey & very light ammunition to 40 officers + 130 hen. nothing was done by us. 40 shell fell in village	
	" 3		Enemy quiet all day. At 7.15 p.m. a mine was exploded by the enemy to the left of the 51st Division on the right of the 17th Battn. No. 1 we stood to arms until 8.15 p.m. the crater was occupied by the 51st Division. At 10.5 a.m. a german aeroplane was brought down by two of our troops an English aeroplane. Officer & men were killed. Enemy was observed by our own troops. German who claim to have hit the German trenches. 100 m. went up at night 2 work on BH crater, under R.E. 100 shell turned in village. D Coy was relieved by E boy which marched up from ECOURES from rest.	
	" 4		Enemy quiet all day. Work started on parallel 6 or Roy Road from the Chapel to junction to PORTIQUE. Working parties of 2 officers 40 men found to work on no. 2 BH. 25 Shell fell in village	

WAR DIARY
or
INTELLIGENCE SUMMARY
(Erase heading not required.)

Army Form C. 2118

Instructions regarding War Diaries and Intelligence Summaries are contained in F.S. Regs, Part II. and the Staff Manual respectively. Title Pages will be prepared in manuscript.

Place	Date	Hour	Summary of Events and Information	Remarks and references to Appendices
NEUVILLE ST VAAST	Ap 15		Work continued on ROY Trench. This trench has now been connected up from PORTIQUE to BUZZRA Headquarters. Two mines exploded by enemy in front of 139.2 Bde on left at 6.45 pm. The other on left of 5th Division on our right at 7.25 pm no artillery activity followed. 25 shell fell in village.	
	Ap 16		Roy trench completely dug through to BOYAU MERPILLAT. Every quiet. 10 shells fell in village. Lt Lee Evans went on weeks leave.	
	Ap 17		Work carried on as usual enemy particularly quiet 25 shells fell in village. Party of Germans observed working at 11 am in front of MEZUS the artillery was informed and fire was opened at at that dispersed the party	
	Ap 18		C.R.E. 46th Division inspected accouter defences afternoon on enemy again very quiet all day. 10 shells fell in village.	
	Ap 19		Work carried on as usual Parallel VI completed enemy very active and made into a communication trench from Chassery to the main road. From 8.10 - 8.30 pm our 9.2 + 8" heavy gun fired on B6 crater. The enemy retaliated by firing heavy shells - 77 mm shells on the support line - N.B. shrapnel on Parallel VIII 25 shell fell in village. A boy returned by D Coy.	
	Ap 20		Working party found as usual, the enemy burst shrapnel over N. Head of village at 12 noon + 1 pm except for this the enemy was quiet all day. 30 shells fell in village.	
	Ap 21		Lt-Col HOME + Major THORPE, GSO, 1+2 of the 46th Division inspected defences of village. Work re-started on the CENTRAL REDOUBT	

Army Form C. 2118

WAR DIARY
or
INTELLIGENCE SUMMARY
(Erase heading not required.)

Instructions regarding War Diaries and Intelligence Summaries are contained in F.S. Regs., Part II. and the Staff Manual respectively. Title Pages will be prepared in manuscript.

Place	Date	Hour	Summary of Events and Information	Remarks and references to Appendices
NEUVILLE ST VAAST	Ap 11		25 Shells fell in village. Brigsy HQ'rs all day	
	Ap 12		Platoon at CENTRAL REDOUBT work on wire all day. CENTRAL REDOUBT and Panel VI. 50 Shells fell in village.	
	Ap 13		Weather unsettled & bright now & again. Rifle Battery placed up in LUNDY ISLAND REDOUBT which fires upwards THELUS. 25 Shells fell in village.	
	Ap 14		Weather unsettled. 3 Officers & 120 other ranks arr'd off to MONT ST ELOY to form part of a composite company made up from the Gren. Bn attached to the 17th Corps to work the Light Railway. Enemy firing very fiercely 25 shells fell in village	
	Ap 15		C.O. and Adjutant of 6th S.W.B came up to reconnoitre as they relieve us the 22nd inst. in Cy B. Lieut "B" Coy. I casualty (wounded) 25 Shells fell in village. Snow 10pm to 11am an enemy aeroplane flew over village & dropped a bomb, no damage done	
	Ap 16		Fine, warm day, a villager on both sides being ordered working party on fatigue. Lieut C. KIRBY Machine Gun Officer wounded by shrapnel, 200 other ranks employed. Casualties 1 Officer wounded (as above)	
	Ap 17		At 12 midnight 16-17 we rec'd orders to move forward to the left of Bn in the area of the 139th Brigade, our heavy shelling followed. C.R.E 25th Division came up to inspect defences. Report made by C.R.E, 146th Division and R-Col Blewitt 6th S.W.B 150 Shells fell in village. Lt J.M PHILLIPS admitted to Hospital, Sick.	

WAR DIARY or INTELLIGENCE SUMMARY

Army Form C. 2118

Place	Date	Hour	Summary of Events and Information	Remarks and references to Appendices
NEUVILLE ST VAAST	Apl 18		Enemy quiet except for occasional bursts of shells. At 6.45 p.m. the Germans delivered an attack more known a picture of part of our front line, attack being noticed by any to our regiment, forced 150 shells fell on village.	
	Apl 19		From 8.30 a.m to 9 a.m the enemy shelled the Neuville area from CHEPSTOW trench to 92 m.h.g.s 50 shells fell. Actually shells were watched and reported it the recces received. At 2 p.m bombs were used (17/5) by Gen. Hon. J. BYNG, employed officers of NEUVILLE in matter, 50 shells fell in village. Relief of H.B. Division by 25th Division carried out.	
	Apl 20		Working parties carried on as usual. Periscopes again shelled in early morning 50 shells fell in village.	
	Apl 21		Working parties carried on as usual, owing to many of the trenches now allotted to follow places selected by 6th S.W.B. Arrived with signallers and from NEWPORT Demolition Officer VIII Grace in attendance in reconnoitre.	
ACQ	Apl 22		Battalion relieved by 6th Bath. R. Welsh Borderers relieving picket by 10 p.m. Battalion marched to rest billets at B Boys to AGNIERES, C & D Coys to ACQ. Battalion Headquarters to ACQ.	MOVE
TILLOY-LES-HERMAVILLE	Apl 23		Battalion Headquarters moved to TILLOY-LES-HERMAVILLE. Companies working only necessary work and but improving being done. All billets inspected by Major Dump & Adjutant & being done.	
	Apl 24		Work started on roads in vicinity of AGNIERES, ACQ & ECOIVRES. The work consists of widening roads at MONT ST ELOY and FREVIN-CAPELLE and laying down roads under the supervision of the Chief Engineer 17th Corps.	
	Apl 25		Work at ACQ continued also billets. Leave re-opened at the same allotment as previously, e.g. one passage on leave boat per day.	

Army Form C. 2118

WAR DIARY
or
INTELLIGENCE SUMMARY
(Erase heading not required.)

Place	Date	Hour	Summary of Events and Information	Remarks and references to Appendices
TILLOY-LES-HERMAVILLE	April		Work continued as usual for the last 4 days the weather has been very warm with bright sunshine.	
	27		Chief Engineer 1st Corps inspected work in hand with C.O. & Adjutant. Orders received to send working party to MAROEUIL to construct transfer station for Light Railway. LT-COL C.R.EVILL & 2LTN.J SELINE went on leave.	
	28		"B" Company marched to MAROEUIL. 1 other rank killed (Rfn Osborn B)	MOVE
AGNIERES	29		C.O, Adjutant & made to ACQ to inspect work Battalion Headquarters moved from TILLOY-LES-HERMAVILLE to AGNIERES	
	30		C.O, Adjutant inspected work and billets of Company at MAROEUIL. Bugle band again assembled with 16 buglers.	

T. J. Duvett
Major Commanding
1/1st Bn The Monmouthshire Regt

11/5/16.

46

Vol 12

Confidential

War Diary

1/1st Batt. the Monmouthshire Regt T.F.

from 1st May 1916 to 31st May 1916.

Army Form C. 2118

WAR DIARY
or
INTELLIGENCE SUMMARY   1st Monmouthshire Regt.
(Erase heading not required.)

Place	Date	Hour	Summary of Events and Information	Remarks and references to Appendices
AGNIERES	May 1		Work carried on as usual. A box of gifts having been received from H.M. Queen Alexandra on April 20th consisting of Cigarettes, scarves & sweets, the following letter was sent to Her Majesty	

B.E.F.
1st May 1916

As Commanding Officer of the 1st Battalion Monmouthshire Regiment, I desire to express to your Majesty the gratitude of my men for the comforts you so graciously sent them. The gifts are appreciated and valued by them not only on account of their intrinsic value and utility, but as evidence of your Majesty's constant care and thought for the soldiers of the Field

(Signed) F.J. TRUMP, Major Commdg
1/1st Batt. Monmouthshire Regt.

2/Lt R K WELLSTEED reported for duty from 3rd line

Copy of letter received from Her Majesty Queen Alexandra

Marlborough House
Pall Mall
5th April 1916

Dear Sir, I am despatching to you today some comforts for Queen Alexandra which the Rangers have knitted

Army Form C. 2118

WAR DIARY
or
INTELLIGENCE SUMMARY
(Erase heading not required.)

Instructions regarding War Diaries and Intelligence Summaries are contained in F.S. Regs., Part II. and the Staff Manual respectively. Title Pages will be prepared in manuscript.

Place	Date	Hour	Summary of Events and Information	Remarks and references to Appendices
AGNIERES	May 1		amongst the men under your command, and which I hope will be acceptable to them. Perhaps you will be good enough to acknowledge the receipt direct to Her Majesty. I am, dear Sir, Yours faithfully, (sgd) HENRY STREATFIELD Private Beauchamp to H.M. Queen Alexandra.	
	May 2	6 p.m.	"A" Company & details of "B" "C" & "D" Coys inspected by the C.O.	
	May 3		Orders received that the regiment would be relieved on the night of 4/5 & that the Battalion would concentrate at MAIZIERES on the 5th. Orders issued to effect exchange of 30 officers and 120 men now lodged on light Railway work, to rendezvous at AGNIERES on night of 4/5. C.O. inspected C & D Companies at ACQ.	
	May 4		All companies arrived at AGNIERES by 11 p.m. and were billeted for the night. Lt J.R. EVANS went on leave. A draft of 153 men arrived from Base. These men with one draft of 19th Reserve Battalion found at nearly old 2nd line men who were out to the 3rd line when the 2nd line was reorganized to form 3rd line Reserve. 110 old BEF men arrived with the draft.	
MAIZIÈRES MOVE	May 5		Battalion paraded 9.30 a.m. & marched to MAIZIÈRES, the day was exceedingly hot and although the distance was only 8 miles a considerable number of men felt it owing to the great heat & want of training. Battalion marched into MAIZIÈRES about 1 p.m. & billeted there the night.	

Army Form C. 2118

WAR DIARY
or
INTELLIGENCE SUMMARY
(Erase heading not required.)

Instructions regarding War Diaries and Intelligence Summaries are contained in F. S. Regs., Part II. and the Staff Manual respectively. Title Pages will be prepared in manuscript.

Place	Date	Hour	Summary of Events and Information	Remarks and references to Appendices
MAIZIERES BEAUDRICOURT	May 6		Battalion paraded 7a.m. and marched to BEAUDRICOURT (6½mls) arrived at 9.30 a.m. No men fell out. The day was much hotter than yesterday. Billeted the night at BEAUDRICOURT	MOVE
POMMIER	" 7		Battalion paraded 11 a.m. and marched to POMMIER (11 miles) no men fell out. A halt was made at 1 p.m. for dinner. Battalion arrived at 4.30 p.m. no men killed. This village is about 2½ miles behind the line but has not been shelled.	MOVE
	" 8		Companies at disposal of O.C. Companies.	
	" 9		Companies at disposal of O.C. Companies	
	" 10		Companies at disposal of O.C. Companies. Concentration of a large train for the evacuation of May 8th 1915 (2nd Battle YPRES)	
	" 11		Companies at disposal of O.C. Companies.	
	" 12		Companies at disposal of O.C. Companies. 2/Lts T.O. JONES, S. MURRAY, C.H. CHAPMAN reported for duty marked billets. 2/Lts T.O.JONES, S MURRAY, C.H CHAPMAN reported for duty from the Reserve Battalion.	
	" 13		Companies at disposal of O.C. Companies. Rapid Wiring training and bayonet fighting is being carried out. 2/Lts E.P.H LANG, G. HARLEY reported for duty from Reserve Battalion.	
	" 14		As on the 13th. Draft of 8 men arrived from Base	
	" 15		As on the 14th. 100 men inoculated	
	" 16		As on the 15th. 100 men inoculated	

WAR DIARY or INTELLIGENCE SUMMARY

Army Form C. 2118

Place	Date	Hour	Summary of Events and Information	Remarks and references to Appendices
POMMIER	May 17	—	100 men inoculated. Lt. Col. E. VIII returned from leave and resumed command of the Battalion.	
	" 18		Companies at disposal of O.C. Coys.	
	" 19		A party of 2 Officers and 100 others to be detailed to work on HUMBERCAMP — ST AMAND ROAD. Remainder of Regiment carried on with training (Bayonet fighting, Bomb etc.)	
	" 20		Companies carried on as usual with training.	
	" 21		Church parade 12 noon. Companies at disposal of O.C. Coys for remainder of day. Personnel of Transport inspected at 10 a.m. by C.O.	
	" 22		A fatigue party of 320 other ranks to be found for digging a cable trench. Telephone wires from SOUASTRE to FONQUEVILLERS. Dimensions of trench 2ft wide x 6ft deep. Fatigue also found of 1 Officer and 25 men for work on Advanced Divisional Headquarters at ST AMAND. Total number of men daily on fatigue work 425 men with NCOs + Officers in proportion.	
	" 23		C.O. inspected D Coy at 3.30 p.m. Fatigue parties found as yesterday. One NCO or man per platoon to be on parade every day under 2/Lt R.H. WELLSTEED for a week for instruction in bayonet fighting. These 16 NCOs + men when trained will be used for instructing their platoons at the first opportunity.	
	" 24		Fatigue parties as usual. C.O. inspected the 2 platoons of C + D Coys HQs as on day fatigue.	
	" 25		Fatigues found as usual. 2/Lt N.T.G. LLEWELLIN went on leave	

Army Form C. 2118

WAR DIARY
or
INTELLIGENCE SUMMARY
(Erase heading not required.)

Instructions regarding War Diaries and Intelligence Summaries are contained in F.S. Regs., Part II. and the Staff Manual respectively. Title Pages will be prepared in manuscript.

Place	Date	Hour	Summary of Events and Information	Remarks and references to Appendices
PONNIER	May 26		Fatigue found as usual. Draft of 36 other ranks arrived from Rouen Base, 30 from Rouen Base & 6 from Base Hospitals. Company started to dig shelter trenches behind the village for use in case the villages are shelled. This appears likely as heavy guns are being placed behind the Coldstream Lines, one 15" gun will probably be placed near the tramway.	
	27		C.O. inspected the 2 platoons of C + D Coys that are working by night. Fatigues found as usual.	
	28		Church Parade 12 noon. Orders received to arrange 6 Officers and 186 men to consist of Rouen boys from the fifth line out towards the German trenches. These Rouen boys are turned out from the front trench apparently 18" below the ground level. Details found as usual. After tonight the digging of the Cable trench is to be handed over to 138 & Bde. and complimentary message received from GOC	Officers 1 Bn from OOC 138/5/6
	29		"B" Coy marched out at 9 a.m. to FONQUEVILLERS this Coy is to be billeted there and carry on the work of making the Rouen Bays C.O. and Major Dunn marched to 139 Bde H.Q. and afterwards inspected point where Regt. is to be made. "A" Coy marched to FONQUEVILLERS at 8.30 p.m. to billets. These two companies to work on dug outs and advanced trenches headquarters for the 139 Bde.	
	30		Major Dunn & Lieut Royston & other officers at FONQUEVILLERS took on sap commenced the following officers	

1875 Wt. W593/826 1,000,000 4/15 J.B.C. & A. A.D.S.S./Forms/C. 2118.

WAR DIARY
or
INTELLIGENCE SUMMARY

Army Form C. 2118

Place	Date	Hour	Summary of Events and Information	Remarks and references to Appendices
POMMIER	May 3		reported for duty from the Reserve Battalion. Lieut J. Jordan-Lloyd, 2/Lt P.D. Malone Skinner, 2/Lt T.R.S. Jones, 2/Lt A.W. Bent, 2/Lt G.S.J, 2/Lt W. E. J Huggins	
	31		C.O. Major Trump worked ours in line trap ordered each one to be drawn about 8 yards straight of line today 37 Officers and 736 other ranks	

Commanding 1/1st Bn The Monmouthshire Regt J.S.
Lieut Colonel

APPENDIX NO. 1.

Wire received from General Officer Commanding, 46th Division.

To. 1st Monmouths.

G. 719.   28th   —   AAA

The General Officer Commanding wishes to congratulate the Battalion on the excellent work done last night in digging the cable trenches. AAA

46th Division.
9.5 p.m.

Vol/13 4b

Confidential
War Diary
of
1/1st Battalion The Monmouthshire Regt.
from 1st June 1916 to 30th June 1916

A.C.Hill
Lieut-Colonel.

Comdg. 1/1st Bn. The Monmouthshire Regt.

Army Form C. 2118

1/1st Bn Monmouthshire Regt TF

WAR DIARY
or
INTELLIGENCE SUMMARY

(Erase heading not required.)

Instructions regarding War Diaries and Intelligence Summaries are contained in F. S. Regs., Part II. and the Staff Manual respectively. Title Pages will be prepared in manuscript.

Place	Date	Hour	Summary of Events and Information	Remarks and references to Appendices
POMMIER	1 June		C.O. & Major TRUMPIN inspected saps. Length to noon :— No 1. 33 feet total length " 2. Delayed by old trench " 3. 36 feet total length " 4. 30	
	2 June		As yesterday. Length of saps to noon :— No 1. 35 feet total " 2. 36 " " 3. 60 " " 4. 52 " One Platoon "D" Coy sent to FONQUEVILLERS and attached to "B" Coy to act as carrying party for saps. 2 Platoons "C" Coy sent to FONQUEVILLERS for work in conjunction with "A" Coy	
	3 June		As yesterday. Length of saps. No 1. 73 feet total No 2. 50 " No 3. 80 " No 4. 62 " Extract from Supplement to London Gazette dated 2nd June 1916. "To be a Companion of the Distinguished Service Order Captain (A/Lty Col) C DEVILL Monmouthshire Regt TF.	

1875 Wt. W593/826 1,000,000 4/15 J.B.C. & A. A.D.S.S./Forms/C. 2118.

Army Form C. 2118

WAR DIARY
or
INTELLIGENCE SUMMARY
(Erase heading not required.)

Instructions regarding War Diaries and Intelligence Summaries are contained in F. S. Regs., Part II. and the Staff Manual respectively. Title Pages will be prepared in manuscript.

Place	Date	Hour	Summary of Events and Information	Remarks and references to Appendices
POMMIER	4 June		Major TRUMP & Adjutant visited work and saps at FONQUEVILLERS. Length of saps:- No 1. 97 feet total No 2. 70'1" " No 3. 100 " " No 4. 86 " "	
	5 June		C.O. & Major TRUMP inspected saps at FONQUEVILLERS. Length of saps:- No 1. 120½ feet total No 2. 93 " " No 3. 122 " " No 4. 107 " "	
	6 June		C.O. & Major TRUMP inspected saps at FONQUEVILLERS. Length of saps:- No 1. 136½ feet total No 2. 117 " " No 3. 142 " " No 4. 130 " "	
			Captain & Adjt R.C.L. THOMAS went on leave.	
	7 June		C.O. & M.G.O. inspected saps. Major Trump & 2.Lt Harley attended demonstration of Stykowski Jacko & boring instruments.	

Army Form C. 2118

WAR DIARY
or
INTELLIGENCE SUMMARY
(Erase heading not required.)

Instructions regarding War Diaries and Intelligence Summaries are contained in F. S. Regs., Part II. and the Staff Manual respectively. Title Pages will be prepared in manuscript.

Place	Date	Hour	Summary of Events and Information	Remarks and references to Appendices
PONNIER	7 June		Length of saps:— No 1 159 ft total " 2 139 " " 3 169 " " 4 152 "	
	8 June		C.O. at FONQUEVILLERS reconnoitring new work to be done by the Battalion. Major TRUMP inspected saps. Length of saps No 1 176 feet total length " 2 149 " " 3 191½ " " 4 171 "	
			Progress of No 1 & 2 delayed owing to steel holes being encountered	
	9 June		C.O. & Major TRUMP at FONQUEVILLERS. Length of saps No 1 195 feet total length " 2 168½ " " 3 214½ " " 4 191½ "	
			An old French encountered in No 1 work French cartridge caps. The following officers reported for duty from the Reserve Battalion: 2/Lieut. Jendeyn, 2/Lt. J. Edwards, 2/Lieut. C. Joffe	

1875 Wt. W 593/826 1,000,000 4/15 J.B.C. & A. A.D.S.S./Forms/C. 2118.

Army Form C. 2118

WAR DIARY
or
INTELLIGENCE SUMMARY
(Erase heading not required.)

Instructions regarding War Diaries and Intelligence Summaries are contained in F.S. Regs., Part II. and the Staff Manual respectively. Title Pages will be prepared in manuscript.

Place	Date	Hour	Summary of Events and Information	Remarks and references to Appendices
HQ POMMIER	June 10		C O to FONQUEVILLERS. Major TRUMP attended demonstration of Hydraulic Pipe Boring Jacks at BRIQUETTERIE. Length of saps	
COYS AT FONQUEVILLERS			No 1. 214 feet total length	
			" 2. 188 " " "	
			" 3. 235 " " "	
			" 4. 212 " " "	
	" 11		Casualty. Captain A. I. EVANS wounded in head by shellfire today. Lieut Jordan Lloyd assumed command of B Coy as from	
			C.O. Major Trump inspected saps at FONQUEVILLERS. Length of saps	
			No 1. 231 feet total length	
			" 2. 205 " " "	
			" 3. 256 " " "	
			" 4. 230 " " "	
	" 12		C.O. Major Trump inspected work at FONQUEVILLERS with C.R.E., 46th Division. Length of saps.	
			No 1. 231 feet total length	
			" 2. 225 " " "	
			" 3. 275 " " "	
			" 4. 249 " " "	
			A draft of 35 Other Ranks arrived from the Base of which 2 Sgts & 5 Pte had previously been with this Unit in France. These men were Pte Recruits from the Reserve Battalion	

Army Form C. 2118

WAR DIARY
or
INTELLIGENCE SUMMARY
(Erase heading not required.)

Instructions regarding War Diaries and Intelligence Summaries are contained in F.S. Regs., Part II. and the Staff Manual respectively. Title Pages will be prepared in manuscript.

Place	Date	Hour	Summary of Events and Information	Remarks and references to Appendices
H.Q. at POMMIER	June 13		C.O. & Major TRUMP up to FONQUEVILLERS. Length of sap. No 1. 271 feet total length " 2. 246 " " " " 3. 299 " " " " 4. 266 " " "	
COMPANIES AT FONQUEVILLERS		14	C.O. & Major TRUMP up to FONQUEVILLERS - C.R.E. (46th Division) interviewed C.O. regarding alteration of No 4 sap & Plans of Trench Mortar positions. Length of saps:- No 1. 290 feet total length " 2. 263 " " " " 3. 321 " " " " 4. 284 " " " In accordance with Army Order and in conformity with French Daylight Saving Act all watches were advanced 60 minutes at 11 p.m. making new time midnight. 2/Lt. FISHER went on short leave.	
		15	C.O. & Major TRUMP up to FONQUEVILLERS to meet C.R.E. Work on saps Nos. 2, 3, 4 to be discontinued during the night. A trench mortar position is to be constructed off No. 1 and off No. 4 sap. Length of saps No 1. 312 feet total length " 2. 279 " " " " 3. 340½ " " " " 4. 305½ " " "	

WAR DIARY or INTELLIGENCE SUMMARY

Army Form C. 2118

Place	Date	Hour	Summary of Events and Information	Remarks and references to Appendices
HQ PONNIER	June 15		In the afternoon G.O.C. Division (Maj-Gen. Hon: E.J STUART-WORTLEY) called at Battn. H.Qrs. and congratulated the C.O. on the excellent work done by this unit, especially in regard to the Russian sap. Major THORPE (G.S.O.1) who was with him also expressed admiration for the way the Battalion had worked. The G.O.C. desired a complementary message to appear in tonight's orders.	Appendix 1
COMPANIES AT FONQUEVILLERS	" 16		C.O. & Major Dump all day at FONQUEVILLERS. Length of sap. No 1. 328 feet some length " 2. 316 " " " 3. 359 " " " 4. 329 " "	
			Nos 1 & 4 have been turned on preparations for making Trench Mortar emplacements. This was the first fine day for the past fortnight. It continued rain has made the trenches in all respects a condition. Parapets had been made knee-high in many places. Casualty 1 O.R. wounded in head - not serious.	
	" 17		C.O. & Major Dump inspected work at FONQUEVILLERS. Length of sap:- No 1. 328 feet total length " 2. 316 " " " 3. 379 " " " 4. 329 " " Trench Mortar emplacements have been made on nos 2-4	

Army Form C. 2118

WAR DIARY
or
INTELLIGENCE SUMMARY
(Erase heading not required.)

Instructions regarding War Diaries and Intelligence Summaries are contained in F.S. Regs., Part II. and the Staff Manual respectively. Title Pages will be prepared in manuscript.

Place	Date	Hour	Summary of Events and Information	Remarks and references to Appendices
H.Q. POMMIER	Jan 17		by driving an extra length of shaft to the right for about 6 yards at 320 feet on No 2 × 317 ft on No 1.	
COMPANIES AT FONQUEVILLERS	18		Work inspected by C.O. & Major Dunup. Length of sap:— No 1 3393 ft total length , 2 329½ " " , 3 400 " " , 4 348 " " Casualties 2 O.R. wounded by shell. The following Officers of this Unit were mentioned in a dispatch from Sir Doug Haig to the Secretary of State for War dated April 30th 1916. EVILL, Capt (Temp. Lt. Col.) C.A. KIRBY, 2nd Lt (Temp Lt) C.	
	19		Usual inspection of work. Casualties 1 killed 5 wounded caused by shell bursting in a dugout by FONQUEVILLERS Church. Length of sap:— No 1 359 feet total length , 2 338 " " , 3 418 " " , 4 366 " "	
	20		Got 1 Battery of RGA 9.2 Howitzers have been moved into POMMIER. Usual inspection of work. The Platoon of D Coy which has been working on Advanced Divisional HQ at ST AMAND have now completed the work and is being sent up to FONQUEVILLERS to help with work here.	

1875 Wt. W593/826 1,000,000 4/15 J.B.C. & A. A.D.S.S./Forms/C. 2118.

WAR DIARY
or
INTELLIGENCE SUMMARY
(Erase heading not required.)

Army Form C. 2118

Place	Date	Hour	Summary of Events and Information	Remarks and references to Appendices

H.Q. POMMIER
 	
COYS AT FONQUEVILLERS
	June 20
	
	.21
	
	.22
			Length of sap: No 1. 378 feet total length
			      " 2. 354 " "
			      " 3. 436½ " "
			      " 4. 386½ " "
			
			Usual inspection of work. Conference of O.C. Companies with C.O. at FONQUEVILLERS. Length of sap:
			      No 1. 393 feet
			      " 2. 375 "
			      " 3. 459 "
			      " 4. 408 "
			
			Divisional Orders received that on the night of 22nd-23rd the front line of the Division will be advanced a distance of 150 yards.
			
			Usual inspection of work. Length of sap:-
			      No 1. 410 feet.
			      " 2. 399 "
			      " 3. 476 "
			      " 4. 430 "
			
			Orders received to move tomorrow to huts at PAS. Divisional front line advanced 150 yards as desired yesterday. Lt. C.T. VACHELL rejoined from Hospital & rooted & command "A" Coy.	

Army Form C. 2118

WAR DIARY
or
INTELLIGENCE SUMMARY
(Erase heading not required.)

Place	Date	Hour	Summary of Events and Information	Remarks and references to Appendices
PAS. HUTS	June 23		Orders received to all details at FONQUEVILLERS to proceed to PAS HUTS after dusk, with the exception of 96 men of B Company under Lt. JORDAN-LLOYD + 2 Lts. HARLEY + EDWARDS who are being left up to push on the 2nd day to the advanced front line trench. Remainder of batt. and transport moved to PAS Huts starting at 12 noon. From 3 p.m. to 5 p.m. a very heavy thunderstorm passed over with intense rain and on 2/Lt. + 2 Lt. R.H. MARTIN was riding on to the new transport lines at PAS he was struck by lightning, thrown from his horse and badly injured. Details from FONQUEVILLERS arrived at 2.30 a.m. to the above. Rain had fallen very heavily from 8 a.m. to 3 a.m. 24th. The front line trenches at FONQUEVILLERS were thigh high in water and the communication trenches were also about 3 feet deep.	MOVE
	24		Whole of day spent in cleaning up men and their clothing and equipment after being a month at FONQUEVILLERS. The clothes had got into an extremely bad condition. 362 Brigade had Baths at GRINCOURT allotted to the Unit from 2 p.m. to 7 p.m. Heavy rain fell at intervals during the morning but cleared off about midday. In the afternoon Orders, today is known as "U" day and is the first of the bombardment, which will last 5 days, days being designated U.V.W.X.Y.Z. days. ZERO being the hour of attack on "Z" day.	

Army Form C. 2118

WAR DIARY
or
INTELLIGENCE SUMMARY
(Erase heading not required.)

Instructions regarding War Diaries and Intelligence Summaries are contained in F.S. Regs, Part II. and the Staff Manual respectively. Title Pages will be prepared in manuscript.

Place	Date	Hour	Summary of Events and Information	Remarks and references to Appendices
PAS	Jun 24 (con'd)		A letter "M" cut in black cloth 2 inches square has been adopted as a distinguishing mark to be worn by the N.C.Os and men with the approval of the G.O.C. 46th Division. The "M" is sewn on the back of the jacket in the centre and 1 inch below the collar.	
	Jun 25		Battalion inspected at 9.15 a.m. by G.O.C. 46th Division who first addressed the Regt and then inspected it. At 10.30 a.m. 15 German aeroplanes flew over PAS and surrounding villages and bombed all camps in a thy paced orchard, a number of bombs were dropped near the two occupied by this Unit but no damage was done. The 3 Officers and 96 men left behind at FONQUEVILLERS to finish the 2 days marched into camp at 8 p.m. having completed the work. The trenches are still very wet, the walls being once deep & our own in most places. V day of bombardment.	Appendix 2
	Jun 26		Companies at disposal of O.C. Coy. B Company bathed. VI day of bombardment.	
	" 27		"B" Company paraded 2 p.m. and marched to FONQUEVILLERS. This Company is to to open up the Russian sap under the direction of Major Dump. Work is to commence about 8 p.m. Officers marching out with this Company 2/Lt. T. EDWARDS i/c Claering No 1. Sap " " C.H. CHAPMAN " " No 2.	

1875 Wt. W593/826 1,000,000 4/15 J.B.C. & A. A.D.S.S./Forms/C. 2118.

Army Form C. 2118

WAR DIARY
or
INTELLIGENCE SUMMARY
(Erase heading not required.)

Place	Date	Hour	Summary of Events and Information	Remarks and references to Appendices
PAS	June 27 (cont)		2/Lt. M.C.D. HARRIS i/c cleaning No 4 coy	
			" G. HARLEY " " " 3	
			" L.C. W.S. JONES Runner to Major TRUMP	
			Lt. J. JORDAN LLOYD O.C. B Coy. i/c No.1 & 2 coys	
			Lt. R. RUTHERFORD i/c 3 & 4 coys	
			Major F.J. TRUMP in charge of operations	
			X day of bombardment.	
	28		Orders received at 2.30 p.m. that all moves are postponed for the present. This necessitated recalling the transport and details which had marched a short distance from Camp to LA BAZEQUE FARM viâ HUMBERCAMPS where Battalion Headquarters is to be established and transport parked.	
			Y day of bombardment.	
	29		Battalion remained in camp at PAS and was inspected by C.O. at 2.30 p.m. Major TRUMP returned from FONQUEVILLERS during the night and reported the work satisfactory and that the dugouts were ready to be opened the following night.	
			Y1 day of bombardment.	
			During the night orders were received from the 46th Division that the Battalion would continue the advance by open trench to within 100 yds of the German line, by the following night previous to the advance.	

Army Form C. 2118.

WAR DIARY
or
INTELLIGENCE SUMMARY
(Erase heading not required.)

Place	Date	Hour	Summary of Events and Information	Remarks and references to Appendices
FONQUEVILLERS	June 30		Battalion less B Coy paraded at 10.30am and marched to SOUASTRE where dinners were given to the men by the side of the road. The C.O. saw the G.O.C. 139th Brigade in order to arrange details of assembly trenches in consequence of the new scheme. It was decided by the Brigadier that the men, working on the two caps in the wood and proceeding in the caps for the night and proceed with the work as soon as the barracks was finished. The Batt. then proceeded through SOUASTRE along the SOUASTRE-BIENVILLERS Road by Coy trains and debouched across the open country to the right. Nos 1, 2 cap parties proceeding by "D" track and Nos 3, 4 cap parties by "C". track to the western edge of FONQUEVILLERS. The country was under observation and open, but no artillery fire was drawn on the parties. The C.O. then proceeded to the 137th Brigade for instructions as to place of assembly for Nos 1, 2 cap parties, and after a lengthy discussion owing to the difference arising from the withdrawal of the cap parties moving the blocking the assembly of the attacking battalions, it was decided to withdraw these parties to assembly trenches in rear at 2am. During the discussion a message was received to the effect that ZERO would be at 7.30 am the next morning (ZERO being the code word for the time of the attack) as they boys had been ordered to be opened. It was ascertained that the men vaccinated in them would be visible to the enemy for about 3 hours of	MOVE

1875 Wt. W593/826 1,000,000 4/15 J.B.C. & A. A.D.S.S./Forms/C. 2118.

WAR DIARY
or
INTELLIGENCE SUMMARY

(Erase heading not required.)

Army Form C. 2118

Place	Date	Hour	Summary of Events and Information	Remarks and references to Appendices
FONQUEVILLERS	Jun 30		daylight, the saps being ploughed and the ground sloping away towards the enemy's position, this necessitated an alteration of the arrangements made early in the day with the 139th Brigade who had decided to assemble the troops in the saps themselves. The C.O. then interviewed the Brigadier 139th Bde. and arranged for them to be withdrawn. This was at 11pm and the parties had to be removed. After consultation with the officers "B" Coy parties were moved up at once to proceed with the opening of the saps as soon as it was dark and the remaining parties composed as follows:-	
			No 1. Sap. 1, 2, 3 platoons under 2/Lts. T.G. FRY & E.P.H. LANG	Under Lt. W.L. ROBERTS. These 2 saps were in the 137th Bde. front and the platoons detailed were attached to this Brigade.
			No 2. " 4, 11, 12 platoons under 2/Lts. G. SMART & A.W. GOLDSWORTHY	
			No 3. " 9, 10, 15 platoons under 2/Lts. N.J. SELINE & C. JEFFS	Under Capt. K.C. RAIKES. These 2 saps were in the 139th Bde. front and the platoons detailed were attached to this Brigade.
			No 4. " 13, 14, 16 platoons under 2/Lts. S. MURRAY & J. JENKYN	
			were moved to their assembly trenches. Instructions were now received that there would be an artillery bombardment up to 11pm and no work would be proceeded with before that hour, also that the Lewis Guns	

WAR DIARY or INTELLIGENCE SUMMARY

Place: FONQUEVILLERS
Date: Jun 30

would be firing on the gaps in the German wire during the work and knowing that this would have to keep close to the alignment of the trench.

"B" Company completed the whole of their work in the allotted time and withdrew to FONQUEVILLERS where they marched to POMMIER at 3.30 a.m. July 1st. The whole of the work was planned by Capt of 2/1 Coys. B Company under the direction of Major F.J. TRUMP and carried forward noise from the G.O.C. and C.E.'s of the 3rd Army and 7. Corps.

No. 1 Bat. party proceeded with their work on the termination of the bombardment and succeeded in digging a trench in continuation of the sap for about a distance of 60 yards.

No. 2 Sap party did likewise.

No. 3 Sap party succeeded in marking out their trench and getting out their covering party, when a very severe fire was opened by the enemy all down the line, forcing a great number of casualties at one time. 2nd Lt. N.J. SELINE was badly wounded and lay for some time close to the German wire and refused to be moved until the work was in progress. He was brought in by 2/KI JEFFS and an Officer of the 5th SHERWOOD FORESTERS who had been sent by Lieut. Col. WILSON the C.O. of the 5th SHERWOODS for this purpose. It is thought that the parties sent out to cut the German wire were discovered and drew the fire which effectually stopped further digging.

Army Form C. 2118

WAR DIARY
or
INTELLIGENCE SUMMARY
(Erase heading not required.)

Place	Date	Hour	Summary of Events and Information	Remarks and references to Appendices
FONQUEVILLERS	Jun 30		Recce party did not succeed in reaching their objective owing to the congested state of the trenches and the deep slush. Lt MURRAY however reconnoitred the ground ready for work during the assault ½ day. STRENGTH of Battn (less B. Coy) marching up to FONQUEVILLERS on June 30th 1916 :- 13 Officers and 346 Other Ranks. Battn. H.Q.rs marching up included in above but not previously detailed :- Lt. Col. CAEVILL, D.S.O., Capt. & Adjt. R.C.L. THOMAS. Lt. W. SHANKS, R.A.M.C. Strength of Battalion on June 30th 1916 :- 36 Officers. 714 other ranks. [signature] Lieutenant-Colonel. Comdg. 1/1st Battalion The Monmouthshire Regt.	

Army Form C. 2118

WAR DIARY
or
INTELLIGENCE SUMMARY
(Erase heading not required.)

APPENDIX. NO. 1

Place	Date	Hour	Summary of Events and Information	Remarks and references to Appendices
POMMIER	Jun 15		Extract from Battalion Orders:– The G.O.C. has expressed his admiration for the splendid work being done by this Battalion at the present time and that this should be published in Battalion Orders. The Commanding Officer feels sure that all ranks will be spurred to even greater efforts by this congratulatory message.	

Army Form C. 2118

WAR DIARY
or
INTELLIGENCE SUMMARY
(Erase heading not required.)

APPENDIX NO. 2

Place	Date	Hour	Summary of Events and Information	Remarks and references to Appendices
PAS	June 21	9.15 a.m.	Address of Major-General E. J. MONTAGUE-STUART-WORTLEY, C.B., C.M.G., M.V.O., D.S.O., G.O.C. 46th Division, to the Battalion:- "I wish to thank the Officers, Warrant Officers, N.C.Os and men of this Battalion for the splendid manner in which they have carried out the work allotted to them recently, more especially with regard to the Russian Saps. Ever since this Battalion has been in my Division it has done its work to the greatest satisfaction of all concerned and I look forward with the utmost confidence to the work to be done by this Regiment in the near future."	

T.M.N.800/8.

46th Division.

Reference your No. A/2764/1, I beg to enclose the War Diary of this Unit for the month of July 1916.

[signature]
Major.

5/8/16.   Commanding 1/1st Batt: Monmouthshire Regiment.

Army Form C. 2118

P/Lib.
1/1 Monmouth Regt

WAR DIARY
or
INTELLIGENCE SUMMARY
(Erase heading not required.)

Vol 14

War Diary
of
1/1st Batt. The Monmouthshire Regiment
from 1st July to 31st July 1916 inclusive.

J.S. Drury
Major
Comdg 1/1 B. Monmouthshire Rgt

WAR DIARY
of 1/1st Bn Monmouthshire Regt T F
INTELLIGENCE SUMMARY
(Erase heading not required.)

Army Form C. 2118

Place	Date	Hour	Summary of Events and Information	Remarks and references to Appendices
FONQUEVILLERS	July 1st		Z day The period up to 3.0 a.m. has been dealt with in the account already given. The bombardment was kept up during the early hours and at 6.25 a.m. a very intense bombardment was started which lasted for 65 minutes. The assault was launched at 7.30 a.m. The right Brigade did not succeed in reaching the German line. The left Brigade the first waves of the S.F. + 7.SHERWOODS succeeded in taking the German 1st line and possibly the 2nd line. The enemy's artillery was found to be very much stronger than was anticipated and a very heavy rapid fire was kept away the preceding ranks. The digging parties of the Batt although they had been moved up to their appointed places were unable to go forward owing to the necessity for their doing so never arose. They were withdrawn to their places of assembly and remained there during the bombardment by the enemy suffering considerable casualties. About 3.30 p.m. the G.O.C. 139th Brigade ordered nos 3+4 parties to withdraw to FONQUEVILLERS and nos 1+2 parties to withdraw were be west of FONQUEVILLERS about 5.30 pm	G.O.C. 137 TMC

Army Form C. 2118

WAR DIARY
or
INTELLIGENCE SUMMARY
(Erase heading not required.)

Place	Date	Hour	Summary of Events and Information	Remarks and references to Appendices

FONQUEVILLERS	July 1st		Subsequently orders were received from the Division for the Battalion to assemble at POMMIER and they were withdrawn without casualty arriving there about 9p.m. The casualties sustained during the whole operation were:-
			
			 Officers:- Wounded 2/Lt. N.J. SELINE,
			                       " T. JENKYN.
			
			 Other ranks:-
			       Killed 15.
			       Wounded 76.
			       Wounded & Missing 2.
			       Missing 4
			                     97
			
			 Total: 2 Officers and 97 other ranks
				MOVE

POMMIER	2		Companies at disposal of O.C. Companies for Rising actions. Draft of 44 other ranks arrived from the Base composed of:- 40 Recvr Batt men (old third line men) 4 men from Base Hospitals.	

Army Form C. 2118

WAR DIARY
or
INTELLIGENCE SUMMARY
(Erase heading not required.)

Instructions regarding War Diaries and Intelligence Summaries are contained in F. S. Regs., Part II. and the Staff Manual respectively. Title Pages will be prepared in manuscript.

Place	Date	Hour	Summary of Events and Information	Remarks and references to Appendices
LA CAUCHIE	3.7.43	4	Battalion moved by companies to LA CAUCHIE to billets. B Coy on fatigue work for billeting officer at FONQUEVILLERS	
BERLES-AU-BOIS			Battalion (less A Coy) moved to BERLES-AU-BOIS and took over billets vacated by 6th NORTH STAFFORDS Pioneer Battalion of the 37th Division. "D" Company QM Stores and Transport are remaining at LA CAUCHIE. A Coy being detailed to work on roads. Lt Col EVILL appointed Commandant BERLES by H.Q. 46th Division. Very heavy rain fell from 12 noon – 6 p.m.	
D. COY AT LA CAUCHIE		5	By 9 a.m. of village worked and allotted to Coys by C.O. Draft of 85 other ranks arrived from Base, all old second line men. The draft included 6 trained Lewis Gunners and 5 trained Signallers. Companies worked on improving their second defences.	
		6	P.B.P. of 85 other ranks to what arrived yesterday was inspected by the C.O. at 10 a.m. Coys worked on their portion of village defences. The defences encircling the village form part of the DIVISIONAL defence line and consist of a series of fire trenches on the N. E. & S. sides and a double line of wire what connects to the village by communication trenches. I have the Divisional line in a high state of wire completely encircling the village. The village is only harassed with about five breaks at a few open ends of roads. Major General of H.Q. Division and was accompanied by Major Gen. W. THWAITES. MONTAGUE STUART-WORTLEY took charge of village agreed.	Appendices
		7	Companies at work upon their sector of village defences. Extremely heavy rain fell at intervals throughout the day. C.R.E. Lt.-Col. THORPE (G.S.O.) had a conference with the C.O. re the defences.	

Army Form C. 2118

WAR DIARY
or
INTELLIGENCE SUMMARY

(Erase heading not required.)

Instructions regarding War Diaries and Intelligence Summaries are contained in F. S. Regs., Part II. and the Staff Manual respectively. Title Pages will be prepared in manuscript.

Place	Date	Hour	Summary of Events and Information	Remarks and references to Appendices
BERLES-AU-BOIS	July 8th		No work done by day. The whole Battalion less D Coy being detailed for carrying cylinders of gas up to the front line trenches opposite MONCHY. The gas is a new kind-diphenylchlorarsine hydrogen.	
'D' COY AT LA CAUCHIE	July 9th		Battalion engaged as yesterday on carrying up gas cylinders to the front trenches. No other work done. Orders received to attach one company to 137 F. Bde for work with the 1/2 North Midland Field Co. R.E. "A" Coy detailed.	
	July 10th		Battalion again on fatigue carrying gas cylinders and material in connection with gas. 2/Lt M.G. ALLPRESS has opened to England.	
	July 11th		Battalion worked on their sector of village defences. Weather much better and warmer.	
	July 12		G.O.C., G.S.O.1, C.R.E., C.O. inspected Divisional line when it was decided that work on the village defences is to be suspended for the present and that all coys should be directed on to improving communication trenches up to the front line.	
	July 13		Coys were now allotted to work as follows. A Coy working for 137 F. Brigade on NEWARK ST. Communication trench. B Coy 2 platoons on FARNBORO' ROAD and 1 platoon each on RENFREW ST. and LINCOLN LANE. "C" Company at work on Div: reserve line (village defences) "D" Coy on roads in 46. Divisional Area.	
			Coy again worked as yesterday. 2 Lt D WALROND SKINNER transferred to R.F.C. as pilot.	

WAR DIARY or INTELLIGENCE SUMMARY

Army Form C. 2118

Place	Date	Hour	Summary of Events and Information	Remarks and references to Appendices
BERLES-AU-BOIS	15/6/15		Companies at work as yesterday except that 'C' Coy worked by night on ST. CROSS Trench for 138? Bde. Capt Wm B. BURNYEAT reported for duty from Reserve Battalion & posted to 'B' Coy.	
D.COY AT LA CAUCHIE	16		Companies at work as yesterday except that C Coy tracks & employment started by B Coy on NOBS LANE.	
	17		Companies at work as yesterday except that motion was received to transfer C Coy to LA CAUCHIE for work or raids. Coy was discharged from our front line trenches opposite MONCHY at 10 p.m. This was officered by any attack or raid, it was / worded by an artillery bombardment. Two gas men went next - suffered with hydrogen what was received and Chlorine which was released shortly afterwards. The idea being that the fumes discharge would make the enemy duck & the second discharge would make him the enemy only retaliated slightly and there was principally gunfire of rifle & machine gun fire directed on our front trenches. 2LT. H.E. SHARPE reported for duty from the Reserve Batt.	
	18		Telegram received from 46th Div. in ever stating that the Commander-in-Chief had awarded a Military Cross to C.S.M. CHEEK R. (D.Coy). I strongly received that Battalion would be inspected by G.O.C. 46th Division on July 20th Coy's worked as yesterday. C Coy stood by for orders at LA CAUCHIE from VII Corps.	

1875 Wt. W593/826 1,000,000 4/15 J.B.C. & A. A.D.S.S./Forms/C. 2118.

Army Form C.2118

WAR DIARY
or
INTELLIGENCE SUMMARY
(Erase heading not required.)

Instructions regarding War Diaries and Intelligence Summaries are contained in F.S. Regs., Part II. and the Staff Manual respectively. Title Pages will be prepared in manuscript.

Place	Date	Hour	Summary of Events and Information	Remarks and references to Appendices
	July 18		Bombardment were carried out by our guns on the enemy's tracks & trenches to such by MONCHY for the period of 30 minutes during the night.	
	" 19		Work suspended from 12 noon for companies to clean equipment for GOC's inspection. At 5 p.m. leave received instructions 9 GOC's inspection. Bombarding during the night just to the north of MONCHY heavy firing by both sides.	
	" 20		Companies worked as usual upon their company work.	
	" 21		C Company moved from BERLES to BAILLEULVAL for work upon roads particularly the BAILLEULMONT - BAILLEULVAL - BASSEUX road. The company was ordered upon this work by the Corps (1st) in view of possible advance.	
	" 22		Work carried on as usual by companies. Lt. COLEVILL left for SAULTY to take over command of H.Q. Division School.	
	" 23		Work carried on as usual by companies. Work ceased at 12 noon to let companies prepare for GOC's inspection tomorrow.	
LA CAUCHIE	" 24		Bn. to be handed at 11 a.m. at LA CAUCHIE for L. Yuckles by GOC 46th Division. Major Genl W. THWAITES, who addressed the Battalion (during the inspection)	APPENDIX 2
BERLES-AU- BOIS	" 25		Work carried on as usual.	
	" 26		Work carried on as usual. At 7 p.m. Capt. WM. B. BURNYEAT R.A.M.C. pigeon on the roof of his billet, he photographed that they was a message rolled round its leg. The bird was sent to the H.Q. Division for examination & on opening turned out that he had carried a message from the 12 GLOUCESTERS at LONGUEVAL to	

Army Form C. 2118

WAR DIARY
or
INTELLIGENCE SUMMARY
(Erase heading not required.)

Instructions regarding War Diaries and Intelligence Summaries are contained in F. S. Regs., Part II. and the Staff Manual respectively. Title Pages will be prepared in manuscript.

Place	Date	Hour	Summary of Events and Information	Remarks and references to Appendices
LACOUCHE	July 7th		(continued) The battalion then marched past in column of route, the G.O.C. taking a salute, after which the rode to the field where the first line transport was paraded which was first inspected at the halt and then on the march.	

WAR DIARY or INTELLIGENCE SUMMARY

Army Form C. 2118

Place	Date	Hour	Summary of Events and Information	Remarks and references to Appendices
BERLES-AU-BOIS	Sept.		A heavy bombing raid that a heavy shell had dropped in the trench not inflicted many casualties. Enemy was active 7 a.m. to 1 a.m. the same day. 2/Lt SE RICHARDS reported for duty from Base Battalion.	
	27		Work as yesterday. Weather becoming much warmer. Lt A. MITCHELL reported at NUBIGNY for an interview with a flying Corps Officer, was accepted for training as a Pilot. 2/Lt Fontenoil was struck off the strength accordingly.	
	28		Work as yesterday. A draft of 43 other ranks arrived from the Base. 35, 1st Mon men from Reserve Battn as hearty as hardly finest. 2, 2nd Mon men from Base Hospital. 1, 3rd Mon men from Base Hospital. 5, 1st Mon men from Base Hospital. Total draft 43. This is the first draft of partially trained men received by this Unit.	
	29		Work carried on as usual. Draft of 22 3rd other ranks all from the 3rd Monmouths reported for duty from the Base. The draft is composed of old second line men of the 3rd Mon and with the exception of a few of the 3/3 Mon men, All have had about 1½ years training. After being inspected at 60 COYCIE by the 700th draft was divided equally between companies.	

Army Form C. 2118

WAR DIARY
or
INTELLIGENCE SUMMARY
(Erase heading not required.)

Instructions regarding War Diaries and Intelligence Summaries are contained in F. S. Regs., Part II. and the Staff Manual respectively. Title Pages will be prepared in manuscript.

Place	Date	Hour	Summary of Events and Information	Remarks and references to Appendices
BERLES AU BOIS	July 29		(1) Duplicate copy of War Diary from 3rd May 1915 to June 30th 1916. (2) Old copies of Operation Orders and Documents of a historic nature from about 31/5/15 to 31/5/16, numbered consecutively from A1 to A105. Both the above were today put in two parcels by registered post to the O.C. Home Records SHREWSBURY for safe keeping until the conclusion of the war.	
	30		Work carried on as yesterday. The draft men remained off fatigues for Pit & rifle inspection etc scattered for the last 3 days. The day extremely hot. Casualties 1 man wounded 1803 Pte W E THOMAS (shrapnel)	
	31		Extremely hot day. Work carried on as usual. P.O. & Q.s inspected FARNBOROUGH ROAD work. Strength of Battalion 31/7/16- Officers 36. Other ranks 1009. During the period the Batt. has been at BERLES, 12 N.C.O.s and men have been away from the front line, who have not been put on duty of providing and in addition to digging the enemy has been kept under observation particularly in the vicinity of MONCHY. Several tips have been obtained.	

F. J. Drury
Major
Commdg. 1/1st Monmouthshire Regiment

Army Form C. 2118.

WAR DIARY
or
INTELLIGENCE SUMMARY
(Erase heading not required.)

APPENDIX NO. 1.

Instructions regarding War Diaries and Intelligence Summaries are contained in F.S. Regs., Part II. and the Staff Manual respectively. Title Pages will be prepared in manuscript.

Place	Date	Hour	Summary of Events and Information	Remarks and references to Appendices
	5 July		Copy of wire received from 46th Division.	
			To 1st Monmouths.	
			A991 5th AAA	
			On relinquishing the command of the Division, General STUART WORTLEY wishes to thank all ranks & specially those who have been with the Division since mobilization for their loyalty to him and their unfailing spirit of devotion to duty AAA He trusts the friendships formed may be lasting and wishes the Division good luck and God Speed	
			From 46th Division	

WAR DIARY or INTELLIGENCE SUMMARY

Army Form C. 2118

Appendix 2

Place	Date	Hour	Summary of Events and Information	Remarks and references to Appendices
LA CAUCHIE	24/7/16		Speech by G.O.C. 46th Division to Battalion after inspection on July 24th. "Officers, N.C.Os and men of the 1/1st Monmouth Regiment, I have inspected you and your attached body of men. Of good spirit and I congratulate Col. Evill on being in command of you. You are the best Battalion I have seen in the Division. I realise that as a Pioneer Battalion you are called upon to do a lot of work for which there is little to be shown and of apparently humdrum nature, particularly the look of upkeeping roads. But I wish to point out that the work you are engaged on and in particular the work of repairing roads is of an extremely important nature and is probably will have actually most important bearing upon distant operations. Therefore while as a Pioneer Battalion you are not called upon except in exceptional circumstances to hold the front line, you are doing just as important work as your own men in the front line. I realise the full teaching and continuous nature of the work this unit was called upon to in preparing for the recent attack and hope to receive some recommendations from the commanding officer.	

Army Form C. 2118

Confidential

WAR DIARY
or
INTELLIGENCE SUMMARY
(Erase heading not required.)

Vol 15

War Diary

1st Batt. The Monmouthshire Regt. IJ

1st August 1916 to 31st August 1916

WAR DIARY
or
INTELLIGENCE SUMMARY

Army Form C. 2118

Place	Date	Hour	Summary of Events and Information	Remarks and references to Appendices
BERLES-AU-BOIS	Aug 1st	1	Work inspected in morning by C.R.E., G.S.O.1 & C.O. Another exceedingly hot day.	
	"	2	Work carried on as usual. Orders received to send 2 Officers, 6 N.C.O.s & 60 men to the Pioneer Battalion of the 56th Division. The 1/5 CHESHIRES, the men to be sent being picked from the new who arrived the Russian arm at FONQUEVILLERS.	
	"	3	The party ordered to report to the 5th CHESHIRES paraded at 9am under 2/Lts M^cD HARRIS & CHARLEY when they were inspected by the C.O. before marching off. A party from the 5 CHESHIRES in exchange reported for duty at 5pm & was attached to "B" Coy. At 7am a British Aeroplane was hit by a German A.A. Aircraft shell and was compelled to descend in W.22.a. (sheet 51c) just 50 yards to the left of NOBS WALK and about 50 yards in front of the CALVAIRE on Ridge Road. The machine was in full view of the enemy and only about 1000 yards from their front line. It was shelled intermittently throughout the whole day but was not hit. All pontoons of value were removed during the night.	
	"	4	At 4.10 a.m the enemy opened a heavy fire on the front line trenches opposite MONCHY and to the South towards BIENVILLERS and also put up a barrage. This lasted until 5.10 a.m when the situation became normal. "A" & "B" Coys "stood to" and manned their defences while C.T.D "stood to" at billets. The order to "stand down" came at 5.15am from the 137th Brigade. The cause of the bombardment was an attempted German raid on Trenches held by front line troops but the enemy did not succeed in entering our front line. Work carried on as normal	

Army Form C. 2118

WAR DIARY
or
INTELLIGENCE SUMMARY
(Erase heading not required.)

Instructions regarding War Diaries and Intelligence Summaries are contained in F. S. Regs., Part II. and the Staff Manual respectively. Title Pages will be prepared in manuscript.

Place	Date	Hour	Summary of Events and Information	Remarks and references to Appendices
BERLES-AU-BOIS	Aug 5		Work carried on as usual tocyl where interfered with by the bombardment. At 11.5 to 11.45 a bombardment was carried out on the trenches in the vicinity of MONCHY and in redoubt neighbourhood, during the bombardment two working parties of 4th Lincolns & 5th South Staffs were sent out, owing to the enemys wire being uncut - they did no damage. Sergt W. H. TIDMAN /A. Coy awarded Military Medal for his conduct during the recent operations at GOMMECOURT on July 1916.	
"	6		FARNBORO RD was completed with the exception of a few minor details by "B" Coy, which Coy was relieved by "D" Coy from 40 CRUCHIE. "B" Coy will now carry on with road repairs & D Coy will take over work on the Divisional line consisting of clearing trenches A & H. 2/Lieut FAIRBURN reported for duty from 3 Base	
"	7		Additional party of 10 men sent to the 5th CHESHIRES for carrying work. GOC, CRE, GSO1 & the CO inspected a portion of the Divisional line from hours 147 (W16a 2 8) Sheet 51c to the north about W17a 5 6 and gave instructions as to future work.	
"	8		Instructions received from Division to send party of 90 other ranks to work on a Heavy Trench Mortar Emplacement. Working parties in neighbourhood of NEWARK ST by night were ordered to cease work and stand to man the outpost line by the OC 6th Lincolns. Parties stood down at dawn & 2nd I Cawacky. [?] returned to BERLES, a German raid was attempted. 3890 Rfn WILKS ME R. Coy (Wounded - Shrapnel)	

Place	Date	Hour	Summary of Events and Information	Remarks and references to Appendices
BERLES-AU-BOIS	Aug 9		Work carried on as usual. Parties again sent to the Heavy Trench Mortar Battery.	
"	10		Work carried on as usual. 2/Lt R.K. WELLSTEED accepted for training as Pilot R.F.C. and transferred to England. 2/Lt A.E. WILKS of "A" Coy died of wounds received 8/8/16.	
"	11		Work carried on as usual. 2/Lts C.S. HALL "D" Coy, E.E. DAVIES "C" Coy, R. DEDMISTON "B" Coy, N.F. KIRBY "A" Coy reported for duty and posted to companies as shown. Acct. Head officers are from the Barnsley Battalion. NEWARK ST finished and handed to 138th Bde.	
"	12		"D" Company worked on personal line. "D" Coy on their picton of the village. Orders received from 119th Division to attack two craters each to the 137th & 138th Brigades. For employment of 2/Lt J.G. BLAKE, E.R.J. EDWARDS, H.C.D. HARRIS, "B" Coy, attached to provide 2/Lt H.C.D. HARRIS. "B" Coy relieved by 2/Lt D. EDWARDS at HEBUTERNE about 66 men of "B" Coy who are attached to the 5th CHESHIRES and billeted.	
"	13		C.R.E. & Co. again inspected Divisional line. "D" Coy worked on Pvt line. "A" Coy commenced work upon instructions issued yesterday.	
"	14		Work carried on as yesterday. Heavy rain fell at intervals the final for fuel over Barakes.	
"	15		C.R.E. & Co. inspected Divisional line. Working parties went out as yesterday. For the last 4 nights gas has been carried up in cylinders to the front line in the neighbourhood of MONCHY and placed in position.	Trench maps refs:- E.4 & 30.60 (57D N.E. Sheet 1,2) BIENVILLERS-MONCHY RD C2 D.293 to W.29 & 55.90 (51c S.E. Parts 3 & 4).

WAR DIARY
or
INTELLIGENCE SUMMARY

(Erase heading not required.)

Army Form C. 2118

Instructions regarding War Diaries and Intelligence Summaries are contained in F. S. Regs., Part II. and the Staff Manual respectively. Title Pages will be prepared in manuscript.

Place	Date	Hour	Summary of Events and Information	Remarks and references to Appendices
BERLES-AU-BOIS	August 15		Operation orders received that at the first opportunity after tonight the gas would be discharged. The gas was not discharged as the wind was unfavourable.	
	16		Work carried on as usual. The gas was not discharged again today. 2 men put to the Base for discharge owing to their gunshot wounds, the remainder to be of "already this nature" who have Op's wounds & not to the Base by this ground. 3 N.C.O (Sergeants) arrived from Base and 1 Corporal for duty, that had been put in exchange for 3 N.C.O of the rank N.C.O's who are to go to the Bourne Battalion to help in training of recruits.	
	17		Operations today as yesterday, no gas discharged. 1 reinforcement arrived from Base. Hi grieff from Base Hospital.	
	18		Work carried on as usual. Casualty 1/2503 Pte PIDGET A B.C. Wounded at HEBUTERNE	
	19		No. 9 Platoon at intervals. The detachment of 1/15 CHESHIRES, 56th Div: Division attached to this Battalion reported their own Battalion today. The 56th Provision. Division, the other Division of the 1st Corps, being relieved by the 17th Division.	
	20		Work & parties as usual. 2/Pte R.A. BARR reported for duty from Base as reinforcement from Res. Batt: Barracks. 2 O.R's marked wounded "B.Co"	
	21		CRE inspected village trenches with C.O. Working parties: "A" Coy 40 o.r's, Party working on trench 76 in front of BIENVILLERS for 138th Bde. Gas shelled barracks 1. O.R Sticks, (R/Richard. P. 13435) & 5 other ranks wounded.	
	22		Work carried on as yesterday except that "A"bay owing to shelling is now working by night. Orders received that	

WAR DIARY or INTELLIGENCE SUMMARY

Army Form C. 2118

Place	Date	Hour	Summary of Events and Information	Remarks and references to Appendices
BERLES-AU-BOIS	May 22 (cont'd)		Major F.J. TRUMP has been D/F promoted to command the 1/6 South Staffs and that Lt Col EVILL will hand over the Brigade School and return to the Battalion on Saturday next 26th. Village Ducks from Bn to Bn as ordered by C.O. Adjutant.	
	23		Working parties as yesterday. One detachment of 'B' Coy that has been working at the Russian Sap at HEBUTERNE at Divisional H.Q. of 1/5 Bn Lincolnshire R according to pl. 181 D.R. All 'B' Coy R.E. today rejoined the Battalion.	
	24		Working parties as usual. Arrangements made for 'A' Coy to be relieved by 'C' Coy on 25th. CRE and CO inspected work.	
	25		Working parties as usual. Parade held at 3½ pm at BAILLEULMONT for the distribution of honours and Military Medals to N.C.O's + men of 'A' Coy under 2/Lt T. EDWARDS as sent by the Battalion to attend the parade. The following Officers and O.R's represented the Battalion: Major R Gordon by the Corps Commander VII Corps 2/Lt - Gen Sir T.D O'SNOW, K.C.B Lt. Col. C.A. EVILL D.S.O. C.S.M. Meek R. Military Cross Sgt Dickman T.N. Military Medal 2/Lt Moldrum B. Coy moved up to BERLES to act as an addition working party - they are to work on STONYGATE Communication Trench in 138 Brigade.	

WAR DIARY
or
INTELLIGENCE SUMMARY
(Erase heading not required.)

Army Form C. 2118

Place	Date	Hour	Summary of Events and Information	Remarks and references to Appendices
BERLES-AU-BOIS	Aug 25		C Coy relieved "A" Coy after work had been finished for the day. The usual dispositions of the Battalion are	

	" 26		Headquarters ———— BERLES-AU-BOIS
			Q.M. Stores + Transport Lines — LA CAUCHIE
			"A" Company on road work ———— BAILLEUVAL
			"B" " 2 platoons ———— LA CAUCHIE
			"B" " 2 platoons
			"C" " 2 platoons working
			       for 137th " 2 platoons ———— BERLES-AU-BOIS
			       for 138th /Bde
			"D" At work on
			       Divisional Line ———— Do.	

	" 26		Working parties as usual C.O. + C.R.E. inspected work, exceptionally heavy rain haver shower.	
	" 27		Working parties as usual. Lt-Col CAE VILL returned to the Battn from the 46th Divisional School and resumed command of the Battalion. Heavy rain continued at intervals throughout the day.	
	" 28		Major F.J. TRUMP left the Battalion to take over the command of the 1/6th Batt 2nd South Staffordshire Regt. D.S. Major W.A. LEWIS, 3rd Mon. Regt. reported for duty and took up duties of Senior Major. Working parties as usual.	
	" 29		Instructions received from 46th Division that the two platoons C Coy working for the 138th Bde would work as before today on the construction of a new portion of the Divisional Line	

WAR DIARY or INTELLIGENCE SUMMARY

Army Form C. 2118

Place	Date	Hour	Summary of Events and Information	Remarks and references to Appendices
BERLES-AU-BOIS	Aug 29		in front of BIENVILLERS. The first work being the construction of a Strong point off STONYGATE ROAD Communication Trench. The CRE met the CO in the morning to point out the work. 2/Lt. S.E. RICHARDS died of wounds at No.20 Casualty Clearing Station and was buried at Cemetary adjoining Sheet 51C. V.18.d.3.3.	
	30		Working parties as usual except that the 2 platoons of C Coy commenced their new work at BIENVILLERS. Occasional heavy rain all day. A draft of 17 other ranks reported as reinforcement from the Base. The draft was composed of all 1st (Monmouth) Regt Bn men. The ground was carried up to the front line trenches by route MONCHY on night of 31st to 1st and was relieved at 10 p.m. The enemy retaliated only slightly with rifle & machine gun fire and a few trench mortar bombs. No casualties.	
	31		Working party as usual – weather much improved today. 1st Quartermaster W.M. PORTER took Quartermaster's 3° duties of Quartermaster as a R.E. forenoon and took over on that capacity since 2/Lt. L.F. BEYNON was transferred to R.F.C. Strength of Battalion 40 officers and 974 other ranks.	

C.A. Elliot
Lt-Col
Comdg. 1st (Monmouth) Regt

War Diary
for
September 1916
of
1/1st Bn Monmouth Rgt.

46th DIVISION

CONFIDENTIAL.

T.M.N. 971.

46th Division.

      Herewith please find the War Diary of this Battalion for the month of September 1916.

                                    E. Emerson Davies.
                                            2/Lieut & A/Adjutant.

4-10-16.   for O/C 1/1st Batt The Monmouthshire Regiment T.F

Army Form C. 2118

WAR DIARY
or
INTELLIGENCE SUMMARY
(Erase heading not required.)

Confidential

Instructions regarding War Diaries and Intelligence Summaries are contained in F.S. Regs., Part II. and the Staff Manual respectively. Title Pages will be prepared in manuscript.

War Diary

1/1st Batt. The Monmouthshire Regiment T.F.

1st September 1916 to 30th September 1916

Place	Date	Hour	Summary of Events and Information	Remarks and references to Appendices

Army Form C. 2118

WAR DIARY
or
INTELLIGENCE SUMMARY
(Erase heading not required.)

1st Monmouth R[egt]

Instructions regarding War Diaries and Intelligence Summaries are contained in F.S. Regs., Part II. and the Staff Manual respectively. Title Pages will be prepared in manuscript.

Place	Date	Hour	Summary of Events and Information	Remarks and references to Appendices
BERLES-AU-BOIS	Sept 1st		Working parties as usual. C.O inspected "A" Company at 6.30 pm at BAILLEULVAL. Casualties, 1 other rank wounded.	
	Sept 2nd		Working parties as yesterday. C.O inspected D. Company at 6.30 pm at BERLES. At 11 pm a raid was carried out on the enemy trenches from to by the 1/6th South Staffords. 1 Officer & 3 other ranks were taken prisoners and several Germans killed.	
	" 3rd		The C/O inspected the Battalion First Line Transport at 10 am at LA CAUCHIE.	
	" 4th		Working parties as yesterday.	
	" 5th		Working parties as usual. Very heavy rain at intervals during the day.	
	" 6th		Working parties as yesterday. Heavy showers of rain again to-day. Working parties as usual. The C.O inspected "A" Coys G.S Tool Wagons and Tool Wagons with a view to seeing whether Officers kits could be carried on the pack animals in addition to the Tools. This was found to be very easily possible provided that the kits were only 35 lbs in weight.	
	" 7th		Working parties as usual	
	" 8th		Work as yesterday Lieut W. Shanks went on 14 days leave and was replaced by Capt. H. Dyer R.A.M.C.	

1875 Wt. W593/826 1,000,000 4/15 J.B.C. & A. A.D.S.S./Forms/C. 2118.

Army Form C. 2118

WAR DIARY
or
INTELLIGENCE SUMMARY

(Erase heading not required.)

Instructions regarding War Diaries and Intelligence Summaries are contained in F. S. Regs., Part II. and the Staff Manual respectively. Title Pages will be prepared in manuscript.

Place	Date	Hour	Summary of Events and Information	Remarks and references to Appendices
BERLES AU BOIS	Sept 8th		6. 5.9" shells fell in village at 9 pm, damaging one house and inflicting several casualties on R.G.A.	
	" 9th		Working parties as usual.	
	" 10th		Working parties as usual.	
	" 11th		Work as usual. Draft of 5 O.R. reported from Base all 1st Monmouth men. Lieut J.A. WILSON and 2/Lieut B. JESSEMAN reported for duty from Base (from reserve Battalion.) The 33rd Division marched into VII Corps area and in future will form part of the Corps. The 33rd Division has just come up from the SOMME. The reorganization of the Corps line will now be as follows:- 46th, 33rd, 56th from North + South.	
	" 12th		No work done owing to all Companies billeted in BERLES being engaged last night in carrying up Gas cylinders to the front line trenches. Casualty 1 man wounded.	
	" 13th		No work done as whole of Battalion billeted in BERLES engaged on carrying fatigue to the front line (Gas cylinders) Company parades held in afternoon + evening	

Army Form C. 2118

WAR DIARY
or
INTELLIGENCE SUMMARY
(Erase heading not required.)

Instructions regarding War Diaries and Intelligence Summaries are contained in F. S. Regs., Part II. and the Staff Manual respectively. Title Pages will be prepared in manuscript.

Place	Date	Hour	Summary of Events and Information	Remarks and references to Appendices
BERLES AU BOIS	Sep 13th		C/O inspected "C" Company & details of B. Company at 6pm. Road working parties as usual.	
	" 14th		Working parties as usual. C/O inspected details of B. Company billeted at LA CAUCHIE at 6.30 pm. Draft of 9 arrived from Base, all 1st Monmouth men from Base Hospitals.	
	" 15th		Work as usual. 2/Lieuts W.G. RAMSDEN } 3rd Mon Regt. " A. LEWIS } arrived as reinforcements. " H.C. MORRIS } The Gas carried up to the front line by this and other units is now prepared for discharge, which will be carried out with the first favourable wind.	
	" 16th		Draft of 85 arrived from Base all 1st Monmouths. Working parties as usual. Capt R.C.L. THOMAS left for course at 3rd Army School also Lieut W.L. ROBERTS	
	" 17th		C/O inspected draft; Capt Martyn left for 7 days rest at BOULOGNE also 5 men. Lieut. Llewelyn returned [with] 12 men from rest Camp BOULOGNE. Working parties as usual. 1 man wounded.	

Army Form C. 2118

WAR DIARY
or
INTELLIGENCE SUMMARY

(Erase heading not required.)

Instructions regarding War Diaries and Intelligence Summaries are contained in F.S. Regs., Part II. and the Staff Manual respectively. Title Pages will be prepared in manuscript.

Place	Date	Hour	Summary of Events and Information	Remarks and references to Appendices
BERLES AU-BOIS	Sept 18th		2/Lieut E.J. Jenkins and three men went on leave to England. Very wet all day. Working parties as usual.	
	" 19th		Work as usual. Raid by 5th North Staffords, no prisoners taken	
	" 20th		Work as usual, one man wounded. C.O. to Divisional Headquarters re scheme of work	
	" 21st		Work as usual. Major W.A. Lewis, Medical Officer & O's.C. Companies went to demonstration of small Box Respirators at Divisional School. Raid by 8th Sherwoods, 5 prisoners taken.	
	" 22nd		Work as usual. C.O. & O.C. "A" Company went to Engineer St to arrange plan of new work	
	" 23rd		Work as usual. C.O. held weekly conference with Os. C. Companies Mess Dinner held at Headquarters. Captain T.J. Jordan Lloyd reported from Base.	
	" 24th		'D' Coy relieved at BERLES by A. Coy, D Coy going to BAILLEUVAL	
	" 25th		Work as usual. Ten men sent to BOULOGNE for week's rest.	

Army Form C. 2118

WAR DIARY
or
INTELLIGENCE SUMMARY
(Erase heading not required.)

Instructions regarding War Diaries and Intelligence Summaries are contained in F.S. Regs., Part II. and the Staff Manual respectively. Title Pages will be prepared in manuscript.

Place	Date	Hour	Summary of Events and Information	Remarks and references to Appendices
BERLES AU BOIS	Sep 26th		Work as usual. Raid 1/5 North Staffords on RANSART. Good news from the SOMME, COMBLES, THIEPVAL & GUEDECOURT captured. Capt DYER left.	
	27th		Work as usual. C.O. and Major Lewis inspected the miners and party at CHURCH STREET. Miners relieved by another party from "C" Coy.	
	28th		Work as usual. Working parties as usual. 2/Lieuts BARR & FAIRBURN returned from Divisional School.	
	29th		Working parties as usual. Conference & Mess dinner.	
	30th		Three men gassed, owing to a broken cylinder. The progress on the Battle front of the SOMME can be heard in the distance by the position of the German balloons, which have been seen to retire in a northerly direction.	

Arthur [signature]
Lieut Colonel
Commanding 1/1st Batt Monmouthshire Regt T.F.

WAR DIARY
or
INTELLIGENCE SUMMARY
(Erase heading not required.)

Army Form C. 2118

Vol 17

WAR DIARY

1ST MONMOUTHSHIRE REGIMENT. T.F.

1ST OCTOBER 1916 TO 31ST OCTOBER 1916.

Army Form C. 2118

WAR DIARY
or
INTELLIGENCE SUMMARY
(Erase heading not required.)

1st Monmouths

Instructions regarding War Diaries and Intelligence Summaries are contained in F.S. Regs., Part II. and the Staff Manual respectively. Title Pages will be prepared in manuscript.

Place	Date	Hour	Summary of Events and Information	Remarks and references to Appendices
BERLES AU-BOIS	Oct 1st		Working parties as usual. 2/Lieut A.C. CORRY SMITH to Divisional School, 2/Lieut H.C.D. HARRIS to Bombing School. Battalion Church parade on recreation field. Winter time came into operation.	
	2nd		Working parties in the morning. Gas carrying fatigue, removing cylinders from trenches. The C/O gave a dinner in honour of Lieut Colonel TRUMP's promotion	
	3rd		No working parties, Lieut TISDALL and 1.O.R. to England on leave	
	4th		Working parties as usual.	
	5th		Working parties as usual. Raid by 1/5th LEICESTERS, no prisoners taken. The C/O left to take charge at Divisional school	
	6th		Working parties as usual. A draft of 12 O.R. reported for duty. 6 - 3rd Bn Monmouthshire Regt, 6 - 1st Bn Monmouthshire Regt	
	7th		Working parties as usual.	

1875 Wt. W593/826 1,000,000 4/15 J.B.C. & A. A.D.S.S./Forms/C. 2118.

Army Form C. 2118

WAR DIARY
or
INTELLIGENCE SUMMARY
(Erase heading not required.)

1st Monmouths.

Place	Date	Hour	Summary of Events and Information	Remarks and references to Appendices
BERLES AU-BOIS	Oct 4	8⁴⁵	Working parties as usual. Three officers and 117 O.Rs of "C" Company went to FONQUEVILLERS to make T.M. emplacements for 49th Division. Cpl BLAND was accidentally shot by a Stafford while out wiring. Casualties at FONQUEVILLERS 1 killed and 4 wounded. Capt B.T. REES, 2/Lieuts MARRABLE, MOORE and CLERY reported from the Base. BERLES heavily shelled for two hours, casualties 2 killed and 4 wounded, all STAFFORDS.	
		9⁵	Working parties as usual. BERLES was shelled three hours during the morning with 4.2s and 5.9s and again at 10.30 pm up to 12 midnight. 2/Lieut BLOW went to LUCHEUX as Town Major	
		10⁵	Working parties as usual. 2/Lieuts HALL and RICHARDS reported having seen strange lights the previous evening immediately before the bombardment.	
		11⁵	Working parties as usual. 2 men wounded at FONQUEVILLERS. Court of enquiry held re Cpl BLANDS death. One man to England on leave.	

WAR DIARY
or
INTELLIGENCE SUMMARY
(Erase heading not required.)

Army Form C. 2118

1st Monmouths

Place	Date	Hour	Summary of Events and Information	Remarks and references to Appendices
BERLES AU-BOIS	Oct	12th	Working parties as usual. 3 men killed and 1 man wounded at FONQUEVILLERS	
		13th	Working parties as usual. 1 man wounded at FONQUEVILLERS	
		14th	Working parties as usual. 2 inch Trench Mortar emplacements completed at FONQUEVILLERS. BERLES very heavily shelled by 4.7" and 5.9" from 7am. to 2 pm.; Casualties, 1 killed and 3 wounded Monmouths. Lieut WILSON and 2 N.C.O's of Lieut MURRAY applied to 46th Division to make to Third Army school. Permission given in the latter case. Inquiry in the outskirts of BERLES in the war granted. The whole of working parties making shelters and dug-outs on outskirts of village in case of further shelling.	
		15th	2/Lieut RAMSDEN to England on ten days special leave. "B" Company came to BERLES in relief of "C" Company.	
		16th	Working parties on dug-outs and shelters	

Army Form C. 2118

WAR DIARY
or
INTELLIGENCE SUMMARY
(Erase heading not required.)

1st Monmouthshire

Place	Date	Hour	Summary of Events and Information	Remarks and references to Appendices
BERLES AU-BOIS	Oct.	17	Working parties on dug-outs and shelters. The G.O.C. interviewed 2/Cpl Sheldon re commission and inspected work at GASTINEAU	
		18	Working parties on dug-outs and shelters. 2/Lieut RICHARDS and 2/Lieut A. LEWIS to Divisional school. The C/O came over from SAULTY to inspect work on dug-outs.	
		19	Working parties on dug-outs and shelters.	
		20	Working parties in dug-outs and shelters. The G.O.C inspected the 1st line transport on valley road to BAILLEULMONT. He was very pleased with the turn out.	
		21	Working parties on dug-outs and shelters. The C/O to England on 10 days leave.	
		22	Working parties on dugouts and shelters. 2/Lieut T.O. TONES to 3rd Army Snipers school, seven days. All instructs to reach the D.A.D.O.S. by 12 midnight, after which none accepted as move anticipated. Football match at BAILLEULVAL between C and D Companies result, a draw, 4 goals each.	

WAR DIARY
or
INTELLIGENCE SUMMARY

(Erase heading not required.)

Army Form C. 2118

1st Monmouths.

Place	Date	Hour	Summary of Events and Information	Remarks and references to Appendices
BERLES AU-BOIS	Oct.	23rd	Working parties as usual. C.R.E. gave instructions for new work at GASTINEAU and L'ALOUETTE	
		24th	Working parties as usual. 2/Lieut J.R. EVANS returned from Transport course at HAVRE. Divisional school broken up. 2/Lieut RICHARDS and LEWIS rejoined Battalion. 8 O.R. reported from Base as reinforcements.	
		25th	Working parties as usual. 2/Lieut MOORE returned from Divisional school. The 6th South Staffords made a successful raid at W.24.a.15.45 + took six prisoners.	
		26	Working parties as usual. 2 Officers and 70 O.R. on gas carrying fatigue to trenches. 3262 Rfn Thomas F. "A" Coy sniper wounded by a shell.	
		27th	Working parties as usual. Orders received that 46th Division will be relieved by the 30th Division on 28th, 29th, 30th & 31st but 1st Monmouths and Divisional artillery will remain & be attached to new Division. Court martial on 15599 Rfn BARTLETT. H. "B" Co	

Army Form C. 2118

WAR DIARY
or
INTELLIGENCE SUMMARY
(Erase heading not required.)

1st Monmouth

Instructions regarding War Diaries and Intelligence Summaries are contained in F.S. Regs., Part II. and the Staff Manual respectively. Title Pages will be prepared in manuscript.

Place	Date	Hour	Summary of Events and Information	Remarks and references to Appendices
BERLES AU-BOIS	Oct 27th		for franking a letter with 2/Lieut A. LEWIS signature. C.R.E. 30th Division took over from C.R.E. 46th Division	
	28th		Working parties as usual. Relief of 46th Division by 30th Division continued. Adjutant returned from 3rd Army school	
	29th		Working parties as usual. extremely wet weather. Work inspected by C.O.	
	30th		Work as yesterday. Heavy rain continued.	
	31st		Work as yesterday. The 30th Division took over command of Line from 46th Division at 10 a.m. The 30th Division is composed of :- (CENTRE) 21st Brigade (Regulars) (RIGHT) 89th " (Service Btn) (LEFT) 90th " (Service Btn) G.O.C. is MAJ-GEN. J.S. SHEA. C.B. D.S.O The Pioneer Battalion of the 30th Division is at present engaged on building a Railway in the SOMME area, therefore	

1875 Wt. W593/326 1,000,000 4/15 J.B.C. & A. A.D.S.S./Forms/C. 2118.

Army Form C. 2118

WAR DIARY
or
INTELLIGENCE SUMMARY

(Erase heading not required.)

1st Monmouths

Place	Date	Hour	Summary of Events and Information	Remarks and references to Appendices
BERLES AU-BOIS	Oct.	31st	This unit is replacing it until such time as we are relieved. The VII Corps is now composed of 49th and 30th Divisions. Strength of Battalion, 48 Officers and 921 O.R.	

C.H. Evill
Lieut. Colonel
Commanding 1st Monmouthshire Regiment T.F.

Army Form C. 2118

CONFIDENTIAL Secret

Vol 18

WAR DIARY
~~INTELLIGENCE SUMMARY~~
(Erase heading not required.)

1st MONMOUTHSHIRE REGIMENT T.F.

NOVEMBER 1st 1916 TO NOVEMBER 30th 1916

Instructions regarding War Diaries and Intelligence Summaries are contained in F. S. Regs., Part II. and the Staff Manual respectively. Title Pages will be prepared in manuscript.

Place	Date	Hour	Summary of Events and Information	Remarks and references to Appendices

Army Form C. 2118

WAR DIARY or INTELLIGENCE SUMMARY

(Erase heading not required.)

1st Month 16

Place	Date	Hour	Summary of Events and Information	Remarks and references to Appendices
BERLES AU-BOIS	Nov	1st	Working parties as usual. Capt O.W.D. STEEL. M.C reported for duty as M.O. Capt Steel held a commission in the 3rd MONMOUTHS and transferred to the R.A.M.C when he was attached to the 3rd MONMOUTHS as M.O. Lieut Col. C.A. EVILL. D.S.O returned from leave and resumed command of the Battalion. News received unofficially that the Battalion will rejoin the 46th Div on Nov 6th.	
		2nd	C.O inspected working parties. Draft of 5 other ranks arrived from Base. 4-1st MONS and 1-2nd MONMOUTH. 1 casualty, RFN SHEPHERD (Shell shock)	
		3rd	Working parties as usual. Capt DICKSON, 11th SOUTH LANCS REGT, pioneer Battn to the 30th Division, arrived to take over and reconnoitre works.	
		4th	C.R.E, 30th Division was taken round works by C.O. He said that he considered the work done by this Battalion to the Village defences was extremely good. Duplicate copies of War Diary for the months of July, August, September and October sent by registered post to Home records.	
		5th	Working parties as usual. Orders that Battn will not move until hour of the 11th SOUTH LANCS move into HUMBERCOURT to-morrow where they will remain until 11th when the relief will take place.	

WAR DIARY
INTELLIGENCE SUMMARY
(Erase heading not required.)

Army Form C. 2118

1st Month.

Place	Date	Hour	Summary of Events and Information	Remarks and references to Appendices
BERLES AU-BOIS	Nov	5th	The two days delay is caused because the 11th SOUTH LANCS have not had a bath or change of clothing before starting them on fresh work.	
		6th	One platoon of D Coy moved from Dugouts on S.W. of BERLES to work on village defense trenches B.E.1-6. The heavy rain has caused the unrevetted parts of the above trenches to collapse in many places.	
		7th	Working parties as yesterday. Extremely heavy rain all day.	
		8th	Work as yesterday. O/C Coys and L.G.O. of 11th SOUTH LANCS reconnoitred and took over works. Orders received to march to-morrow to HUMBERCOURT.	
		9th	Battalion rendezvoused at 3.15 pm at LA CAUCHIE and marched off. A halt of 1½ hours was made the east side of the ARRAS-DOULLENS ROAD which could not be crossed until 5 pm. The Battn was formed up in lines of Coys and tea was issued. HUMBERCOURT was reached at 8.30 pm & Battn was billeted. Length of march about 12 miles. The night was beautifully fine with very bright moonlight. Lewis Gun handcarts were used for first time on the march, the coy Lewis Gun detachments pulled	

Army Form C. 2118

WAR DIARY or INTELLIGENCE SUMMARY

(Erase heading not required.)

1st M mmwh.

Instructions regarding War Diaries and Intelligence Summaries are contained in F. S. Regs., Part II. and the Staff Manual respectively. Title Pages will be prepared in manuscript.

Place	Date	Hour	Summary of Events and Information	Remarks and references to Appendices
BERLES AU-BOIS	Nov	9th	Shem by hand without assistance, but found it rather cumbersome.	
HUMBERCOURT	"	10th	Morning devoted to cleaning equipment, afternoon to drill under O/C Coys. Orders received that Battalion will move by motor bus to-morrow to CAOURS (2 miles East of ABBEVILLE) and that transport will march by road. Transport and Lewis Gunners paraded at 3 p.m. and marched to OUTREBOIS (distance 15 miles)	
		11th	Battalion paraded 9.15 am and entrused in 141 buses. Stores required for to-day and to-morrow such as rations, officers valises &c. were carried on H of the buses.	
			At ST RIQUIER both debused having ridden 30 miles, and marched to CAOURS 5 miles distance – This march was trying as men carried blankets and leather jerkins. CAOURS was reached at 4 pm and the Battn was billeted. This village has seldom been used for billeting troops and all billets are extremely comfortable, the country around is unploughed stubble and so very suitable for training. Transport marched from OUTREBOIS to BERNATRE.	

Army Form C. 2118

1st Monmouth

WAR DIARY
or
INTELLIGENCE SUMMARY
(Erase heading not required.)

Place	Date	Hour	Summary of Events and Information	Remarks and references to Appendices
CAOURS	Nov	11th	Draft of 13 other ranks arrived from Base, all hospital cases.	
	"		5 - 1st Monmouths
			2 - 2nd do
			6 - 3rd do
	"	12th	Company parades from 10 am to 12 noon for close order drill. Battalion parade 3 pm for Church service. Transport arrived at 4 pm the 35 mile march having passed off without any hitch excepting for one horse which fell sick and was left at BERNATRE	
	"	13th	Company parades 9 am – 12.30 pm for physical drill, squad, platoon and company drill. G.O.C. the 46th Division visited training ground Afternoon spent at games.	
	"	14th	Parades as yesterday. Weather very suited to training, fine and cold.	
	"	15th	Parades as yesterday. Complimentary letter as under received from Chief Engineer VII Corps.	

" I wish to bring to notice, the very good work done by the two companies of the 1st Monmouthshire Pioneers employed on roads in the advanced area. I fully recognise the monotonous character of this very useful and essential work, and I think that all the more credit is due

WAR DIARY or INTELLIGENCE SUMMARY

Army Form C. 2118

Place	Date	Hour	Summary of Events and Information	Remarks and references to Appendices
CAOURS	Nov	15½	to those who take an interest in it, and do it well. I therefore bring the matter to your notice" (Sd) J. A. TANNER, BRIG. GENERAL CHIEF ENGINEER VII CORPS H.Q. VIIth CORPS 11-11-16	
"	"	16½	Parade 9 am - 12.30 pm. Physical training and Bayonet fighting. Platoon and Company drill followed by 3rd hour Battalion drill. 450 suits of clothing have been received recently from Ordnance and men with new clothing and drill parades have smartened up and appear extremely well on parade. 2/Lieut C.T.A. WATERS from 1st Recc Mor Regt and 2 other ranks also 1st Recc Mor Regt, reported for duty as reinforcements. 2/Lieut C.T.A. WATERS appointed Battalion Signalling Officer	
"	"	17	Parade 9 am - 12.30 pm. Ceremonial and Battn drill. Extremely cold day, frost at night. 2/Lieut A.C. CORRY SMITH proceeded to U K on 10 days leave. 1 Other ranks also.	
"	"	18	Company parade 9 am for Physical drill. 10 am Battn parade for Ceremonial drill which was cancelled owing to bitterly cold weather	

Army Form C. 2118

WAR DIARY
or
INTELLIGENCE SUMMARY
(Erase heading not required.)

1st Monmouth

Place	Date	Hour	Summary of Events and Information	Remarks and references to Appendices
CAOURS	Nov	18th	and Batt'n went for a short route march, snow fell. Batt'n returned at 11 am when as snow had stopped ceremonial drill was proceeded with. Bugle band made up to full complement of 17, much progress has been made in the playing of this band which is now very good.	
"		19th	Voluntary Holy Communion service 10.30 am (C of E) and parade service for Roman Catholics at DRUCAT Church 9.30 am. Battalion parade 11.30 am for ceremonial drill. C/O presented medal ribbon to recent recipients of Military Medal, the N.C.O's and men were paraded in front of the Battalion, the act for which the medal was awarded was read out by the Adjutant, after which the C/O congratulated them individually. Small Box Respirators issued to Battalion in lieu of P.H.G. Gas helmet.	
"		20th	Company parades 9 am – 12.30 for physical training, extended order drill, artillery formation etc. Sergt. Major CURLEY of the Army Gymnastic Staff attached to this unit for 5 days for the purpose of training 1 Officer and 4 senior NCO's per company as instructors in physical training and bayonet fighting.	

Army Form C. 2118

WAR DIARY
or
INTELLIGENCE SUMMARY
(Erase heading not required.)

1st. Monmouths.

Place	Date	Hour	Summary of Events and Information	Remarks and references to Appendices
CAOURS	Nov	21st	Battalion parade 9 am. Physical training by companies until 10 am. 10 am to 12:30 pm Ceremonial drill. Capt G.E.B Stephens (late Rifle Brigade now Lees of Officers) who was adjutant of this Battalion from 1910-1913 and who is now D.A.A.G Lines of Communications came to see Battalion on parade.	
"		22nd	Battalion parade 10.15 am. Batt" marched to COULONVILLERS a distance of about 8 miles. Batt" arrived at 2 pm and was billeted for the night. Great delay on the roads owing to the whole Division evacuating the ST. RIQUIER area while the Royal Naval Division was moving in.	
"		23rd	Battalion parade 8 am. Batt" marched off at 8.20 am to MEZEROLLES via CRAMONT, MAZICOURT, WAVANS, and FROSN-LE-GRAND a distance of about 16 miles. A halt of one hour was made at 1 pm for dinner. The G.O.C Division inspected Battalion as it marched over WAVANS bridge. Batt" arrived at MEZEROLLES about 3 pm and was billeted for the night. Capt S.R.MARTYN while on leave in England, admitted to hospital sick.	

WAR DIARY or INTELLIGENCE SUMMARY

Army Form C. 2118

1st Monmouth

Place	Date	Hour	Summary of Events and Information	Remarks and references to Appendices
MEZEROLLES	Nov 24th		Battalion remained at MEZEROLLES for day. C/O inspected Battalion by companies at 2 pm.	
	25th		Battalion paraded at 8:30 am and marched to LUCHEUX about 11 miles. The weather was very bad, rain fell the whole time. LUCHEUX was reached at 12:30 pm and Battn was billeted. Draft of 6. O.R. arrived from Base composed of {3-1st MONS from hospital, 3.3" draft from England}	
LUCHEUX	"	26th	Companies at disposal of O/C Coys. Rain continued at intervals throughout the day. Draft of 8. O.R. arrived from Base composed of:- 7-1st MONS from Base Hospital 1-1st " Draft from England.	
	"	27th	Fatigue party of 500 men sent to LUCHEUX Forest to make hurdles and fascines under supervision of R.E. Orders received that G.O.C. 46th Division will inspect this Battalion on 30th inst.	
	"	28th	Company parades in morning for Physical training & Bayonet fighting. Battalion parade 2.15 pm for Ceremonial drill. Weather cold and fine but very foggy.	

Army Form C. 2118

WAR DIARY
or
INTELLIGENCE SUMMARY
(Erase heading not required.)

Instructions regarding War Diaries and Intelligence Summaries are contained in F. S. Regs., Part II. and the Staff Manual respectively. Title Pages will be prepared in manuscript.

Place	Date	Hour	Summary of Events and Information	Remarks and references to Appendices
LUCHEUX	Nov 29		Battalion parade 9.30 am on inspection parade ground at (Sheet 51C. U.25.b.7.5) near LE.GROS TISON FARM. Rehearsal parade for to-morrows inspection. Battalion parade again at 2.15 pm for ceremonial drill. The band of 138th Brigade should have attended this parade, but owing to the wagon sent to fetch it going astray, the band did not arrive until too late. Weather again cold and foggy. 2/Lieut. O. HARLEY left for England for R.E course.	
"		30th	Battalion paraded at 10 a.m. on ground near LE GROS TISON FARM and was inspected by Maj. General W. THWAITES, G.O.C 46th Division. The Battn was drawn up in line, the band of the 138th Brigade was lent for the parade. After taking the salute Gen THWAITES inspected the Battalion after which he presented the ribbon of the MILITARY MEDAL to:— SERGT. SWEET. F " HOOKHAM. E CORPL. FISHER. W " DAVIES. S LCE/CPL ROBERTS. J	

1875 Wt. W 593/826 1,000,000 4/15 J.B.C. & A. A.D.S.S./Forms/C. 2118.

Army Form C. 2118

WAR DIARY
or
INTELLIGENCE SUMMARY
(Erase heading not required.)

1st Monmouths

Place	Date	Hour	Summary of Events and Information	Remarks and references to Appendices
LUCHEUX	Nov	30	The Army Commander GEN. SIR E. ALLENBY. K.C.B, G.O.C. 3RD Army arrived on the parade ground at 10.20 am, notice of his coming was only received on parade. After the distribution of medal ribbons, the Battn which was drawn up for ceremonial drill, marched past by companies (the Army Commander taking the salute) and then as a Battn in close column of companies. Line was then reformed and the Battn advanced in Review order and gave a General Salute. The Army Commander then sent for the Officers, shook hands with the C/o & made the following speech. (APPENDIX 1) The Army Commander again shook hands with Lt Col Evill, the Officers rejoined their companies, and the Battalion marched off the parade ground. On the afternoon at 2.45 pm the Battalion took part in the Divisional cross country run, the course was 2¾ miles and had to be finished in 25 minutes. 133 Officers and men	

Army Form C. 2118

WAR DIARY
or
INTELLIGENCE SUMMARY
(Erase heading not required.)

1st Monmouths

Place	Date	Hour	Summary of Events and Information	Remarks and references to Appendices
LUCHEUX	Nov 30th		involving the C/O, completed the course in the specified time. Result of Race :- 1st 4th LEICESTERS 2nd 5th SHERWOODS 3rd 6th N. STAFFORDS Strength of Battalion November 30th 1916. 46 Officers 916 other ranks.	

E. Snell
Lieut- Colonel
Commanding 1st Monmouthshire Regt T.F.

APPENDIX 1

WAR DIARY or INTELLIGENCE SUMMARY

1st Monmouths

"SPEECH BY GEN. SIR. E. ALLENBY. K.C.B. G.O.C. 3RD ARMY
TO THE OFFICERS OF THE BATTALION

"I have called you out to let you know how pleased I am to have had the opportunity of seeing this splendid Battalion on parade to-day. One point which has particularly impressed me, is the steadiness of all ranks on parade, in spite of the cold weather. The men are clean and well turned out, the march was well done, and the whole parade is most creditable. I congratulate COL EVILL on his fine Battalion.

CONFIDENTIAL

Army Form C. 2118

WAR DIARY
or
INTELLIGENCE SUMMARY

(Erase heading not required.)

Vol 19

1ST MONMOUTHSHIRE REGIMENT T.F.

DECEMBER 1ST 1916 TO DECEMBER 31ST 1916

Army Form C. 2118

WAR DIARY
or
INTELLIGENCE SUMMARY
(Erase heading not required.)

1st Monmouths 46 Div

Place	Date 1916	Hour	Summary of Events and Information	Remarks and references to Appendices
LUCHEUX	1 Dec	1st	200 men on fatigue in LUCHEUX FOREST. Box Respirators of "C and D" coys fitted. "C" Company bathed.	
	"	2nd	Fatigue party of 500 sent to Forest. "A" Company bathed.	
	"	3rd	Fatigue party of 500 again sent to Forest. Fitting of Box Respirators proceeded with of all available men.	
	"	4th	Fatigue party as yesterday. D. Company bathed.	
	"	5th	Battalion paraded at 9am and marched to SOUASTRE via MONDICOURT PAS and HENU and relieved the 19th LANCASHIRE FUSILIERS, Pioneer Battalion of the 49th Division. SOUASTRE was reached at 12.30 pm and the Battalion was billeted. LIEUT and Q.M R.H.MARTIN rejoined Battalion as reinforcement from Base.	
SOUASTRE	6		Battalion took over dispositions of work of outgoing unit. The Battalion with Headquarters, Transport and Quartermasters stores are all in SOUASTRE. Two companies A and D are working for the Chief Engineer VIIth Corps on roads, the two remaining companies B and C are working in the FONQUEVILLERS sector for the 139th Brigade on the communication trenches LINCOLN LANE, ST MARTINS LANE, NOTTINGHAM ST and on the support line. The C/O visited working parties.	

Army Form C. 2118

WAR DIARY
or
INTELLIGENCE SUMMARY
(Erase heading not required.)

1st Monmouths 46 Div.

Instructions regarding War Diaries and Intelligence Summaries are contained in F.S. Regs., Part II. and the Staff Manual respectively. Title Pages will be prepared in manuscript.

Place	Date 1916	Hour	Summary of Events and Information	Remarks and references to Appendices
SOUASTRE	Dec	7th	Working parties as yesterday. C/O visited parties this morning. Extremely foggy weather. Major W.A. LEWIS went on leave.	
"		8th	Work as yesterday. 2 platoons of D coy moved to POMMIER, it being a more convenient centre for that sector of the roads.	
"		9th	Heavy rain with brief intervals all day. Work as yesterday. Draft of 13 other ranks arrived. Composed of :- 2ND MONMOUTHS from England, 3RD MONMOUTHS, 1 man of this unit from Base Hospital, 1 man of 1st MONMOUTHS from England. Voluntary Church services this evening.	
"		10th	Working parties as yesterday. Rain fell almost continuously.	
"		11th	Working parties as yesterday. Snow fell during the morning and turned to rain about mid-day. Owing to bad weather all working parties were withdrawn at 2 pm. The C/O, Adjutant and O/C B. Coy reconnoitred new work on support line off ROBERTS AVENUE and LINCOLN LANE.	
"		13th	Road parties only sent out owing to an organised bombardment being arranged of the MONCHY SALIENT, which was carried out from 11 am to 4 pm.	
"		14th	Working parties as usual. Owing to a new programme of work being drawn up by the 139th Brigade as from to-day a rearrangement is being made in working parties. All work now being done on	

Army Form C. 2118

WAR DIARY
or
INTELLIGENCE SUMMARY
(Erase heading not required.)

Place	Date	Hour	Summary of Events and Information	Remarks and references to Appendices
SOUASTRE	Dec	14th	communication trenches is being handed over to the R.E's and the parties found by this Battalion are to work on the support line. Present allocation of works:— RIGHT SECTOR. "C" Coy working on support line off 5TH AVENUE, ST MARTINS LANE and HURST AVENUE. LEFT SECTOR. B Coy. working on support line off ROBERTS AVENUE, LINCOLN LANE and GOMMECOURT ROAD. All work with the exception of small parties is carried out by day.	
"		15th	Working parties as yesterday, considerable shelling by enemy greatly interfered with work. A German aeroplane flew low over our line and fired at a party of B Coy working in the support line off ROBERTS AVENUE, with a machine gun.	
"		16th	Working parties to FONCQUEVILLERS sent up by night, instead of day owing to shelling. Road parties carried on as usual.	
"	17th (SUNDAY)		Under arrangements made with Division no working parties in the line are to be found on Sundays. Road parties worked until mid-day only. Remainder of day spent over kit inspections etc. Church parade services held in evening.	
"		18th	Working parties as usual. C/O inspected works with Lt-Col THORPE.	

/St M[?] 26 Dec

Army Form C. 2118

WAR DIARY
or
INTELLIGENCE SUMMARY
(Erase heading not required.)

1st Mons. 46 Div.

Place	Date	Hour	Summary of Events and Information	Remarks and references to Appendices
SOUASTRE	DEC 1916	18th	(G.S.O.1. 46th Division) and Brig. Gen SHIPLEY, G.O.C. 139th Brigade.	
		19th	Working parties as usual. After work to-day a relf. of the companies working at FONCQUEVILLERS was carried out by the companies working on roads. A and D coys relieved B and C coys respectively.	
		20th	Total of 5 other ranks reported from Base, all five being new from Base Hospitals, after being evacuated from this Battalion. Working parties as usual.	
		21st	Working parties as usual. About 120 men paraded for interviews by Ordnance and R.F.C. Officers as to their qualifications for fitters plumbers etc.	
		22nd	Working parties as usual. Casualties 2/Lieut G. SMART and 3 other ranks of "A" Coy wounded by shell fire at FONCQUEVILLERS. Under orders from 46th Division, 1 Officer and 50 other ranks are to be withdrawn from working parties in the line they are to form a party for the construction of deep dug-outs in the Divisional line at FONCQUEVILLERS. Work was to have been commenced to-day, but 2/Lieut G. SMART was wounded and he was to have been in charge. the start is delayed until to-morrow. Party of 1 Officer & 30 other ranks moved to WARLINCOURT to billet for road work.	

1875 Wt. W593/826 1,800,000 4/15 J.B.C. & A.   A.D.S.S./Forms/C. 2118.

Army Form C. 2118

WAR DIARY
or
INTELLIGENCE SUMMARY
(Erase heading not required.)

1st Manc 46 Div

Place	Date	Hour	Summary of Events and Information	Remarks and references to Appendices
SOUASTRE	Dec 1916	23	Working parties as usual. After a frost of several days a thaw has set in. This has caused the trenches in many cases to fall in. The usual Sunday rest is not being observed, the time off being taken to-morrow. The main communication trenches from FONCQUEVILLERS to the line being in such a bad state, LINCOLN-LANE in some places 3 ft deep with water and mud, ST MARTINS LANE being in a similar condition, the Division has ordered that they are to be taken in hand at once and to do this, this Battalion is to withdraw enough men from the other line parties.	
		24th		
		25th	XMAS DAY No working parties sent out. Parade services for all denominations held during the morning. Xmas dinners were arranged by companies of Roast Beef, vegetables, Beer and Xmas pudding. The C/O visited all companies whilst they were at dinner. Sergeants had a Sergts Mess dinner at 6.30 pm. The Officers Mess dinner was held on Xmas eve.	
		26	POMMIER and WARLINCOURT detachments marched to SOUASTRE for the day. Work commenced on C-Ts LINCOLN LANE and ST. MARTINS LANE also a party of 2 Officers and 52 men started work on deep dug-outs in Divisional line in S.P.s off CRAWL BOYS LANE and ROBERTS AVENUE	

Army Form C. 2118

WAR DIARY
or
INTELLIGENCE SUMMARY
(Erase heading not required.)

/A. Mons 46 Div.

Place	Date	Hour	Summary of Events and Information	Remarks and references to Appendices
SOUASTRE	DEC	26th	Weather finer. Aeroplanes on both sides very active. Working parties as usual.	
"		27th	Working parties as usual. The enemy raided front line trenches. Casualties, Other ranks, 1 killed, 2 died of wounds, 1 wounded 'A' Coy in LINCOLN LANE.	
"		28th	Working parties as usual. The enemy raided front line trenches between ROBERTS AVENUE and LINCOLN LANE at 3 a.m. in the morning. The artillery barrage did very considerable damage to LINCOLN LANE.	
"		29th	Working parties as usual. G.O.C. inspected work together with G.O.C Divisions and Brigade. The G.O.C. was extremely pleased with progress made on C.Ts. Dug-out party withdrawn owing to shortage of material.	
"		30th	Very heavy rain in the night which continued throughout the morning. This rain did tremendous damage to the trenches, practically all unrevetted portions collapsing. In some places in the main C.Ts there is 4 feet of slush. Working parties as usual but work was delayed through clearing falls etc.	
"		31st	SUNDAY No parties sent to the line and road companies only worked until mid-day. Church parade services held for all denominations	

Army Form C. 2118

1st Mon 46 Div.

WAR DIARY
or
INTELLIGENCE SUMMARY
(Erase heading not required.)

Place	Date	Hour	Summary of Events and Information	Remarks and references to Appendices
SOUASTRE	DEC 1916	31st	In the evening Draft of 4 other ranks arrived, returned from Base hospital men who have previously served with this unit. Strength of Battalion :— 44 Officers 897 Other ranks	

A. Hill
Lieut-Colonel.
Commanding 1st Monmouthshire Regiment T.F.

APPENDIX I

Army Form C. 2118

WAR DIARY
or
INTELLIGENCE SUMMARY
(Erase heading not required.)

1st Manch. 46th Div.

Summary of Events and Information

Copy of personal letter received by Lieut-Col C.A. EVILL from MAJ-GEN L.J. BOLS G.S.O.1, 3rd Army and late B.G.C. 84th Brigade who accompanied the Army Commander on his inspection of this Battalion at LUCHEUX on 30/11/1916

9th Dec 1916

My Dear Evill,

Thank you very much for sending me your Xmas card of many memories. It is very good of you to remember me and I appreciate it very much. Those were very proud days when I had the honour of having your Regiment under me, what nippers all those fellows were, and now you seem to have collected just as good a lot once more — if not a better — for I have never seen such a steady and well drilled and well turned out lot of fellows as you showed the Army Commander the other day. He was really delighted with your Battalion.

I am very glad to know that Martin is all well again. Please give him my greetings and to any others who may still remember me

All good fortune
From sincerely yours
(Sd) L.J. Bols.

Army Form C. 2118

CONFIDENTIAL

Vol 20

WAR DIARY
or
INTELLIGENCE SUMMARY

(Erase heading not required.)

1ST BATT MONMOUTHSHIRE REGIMENT .T.F.

JANUARY 1ST 1917 TO JANUARY 31ST 1917.

Instructions regarding War Diaries and Intelligence Summaries are contained in F. S. Regs., Part II. and the Staff Manual respectively. Title Pages will be prepared in manuscript.

Place	Date	Hour	Summary of Events and Information	Remarks and references to Appendices

1875 Wt. W593/826 1,000,000 4/15 J.B.C. & A. A.D.S.S./Forms/C. 2118.

WAR DIARY or INTELLIGENCE SUMMARY

(Erase heading not required.)

Army Form C. 2118

Place	Date	Hour	Summary of Events and Information	Remarks and references to Appendices
SOUASTRE	Jan 1917	1st	Working parties as usual. Extract from "London Gazette" dated 1/1/17. "His Majesty the King has been pleased to approve the following awards for distinguished service in the Field. **MONMOUTHSHIRE REGT** "To be a Companion of the Distinguished Service Order - CAPT (TEMP MAJOR) (TEMP LIEUT-COLONEL FREDERICK JOSEPH TRUMP. Military Cross CAPTAIN. ROBERT. CLIFFORD LLOYD THOMAS.	
		2nd	Working parties as usual - Weather bad. Relief of line Companies by road Companies carried out after work.	
		3rd	Working parties as usual - The party of 1 Officer and 54 men working on dug-outs in the Divisional line, being held up for material are now sent daily to report to R.E's for work on Divisional line. This arrangement is being made for the time to-day - The C.O. Division sent a telephone message saying that he was extremely pleased with the progress of work made on Communication trenches	
		4th	Working parties as yesterday - Weather improved - Owing to shelling on LINCOLN LANE all work there is being carried on by night in two shifts	
		5th	Working parties as usual - The following of this unit were mentioned	

Army Form C. 2118

WAR DIARY
or
INTELLIGENCE SUMMARY
(Erase heading not required.)

Instructions regarding War Diaries and Intelligence Summaries are contained in F. S. Regs., Part II. and the Staff Manual respectively. Title Pages will be prepared in manuscript.

Place	Date	Hour	Summary of Events and Information	Remarks and references to Appendices
SOUASTRE	Jan	5th	in SIR. D. HAIG'S Despatch dated January 4th 1917 for distinguished and gallant services and devotion to duty :- TRUMP. CAPT. F.J. TEMP MAJOR, TEMP LIEUT-COLONEL · S-STAFFS REGT. HUGHES No 100, COL SERGEANT, ACT. C.S.M. D. HODGES No 1011. CPL. (ACT L-SERGEANT) G. Draft of 60 other ranks arrived from Base composed of :- 35 - 2ND MONMOUTHS 16 - 1ST " 6 - 3RD " 3 - 1ST " } From Res. Batt. England. Reported from Base Hospitals.	
		6th	Working parties as usual - C.O. inspected draft at 10 am - The physique is exceedingly good also their clothing & equipment.	
		7th	SUNDAY. No working parties sent to the line - Road companies worked for half day only. - Draft fitted with Box Respirators - Parade services for all denominations morning or evening. - Lieut. and Q.M. W.M. PORTER left to report to 2ND MONMOUTHSHIRES.	
		8th	The Army Commander presented ribbons of Decorations awarded to Officers and men of the 46th Division in the New Year honours at Divisional Headquarters HENU at 10 am. LIEUT-COLONEL F.J.TRUMP attended	

WAR DIARY or INTELLIGENCE SUMMARY

Army Form C. 2118

Place	Date	Hour	Summary of Events and Information	Remarks and references to Appendices
SOUASTRE	Jan	8th	and received the ribbon of the D.S.O., CAPT. R.C.L. THOMAS receiving that of the Military Cross. - Detachments from all units attended the parade. - Work commenced by D and C Companies on one section of ST MARTINS LANE about 120 yards long which required revetting badly. This work was practically completed.	
		9th	B. Company resumed working on its normal positions in LINCOLN LANE and support line - C. Company carried on with ST. MARTINS LANE. Working parties as yesterday. - Casualties 2 other ranks wounded by shell fire in FONCQUEVILLERS. - A small balloon was seen to be drifting over lines towards the enemy, it was destroyed by one of our aeroplanes, the pilot flying into it - The balloon fell somewhere between SOUASTRE and POMMIER but no message was discovered.	
		10th	Working parties as usual - snow fell slightly from 10 a.m. to 1 p.m.	
		11th	Working parties as usual - 19th Division relieved 31st Division which was the Division on our right, VI Corps area. Snow sleet fell during the morning and at intervals throughout the day.	
		12th	Our heavy artillery shelled BUCQUOY at 7 p.m. and 10 p.m. - In retaliation the enemy shelled SOUASTRE with about 50-59 shells causing several	

Army Form C. 2118

WAR DIARY
or
INTELLIGENCE SUMMARY
(Erase heading not required.)

Instructions regarding War Diaries and Intelligence Summaries are contained in F. S. Regs., Part II. and the Staff Manual respectively. Title Pages will be prepared in manuscript.

Place	Date	Hour	Summary of Events and Information	Remarks and references to Appendices
SOUASTRE	Jan 1917	12th	Casualties but very little damage. Casualties 2/Lieut C.S. HALL and 1 other rank killed in evening by enemy shelling while working along main road of SOUASTRE	
	13th		G.O.C. Division inspected work with C.O. - He expressed satisfaction at progress made - LINCOLN LANE was completed yesterday and handed over 2/Lieut. C.S. HALL and the man killed last night. NO. 3164 RFN MEREDITH. 1.D.Co. buried in ST. AMAND cemetery.	
	14th		SUNDAY. Working parties on roads returned at mid-day - No parties sent up to the line - Church parade services for all denominations held. LIEUT-COLONEL C.A.EVILL proceeded to AUXI-LE-CHATEAU to attend the Commanding Officers Conference at 3RD Army School.	
	15th		C.O. inspected work accompanied by G.O.C 1/1st FIELD.Co. R.E. - Working parties as usual	
	16th		Working parties as usual - ST. MARTINS LANE. C.T completed up as far as support line and handed over. - Trench mortars, rifle grenades and some shelling interfered with parties in LINCOLN-LANE which had to be withdrawn.	
	17th		Working parties as usual - Snow fell last evening and about 6 inches depth is on the ground.	
	18th		Working parties as usual - Snow remains on ground, slight additional falls.	

Army Form C. 2118.

WAR DIARY
or
INTELLIGENCE SUMMARY
(Erase heading not required.)

Place	Date	Hour	Summary of Events and Information	Remarks and references to Appendices
SOUASTRE	Jan 18th		5 other ranks reinforcements reported from Base composed of :- H - 1st and 1-3rd MONMOUTHS, all signallers.	
	19th		On Divisional orders 1 Officer and 40 men have to be withdrawn from roads and put on Trench work for 137th Brigade. As this party will interfere with rest period it will be found daily in turn by the two Companies on road works. At present this party is working on NAKED STREET nemetting, and on the Divisional line barbed wire, across this trench. – Snow fell slightly and frost still continues. – Road parties are only able to clear the snow from surface of roads. – Draft of 47 other ranks arrived from Base, composed of all 1st MONMOUTHS mostly old 2nd line men except 1 man from 3rd MONMOUTHS	
	20th		Working parties as usual. – C.O. inspected draft. – At 11:30 am about 30 shells fell in the village fired from a 4.2 gun – not much damage was done and very few casualties. At 5 pm in retaliation for this mornings shelling 7th Corps Heavy Artillery shelled ABLAINZEVELLE. Enemy in reply shelled SOUASTRE at 6 pm with about 50 shells 4.2's Capt C. COMELY, 2nd MONS reported for duty as reinforcement from Base	
	21st		SUNDAY No trench parties sent out and road Companies only worked until mid-day – Church parade services held for all denominations.	

WAR DIARY or INTELLIGENCE SUMMARY

Army Form C. 2118

Place	Date	Hour	Summary of Events and Information	Remarks and references to Appendices
SOUASTRE	Jan 1917	22nd	Working parties as usual – Frost still on and ground frozen very hard. LIEUT-COLONEL C.A.EVILL returned from C.O's conference at 3rd Army School and resumed command of the Battalion.	
		23rd	Working parties as usual – Very hard frost during night.	
		24th	LIEUT-COLONEL C.A.EVILL took over command of the 137th Brigade during absence of Brigadier on leave. – Working parties as usual – Enemy aeroplanes very active, one flew on three different occasions along the support line from GOOCH STREET to ST MARTINS LANE and fired a Machine Gun on D.Coys working parties – no casualties were suffered. – At 10am the 46th Div. left the VIIth Corps and became part of the XVIIIth Corps – The VIIth Corps H.Qrs moved to FOSSEUX, the XVIIIth Corps took over the old VIIth Corps H.Qrs at PAS. the other Division in the XVIIIth Corps being the 49th – The new Corps Commander is LIEUT-GENERAL. SIR F.I.MAXSE. K.C.B. C.V.O. D.S.O.	
		25th	Working parties as usual – Draft of 7 other ranks reported from Base composed as follows:– 4 – 1st MONMOUTHS 1 – 2nd " 2 – 3rd " all out for first time from Base Battalion Weather still extremely cold.	

Army Form C. 2118

WAR DIARY
or
INTELLIGENCE SUMMARY
(Erase heading not required.)

Place	Date	Hour	Summary of Events and Information	Remarks and references to Appendices
SOUASTRE	Jan 1917 26th		Working parties as usual - no event of importance occurred.	
	27th		Owing to an organised bombardment of enemy trenches D Company did not parade for work until middle-day. - A Coy working on the Divisional line worked as usual - Draft of 7 reported from Base all men who have previously served with this Battalion and who have returned from Base Hospitals.	
	28th		SUNDAY - No Trench working parties sent out and only C. Coy worked on roads until mid-day. - Church Services held for all Denominations in Evening.	
	29th		Working parties as usual	
	30th		Working parties as usual - Relief of A and D. Coys by B and C Coys carried out after work to-day.	
	31st		Working parties as usual - severe weather still continues - snow fell slightly during day - no signs of the thaw at present. Strength of Battalion :- 41 Officers, 986 Other ranks	

W. Edwards Major for Lieut Col?
Commanding 1st Batt MONMOUTHSHIRE REGT T.F.

CONFIDENTIAL

Army Form C. 2118.

WAR DIARY
~~INTELLIGENCE SUMMARY~~
(Erase heading not required.)

Vol 21

1st Batt Monmouthshire Regiment T.F.

February 1st 1917 to February 28th 1917

Army Form C. 2118.

WAR DIARY
or
INTELLIGENCE SUMMARY.
(Erase heading not required.)

1st Monmouths

Place	Date	Hour	Summary of Events and Information	Remarks and references to Appendices
SOUASTRE	Feb 1917	1st	Working parties as usual - The Corps Commander inspected the trenches of 139th Brigade (X. Sector) - 2/Lieut A.C. Corry Smith left for England for transfer to Royal Engineers.	
"	"	2nd	B. Company worked as usual on the Divisional Line - 100 men of "C" Company were withdrawn from GOOCH ST. C. Trench and put on making French mortar emplacements for 139th Brigade. The emplacements are situated in various places along the front and support line, from the lower Commecourt Road to LINCOLN LANE. The 58th Division, a 2nd line London Territorial Division has started to arrive in the XVIIIth Corps area - This Division has only been out from England a week and is, commencing to-night, doing its French instruction with this Division.	
"	"	3rd	Working parties as usual - Leave allotment increased from 17 to 19 passages per week, for all ranks.	
"	"	4th	SUNDAY No working parties sent out except the half company of "D" at POMMIER who worked on roads during the morning. "A" Company moved to BERLES for work on communication trenches and Divisional line with Z sector 137th Bde.	
"	"	5th	Working parties as usual - Frost still continues.	
"	"	6th	Working parties as usual	
"	"	7th	Working parties as usual - Casualties "A" Coy 3 killed, 2 wounded at BERLES by shell fire.	

Army Form C. 2118.

WAR DIARY
or
INTELLIGENCE SUMMARY.
(Erase heading not required.)

1st Monmouths

Place	Date	Hour	Summary of Events and Information	Remarks and references to Appendices
SOUASTRE	Feb 1917	8th	Working parties as usual - casualties "C" Coy 1 man wounded by shell fire at FONQUEVILLERS	
"	"	9th	Working parties as usual.	
"	"	10th	Working parties as usual - Orders received for one company to proceed to ARRAS for work there. Company will be attached to the 14th Division and is to march tomorrow. D. Company detailed for this duty. "A" Company relieved at BERLES by "D" Company in afternoon.	
"	"	11th	SUNDAY No working parties sent out - Church services held for all Denominations during evening - LIEUT-COL C A EVILL D.S.O. returned to Battalion from temporary command of 137th Brigade and he assumed command of the Battalion. "D" Company moved off from BERLES at 9 am to march to ARRAS - Draft of 48 other ranks arrived from Base as reinforcements, composed of :- 38 - 2/1st MONMOUTHS from England 8 - 2nd " " " 2 - 3rd " from Reserve Battalion.	
"	"	12th	Dispositions of Battalion after change of companies is Headquarters and Transport. SOUASTRE "A" Coy at work on roads, 2 platoons SOUASTRE and 2 platoons POMMIER B Coy SOUASTRE working on Divisional line at FONQUEVILLERS "C" Coy SOUASTRE working for 139th Bde. 2 platoons trench mortar emplacements and 2 platoons working on Trenches on night of X sector. D Coy attached 14th Division at ARRAS	

Army Form C. 2118.

WAR DIARY
or
INTELLIGENCE SUMMARY.
(Erase heading not required.)

1st Monmouths.

Place	Date	Hour	Summary of Events and Information	Remarks and references to Appendices
SOUASTRE	Feb	12th cont'd	LIEUT-COL. C.A. EVILL proceeded on one months leave and MAJOR W.A. LEWIS assumed command of the Battalion. – Draft inspected by the C.O at 3 p.m. – With very few exceptions the men are of good physique and well drilled. Working parties as usual – Thaw started.	
"	"	13th	Working parties as usual. – Thaw continued but freezing continues at night.	
"	"	14th	Working parties as usual. – Thaw continued but very slowly. – Work for 139th Brigade stops as from to day. – MAJOR (TEMP LIEUT-COL) F.J. TRUMP awarded "CROIX DE GUERRE".	
"	"	15th	"C" Company reported for work on Divisional Line at FONQUEVILLERS but was unable to work owing to bombardment. – Other parties as usual. G.O.C Division inspected Divisional line with C.O and expressed himself very pleased with the good work done by this Battalion.	
"	"	16th	"D" Company and 3 platoons "C" Coy worked on Divisional line at FONQUEVILLERS. 1 platoon "C" Coy worked on BIENVILLERS line - "A" coy as usual on roads. Operation orders received to move to GUOY on the 20th instant. The Division has, as from to day, formed a Depot Battalion for the training of reinforcements as they arrive from the Base – Each Infantry Battalion provides 1 platoon and finds instructional Staff. – 2/Lieut C.B. MARRABLE and the 10 draft of 47 other ranks which arrived on the 11th instant moved off at 9am to join Depot Battalion at LE GOUROY – Draft of 17 other ranks arrived from Base including RFN W.J. CORK, under escort. This man deserted while on leave	

Army Form C. 2118.

WAR DIARY
or
INTELLIGENCE SUMMARY.
(Erase heading not required.)

1st Monmouths

Place	Date	Hour	Summary of Events and Information	Remarks and references to Appendices
SOUASTRE	Feb.	16th contd	in September 1915 - Draft composed as follows :- 7 men who have served with this unit before 5 wounded men from England and 2 s/s from base 2. 1st MONMOUTHS from Reserve Battalion. " 2nd " " " " " " 5. 2nd " " " " " " 2. 3rd " " " " " "	
"	"	17	Shawing very hard, the roads are now in a bad state and all motor lorry traffic, except for a few lorries on special duty, is stopped. Working parties were found as yesterday. Instructors have been received from C.R.E. to stop work after to-day - C.O inspected Draft at 11 a.m.	
"	"	18th	SUNDAY. No working parties sent out - Boxing Tournament arranged in the afternoon - L/Cpl W. MORGAN "C" Coy beat PTE MARKS 139th M.G.C for Featherweight championship of Division. C of E parade services cancelled owing to no Padre available - Other denominations held services as usual	
"	"	19th	No working parties found to-day in view of to-morrows move. Day devoted to cleaning kit &c and inspections - Billeting party sent ahead to FOSSEUX to arrange accomodation for to-morrows.	
"	"	20th	Battalion paraded 6 a.m and marched to FOSSEUX via SAULTY arriving about 12.30 pm where it billeted for the night in huts - The thaw has made the roads in a very bad state - This & light rain made marching difficult	
FOSSEUX	"	21st	Battalion paraded at 11.15 am and marched to ARRAS. A halt was made outside WARLUS for dinner. From WARLUS onwards the Battalion had to march by	

Army Form C. 2118.

WAR DIARY
or
INTELLIGENCE SUMMARY.
(Erase heading not required.)

1st Monmouths

Place	Date	Hour	Summary of Events and Information	Remarks and references to Appendices
ARRAS	Feb.	21st 1917 cont'd	Platoons at 200 yards interval and on arriving at the Railway Arch outside DAINVILLE platoons were split up into sections of 12 at 200 yds interval. This greatly delayed march and the last Company did not arrive at ARRAS until 6pm. Companies marched straight to billets. Battalion is now back in VII Corps, the other Divisions being 14th & 31st. Companies at disposal of O/C Corps - C/O inspected billets which are as follows: Headquarters - House off Allyway next to 55 REU D'AMIENS "A" Company 13 RUE DE LILLE "C" " 16 RUE DE LA TERRIE DE CITÉ "B" " French Barracks "D" " 12 & 16 RUE DE L'ABBÉ HALLUIN Very strict standing orders are in force in ARRAS. No one is allowed out of billets by day except those on duty.	
"	"	22nd		
"	"	23rd	"D" Company carried on with its previous work of constructing dug-outs. O/C "A", "B" and "C" Coys met the O/C 466th & 468th Field Companies R.E. and reconnoitred work.	
"	"	24th	Work started last night, companies working as follows:- "A" Company clearing HARDY ST. C.T. "B" " " LIGHT RAILWAY by HAVANA ST. "C" " " HOPE ST C.T. "D" " constructing Dug-outs on Railway embankment at ACHICOURT No material at all is available owing to all Transport except supply transport, being kept off the roads until 2.6.5 on account of the road surface	

Army Form C. 2118.

WAR DIARY
or
INTELLIGENCE SUMMARY.
(Erase heading not required.)

1st Monmouths

Place	Date	Hour	Summary of Events and Information	Remarks and references to Appendices
ARRAS	Feb.	24th cont?	being offered by the Huns. Casualty 1 other rank seriously wounded by M.G. bullet.	
		25th	Working parties as yesterday. C.R.E inspected "C" companies works.	
		26th	Working parties as yesterday.	
		27th	B Company moved 2 platoons from GREEN ST. C.T to deep dug-outs which are to be finished by this Battalion, one for a Brigade Headquarters off Trench Mortar Railway by HARLEY ST and another for a Battalion Headquarters near the front line in the same C.T. — other working parties as usual. An English aeroplane was attacked by 4 Germans over ARRAS this afternoon and fell in flames by B Companies billet. both observer and pilot were killed. Weather very mild.	
	"	28th	Orders received in early morning to stand by in billets to move at short notice At 1 pm orders were received to march to BAVINCOURT to-night. Battalion paraded at 6:30 pm and marched to above place arriving at 11:30 pm. The road taken was the main ARRAS - DOULLENS. At BEAUMETZ the road surface had collapsed owing to passage of heavy guns, and various vehicles were hung up completely blocking the road. This delayed the march very considerably. The Transport which did not leave ARRAS until 9:30 pm was held up for the same reason and did not reach BAVINCOURT until 8 am on March 1st. Strength of Battalion :- 48 officers 1008 other ranks	

W Watkins Major
Commanding 1st Bn Monmouthshire Regt T.F.

CONFIDENTIAL. *Sent*

Army Form C. 2118.

Vol 22

WAR DIARY
or
INTELLIGENCE SUMMARY.
(Erase heading not required.)

1ST MONMOUTHSHIRE REGIMENT T.F.

MARCH 1ST 1917 TO MARCH 31ST 1917

Army Form C. 2118.

WAR DIARY
or
INTELLIGENCE SUMMARY.
(Erase heading not required.)

1st Monmouth Regt.

Place	Date	Hour	Summary of Events and Information	Remarks and references to Appendices
BIENVILLERS	March	12th	Battalion paraded at 11 am and marched to BIENVILLERS arriving at 12.30 pm. The Division now holds a front from GOMMECOURT CEMETERY to W.18.a.0.2 and is track in the XVIII Corps, the other divisions in the Corps being the 58th and 31st. Orders received at 8 pm to move 2 companies to FONQUEVILLERS by 11 am to-morrow. Casualties 5 other ranks wounded.	
"	"	2""	A and B Companies paraded at 9 am and marched to billets in FONQUEVILLERS. Adjutant attended a conference at the CRE's Office on system of work to be adopted under the present general circumstances and obtained programme of work. Conference of O's/C Companies, Adjutant and O/C 435th Field Coy R.E. at FONQUEVILLERS at 2.30 pm, when work to be done was allotted to Companies as follows:- A and B Coys. Work for Infantry Brigade holding line - This consists at present of trench grid paths to GOMMECOURT and digging a C.T. to the same place, to trench also to prepare the FONQUEVILLERS - GOMMECOURT R.D. for traffic. C and D Coys. To clear and prepare the FONQUEVILLERS - GOMMECOURT R.D. for traffic.	
"	"	3rd	3 Companies carried on work allotted yesterday - "D" Coy is working by night and "C" Coy by day on the road - Casualty 1 other rank wounded by shell.	
"	"	4th	Germans retired from present position about 1000 yds East of GOMMECOURT to a line from the South of MONCHY, East of RETTENOY FARM and East of BIEZ WOOD. This makes the FONQUEVILLERS - GOMME COURT Rd extremely urgent for transport and guns. "C" Company worked by day on this road and by 6 pm it had been cleared to permit of G.S. Wagons proceeding up to 600 German front line - D. Coy worked by night on the continuation of the road.	

Army Form C. 2118.

WAR DIARY
or
INTELLIGENCE SUMMARY.
(Erase heading not required.)

1st Monmouth Rgt.

Place	Date	Hour	Summary of Events and Information	Remarks and references to Appendices
BIENVILLERS	March 4th	4 pm	Through GOMMECOURT VILLAGE - The portion of the road was nothing but shell holes and covered with about 12 to 18 inches of mud. By 4 am the 5th men work ceased, all trenches across the road had been filled in for 50 yards and also shell holes. This find 50 yds passed through the old German front and support line. The road being absolutely obliterated.	
		5.5	Snow fell in early morning but cleared at 9 am. Owing to the further German retirement yesterday orders have been received to concentrate on roads and to cease work on the new C.T. and French gun works. "B" and "C" Coys worked by day on road through GOMMECOURT VILLAGE and by 5 pm the surface had been cleared and all holes and trenches filled right through to the Eastern side of the Village. This will enable guns to be taken through tonight. "D" Coy worked by night on clearing HANNESCAMPS - ESSARTS Rd. up as far as our front line. The following complimentary message was received today:- "The Brigadier-General sends congratulations on splendid work on the road through GOMMECOURT last night." 139th BRIGADE	
"	6th		Working parties as usual. "B" Coy moved from road in GOMMECOURT to HEBUTERN to work on the road from here to GOMMECOURT - billets remain unchanged. "A" Coy worked by night on road from FONQUEVILLERS to LA BRAYELLE FARM	

Army Form C. 2118.

WAR DIARY
or
INTELLIGENCE SUMMARY.
(Erase heading not required.)

1st Monmouth Regt.

Place	Date	Hour	Summary of Events and Information	Remarks and references to Appendices
BIENVILLERS	March 7th		Work carried on as yesterday. At 12 noon the 46th Division was taken over by the 5th Corps and so now in the 5th Army. The 5th Corps is commanded by Lt. Gen. FANSHAWE and is composed of the following Divisions:- 7th, 11th, 31st, 62nd and 46th.	
	8th		Working parties as yesterday. D Coy moved back on to road in GOMMECOURT VILLAGE, installing for the road now being available. B Coy finished filling shell holes on half of ROSIGNAL-GOMMECOURT Rd and also bridging German trenches in front of HEBUTERN. Guns are being taken up this route to-night. Snow fell from 8 am to 3 pm freezing hard again in the evening.	
	9th		Working parties as usual. Snow fell slightly during day. Canal D worked on road in GOMMECOURT VILLAGE. A and B worked on GOMMECOURT to ROSIGNAL ROAD.	
	10th		Working parties as yesterday. Weather much warmer, rain fell during evening. Orders received for Battalion to move to HEBUTERN to-morrow. 2/Lieut. F.W. GOWER, R.B. YENDOLL and P.T. WELLSTEED reported as reinforcements.	
	11th		Battalion moved to HEBUTERN. Headquarters and C and D Companies paraded 9.45 am marching via SAILLY - HEBUTERN-ROAD. A and B companies caused by very bad state of SAILLY - HEBUTERN-ROAD. A and B companies marched independently from FONQUEVILLERS also via SAILLY - HEBUTERN (as in bad state in mud), all roads being badly knocked about. The streets of	

Army Form C. 2118.

WAR DIARY
or
INTELLIGENCE SUMMARY.
(Erase heading not required.)

1st Monmouth Rgt.

Place	Date	Hour	Summary of Events and Information	Remarks and references to Appendices
HEBUTERN	March	11th	by heavy gun traffic – all billets in cellars or dug-outs. A and B worked from 5 – 9.30 pm on tracks from HEBUTERN to NAMELESS FARM.	
	"	12th	Working parties as usual – Casualty 1 other rank of D Coy killed by shell fire in GOMMECOURT	
	"	13th	Working parties as usual. G.O.C Division sent a verbal message to this Battalion of good work done by this Unit. 3 other ranks wounded by shell fire in GOMMECOURT	
	"	14th		
	"	15th	Working parties as usual. Lt-Col C.A.E.VILL. D.S.O returned from leave and resumed Command of the Battalion.	
	"	16th	C/O inspected working parties which were found as usual.	
	"	17th	C/O inspected working parties. The Germans evacuated BUCQUOY last night also MONCHY, ESSARTS and BAPAUME and the Division is pressing forward accordingly. 2/Lieuts H. BROWNE, H.B. PERKINS and Lieut J.A. PHILLIPS reported for duty as reinforcements from Base	
	"	18th	The Germans withdrew in the night from DOUCHY, ABLAINZEVELLE ETC. Cavalry were sent forward. Working parties found as under:–	
			"A" Company SOUASTRE – FONQUEVILLERS ROAD	
			"B" do GOMMECOURT – PUYSEUX ROAD	
			"C" do ROSIGNOL WOOD – BUCQUOY ROAD	
			"D" do GOMMECOURT – ESSARTS ROAD	

Army Form C. 2118.

1st Monmouth Bn

WAR DIARY
or
INTELLIGENCE SUMMARY.
(Erase heading not required.)

Instructions regarding War Diaries and Intelligence Summaries are contained in F. S. Regs., Part II. and the Staff Manual respectively. Title pages will be prepared in manuscript.

Place	Date	Hour	Summary of Events and Information	Remarks and references to Appendices
HEBUTERN	March 19th		Further withdrawal of Germans – Cavalry in touch with enemy at ECOUST – ST-MEIN. Companies worked on roads as follows:– "A" Coy. FONQUEVILLERS – GOMMECOURT B and C. Coys. ROSIGNAL WOOD – BUCQUOY D Coy GOMMECOURT to ESSARTS	
			A large crater at cross roads by ROSIGNAL WOOD and another at cross roads by ESSARTS have both been filled.	
	20th		Battalion ordered to concentrate on FONQUEVILLERS – GOMMECOURT – ESSARTS Rd and companies assembled accordingly. Orders received that Battalion will as from to-morrow be attached to 7th Division for work on SERRE – PUISIEUX Rd. German retreat continues and ST LEGER is now occupied by our cavalry. Owing to 7th & 8th Division advancing N.E. and the 46th Division also advancing E. the 46th Division has now been withdrawn from the line and is engaged on Salvage work.	
	21st		Battalion received orders at 10 a.m. to move to COURCELLES which was altered to COUIN at 1.50 p.m. Battalion paraded at 2.30 p.m. and moved to COUIN, marching across country until just east of COLONEAUX. Battalion billeted in huts on S.W. outskirts of that village.	
	22nd		Day utilised for cleaning up generally. 13 Companies route marches left Billets at intervals during day but frozen falls overtakes	
COUIN	23rd		Orders received to move to BERTRANCOURT – Battalion paraded at 3.30 p.m. was bright and sunny and marched off arriving in new billets at 5 p.m.	

Army Form C. 2118.

WAR DIARY
or
INTELLIGENCE SUMMARY.
(Erase heading not required.)

1st Monmouth Regt

Instructions regarding War Diaries and Intelligence Summaries are contained in F. S. Regs., Part II. and the Staff Manual respectively. Title pages will be prepared in manuscript.

Place	Date	Hour	Summary of Events and Information	Remarks and references to Appendices
BERTRANCOURT	March 24th		Battalion paraded at 1 pm and marched to LEALVILLERS, arriving about 2:30 pm and was billeted here for night.	
LEALVILLERS	25th		Battalion paraded at 11 am and marched to VILLERS BOCAGE, distance 11 miles and billeted here for night - no men fell out. A halt was made from 1 pm to 2 pm for dinner just south of HERRISART. After dinner the following complimentary letter received from G.O.C 46th Division was read on parade by Lieut-Col C.A.EVILL (APPENDIX 1)	
VILLERS-BOCAGE	26th		Battalion paraded 11:30 am and marched to main AMIENS Rd where motor lorries were drawn up. These lorries moved off at 2 pm and conveyed Battalion to FERRIERS, about 4 miles S.W of AMIENS where Battalion was billeted. Transport moved by march route via BERTANGLES and AILLY	
FERRIERS	27th		Companies at disposal of O/C Coys for purposes of cleaning up generally and for close order drill. 25% of Battalion allowed to visit AMIENS	
"	28-		Orders received for Battalion to entrain at SALEUX at 11 am on 29th. Companies again at disposal of O/C Coys. Fresh orders for entraining received. The Battalion now entrains at 9 am on 29th. Billeting party paraded at 6 pm and entrained with first party of 137th Brigade to which Brigade this Battalion is attached for move. 25% of Battalion again visited AMIENS	
"	29th		Battalion paraded (less D. Coy) at 5:45 am when Battalion marched to SALEUX station and entrained in train leaving 9:25 am. Transport moved	

WAR DIARY
or
INTELLIGENCE SUMMARY.

(Erase heading not required.)

Army Form C. 2118.

1st Monmouth Bn.

Place	Date	Hour	Summary of Events and Information	Remarks and references to Appendices
	March 29th	5ᵃ	Bn. at 5.30 am in order to get vehicles on in time. The accommodation was limited. HQ men travelling in a truck. LILLERS was reached at 1.30 am where Battalion detrained and marched to ECQUEDECQUES, where billets had been arranged. D Coy travelled with Divisional details on train leaving SALEUX at 1.25 pm, and arrived at ECQUEDECQUES at 5.30 am 30th	
ECQUEDECQUES	"	30ᵗʰ	Battalion roused at 11 am - Day spent in cleaning billets	
	"	31ˢᵗ	Owing to a move to AUCHY being possible this afternoon only physical drill parades were held during morning. Battalion paraded at 2 pm for route march, so impending move was cancelled. The Battalion is now in the 1st Army, commanded by General SIR H.S. HORNE. K.C.B. and the 2ⁿᵈ Corps commanded by Lieut-Gen. SIR CLAUDE JACOB. K.C.B. All Officers of the 137th Brigade groups attended at ST. HILAIRE at 9.45 am to meet Corps Commander, who first addressed the Officers, after which each Battalion's Officers paraded, when they were introduced to GEN JACOB who shook hands with each and asked one or two questions. Strength of Battalion:- 45 Officers 971 Other ranks	

M Scott
Lieut. Colonel
Commanding 1st Monmouthshire Regiment. T.F.

APPENDIX I

WAR DIARY
or
INTELLIGENCE SUMMARY.
(Erase heading not required)

Army Form C. 2118.

Place	Date	Hour	Summary of Events and Information	Remarks and references to Appendices
			Complimentary Letter received from G.O.C. 46th Division	
			O/C 1st Monmouthshires	46th Division p. 651.
			The G.O.C. wishes me to say that he congratulates you and all ranks under your command on the admirable work done by the Battalion during the recent operations, in which the Division has been engaged.	
			He is proud to have such a Pioneer Battalion under his command.	
			Kindly communicate this to all ranks	
			(Sd) W.H.M FREESTUN. LIEUT-COL A.A.&Q.M.G 46th Division	
	23rd March 1917			

Army Form C. 2118.

WAR DIARY
or
INTELLIGENCE SUMMARY.
(Erase heading not required.)

CONFIDENTIAL

P/46

Vol 23

1st Batt Monmouthshire Regiment T.F.

April 1st 1917 to April 30th 1917

Place	Date	Hour	Summary of Events and Information	Remarks and references to Appendices

Army Form C. 2118.

WAR DIARY
or
INTELLIGENCE SUMMARY.
(Erase heading not required.)

Instructions regarding War Diaries and Intelligence Summaries are contained in F. S. Regs., Part II. and the Staff Manual respectively. Title pages will be prepared in manuscript.

Place	Date	Hour	Summary of Events and Information	Remarks and references to Appendices
ECQUEDECQUES	April 1		Sunday. No training parades held. Church parade at 2-30 pm. Battalion parade ground, rain came on, and service was abandoned after 20 minutes.	
	2		Company parades 9am to 12-30 pm for close order drill, physical drill, etc. Recreation in afternoon.	
	3		Considerable fall of snow during night, which continued part of the morning. Companies stood by in billets & carried on with gas drill & inspection. Battalion parade 2 pm for route-march.	
			2nd Divisional Depot Battalion reassembled at ERNY ST JULIEN. 20 of Markable, 4 instructors & 14 partially trained men left Battalion to join depot.	
	4		Company parades for training in morning, also for 1 hours route march. Commanding Officer inspected D Coy. Weather still unsettled	
	5		Company parades as usual. C.O. inspected C Coy. Baker Ky. Bath etc to other ranks arrived from base, all trained	

A 5834 Wt. W.4973/M687 750,000 8/16 D.D. & L. Ltd. Forms/C.2118/13.

WAR DIARY
or
INTELLIGENCE SUMMARY.
(Erase heading not required.)

Army Form C. 2118.

Place	Date	Hour	Summary of Events and Information	Remarks and references to Appendices
ESQUEDECQUES	April 5		Signallers composed 5 - 1st + 4 - 3rd + 1 - 2nd Man Regt all from England except 1st + 1, 3rd Man men.	
"	"	6	Company parades during morning for usual training. C.O. inspected 'B' Coy. Draft of 10 paraded + sent to 1st Batt Battalion.	
"	"	7	Company paraded for training. C.O inspected 'A' Coy. and Transport personnel. Weather fine, but cold. A + B Coys bathed in baths at ST HILAIRE.	
"	"	8	Easter Sunday. Battalion parade 6 + 6. 11.30 a.m. in Head Quarter yard followed by a Communion Service. Roman Catholic service 9.30am in Church. Tactical scheme for Officers in afternoon over C.O. Weather beautifully fine + warm. C.O., C.Adj + Transport personnel bathed. Draft of 6 other ranks arrived, all being men who have previously served with this unit + who have been discharged from Base Hospitals.	
"	"	9	Divisional Route March. Battalion paraded 9 am in marching order + moved off to starting point which was cross roads 300 yards south of COTTES near ST HILAIRE. This Battalion marched in rear of 5th North Staffordshire Regt. + formed part of 137 Brigade group. The route taken was AUCHY, ESTREE BLANCHE, LONGHEM, LINGEM, ROMBAY, NORRENT FONTES + BOURECQ a distance of about 15 miles. No men fell out. The G.O.C. II Corps', G.O.C. 46th DIVISION. inspected all troops en route. The battalion returned to billets at 3.15 p.m. The distinguishing mark of a Khaki M. worn on the back has been attached and a new one introduced of a black dragon flowelled on the back of the Steel helmet.	
"	"	10	Company parades during morning. Training interfered with by high wind + occasional snow. Battalion played 6th North Staffordshire Regiment at football the result being Rugby 1st Mons. 12 Bomb 6 North Stafford Nil. 6366? Seeger 1st Mons Nil. 63 + WELLSTEED sent to 1/5th SOUTH STAFFS Regt for 39 cadre Enforcement attachment.	

WAR DIARY
or
INTELLIGENCE SUMMARY.
(Erase heading not required.)

Army Form C. 2118.

Place	Date	Hour	Summary of Events and Information	Remarks and references to Appendices
EQUEDECQUES	April 11		Very bad weather, snow fell the greater part of the day. Companies paraded as usual for training, but owing to weather it was greatly interfered with. Training of bombers demonstrated, on the basis of each platoon being composed of one Section of bombers, under 2nd Lt R.B. Venall.	
"	12		Training parade as usual, weather again unfavourable, being fine, but cold towards. Musketry commenced on 30 yards range, each man firing a grouping practice of 5 rounds. C.O. + O.C. Coys, Adjutant + M.O. had tactical scheme in afternoon.	
"	13		Weather much finer. 3 platoons A Coy fired grouping practice. Remainder of Battalion carried on with Training parades. Officers learned out twelve practice in evening. Orders received at 10 p.m. for Battalion to move to HOUDAIN. Tomorrow + after arrival there to come under orders of G.E. 1st Army for work.	
HOUDAIN	"	14	Battalion paraded at 10.45 a.m. + marched to HOUDAIN via MARLES-LES-MINES arriving at 4.30 p.m. A halt of 1½ hours was made midway to dinners. Orders received to move tomorrow to ECOIVRES after which Battalion will be under Chief Engineer XIII Corps for work.	
ECOIVRES	"	15	Battalion paraded 10.30 a.m. + marched to ECOIVRES via REBREUVE arriving at 4.30 p.m. The weather was extremely bad, rain falling throughout the march, owing to rain an old 25 minutes halt was made midway when haversack rations were eaten. Dinner being issued on arrival in new billets.	
ST AUBIN	"	16	Battalion paraded 2 p.m. + marched to ST AUBIN. arriving at 3.35 p.m. 1 was killed. All N.C.O.s are very poor. 2 Companies & B being in marquees. The G.O, O.C. Coy rode in advance of the Battalion to reconnoitre work, which we all on roads in the old forward area.	
	"	17	Companies paraded at 7.45 A.M. to work on roads in ANZIN ST AUBIN.	

WAR DIARY or INTELLIGENCE SUMMARY.

Army Form C. 2118.

Place	Date	Hour	Summary of Events and Information	Remarks and references to Appendices
ST AUBIN	Apr 17th cont'd		District MADAGASCAR and ECURIE roads – Returned to billets at 4.30 pm. The weather was very bad, alternate showers of hail & snow falling throughout the day.	
	18th		Working parties as yesterday – Weather still very cold with intermittent showers. At 10.30 pm message received from H.Q. Division for 8 Officers to report to Lovat's Scouts at BULLY-GRENAY as early as possible.	
	19th	3.30 am	At 3.30 am received orders from H.Q. Division to relieve 12th SHERWOOD FORESTERS (Pioneers) 24th Division at BULLY-GRENAY, relief to be carried out by one Company daily commencing on 19th. "C" Coy paraded at 9am to move billets to MAROC on BULLY-GRENAY. Blankets being transported by G.S. Wagons – On the march the Company were redirected to NOULETTE HUTS – Coy reached billets by 4pm – Remaining Coys found working parties as usual, D Coy knocking off at 12.30 as Reg would be moving off to new billets next day. The weather has improved but still showery & cold – NOULETTE HUTS – R.21 d.5.1 map ref 36.3 – At 5.30 am Sgt Barcker and 7 other observers left ST AUBIN with limber to report to LOVATS SCOUTS, BULLY-GRENAY	
	20th		A Coy paraded 9am to move billets to MAROC and A Coy G.S. Wagons were employed for carrying D Coys blankets – The coy arrived on billets at 4.50 pm. A + B Coy paraded for work as usual – B Coy returned from work at 12.30 pm as this coy would move billets on 21st – The Lewis Gun and Bombing Officers carried out training Bombing Officer taking 8 Grenadiers from A + B Coys. District H.Qrs to R.E.3.1.3 and B Coy to NOULETTE HUTS R.21.d.5.1. reached billets at 3.30 pm	
BOEFFLES-BONVIGNY	21st		Headquarters and B Coy paraded at 9am to move billets to BULLY-GRENAY Weather fine generally again fell during lunch hour from 12 midday to 1 pm. 2/Lieut WATERS reported from Base	

Army Form C. 2118.

WAR DIARY
or
INTELLIGENCE SUMMARY.
(Erase heading not required.)

Instructions regarding War Diaries and Intelligence Summaries are contained in F. S. Regs., Part II. and the Staff Manual respectively. Title pages will be prepared in manuscript.

Place	Date	Hour	Summary of Events and Information	Remarks and references to Appendices
BOYEFFLES-BOVIGNY	Apr	22nd	The Commanding Officer accompanied by O/C Coys and Officer of 12th SHERWOOD FORESTERS reconnoitred roads allotted to the Battalion for repair. B & C Coys to work on road running through 26D through ANGRES to LIEVIN. Map ref 36 B SE. – "D" Company to work on road from M.3.6.8.6 to M.14.C.3.0. through M.10.a.4.0. – 2/Lieut F.W. HOLE reported from the Base and posted to D. Company. – 'A' Coy marched from ST AUBIN and reached their billets in CALONNE at 4 pm.	
"		23rd	B, C & D Companies carried on work on roads. 'A' Coy reconnoitred tramway line running from BULLY-GRENAY through M.7.d.0.4. to M.14.C.?.4. 'B' Coy suffered three casualties from shrapnel on COLONELS Rd, one of which died. 1 O'bearer with LOVATS SCOUTS.	
"		24th	Working parties carried on with work on roads as yesterday. "B" Company carrying out grouping and bombing Officers carrying out training. "B" Company carrying out grouping practice on range at AIX NOULETTE in evening. – Weather clear & dry but cold wind.	
"		25th	Working parties working on roads as yesterday. – Draft of 5 N.C.O's reported from Base.	
"		26th	Working parties as on previous days. – Weather continues clear and dry but still cold. N.W. winds prevail.	

Army Form C. 2118.

WAR DIARY
or
INTELLIGENCE SUMMARY.
(Erase heading not required.)

Instructions regarding War Diaries and Intelligence Summaries are contained in F. S. Regs., Part II. and the Staff Manual respectively. Title pages will be prepared in manuscript.

Place	Date	Hour	Summary of Events and Information	Remarks and references to Appendices
BOYEFFLES BOVIGNY	Apr	27th	Working parties as yesterday - Received orders from CRE to find one company to work on strong points - D Coy was recalled from night work in order to carry out this work - At 10.30 pm orders re strong points cancelled	
		28th	Working parties found as yesterday. Four Officers attached to the 5th SOUTH STAFFORDS for instruction reported the Battalion to-day - weather dry and clear but cold as yesterday.	
		29th	Working parties found to-day as yesterday - The Commanding Officer reported to the 46th Division to-day to take over command of the 138th Brigade	
		30th	One Company working on BULLY-LIEVIN Tramway - Two companies cleaning & repairing ANGRES-LIEVIN Rd - One Company repairing Tramway in LIEVIN under 31st A.T. Coy RE - weather continues bright & clear. Strength of Battalion:- 44 Officers 931 Other ranks	

JS Stewart Major
Commanding 1st Monmouthshire Regt. T.F.

CONFIDENTIAL

Army Form C. 2118.

Vol 24

WAR DIARY
— of —
INTELLIGENCE SUMMARY.
(Erase heading not required.)

1st Batt The Monmouthshire Regiment. T.F

May 1st 1917 to May 31st 1917

Instructions regarding War Diaries and Intelligence Summaries are contained in F. S. Regs., Part II. and the Staff Manual respectively. Title pages will be prepared in manuscript.

Place	Date	Hour	Summary of Events and Information	Remarks and references to Appendices

Army Form C. 2118.

WAR DIARY
or
INTELLIGENCE SUMMARY.
(Erase heading not required.)

Instructions regarding War Diaries and Intelligence Summaries are contained in F.S. Regs. Part II. and the Staff Manual respectively. Title pages will be prepared in manuscript.

Place	Date	Hour	Summary of Events and Information	Remarks and references to Appendices
BOUVIGNY-BOYEFFLES	May 1st		Companies carried out work as yesterday — One man C Company wounded by shell fire — Weather continues sunshine, and much warmer.	
	2nd		Companies carried out work as yesterday. The road between ANGRES & LIEVIN is now cleared for about half way — C Company had 5 casualties from shell fire, one of these men died in hospital in the evening — Weather as yesterday.	
	3rd		Working parties as yesterday — The work carried out by B Company in ANGRE-LIEVIN has at no time been interrupted by shell fire although this company have had to stop work several times through Aeroplane reconnaissance — Weather continues clear & warm.	
	4th		All companies carrying out work as yesterday — In the evening 'A' Company two grouping practices on range — Received instructions from C.R.E. in evening to the effect that the company employed burying cable will be required for work on Strong Points, to work by nights commencing Sunday. Three casualties, two in B Company, and one in A Company, all from shell fire.	
	5th		A. B & D Companies carried on with work already in hand — C Company reported to the 468 Field Coy. R.E's for work on wiring of Divisional line — Owing to 137 & 138 Brigades changing over the 468 Field Coy returned 'C Coy to billets to stand by for work the following night — Weather continues dry but so much colder.	
	6th		With exception of 'C' Coy works were carried out as on previous days. C Coy was employed during nights at 5/6 & wiring S. Points under supervision of 468 Field Coy, in area M.11.A — M.11.B and M.11.D. Weather continues fine & much warmer to-day.	

WAR DIARY
or
INTELLIGENCE SUMMARY.
(Erase heading not required.)

Army Form C. 2118.

Place	Date	Hour	Summary of Events and Information	Remarks and references to Appendices
BOUVIGNY BOYEFFLES	May 7		With exception of "C" Company working parties were found as usual :- C Company were not required for work during night 6/7/17. Owing to alterations in work by R.E.s the following Officers reported from Base are taken on the strength and posted to Companies as under:- Lieut. W. M. JAMES D. Company " T. S. SPITTLE A " " F. T. EVANS A " To-morrow being the anniversary of the Second Battle of YPRES, and permission having been obtained from the Division that no work be carried out on that day, the following have read out on parade :- "The Commanding Officer wishes that no parades or inspections of any description will be held to-morrow - the wish is to have the men to themselves." Weather still continues fine	
	8		A memorial service was held at 7am at NOULETTE HUTS, and the following notice was read out :- "No work will be carried out to-day being the second anniversary of the day on which the Battalion suffered such heavy casualties in the Second Battle of YPRES. We honoured memory of our gallant comrades who laid down their lives for King & Country on that day, remain fresh. Their brave example strengthens us in our determination to conquer the enemy." Weather continuous rain up to mid-day but bright & clear & much warmer in the afternoon.	

Army Form C. 2118.

WAR DIARY
or
INTELLIGENCE SUMMARY.
(Erase heading not required.)

Instructions regarding War Diaries and Intelligence Summaries are contained in F.S. Regs., Part II. and the Staff Manual respectively. Title pages will be prepared in manuscript.

Place	Date	Hour	Summary of Events and Information	Remarks and references to Appendices
BOUVIGNY BOYEFFLES	May	9E	'A' Coy continued work on BULLY-LIEVIN TRAMWAY. – B. Coy standing by for work on Strong Points in BOIS-DE-RIAUMONT to-night – C Coy working under 466 Field Coy RE's preparing wire for wiring Divisional Line, on COLONELS Rd M.21.B.2.3. D. Coy standing by for work at night, under the 465 Field Coy RE's. Weather continues fine.	
		10E	Work continued on BULLY-LIEVIN TRAMWAY. – The Company working on Strong Points in BOIS-DE-RIAUMONT got very little work done owing to very heavy shelling. One non many trucks of wounder 465 Field Co on Strong Points at TUNNEL NEG. One Company working under 468 Field Co wiring at M.26.B.6.8. – Weather continues fine.	
		11E	Working parties fixed to-day as yesterday – Weather continues fine.	
		12E	One Company continued work on BULLY-LIEVIN TRAMWAY. Other companies working on Strong Points as on previous day – B. Company working on Strong Points at BOIS-DE-RIAUMONT on night of 11th had to cease work owing to very heavy bombardment of Gas Shells – many of the RE Sappers were gassed – This Company had 1 Officer and 8 O.R. gassed. Weather continued warm and threatening Thunder.	
		13E	Working parties found to-day as usual – Two. O.Rs of 'A' Coy wounded to-day by shrapnel on returning from work.	
		14E	One Company working on Strong Points Nos 2, 6, 7 & 9 on old village defence line – Other Companies carried on with work as on previous day. Weather still warm and dry.	

WAR DIARY
or
INTELLIGENCE SUMMARY.

(Erase heading not required.)

Army Form C. 2118.

Place	Date	Hour	Summary of Events and Information	Remarks and references to Appendices
BOUVIGNY BOYEFFLES	May	15th	Work carried out on Strong Points on village defence line, wiring & work on fire trenches. Company working on Strong Points in BOIS-DE-RIAUMONT wiring & constructing firebays. – Work carried out on TUNNEL WEG and BULLY-LIEVIN TRAMWAY. – Weather close & threatening thunder.	
		16th	Working parties carried on same as yesterday. Weather very dull & much colder.	
		17th	Working parties found as on previous day under 465, 466 and 468 Field Coys R.E.'s. – Weather strong West winds not so cold.	
		18th	Company working under 466 Field Coy R.E's on Strong Points in BOIS-DE-RIAUMONT received instructions that working parties were cancelled for night of 17/18th owing to bombardment taking place. The work on TUNNEL WEG trenches was also cancelled. Other working parties found as yesterday. Weather dull with strong West winds.	
		19th	Working parties carried out work under R.E's as on previous day.	
		20th	No working parties during the day – C of E service was held at NOULETTE HUTS at 3.30 p.m. at which B and C Companies paraded. All companies paraded in the evening for work under R.E's. Weather continues warm. Capt R.C.L. THOMAS returned to duty after 1 months leave in England.	
		21st	Companies paraded in Evening for work under R.E's as on previous day. Weather warm and threatening thunder. – A draft of 11 men reported from the Divisional Depot Battalion, the majority of these men having	

Army Form C. 2118.

WAR DIARY
or
INTELLIGENCE SUMMARY.
(Erase heading not required.)

Place	Date	Hour	Summary of Events and Information	Remarks and references to Appendices
BOUVIGNY BOYEFFLES	May 21st		Been taken on the strength a fortnight previously when they reported to the Divisional Depot Battalion.	
	22nd		Working parties found by 9/C Coys to work under 465, 466 & 468 Field Coys R.E.s Work carried on during night in wiring on Divisional Defence Line. A Company continued work during the day on BULLY-LIEVIN TRAMLINE.	
	23rd		Continuous rain from early morning through the day. Orders received from Division for B & C Companies to work on ASSIGN TRENCH this evening - This trench is situated in CITÉ-DE-RIAUMONT - A & D Companies worked as usual - Weather cleared up, bright sun and very warm	
	24th		A, B and C Companies worked as yesterday - D Company did not work as the 5th SOUTH STAFFORDS attacked a portion of the enemy trenches known as NASH ALLEY and captured it - At 7pm the captured ground was subsequently retaken by the enemy.	
	25th		A, B and C Companies worked as yesterday - D Company commenced work on ABSALOM TRENCH, this work consists of deepening the old German communication trench and cleaning it	
	26th		A & D Companies worked as usual - B and C Companies had their weekly night off. Sentence of General Court Martial on 2/Lt H.C. MORRIS promulgated. This Officer has been sentenced to be dismissed from his Majesty's Service for being Drunk on May 7th 1917. Casualties. 5 O.R. D Coy gassed by Gas shells 1 OR of these has died at C.C.S.	

WAR DIARY or INTELLIGENCE SUMMARY

Army Form C. 2118.

(Erase heading not required.)

Place	Date	Hour	Summary of Events and Information	Remarks and references to Appendices
BOUVIGNY-BOEFFLES	May 27th		SUNDAY – Church Parades held for all denominations – 2nd Lt. H.G. MORRIS handed over to the A.P.M. 46th Division for disposal – 'A' Company had its weekly day off – B, C and D Companies as usual. Draft of 16 other ranks reported from Base to Divisional Depot Battalion, composed of :- 15 – 1st Mon men, 12 from Base Hospitals and 3 from England. 1 – 3rd Mon Warrant Officer from nucleus of 3rd Battalion. Casualties 2/Lt. J.M. HANSON wounded by shell fire – 3 other ranks wounded, one of which is Gas poisoning.	
	28th		LIEUT-COLONEL C.A. EVILL returned to Battalion after having commanded 138th Brigade since 29th of last month, during absence of G.O.C. sick. Companies worked as usual – Casualties :- 1. O.R. Wounded (Gas) 1. O.R. Wounded (shell & duty)	
	29th		Working parties as usual – The following of this Battalion have been mentioned in SIR D. HAIG'S Despatches as being worthy of special mention for their gallantry and Devotion to duty in the field :- MAJOR W.A. LEWIS LIEUT (TEMP CAPT) W.M.B. BURNYEAT " " J.D. GRIFFITHS " K.C. RAIKES LIEUT J.D. GRIFFITHS SERGT R.H. SPOONER (TRANSPORT SERGT) 225402 " A.R. WEATHERLEY (SIGNALLING SERGT) 222587	

A5834 Wt.W4973/M687 750,000 8/16 D.D. & L. Ltd Forms/C.2118/13.

Army Form C. 2118.

WAR DIARY
or
INTELLIGENCE SUMMARY.
(Erase heading not required.)

Place	Date	Hour	Summary of Events and Information	Remarks and references to Appendices
BOUVIGNY BOYEFFLES	May	30th	Working parties as usual. — 2/Lieut H.C.D. HARRIS rejoined from hospital. Casualties :- 3 other ranks wounded.	
		31st	"A" Company commenced work on the CRASSIER SWITCH which is the northern sector of the Divisional Line. — The work consists chiefly of raising in front. B, C and D. Companies worked by night on deepening the Front line Trench between ABSALOM & ASSIGN. C.T's (M.24.c.4.5 — M.30.A.8.4 sheet 36 C). The enemy at about 12 midnight bombarded the Trench with gas shells and trench mortar bombs, and the working party had to put on respirators — This greatly interfered with the work — The Commanding Officer was apparently wounded this week at 2 am — Casualties :- 6 other ranks Wounded (Gas) Strength of Battalion :- 45 Officers 915 men	

A. Sett
Lieut: Colonel,
Commanding 1st Batt. The Monmouthshire Regt. T.F.

Vol 25

SECRET
+
CONFIDENTIAL

WAR DIARY

1st Batt. Monmouthshire Regiment T.F.

June 1st 1917 to June 31st 1917.

Army Form C. 2118.

WAR DIARY
or
INTELLIGENCE SUMMARY.
(Erase heading not required.)

Instructions regarding War Diaries and Intelligence Summaries are contained in F. S. Regs., Part II. and the Staff Manual respectively. Title pages will be prepared in manuscript.

Place	Date	Hour	Summary of Events and Information	Remarks and references to Appendices
BOUVIGNY BOYEFFLES	June 1917	1st	'A' Company worked as yesterday. 'B' Company worked on ASSIGN and 'D' Company on ABSALOM Communication Trenches. 'C' Company had its weekly nights rest. Casualties 3. O.R. wounded, 4. O.R. wounded (Gas poisoning received on night of 31st last)	
		2.20	'A' Company had night off. B, C & D Coys worked on trench as on 31st last which had to be deepened & widened, work interfered with by barrage put up by enemy owing to Canadians attacking & capturing the Central Electric Station on our right. - Casualties 1 O.R. killed - 1 O.R. missing. Reinforcements :- 1 O.R. from Base previously served with 2nd Battalion	
		9.40	All Companies worked by night - A & D Coys worked on digging a new Communication trench from M.30.a.7.10 to M.24.c.85.20. B & C worked on ASSIGN TRENCH - Casualties 1. O.R. killed, 1 O.R. wounded. 2/Lieut T. EDWARDS slightly wounded in hand and remaining at duty. Reinforcement: 1 O.R. from England.	
		4.15	B & C Coys worked on ASSIGN TRENCH erecting screens, deepening trench etc A & D worked on the new communication trench. They dug last night completing it. The Commanding Officer addressed B & C Coys on parade at 7pm informing them of the G.O.C Division's approval of their work, and of his appreciation for the way they had stuck a very long & trying tour of work. The Corps Commander has awarded a MILITARY MEDAL to No 225149 SERGT HODGES. G. 'C' Company for gallantry in the field on May 27th 1917. The Commanding Officer who was with the G.O.C Division who said that the men had worked magnificently	

A 5834 Wt. W4973/M687 750,000 8/16 D. D. & L. Ltd. Forms/C.2118/13.

Army Form C. 2118.

WAR DIARY
or
INTELLIGENCE SUMMARY.
(Erase heading not required.)

Instructions regarding War Diaries and Intelligence Summaries are contained in F.S. Regs., Part II. and the Staff Manual respectively. Title pages will be prepared in manuscript.

Place	Date	Hour	Summary of Events and Information	Remarks and references to Appendices
BOUVIGNY BOYEFFLES	June 1917	4.5	and that he was extremely pleased with results obtained. Casualties 3 other ranks wounded and 1 other rank wounded (shell shock).	
		5th	Extract from "LONDON GAZETTE" dated June 2nd 1917:- "His Majesty The King has been pleased to approve the following awards for Distinguished Service in the Field. To be a companion of the D.S.O. MAJOR W.A. LEWIS, MONMOUTHSHIRE REGT." B and C Coys worked on ASSIGN TRENCH - A and D Coys commenced to dig a new C.T. each from M.24.C.55.95 and M.30.a.70.98 to the railway cutting about 100 yds east of their points. The Commanding Officer addressed A and D Coys at 8.45pm at BULLY-GRENAY before moving off to work, the address being to the same effect as that made to B and C Companies yesterday. Casualties: 2 O Rks wounded, 1 O.R. wounded (shell shock)	
		6th	A and D Coys worked on completing trenches commenced last night. B Coy worked 2 platoons in ASSIGN TRENCH and 2 platoons on construction of observation posts in BOIS DE RIAUMONT. C Coy dug a new C.T. from ASSIGN TRENCH to a house about M.29.d.22.37 (sheet 36. C). Casualties: 2 O Rks killed and 1 O.R. wounded (shell shock)	
		7th	A Coy worked in ABSALOM C.T. deepening & clearing it on part nearest the line. D Coy worked as last night. C and D Coys assisted the R.E.s in carrying & filling parapet bags down to the fire trenches and in some cases the support trenches on the front between ABSALOM & ASSIGN C.T.s.	
		8th	At 10pm the 138th Brigade carried out a large raid two battalions of the 4th LINCOLNS and 5th LEICESTERS being used for this purpose. The trenches raided were from SOUCHEZ RIVER at N.25.c.23. - FOSSE 3 inclusive - ADMIRAL TRENCH - house in M.24.d. The operation was a success although machine guns interfered with the Companies on the sides. This Battalion found 5 parties of 1 Officer and 24 men each, two of which were attached to the 5th LINCS REGT and one to the 4th LEICESTERS for consolidation purposes	

Army Form C. 2118.

WAR DIARY
or
INTELLIGENCE SUMMARY.
(Erase heading not required.)

Instructions regarding War Diaries and Intelligence Summaries are contained in F. S. Regs., Part II. and the Staff Manual respectively. Title pages will be prepared in manuscript.

Place	Date	Hour	Summary of Events and Information	Remarks and references to Appendices
	June	8th	The parties were used for carrying wire to the newly captured positions. 1 Officer & 15 men were posted at LIEVIN to act as an escort to prisoners of which 3 Officers & 18 men were taken.	
	"	9th	Battalion rested - Day devoted to inspections etc	
	"	10th	SUNDAY. Battalion paraded at MARQUEFFLES FARM at 12 noon when the Commanding Officers inspected the Battalion. Dinners were issued near the parade ground at 1pm from the field kitchens and a Church Parade Service was held at 2.30pm. The 136th Brigade Band attended and played during the inspection & Church Parade. Complimentary memo received from O/C Divisional Signals re Operations of 8/9th inst Appendix 1.	
	"	11th	Copy of memo received from G.O.C. 46th Division on June 11th 1917 (Appendix 2). Working parties around. 'A' Coy 1 platoon on Right Railway under 2/Lt CORRY-SMITH Remainder of Company engaged on wiring Strong Points in Brigade Reserve Line in vicinity of ABSALOM TRENCH. 'B' Coy working with 468th R.E. Coy in CITE DE RIAUMONT 'C' Coy with 466th R.E. Coy on LIEVIN - ST PIERRE LINE Right sector } Brigade Reserve Line 'D' Coy with 465th R.E. Coy on LIEVIN - ST PIERRE LINE Left sector } Casualties 1st Other ranks of B. Coy wounded (Gas poisoning)	
	"	12th	Working parties as yesterday. 'C' coy moved billets from NOULETTE HUTS to BULLY-GRENAY in order to be nearer their work. 2 platoon D. Coy moved to dug outs about M.6.a.3.9 (sheet 36.C) for same reason. Draft of 6 other ranks arrived direct from Base composed of H.1st Iron men, 3 of whom are returned hospital men and 2.2nd Iron men, one of whom has previously served with this Battalion.	
	"	13th	Working parties as yesterday. Lieut. Col. C.A. EVILL left to take command of 138th Brigade during absence of G.O.C. on leave. HQ Divisional Horse Show held at MARQUEFFLES FARM	

WAR DIARY
or
INTELLIGENCE SUMMARY.
(Erase heading not required.)

Army Form C. 2118.

Place	Date	Hour	Summary of Events and Information	Remarks and references to Appendices
	June	13th cont'd	This Battalion entered in several classes for Transport Turn-outs, Jump. of Van etc, but only a Third Prize in the G.S. Wagon Turn-out was gained. The Army Commander presented the DSO ribbons at D.H.Q. at 10 a.m. MAJOR W.A. LEWIS attended to receive the ribbon of the D.S.O. a detachment of 15 men under 2/Lt MARRABLE was present to represent the Battalion.	
	"	14th	Working parties as usual. Permission has now been obtained to keep 1 platoon per company out of the line for resting and training purposes.	
	"	15th	A and B Coys worked as yesterday - C and D Coys commenced to clear and re-open the assembly trenches in CITE DE RIAUMONT which was dug for the operation of 8/9 Inst. Draft of 6 O.Rs arrived from Base. All have served with this Unit previously and are returned Base hospital men.	
	"	16th	All Companies worked on completing the new advanced trench from M.18.d.3.8 to M.24.a.7.5. commenced by the LINCOLNS last night. The resting platoons were used for work and in view of coming operations it is unlikely that the arrangement of 1 platoon per Company being out of the line will continue. The work was much impeded by shelling and Trench Mortar fire. Casualties: Other ranks, 2 killed, 1 died of wounds and 1 wounded remaining at duty. Lieut-Col C.A. EVILL returned from 138th Brigade and re-assumed Command of the Battalion.	
	"	17th	B, C and D Coys worked on advanced trench. The work was again interfered with by shelling and Trench Mortar fire. Casualties: Other ranks: 1 killed and 2 wounded. A Coy with 2 platoons continued wiring the Chateau Strong Point. Draft of 2 O.Rks. 1 man from Base hospital and the other from England both 1st Battalion men. The Corps Commander Lieut. General A.E.A. HOLLAND. C.B. M.V.O. D.S.O. has awarded the Military Medal to :- 226027 CPL. L. PASSANT. A. Coy. 325428 RFN. C.J. COLES. B. Coy for acts of gallantry in the field.	

WAR DIARY
or
INTELLIGENCE SUMMARY.
(Erase heading not required.)

Army Form C. 2118.

Place	Date	Hour	Summary of Events and Information	Remarks and references to Appendices
	June	18th 1917	The Commanding Officer presented the Ribbon of the Military Medal to R.S.M. COLES on a parade of Signallers at 9.30 am and to CPL PASSANT on a parade of 'A' Company at 3.30 pm. 'A' Company moved billets to cellars in LIEVIN in order to be nearer the work. A Thunderstorm with very heavy rain occurred about 2.30 pm and lasted for nearly an hour. 'A' Company worked as yesterday. 'B' Company continued digging advanced trench in M.18.d. near FOSSE 9 - 'C' and 'D' Coys worked on widening and deepening advanced trench in CITE ST THEODORE M.18.b.4.2. to M.18.d.3.8. (36.C) Casualties :- other ranks 1 killed, 1 wounded.	
		19th	2 platoons of 'A' Coy worked on Chateau S.P. remainder of Battalion was to have worked on wiring the new French trench known as CAVALRY TRENCH running from FOSSE 9 (M.18.a.7.5) in a S.W. direction to ABSALOM. C.T. and meeting this C.T. at M.24.c.8.7. Owing however to very heavy fire of all sorts it was not possible to work. Casualties 2/LIEUT W.S. JONES seriously wounded, this Officer died on 20th - 2/Lieut C. JEFFS slightly wounded and 3 other ranks wounded	
		20th	'A' Coy took over work of 'B'. Coy including the platoon employed on Light Railways at BULLY-GRENAY. The platoon of 'A' Coy so relieved moved to LIEVIN. 'A' Coy and 2 platoons of 'B' Coy commenced to dig and wire a trench from junction of ALICE & BATH TRENCHES through M.30.c.0.6 to M.30.a.9.8. This trench is required to consolidate the ground captured by the 5th LINCOLNS yesterday at 2.30pm namely the enemy trench system from M.30.d.2.8. to M.30.b.1.5. This work was proceeded with satisfactorily until 12.30 am 21st when heavy shelling caused work to cease Casualties :- 2/Lt F.W. GOWER slightly wounded and 2 other ranks wounded. 'C' and 'D' worked on wiring of trench as last night. A draft of 6 other ranks arrived at Depot Battalion from Base. 5 other ranks hospitals and 1 returned wounded from England. All are 1st Battalion men who have previously served with this Battalion Casualties :- 2 other ranks killed, 3 wounded.	
		21st	'A' and 2 platoons of 'B' Coy worked on trench commenced last night. Good work was done. 'C' and 'D' Coys commenced work on	

WAR DIARY or INTELLIGENCE SUMMARY

Army Form C. 2118.

Place	Date	Hour	Summary of Events and Information	Remarks and references to Appendices
AUBURN TRENCH (M.34.C.4.6 TO M.34.C.8.9) and the South Bink house to 2 only 2ft deep and has to be completed. Billets: from BULLY-GRENAY to LIEVIN	June	21st cont.d	This trench which was commenced by the 7 Corps Cyclists was found on 2 only 2ft deep and has to be completed. - 'C' Company moved	
		22nd	Working parties found as usual. Arrangements again made for 1 Platoon per Company to be left off work. All Coys worked from 'ASSIGN'. C.O. up to AFRICA, BOOT and BOTT trenches. 3 casualties other ranks. 3 gassed previously reported sick.	
		23rd	Work proceeded excellent as last night. Commanding Officer held a conference of O/C Coys in LIEVIN at 5 p.m. Casualties other ranks 2 Killed, 5 Wounded 8 gassed (gas shells) 2/Lt W.L. ROBERTS (A/CAPT) MIDDLESEX REGT. O/C 'A' Coy awarded Military Cross by Commander-in-Chief. Authority MS/H/5897 dated 19/6/17	
		24th	Acting under orders from Division no working parties were sent out. Commanding Officer held conference of O/C Coys at 5 p.m. No 325777 Sergt. F.R. ELMS 'D' Coy awarded Military Medal by Corps Commander for an act of gallantry on night of 19/20th inst.	
		25th	Orders received from Division for relieving Battalion of 137 Brigade to move up into LIEVIN and take over billets of supporting Battalion of 137 Brigade. This was completed by 9 p.m. This Battalion relieved the 5 SOUTH STAFFORDS and became the Battalion in support for the above Brigade. Working parties found for work on assembly trenches in CITE DE RIAUMONT. Casualties Nil. A subsidiary operation last night had gained the system of trenches on the W. of HILL 65 and the enemy had retired to the Eastern slopes. This had given us possession of FOSSES 3 also and rendered the approach to CITE DE RIAUMONT free from direct observation, making the position rather more comfortable for all concerned. Up to this date the trenches leading to the forward posts, where all the work has been, has been under direct observation from HILL 65 and FOSSE 3. The enemy took full advantage of this in order to shell and snipe all parties who crossed themselves. The advanced patrols could be seen walking on top of the LIP that were shelled off by the enemy. Posts were established on the reverse slopes of the hill by the 6 SOUTH STAFFORDS (Lt.-Col. TRUMP D.S.O)	
		26th	A, B & C Coys worked on assembly trenches on East of Louvignal sector, is BRICK, BATT and BOOT trenches. 'D' Coy took over a sector of the Front Line from the 4 & 6th Canadian Infantry Battalion. The exact front taken being from the SOUCHEZ RIVER at M.30.d.3.1 to N.35.C.1.9	

WAR DIARY
or
INTELLIGENCE SUMMARY.
(Erase heading not required.)

Army Form C. 2118.

Place	Date	Hour	Summary of Events and Information	Remarks and references to Appendices
	June 26th cont?		The relief was completed at 1.18 a.m. on 27th including 3 advanced posts. This Company on completion of relief came under command of the O/C. 5th LINCOLNS REGT. the Battalion on the right. The posts on the right on the South of the river being the 48 Canadian Brigade. The Commanding Officer visited this Company during the night. Casualties : 2/Lt A RICHARDS A Coy died of wounds, 5 other ranks killed and 13 wounded. The working parties were very heavily shelled this night the enemy evidently expecting an attack and putting down a heavy barrage. These assembly trenches were needed for the Right Battalion for the coming operation. They had to be cleared of the debris from a previous attack and there was some difficulty in dealing with the slag. The position is a very strong one from the enemy point of view and it seems strange that it was taken at so small a cost. The FOSSE 10 itself with the enemy ahead, who were caught retiring from their trenches, by the M.G. barrage.	
	27th		Orders received from Division to move into billets of Battalion in Divisional reserve in LIEVIN at present occupied by the 11th SHERWOOD FORRESTERS - This was completed by 9pm by A,B,& C Coys these Coys then moved off to work on assembly trenches in CITE DE RIAUMONT, ASIA AUCTION and ALICE trenches were unformed. D Coy relieved in the front line by the 5th LEICESTERSHIRE REGT the relief being completed by 11 a.m June 28th and then marched to billets in LIEVIN . Battalion Headquarters moved at 10pm to Brigade H.Q. dug outs at ANGRY CORNER by ANGRES CHURCH. The billets vacated by this Battalion in the support area were taken over by the 6th SOUTH STAFFORDS on completion of the above move this Battalion came under command of 138th Brigade. Casualties: 2/Lt F T EVANS wounded (at duty) Other ranks, 1 wounded, 3 wounded remaining at duty	
	28th		at 7.10 pm the 137th and 138th Brigades attacked HILL 65 and occupied ADULT ADJACENT & ADROIT trenches to the east of the Hill. Owing to the Canadian Division on the right flank pushing forward last night to ELEU DIT LEAUVETTES and AVION no resistance was offered by the enemy who ran from the trenches when the assault was launched. This Battalion was detailed to consolidate the captured position by digging a support line on the Western and N.W slopes of HILL 65 from M.24.d.40.35 to M.30.B.8.7 and the Reserves at M.30.B.95.50 to	

WAR DIARY
or
INTELLIGENCE SUMMARY.
(Erase heading not required.)

Army Form C. 2118.

Place	Date	Hour	Summary of Events and Information	Remarks and references to Appendices
	June	28th	ALMANACK TRENCH at N.26.a.10.15 (Sheet 36 C). This was done although a very heavy Thunderstorm at 7.30 p.m. which lasts several hours, made digging very difficult. Casualties. Other ranks 1 wounded, 3 wounded but remaining at duty. Draft 11 other ranks arrived at Depot Battalion from Base. The night was fairly quiet although ASSION TRENCH was shelled heavily at times & FOSSE.3 Our men got up by the road under the wood thus avoiding the shelling. On the way up two men of "D" Coy collapsed under the strain of their recent experiences - One of these men had killed 3 Germans with his Bayonet and shot a German Officer, in receiving his comrades at the HOHENZOLLERN REDOUBT in October 1915. Machine Guns swept the hill from time to time. It was in a state of churned up earth from Artillery fire but the enemy had not constructed any defences on the hill itself. The observation to the West is remarkable fine and the French may be right in saying it is the key to LENS - The men did some very fine digging on difficult ground and made a valuable trench for defence.	
		29th	Working parties provided to dig a communication trench on HILL 65 from ACORN TRENCH at N.25.a.65.20 to N.26.a.20.05. All positions occupied yesterday were maintained. Casualties. Other ranks 2 killed, 2 wounded.	
		30th	Operation orders received from Division that an attack on a three Brigade front will be made to-morrow at dawn and that this Battalion together with the 9th NORFOLKS and 2nd Cavalry Division Pioneer Battalion will form the Divisional reserve - Working parties were sent out as usual but were withdrawn at 1 am 1st owing to impending attack. The parties worked on trench commenced last night and in addition coupled up the trench from N.25.a.20.05 to existing trench at point N.25.a.05.05 - Casualties. Other ranks 1 wounded (Gas) 1 wounded (Gas) still at duty. - Commanding Officer held a conference of O/Cs Coys at 3 pm to discuss arrangements for to-morrows Operations. Orders were received from Brigade for the Battalion in the evening ordering it to be prepared to move at 1 hours notice after 2.30 am. All preparations were accordingly made - During the last month

Army Form C. 2118.

WAR DIARY
or
INTELLIGENCE SUMMARY.
(Erase heading not required.)

Instructions regarding War Diaries and Intelligence Summaries are contained in F. S. Regs., Part II. and the Staff Manual respectively. Title pages will be prepared in manuscript.

Place	Date	Hour	Summary of Events and Information	Remarks and references to Appendices
	June	30th '17	The Battalion has been doing very strenuous work. It has been all night work, and every weary heavy shell fire which has had its effect on the men who are in need of a rest. The strain on all ranks has been very severe. The back areas and roads are daily shelled and casualties caused. In spite of this much valuable work has been done. Assembly trenches have been dug in exposed positions in spite of all difficulties and the officers which have been successful in gaining HILL 65 have been rendered possible by this work. There has been much congestion owing to the scarcity of C.T's. There are old German ones and are not wide so as to give any protection on the eastern slopes. Much hard work was required to make ASSIGN a safe trench and even after digging it very deep it had to be camouflaged as well. ABSALOM TRENCH has been a very unhealthy place owing to shelling and heavy trench mortar fire. The assembly trenches through RIAUMONT were continually being blown in and houses falling across them blocking them up. These trenches were on the forward slope facing HILL 65 rendering their construction a difficult and dangerous work. When the Battalion reached the sector the roads were blocked with the "spoil" from German dug-outs but the DOURY/LIEVIN & D'LIEVIN-RIAUMONT were in a comparatively good condition. As an instance of hard work, one Company (B) cleared a road of "spoil" 6ft deep 5ft shafts & each and 150 yds in length in 3 days, and this road was taking lorry traffic on the third day - This was done under shell fire.

Strength of Battalion:-
42 Officers
812 Other ranks | |

[signature] Major
Commanding 1st Batt The Monmouthshire Regt. T.F.

APPENDIX 2

Copy of memo received from G.O.C. 46th Division on June 11th 1917

46th Division
2679/G

1st Monmouths

Kindly convey to all ranks my great appreciation of the work done by the Battalion in preparation for the operations of the 8th inst.

(Sd) W. Thwaites
Major-General
Commanding 46th Division

June 10th 1917

APPENDIX 1.

Copy of memo received from MAJOR E.A. LEWIS. D.S.O, Commanding Divisional Signal Company.

I beg to express my appreciation of the work carried out by 2/Lieut WATERS and the men under his command in connection with visual signalling during the recent operations. The system formed a very valuable adjunct to the communications and was the means of keeping signalling touch with the Artillery.

I am greatly obliged for the services of your signal section.

(S) E.A. Lewis, Major RE(T)
46th Divisional Signal Coy R.E.

June 10.17.

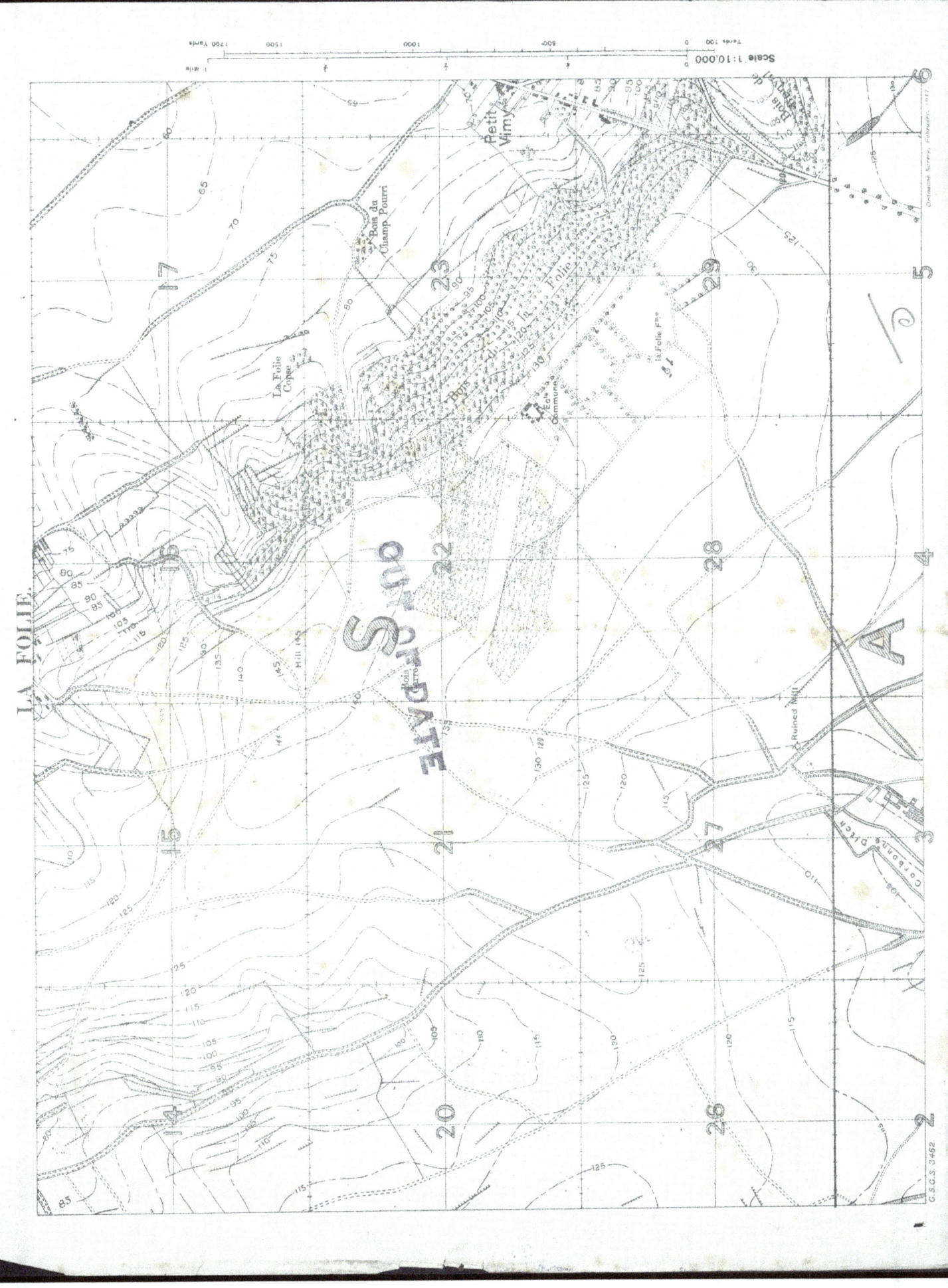

Secret
CONFIDENTIAL

Army Form C. 2118.

Vol 26

WAR DIARY
or
INTELLIGENCE SUMMARY
(Erase heading not required.)

Instructions regarding War Diaries and Intelligence Summaries are contained in F. S. Regs., Part II. and the Staff Manual respectively. Title Pages will be prepared in manuscript.

1ST BATTALION

THE MONMOUTHSHIRE REGIMENT. T.F

JULY 1ST 1917 TO JULY 31ST 1917

WAR DIARY or INTELLIGENCE SUMMARY

Army Form C. 2118.

Place	Date	Hour	Summary of Events and Information	Remarks and references to Appendices
	July 1917	1st	At 2.47 am the Division on our their Brigade front attacked the enemy to secure the line from the SOUCHEZ RIVER at N.25.a.8.8.6 to N.20.c.0.2. ACONITE TRENCH and ALOOF TRENCH thence to N.13.a.9.5.6.5. Orders were received that as from 2.30am onwards this Battalion is to be prepared to move at one hours notice. All objectives were gained except at 3 points but very serious opposition was made by the enemy in the CITE DU MOULIN where two companies of the 1/6th NORTH STAFFORDS were cut off. The 139th Brigade on the left of the attack were heavily counter attacked and gave up most of the captured ground. At 8 pm orders were received from 138th Brigade to dig a Support trench on the Eastern crest of HILL 65. Lt. TISDALL went forward with four R.E. Officers who was to tape this trench out, but much delay was caused by the R.E. not knowing the exact site of trench, and the delay in finding up the material. The Companies eventually left QUARRY DUMP at 11.7pm having previously picked up wire and trestles from LIEVIN Square Dump for the use of the R.E. who were to meet the trench. The rate of the trench was not marked out until about 1am but owing to heavy shelling the line had not been taped out. The material was therefore dumped and the parties returned as dawn was approaching. The whole Battalion was sent out on the above working party and 150 men of the 1/4th LINCOLNS and 5th LEICESTERS was attacked for work owing to orders being received to take the necessary preliminary arrangements could only be made. Running made the LINCOLNS and LEICESTERS failed by sending officers but there was no time to collect them men from trenches near the line and the only work accomplished was the carrying of the R.E. material to the site of the trench. The men were had very hard and fatiguing work and are in need of rest. Casualties NIL	

Army Form C. 2118.

WAR DIARY
or
INTELLIGENCE SUMMARY
(Erase heading not required.)

Instructions regarding War Diaries and Intelligence Summaries are contained in F. S. Regs., Part II, and the Staff Manual respectively. Title Pages will be prepared in manuscript.

Place	Date 1917	Hour	Summary of Events and Information	Remarks and references to Appendices
FOSSE 10	July 2nd	2-	The attack has now developed into a series of small strong points held by small parties. The enemy counter attacked up the early morning regaining some of their ground and it appeared as though the Battalion would have to move up into the support, but no orders to the effect were received and at mid-day instructions were received to withdraw the Battalion to FOSSE 10. This was effected by moving the companies out in twos and threes across country. Battalion Headquarters were heavily shelled together with the whole of ANGRY CORNER from 10am to 8pm - several direct hits were made. The Battalion was assembled in FOSSE 10 by 7pm and billeted for the night. Casualties:- 1 other rank wounded.	
		6.30	Battalion paraded at 6pm and marched to SAINS-EN-GOHELLE - Lire motor buses were provided to convey the Battalion to OURTON which was reached at 9.30pm. This village is to be the resting & training place. The whole Division has been withdrawn from the line being relieved by the 2nd CANADIAN DIVISION, the 137th and 138th Brigades were relieved last night and the 139th Brigade is to be relieved to-night.	
		11K.	Day devoted to Kit etc inspections by companies.	
		5K.	Hot baths and a change of under clothing arranged for all companies. Remainder of day Companies placed at disposal of O/C coys. Draft of 26 men arrived from Base 8th Depot Battalion. Complimentary message received from G.O.C. 46th Division (appendix I)	
		6-	Companies at disposal of O/C coys for close order drill. Parade to 12.30pm. Weather with Anthem and sunny. 2/Lieut A.W. GULLIVER, 2nd MON REGT	

WAR DIARY or INTELLIGENCE SUMMARY

Army Form C. 2118.

Place	Date	Hour	Summary of Events and Information	Remarks and references to Appendices
OURTON	July	6th 1917	Joined Battalion as reinforcement from Base also Draft of 23 other ranks.	
		7	Training parades held during morning from 9am to 1pm for Physical training bayonet fighting Company and Battalion drill. Arrangements made to use a 200 yds range to carry out Battalion musketry.	
		8	SUNDAY. No training parades held. Battalion parade for C of E Service at 6pm. Rain fell during the greater part of the day but cleared off at 5pm. Draft of 7 other ranks arrived at Depot Battalion from Base.	
		9	Training parades held as follows:- 8.30am - 9.45am Company parades for physical training & Bayonet fighting. 10.30am - 1pm Battalion parade for Battalion drill. The G.O.C. Division visited the Battalion parade and remained for about 1 hour.	
		10	Training parades as yesterday. Ceremonial drill was practised on the Battalion parade in view of Battalion inspection by the G.O.C. on the 12th inst. Boy parades for musketry instruction held from 3pm to 4pm. 2/Lt. J.L. SIMPSON joined as reinforcement from Base	
		11	Battalion parade 10.30am for Ceremonial drill and again at 3pm on marching order, a rehearsal for to-morrows inspection.	
		12	Battalion parade 1.30pm on the cavalry training field when the march past was practised once. The G.O.C. 46th Division arrived at 2.45pm and was received with a General Salute. The Battalion being drawn up in line. The G.O.C. then inspected the Battalion dismissing each Company after inspection to remove packs. After the Battalion was inspected Companies were fallen in again	

WAR DIARY or INTELLIGENCE SUMMARY

Army Form C. 2118.

Place	Date	Hour	Summary of Events and Information	Remarks and references to Appendices
OURTON	July 12 1917		and the march past was made. On completion of the first movement of advancing in Review Order the G.O.C sent for all Officers and said that although generally pleased with the parade there were one or two men whose equipment needed more careful fitting, which reflected on the Platoon Commanders. Practices were then placed out and the Battalion fell in, in threes, each man falling in with his own platoon. The Battalion had been aged and Companies equalized for the Inspection. The G.O.C then ordered the Adjutant to drill the Battalion for 10 minutes. He then fell out three platoons and investigated their organization of Lewis Gunners, Rifle bombers, bombers & riflemen. In each case, this was satisfactory. The General then addressed the Battalion saying that the 1st MONMOUTHS in the last sector the Division had been in, had had a hard time, hard digging under shell fire and many casualties but he was pleased to say they had stuck it and had always done their job. He wished to remind them that when once out of the line every effort was to be made to be paid to training the fighting qualities, as at any minute and without warning the Battalion might be called upon to take front in operations. The Band of the 138th Brigade attended the inspection. The Transport was inspected immediately after the Battalion, the G.O.C saying that it was cleaner than he had ever seen it.	
	13		A & B. Companies paraded 7am and marched to a range near BRUAY - 3 practices were fired. 100 yds 5 rounds grouping 200 yds 10 rounds application 200 yds 5 rounds application with fixed bayonet.	

Army Form C. 2118.

WAR DIARY or INTELLIGENCE SUMMARY

(Erase heading not required.)

Instructions regarding War Diaries and Intelligence Summaries are contained in F. S. Regs., Part II. and the Staff Manual respectively. Title Pages will be prepared in manuscript.

Place	Date	Hour	Summary of Events and Information	Remarks and references to Appendices
OURTON	July	13th cont'd	C and D Companies carried on Company drill and instruction of platoons in the attack. Leave allotment increased from 3 to 5 per day.	
		14th	D. Company went to range and carried out same practices as Companies yesterday. A and C Companies carried on with training platoons in the attack etc.	
		15th	SUNDAY. C Company carried out range practices. No training parades held to-day. Church parade service for R.C's only. 2/Lieut. S. MURRAY. D. Coy awarded the "Military Cross" by Commander-in-Chief for an act of gallantry in the field on 16th June 1917.	
		16th	Battalion paraded at 6 pm and was conveyed in Buses to 6th Division area. Headquarters B and C Companies to MAZINGARBE, A and D. Companies to NOYELLES. Quartermasters Stores and Transport to SAILLY LABOURSE. The Battalion arrived in new billets at midnight. The delay being caused owing to the Buses being 3 hours late. A rear party of 6 Officers and 72 other ranks has been left at OURTON until 21st inst. This party forms the entries from the unit for the Divisional Rifle meeting to be held on 19th and 20th inst. Lt Col C.A.EVILL returned from leave and resumed Command of the Battalion.	
MAZINGARBE		17th	On arriving in present billets this Battalion comes under orders of 6th Division for work. The 6th Division commanded by MAJOR GENERAL C.ROSS C.B. D.S.O is composed of 16th, 18th and 71st Infantry Brigades. The Division holds the line on a two Brigade front, at present the 71st Brigade being on the left and the 16th Brigade on the right. Orders received from C.R.E. for A and D. Coys to work under direction of N°59 FIELD COY R.E., B and C Coys under the 509 FIELD COY R.E.	

Army Form C. 2118.

WAR DIARY
or
INTELLIGENCE SUMMARY
(Erase heading not required.)

Instructions regarding War Diaries and Intelligence Summaries are contained in F. S. Regs., Part II. and the Staff Manual respectively. Title Pages will be prepared in manuscript.

Place	Date	Hour	Summary of Events and Information	Remarks and references to Appendices
MAZINGARBE	July 17th 1917		The Commanding Officer and O/C Coys reconnoitred and arranged work, some of which is to commence to night. The work principally consists of revetting communication trenches with "A" frames.	
		18th	B and C Coys moved billets from Southern to Northern part of MAZINGARBE owing to the southern half of the village being handed over to the 1st Canadian Division.	
			A Coy worked on HULLUCH ALLEY and STANSFIELD ROAD Communication Trench.	
			B Coy 2 platoons VENDIN ALLEY Communication Trench	
			D Coy 3 platoons CHAPEL ALLEY "	
			1 platoon constructing Trench Mortar emplacements in CHAPEL ALLEY (Trench O.G.1)	
			C Coy and remainder of B Coy did not work owing to change of billets.	
			Commanding Officer visited work in 16th Brigade area with O/C 509 FIELD COY	
		19th	Work as yesterday except Hqrs "C" Coy and 2 platoons of B Coy commenced work by night on VENDIN ALLEY and PONSEN ALLEY. Draft of 7 other ranks arrived from Havre are C.S. Major and 6 Signallers. Commanding Officer inspected works in 71st Brigade area. Casualties - one other rank wounded.	
		20th	Day parties worked as usual. Night parties did not go out owing to a raid made by 2nd YORK & LANCS Regt on enemy trenches opposite 6 Divisional front. Leave allotment increased to 7 passages a day.	
		21st	Owing to arrangements being made for the Battalion to rest on Sundays no night parties were sent out. Day parties worked as usual.	
		22nd	SUNDAY No day work working parties sent out - night parties proceeded as usual. Draft of 1 Lieut W.E. WILLIAMS and 11 other ranks reported as reinforcements from Base.	

Army Form C. 2118.

WAR DIARY
or
INTELLIGENCE SUMMARY

(Erase heading not required.)

Instructions regarding War Diaries and Intelligence Summaries are contained in F. S. Regs., Part II. and the Staff Manual respectively. Title Pages will be prepared in manuscript.

Place	Date	Hour	Summary of Events and Information	Remarks and references to Appendices
MAZINGARBE	July 22nd		The 138th Brigade relieved the 16th Brigade on the right sector.	
	23rd		All working parties except the night parties in the left sector proceeded as usual. The lorries could not be sent out owing to a raid being made on the enemy trenches on that front by the 1st LEICESTERS. The 139th Brigade relieved the 71st Brigade on the left sector.	
	24th		Working parties as usual. Casualties 1 other rank wounded at duty. "B" Company moved with 3 platoons to dug-outs in tenth avenue. The 4th platoon will remain at MAZINGARBE for 4 days when it will relieve one of the 3 in dug-outs which will in turn rest for 4 days.	
	25th		G.O.C. 46th Division took over command of the Divisional sector at 10 am. Working parties found as usual. Heavy rain fell during day with a thunderstorm in the evening.	
	26th		Working parties found as usual. Orders received from Division for one platoon per company to rest in turn for 4 days, for the purpose of resting and training. This will mean that each platoon works for 12 and then rests for 4 consecutive days.	
	27th		Working parties as usual. Heavy thunderstorm in morning. Conference of O's/C Coys at 4 pm to discuss training of resting platoons. It was decided that the first day should be devoted to cleaning up and the next three to close order drill and general instructions in Lewis Guns and bombs. The training of the specialist sections to proceed independently to the above	

Army Form C. 2118.

WAR DIARY
or
INTELLIGENCE SUMMARY
(Erase heading not required.)

Instructions regarding War Diaries and Intelligence Summaries are contained in F. S. Regs., Part II. and the Staff Manual respectively. Title Pages will be prepared in manuscript.

Place	Date	Hour	Summary of Events and Information	Remarks and references to Appendices
MAZINGARBE	July 1917 28th		Working parties as yesterday. The Commanding Officer visited platoons under training.	
	29th		Heavy rain nearly all day. "C" Coy did not work as orders have been received for this Company to move into dug-outs in Tenth Avenue and work on clearing these will be commenced early to-morrow. Remaining Companies carried on as usual. Draft of 2 men arrived from Base – Leave allotment increased to 10 per day.	
	30		Commanding Officer inspected platoons training in morning – Working parties found as usual – heavy rain in afternoon.	
	31st		Working parties as usual. Commanding Officer reconnoitred Divisional Line which is allotted to this unit to defend in case of attack. Commanding Officer inspected the H. working platoons at 10.30 am. They return to work to-morrow. Strength of Battalion:– Officers 44 Other ranks 855	
			Appendix 2. Summary of Work. July 1917.	

Ed Evit
Lieut-Colonel
Commanding 1st Batt. The Monmouthshire Regt. T.F.

APPENDIX I

Army Form C. 2118.

WAR DIARY
or
INTELLIGENCE SUMMARY

(Erase heading not required.)

Instructions regarding War Diaries and Intelligence Summaries are contained in F. S. Regs., Part II. and the Staff Manual respectively. Title Pages will be prepared in manuscript.

Place	Date	Hour	Summary of Events and Information	Remarks and references to Appendices
			Complimentary letters received from G.O.C. 46th Division	46th Division 2959/G.
			O/C 1st Monmouths	
			The G.O.C wishes you to convey to all ranks under your command how very pleased he is with the excellent work done by them during the period the Division was in the line in front of LENS, and especially for the work done in preparation for the offensive action on the 28th June.	
	5th July 1917		(Sd) V. Johnson, Major General Staff, 46th Division	

WAR DIARY or INTELLIGENCE SUMMARY

Army Form C. 2118.

APPENDIX 2

Summary of Events for JULY 1917

The events of the past month can be summarised as follows:

The first two days were marked by very heavy fighting on the outskirts of LENS and there seemed every probability that the Battalion would have been thrown in a great measure to close a serious hack of three openings. The relief of the Division thought to take a strenuous turn of duty for the Battalion during which it suffered not only considerable casualties, but the strain of an incessant shelling with gas which marked the whole area where they were situated.

The Battalion were in Reserve to the right Brigade area. This Brigade fought with great tenacity throughout and held their ground against all counter-attacks, although it was doubtful that the Battalion would have been involved in the actual fight. The Cavalry who were in support to the Centre Brigade, were called upon to help extricate a part of the Centre Brigade.

The first half of the month was devoted to training & musketry. At the Divisional Rifle Meeting the Battalion did well securing the Runners-up position at the meeting — the O.C.'s Roup for the best Battalion Team — H.E. Rim & ym team, company competitions 2nd out of 50 teams.

The second half of the month was occupied in working on a new Sector, adjoining the scene of the operations in which this Battalion was engaged on 13th October 1915, when the HOHENZOLLERN REDOUBT was attacked and captured by the Division. The Redoubt can be seen on our left flank, but nearly two years of fighting has altered its appearance — whereas formerly it was a mining slope scarred with all manner of trenches, it is now a mass of craters and bomb cants.

The difficulty of sitting the working parties within reach of their work is considerable. The whole should by the Battle of Loos renders it necessary for the men to march across the Plains de la RUTOIRE to their work as the accommodation in the line is

Summary of Events for JULY 1917 (continued)

very quiet. Shelters for a company have been made in the C.T's ready for the winter as men progressing faster.

The PLAINE de la RUTOIRE has been ablaze with colours of the wild flowers,— poppies, cornflowers and daisies, and is the hunting ground of great numbers of butterflies.

Army Form C. 2118.

WAR DIARY
or
INTELLIGENCE SUMMARY
(Erase heading not required.)

1st BATTALION THE MONMOUTHSHIRE REGIMENT T.F.

AUGUST 1st 1917 To AUGUST 31st 1917

CONFIDENTIAL.

Instructions regarding War Diaries and Intelligence Summaries are contained in F. S. Regs., Part II. and the Staff Manual respectively. Title Pages will be prepared in manuscript.

Place	Date	Hour	Summary of Events and Information	Remarks and references to Appendices

APPENDIX 1

Army Form C. 2118.

WAR DIARY
or
INTELLIGENCE SUMMARY
(Erase heading not required.)

Place	Date	Hour	Summary of Events and Information	Remarks and references to Appendices
			Copy of memo received from C.R.E. 46th Division containing complimentary message from Corps Commander	
			O/C 1st Monmouthshire Regt. E.1777.	
			G.O.C. 46th Division has directed me to inform you that the Corps Commander expressed his satisfaction this afternoon of the works done by your pioneers.	
			(Sd) C. WINGFIELD STRATFORD. B.G. C.R.E. 46th Division	
	11/8/17			

WAR DIARY
or
INTELLIGENCE SUMMARY

Army Form C. 2118.

Place	Date	Hour	Summary of Events and Information	Remarks and references to Appendices
MAZINGARBE	Aug 1917	1st	Rain fell the whole of the day and working parties were not sent out. 'C' Company moved from Billets in MAZINGARBE to dug-outs in 10th AVENUE, leaving one platoon in rest billets in the former place. Divisional Defence scheme received. This Battalion is allotted the Divisional line known as the Village line to defend and a hole in case of attack.	
		2nd	Working parties found as usual. Rain fell with short intervals throughout the day. Draft of 10 other ranks arrived from Base. All with exception of 2 out from England being men returned from Base Hospitals. The present dispositions of the Battalion are:- Headquarters MAZINGARBE 'A' Company NOYELLES 'D' do 3 platoons NOYELLES 1 platoon VERMELLES on Right Railway 'C' do 1 platoon PHILOSOPHE do 2 " 10th AVENUE dug-outs 1 " MAZINGARBE do B do 1 " MAZINGARBE do 3 " 10th AVENUE dug-outs	
"		3rd	Rain fell nearly all day. Working parties as usual except that 'D' Company commenced work on DEVON LANE C.T.	
"		4th	Working parties as usual. Rain fell again very heavily with short intervals all day. The continuous rain for the last few days has caused all the trenches to get into an exceedingly bad state, many of the main trenches are almost knee deep in water & mud and large falls of earth have occurred in all trenches not securely revetted. Leave allotment given to this unit at present, 9 Officers and 160 other ranks owing to the large leave amounts to almost ⅓ of the Battalion.	
"		5th	Weather much improved, no rain all day. Working parties found as usual by 'A' & 'D' Coys. 'B' & 'C' Companies about by for orders for special work on the support line under 157th Brigade. This however was cancelled and normal work on VENDIN ALLEY was resumed during the evening.	

Army Form C. 2118.

WAR DIARY
or
INTELLIGENCE SUMMARY

(Erase heading not required.)

Instructions regarding War Diaries and Intelligence Summaries are contained in F. S. Regs., Part II. and the Staff Manual respectively. Title Pages will be prepared in manuscript.

Place	Date	Hour	Summary of Events and Information	Remarks and references to Appendices
MAZINGARBE	Aug 1917	6	Working parties as usual. B and C Companies commenced clearing ESSEX LANE a communication trench from support to front line, which is required for the evacuation of wounded in a forthcoming raid. Heavy rain in afternoon.	
"	"	7th	Working parties as yesterday. ESSEX Trench completely cleared by B and C Companies.	
"	"	8th	Working parties as yesterday. D & C Companies continued work on ESSEX LANE, deepening it where necessary. Commanding Officer and Adjutant visited 46th Divisional Depot Battalion at ALLOUAGNE where all drafts from the base are put through a general course of instruction before being sent to their unit. Very heavy rain and thunderstorm from 7-8 pm.	
"	"	9th	Working parties as usual. B and C Companies resumed work on VENDIN ALLEY.	
"	"	10th	Working parties as yesterday. A Company moved 1 platoon from NOYELLES to JUNCTION KEEP in Village Line. This platoon is a permanent garrison and will hold the post in event of attack.	
"	"	11th	Working parties as usual. The following changes of Regimental Medical Officers have occurred recently:- July 16th Capt. O.W.D. STEEL went on leave. " 14th Capt. F. CHAMBERLAIN reported as relief for Capt. Steel. Aug 11th Capt. STEEL returned from leave and reported on the 12th A D M S 46th Div. for duty in this office. Aug 11th Capt. W.H. TALFOURD JONES reported to this unit as relief for CAPT. F CHAMBERLAIN. Aug 13th CAPT. F CHAMBERLAIN left this unit to report to A.D.M.S 25th Division. Memo received from C.R.E. 46th Division containing complimentary message from Corps-Commander.	APPENDIX 1.
"	"	12th	SUNDAY - Working parties sent out as usual. DEVON LANE heavily shelled and much damaged. D Company which was working there had to withdraw. The 2 platoons of 'C' Company in dug-outs in 10th AVENUE were withdrawn to MAZINGARBE HUTS as the accommodation	

Army Form C. 2118.

WAR DIARY
or
INTELLIGENCE SUMMARY
(Erase heading not required.)

Instructions regarding War Diaries and Intelligence Summaries are contained in F. S. Regs., Part II. and the Staff Manual respectively. Title Pages will be prepared in manuscript.

Place	Date	Hour	Summary of Events and Information	Remarks and references to Appendices
MAZINGARBE	Aug 1917	12th	As required by Brigade. These 2 platoons will eventually move to the cellars of LA RUTOIRE FARM. Strict at present are being strengthened by the R.E's. The Commanding Officer inspected resting platoons at 10 a.m. — Casualties 1. O.R. wounded.	
		13th	Working parties as usual. Owing to raids by the 5 and 6th SHERWOODS in the ST ELIE sector, all night parties withdrawn at 10 p.m. Draft 18 other ranks arrived from Base; all are from Hospital and have previously served with this Battalion.	
		14th	Day working parties found as usual. The 3 platoons of B Company in 10th AVENUE were withdrawn to billets in MAZINGARBE as the accommodation is required for the 5th LEICESTERS who are assembling there tomorrow for a large raid. Owing to the 138th BRIGADE requiring ESSEX LANE to be improved the resting platoons of B and C Coys worked on this C.T. by night. Draft of 7 other ranks arrived from the Base, all returned men from Hospital &c.	
		15th	A and D Companies worked as usual by day on STANSFIELD ROAD and CHAPEL ALLEY respectively. B and C Coys did not work owing to an attack being carried out on HILL 70 and the Eastern half of BOIS HUGO by the Canadian Corps - all the above objectives were reached. No night parties sent out owing to a raid on enemy trenches West of HULLUCH by 5th LEICESTERS. This raid was postponed at the last minute owing to the wire being uncut. The Commanding Officer held conference of O's/C Coys at 5 p.m. re Defence of the Village line.	
		16th	All Companies worked by day, A and D as usual, B and C on LONE TRENCH as no night party being sent to dig in VENDIN ALLEY made work impossible in half trench by day. Commanding Officer inspected Resting Platoons at 11 a.m. The raid by 5th LEICESTERS, postponed from last night, took place to-night at 11.45 p.m. No prisoners were taken. C Company moved 1 platoon from MAZINGARBE to LA RUTOIRE FARM G.15.d.(36.C). This platoon is accommodated in cellars, the rest of the buildings are in ruins. Leave allotment reduced from 10 to 1 passage a day as from 19th inst.	
		17th	Working parties as yesterday.	

WAR DIARY or INTELLIGENCE SUMMARY

Army Form C. 2118.

Place	Date	Hour	Summary of Events and Information	Remarks and references to Appendices
MAZINGARBE	Aug 1917	18th	Working parties as yesterday except that B and C Companies worked on VENDIN ALLEY. 'C' Company moved the remaining platoon available for work, from MAZINGARBE to the cellars in CORONS DU RUTOIRE G.14.c.9.5 (36.C). This platoon will eventually move to LA RUTOIRE FARM when additional accommodation is available there.	
		19th	SUNDAY. Working parties as usual.	
		20th	Work as yesterday. Commanding Officer inspected Resting Platoons at 4 pm. B. Company moved 1 platoon from 10th AVENUE Dugouts to NORTHERN SAP REDOUBT - this platoon will act as a garrison for this Redoubt which is part of the Village line.	
		21st	Working parties as usual - he went of special interest occurred. 2 platoons from B and C Companies moved from work on VENDIN ALLEY to 64 STREET for the purpose of clearing the latter for use as a C.T.	
		22nd	Work as yesterday except that all work on NORTHERN SAP REDOUBT has been stopped as this portion of the line is shortly to be handed over to the 6th Division. Casualties 4 other ranks wounded and 2 other ranks wounded (Gas). The 4 casualties were sustained at the Right Railway station VERMELLES on the night of the 21st. While a train was in the siding a shell struck a truck of French howitzer ammunition which exploded causing an immense amount of damage. About 200 men of all were at the dump when the explosion occurred and about 190 of them became casualties. One mule belonging to this Battalion was killed and another wounded.	
		23rd	Working parties as usual. Very heavy rainstorm in evening.	
		24th	Working parties as usual. Commanding Officer inspected Resting Platoons at 10.30 am and the Transport Lines in the afternoon. Draft of 14 other ranks arrived from the Base.	
		25th	Working parties found as usual. Owing to Gas being projected in the HULLUCH sector parties were withdrawn from 11 pm to 1 am (26th) to the reserve line. Casualties 1 other rank wounded.	

Army Form C. 2118.

WAR DIARY
or
INTELLIGENCE SUMMARY
(Erase heading not required.)

Instructions regarding War Diaries and Intelligence Summaries are contained in F. S. Regs., Part II. and the Staff Manual respectively. Title Pages will be prepared in manuscript.

Place	Date	Hour	Summary of Events and Information	Remarks and references to Appendices
MAZINGARBE	Aug 1917	26th	Working parties as yesterday. Commanding Officer & O/C B and D Companies reconnoitred the CAMBRIN sector which is being taken over from the 2nd Division at 5 pm 27th. This sector is the one immediately north of the present Divisional front.	
		27th	A and D Companies worked as usual on CHAPEL ALLEY. B Company withdrawn from No 10 AVENUE dug-outs and NORTHERN SAP REDOUBT to MAZINGARBE HUTS prior to moving to the CAMBRIN sector to-morrow. 1 platoon of C Coy relieved 1 platoon of B Coy in NORTHERN SAP REDOUBT. C Company did not work owing to a very heavy gale which kept on all night, very heavy rain fell at intervals. Battalion Headquarters and the one Working platoon per Company moved billets to huts at SAILLY in the afternoon. The billets are very good and include an Officers mess and gravel Tennis court. Commanding Officer inspected the working platoons at 10.30 am. A and D Companies worked as yesterday. C Company unable to work by night owing to a raid by the 5th and 6th SOUTH STAFFORDS on the enemy trenches in the HULLUCH SECTOR. B Company moved 1 platoon to dug-outs off RAILWAY ALLEY in the CAMBRIN sector, held by the 139th Brigade. Two more platoons of this Company were to have moved as well to the above dug-outs but this was delayed for 24 hours late in the afternoon by the 139th Brigade and the 2 platoons were billeted at NOYELLES for the night. A Company moved the one platoon remaining at NOYELLES to JUNCTION KEEP also Company Headquarters.	
		28th		
		29th	Gale continued throughout the whole day and night. Two remaining platoons of B Company moved to dug-outs in FACTORY TRENCH off RAILWAY ALLEY. Very heavy rain at intervals throughout the day - Work as usual.	
		30th	Very heavy rain again fell in frequent showers during the day. The dispositions of the Battalion are now as follows:— Battalion Headquarters, Transport Lines, Quartermasters Stores and Resting Platoons — SAILLY LABORSE A Company - 3 platoons — JUNCTION KEEP	

Army Form C. 2118.

WAR DIARY
or
INTELLIGENCE SUMMARY
(Erase heading not required.)

Place	Date	Hour	Summary of Events and Information	Remarks and references to Appendices
SAILLY	Aug	30th	B Company 3 platoons FACTORY TRENCH DUG-OUTS	
			C " 1 " LA RUTOIRE FARM	
			" 1 " NORTHERN SAP REDOUBT	
			" 1 " R.T.O. PHILOSOPHE on Light Railway	
			D " 2½ " NOYELLES	
			" ½ " R.T.O. VERMELLES on Light Railway	
			Companies are working as follows:-	
			'A' Company CHAPEL ALLEY	
			B do OLD BOOTS TRENCH and Reserve Line in CAMBRIN sector	
			C do POSEN ALLEY	
			D do CHAPEL ALLEY	
			Leave allotment increased to 3 per day	
	"	31st	Working parties as yesterday. Weather still very unsettled.	
			Strength of Battalion:-	
			41 Officers	
			882 other ranks.	

(signed) C. Evill
Lieut. Colonel
Comdg. 1st Batt. The Honourable Artillery Regiment T.F.

SECRET AND CONFIDENTIAL.

Army Form C. 2118.

WAR DIARY
or
INTELLIGENCE SUMMARY

(Erase heading not required.)

Vol 28

1st BATTALION THE MONMOUTHSHIRE REGIMENT T.F.

SEPTEMBER 1st 1917 TO SEPTEMBER 30th 1917

Army Form C. 2118.

WAR DIARY
or
INTELLIGENCE SUMMARY

(Erase heading not required.)

Instructions regarding War Diaries and Intelligence Summaries are contained in F. S. Regs., Part II. and the Staff Manual respectively. Title Pages will be prepared in manuscript.

Place	Date	Hour	Summary of Events and Information	Remarks and references to Appendices
SAILLY-LABOURSE	Sept 1916	1st	Working parties as usual except that D. Coy commenced work on SAVILLE-ROW. C7 in the CAMBRIN SECTOR. A draft of 26 other ranks reported at the Div Depot from the Base. Casualties 1 other rank wounded on fatigue duty. The Commanding Officer inspected Resting platoons at 10:30 am.	
		2nd	Working parties as usual - Weather cleaner and warmer	
		3rd	C and D Companies changed billets and work - This was carried out without any interruption of working parties except that 'C' Company did not send out any parties by night, owing to orders being received late in the evening for 'C' Coy to move to cellars in CORONS DU RUTOIRE for work on the HULLUCH SECTOR. A draft of 8 other ranks reported at Depot Battalion from Base.	
		4th	'C' Company moved to cellars in CORONS DU RUTOIRE. Remainder of Companies carried on with work as usual. Weather very hot and sunny.	
		5th	The Commanding Officer inspected Resting Platoons at 10 am. In the early hours of the morning the enemy discharged gas on the left of the Division front (2nd Div sector) from 12:28 am. At 1pm the gas was strongly smelt at SAILLY-LABOURSE and Battalion Headquarters and Resting Platoons were aroused by the gas guard. Box Respirators were worn except for short intervals up to 3 am when the gas had cleared. In addition to the above gas discharge from cylinders the enemy very heavily shelled PHILOSOPHE with gas shells. 'C' Company in CORONS DU RUTOIRE were in the Route of the gas shells. Casualties Lieut. T.O. JONES and 23 other ranks wounded (Gas). All the above are 'C' Company and the cases are believed to be slight.	

Army Form C. 2118.

WAR DIARY
or
INTELLIGENCE SUMMARY

(Erase heading not required.)

Instructions regarding War Diaries and Intelligence Summaries are contained in F. S. Regs., Part II. and the Staff Manual respectively. Title Pages will be prepared in manuscript.

Place	Date	Hour	Summary of Events and Information	Remarks and references to Appendices
SAILLY-LABORSE	Sept. 1917	6th	Working parties as usual. Weather very hot and close. At 6 pm most intense rain fell for half an hour accompanied by thunder and vivid lightning. No casualties. Corpl. J. A. WILSON and 4 other ranks 'C' Coy wounded (Gas). These are from the shelling of PHILOSOPHE on night of 4/5th instant. Draft of 10 other ranks arrived at Div Depot Batt from Base as reinforcements.	
		7th	Working parties as yesterday. 23 men arrived from the Depot Batt. These have been previously stated as a draft when they joined the Depot Batt.	
		8th	Work as usual. G.O.C. 46th Division dined with the Officers. Casualties. 2 other ranks wounded. (Gas)	
		9th	Received orders to the effect that Gas Cylinders will be installed in front line at (Map 36.C.N.W) A.28.C.5.2 to A.27.6.5.2. Work to be carried out under C.R.E. Le Two Companies in CAMBRIN Sector, A and B. 1st Monmouths, to carry out the work. O's/C Companies reconnoitred the ground. There were about 50 emplacements selected to carry in all 270 cylinders. (Orders received for two Companies to be placed at disposal of the 6th Division for work on Tram lines and water supply.	
		10th	One Officer from each Coy, C and D, reported at Headquarters of 128th Field Coy. R.E. LES BREBIS at 10 am to arrange billets and work. Billets were found as follows Headquarters LES BREBIS, L.35.d.70.60. - D.Coy M.2.d.90.90 - C.Coy MAROC M.2.d.20.80. Major LEWIS has taken over command of Left Half Battalion with H.Q. at LES BREBIS. Platoons from A and B. Coys relieved those of Canad. on Right Railways at VERMELLES and PHILOSOPHE. 'C' Coy will work under the 31st A.T. Coy on a 9ct. track at N.I. Central	

Army Form C. 2118.

Instructions regarding War Diaries and Intelligence Summaries are contained in F.S. Regs., Part II. and the Staff Manual respectively. Title Pages will be prepared in manuscript.

WAR DIARY
or
INTELLIGENCE SUMMARY
(Erase heading not required.)

Place	Date	Hour	Summary of Events and Information	Remarks and references to Appendices
SAILLY-LABOURSE	Sept 1917	10	D. Coy will work under the 560th A.T. Coy R.E's on laying a 2" water pipe from LOOS water line to about H.31 central. A & B Coys on night 9/10 carried Rat-Traps (Frames for gas cylinders) to junction of Tramway and RAILWAY ALLEY. G.3.b.9.4. During the day B. Coy employed digging emplacements for Rat Traps - Weather continues fine. Casualty 1 O.R. wounded	
		11	C and D. Coys, less Rioting Platoons, moved to new billets in MAROC moving off at 9.30 am. B. Coy making emplacements and fixing Rat Traps during day. 'A' Coy carrying rat-traps and sand bags to front line on night 10/11th. Weather continues dry & bright.	
		12	The Rioting Platoons of C and D moved to MAROC to join their Companies, which now leaves A and B Rioting platoons only in camp at SAILLY. 'A' Company carrying rat-traps and sandbags on night of 11/12th. 'B' Coy digging emplacements and fitting Rat-Traps 'C' and D. Companies commenced work to-night in new area. Weather fine.	
		13	Both A and B. Coys carried out work on front line on rat-traps. C and D. Coys carried out work on Tram line and water pipe laying at CITÉ ST PIERRE. Weather continues fine	
		14	A + B. Coys continued work on front line on emplacements for gas cylinders While digging Rear emplacements quite a number of old gas cylinders were unearthed. C & D Coys carried on work at CITÉ ST PIERRE as yesterday. Gas cylinder emplacements now completed - Weather fine.	
		15	'A' Coy working on JUNCTION KEEP on repairing & strengthening. 'B' Coy on rest today as they will be employed carrying gas cylinders from G.3.b.9.4. to front line from BOYAU 2 to 15.	

Army Form C. 2118.

WAR DIARY
or
INTELLIGENCE SUMMARY
(Erase heading not required.)

Instructions regarding War Diaries and Intelligence Summaries are contained in F. S. Regs., Part II. and the Staff Manual respectively. Title Pages will be prepared in manuscript.

Place	Date	Hour	Summary of Events and Information	Remarks and references to Appendices
SAILLY-LABORSE	Sept 1917	15th cont.d	'C' and D Coys worked as yesterday. Draft of 42 arrived at Depot Batt from Base. Weather continues fine. (Casualty 1 O.R. wounded)	
		16th	'A' Coy working on CHAPEL ALLEY & JUNCTION KEEP. 'B' Coy carrying gas cylinders night 15/16th. C and D Coys work as usual. – Weather – Sun all day & very warm	
		17th	Working parties found as usual. Weather warm and sun all day.	
		18th	Working parties found as usual. – Weather as yesterday.	
		19th	Working parties found as usual. The 139th Infantry Brigade are relieving the 71st and 18th Infantry Brigades on 21/22nd and 22/23rd on a front from CHALK PIT ALLEY to ENGLISH ALLEY. 'A' Company will move to dug-outs in GUN TRENCH and B Coy to dug-outs in NORTHERN SAP REDOUBT on 22nd inst. A draft of 42 other ranks arrived from Divisional Depot Batt. – These men are of good physique and well turned out. The G.O.C. inspected these men at the Depot Battn and commented on their good appearance and general turn out. Weather dry and clear.	
		20th	'B' Coy carried out work as yesterday on OLD BOOTS Trench and 'A' coy as yesterday. In the evening B. Coy moved from billets to camp SAILLY and will rest until 22nd inst when they move to dug-outs in NORTHERN SAP REDOUBT. The Commanding Officer inspected the draft whose turn out was particularly good – Weather continues fine. B. Coy (parades in accordance with programme of work for working platoons. 'C' and D Coys as work as yesterday in CITE ST PIERRE – Weather as yesterday	
		21st	'A' Coy carried out work as yesterday (remaining at duty) 21st 1 O.R. (wounded) Casualties 20th 1 O.R. Killed 1 O.R. wounded	

WAR DIARY
or
INTELLIGENCE SUMMARY

(Erase heading not required.)

Army Form C. 2118.

Place	Date	Hour	Summary of Events and Information	Remarks and references to Appendices
SAILLY-LABOURSE	Sept.			
	22nd		'A' Coy moved into new billets in GUN Trench which are in very bad condition. An Officer of this Company in conjunction with an Officer from 465 Field Coy RE reconnoitred the work in Reserve trench of HILL 70. 'B' Company moved to new billets in NORTHERN SAP REDOUBT. 'C' and 'D' Coys continued works in CITE ST PIERRE. Weather excellent, warm and sunny.	
	23rd		The ricoting platoons paraded for Church Service in the morning. 'C' and 'D' Coys carried out work as yesterday. A and B coys did not work about from putting their dug-outs in order – Weather as yesterday.	
	24th		B Coy carried out work on Light Railway, repairing track at G.36.a.9.0 to G.36.b.7.9.70 'A' Coy carried out repairs to Reserve trench of HILL 70 (map 36.C.N.W) H.31.a.6.9 to 31.b.9.5 Instructions received for return of C & D. Coys from 6th Division. 'C' and 'D' Coys did not work owing to their moving to-morrow. Weather as yesterday.	
	25th		A and B. Coys carried out work as yesterday. 'C' Coy moved off from MAROC at 9.30, 3 platoons direct to billets in CORONS DU RUTOIRES and 1 working platoon to camp SAILLY. D. Coy moved from MAROC at 2.30, 3 platoons direct to dug-outs just South of NORTHERN SAP REDOUBT and one working platoon to camp SAILLY D Coys dug-outs are in bad repair and are merely shelters. 'C' and D Coys had 2 OR wounded. not work to-night. Weather continues fine. Casualties	
	26th		'A' Coy carried on work as yesterday. B Coy carried on with work on Light Railway from HULLUCH – LOOS ROAD to G.31.a.20.80 and on to Old British Front Line	

WAR DIARY
or
INTELLIGENCE SUMMARY
(Erase heading not required.)

Army Form C. 2118.

Place	Date	Hour	Summary of Events and Information	Remarks and references to Appendices
SAILLY-LABORSE	Sept.	26th cont.	C and D Coys carried out repairs to billets. The frontage for defence of VILLAGE LINE is now as follows:— 'A' Coy in Reserve trench HILL 70 under orders of O/C Support Battalion. 139th Bde. 'D' Coy from RAILWAY ALLEY inclusive to NORTHERN SAP REDOUBT inclusive. 'B' Coy from NORTHERN SAP REDOUBT inclusive to LONE TRENCH inclusive. 'C' Coy from G.16 central to CHAPEL KEEP inclusive. Weather warm & threatening rain.	
		27th	'A' Coy worked as yesterday. 'B' Coy worked on tracks from VERNELLES - LOOS ROAD to North of LOOS. 'C' Coy commenced work in POSEN ALLEY revetting etc. 'D' Coy carried on with repairs to billets. Draft of 54 other ranks arrived at Depot from Base as reinforcements.	
		28th	All Companies worked as yesterday. A draft of 60 other ranks reported for duty with the Battalion from the Depot Battalion.	
		29th	A, B & C Coys worked as usual. D Coy commenced work on new Tramway tracks near LOOS. The Commanding Officer inspected resting platoons at 10 am and also the draft which arrived from the Depot yesterday.	
		30th	SUNDAY. All Companies worked as yesterday. Church Parade services for all denominations of the Resting platoons held during the morning. Lieut. T. O. Jones rejoined the Battalion	

Army Form C. 2118.

WAR DIARY
or
INTELLIGENCE SUMMARY
(Erase heading not required.)

Instructions regarding War Diaries and Intelligence Summaries are contained in F. S. Regs., Part II. and the Staff Manual respectively. Title Pages will be prepared in manuscript.

Place	Date	Hour	Summary of Events and Information	Remarks and references to Appendices
SAILLY-LABORSE	Sept	30 cont.d	from Base as reinforcement, after being discharged from Hospital. 6 other ranks arrived at Depot Battalion as reinforcements from Base. <u>Casualty</u> 1 other rank wounded. Strength of Battalion :- 39 Officers 1003 other ranks.	

C Gill
Lieut Colonel
Comdg 1st Batt The Monmouthshire Regt TF.

WAR DIARY or INTELLIGENCE SUMMARY

SUMMARY OF EVENTS FOR AUGUST 1917

The work for the month has been unsuccessful consisting of the construction of Communication Trenches etc. The attack by the Canadian Corps on our right has made the enemy active with Rum Artillery especially on Artillery positions and back billets. The Counter attacks by the Prussian Guard against the position captured by the Canadians North of LENS was observed easily from the front of this Division and enfiladed by Machine Guns & Divisional Artillery. A German Officer leading the Division on a white charger was very plainly. The attack was broken up before reaching HILL 70.

The Commanding Officer dined with the G.O.C. 3rd Canadian Division and was told but him that he remembered the Battalion at YPRES in April 1915. General LIPSETT then commanded the 8th Canadian Battalion, known as "The Little Black Devils" who were holding the line during the Gas attack on the 9th April 1915. He remembered "C" Company of this Battalion coming to his support during the fight and gave the O/C "C" Coy (Capt. B. L. PERRY who was killed in action) his orders to deliver a counter attack against a Barrie in which the Germans had Machine Guns. Captain PERRY was killed on this attack. General LIPSETT said that in spite of experiences of this war at was improbable that the counter attack could have succeeded.

R.H. Thomson Capt. & Adjt.
for Lieut. Colonel
Comdg. 1st Batt. The Lancashire Regt. T.F.

SUMMARY OF EVENTS FOR SEPTEMBER 1917

The this week has been the taking over of the HILL 70 sector, and the works of 3 Companies has been averted to this sector. There is a great deal of work to be done here for communication and consolidation of the captured ground. The carrying of rations and material is a great difficulty, and great efforts are being made to get tram lines and water pipes and tracks available. The area is heavily shelled every day, making work very arduous, and mostly done by night. The observation from Hill 70 is exceedingly good. Billeting of the troops is a difficulty now, there are work and the men have to live in temporary shelters. Fortunately the weather has been very fine, although the nights are cold.

MMNixon
Capt ??
In Lieut-Colonel.
Comdg 1st Batt The Monmouthshire Regt T.F.

Army Form C. 2118.

SECRET AND CONFIDENTIAL

WAR DIARY
or
INTELLIGENCE SUMMARY
(Erase heading not required.)

Vol 29

1st BATTALION THE MONMOUTHSHIRE REGIMENT T.F.

OCTOBER 1st 1917 TO OCTOBER 31st 1917.

Place	Date	Hour	Summary of Events and Information	Remarks and references to Appendices

Instructions regarding War Diaries and Intelligence Summaries are contained in F. S. Regs., Part II. and the Staff Manual respectively. Title Pages will be prepared in manuscript.

2449 Wt. W14957/M90 750,000 1/16 J.B.C. & A. Forms/C.2118/12.

WAR DIARY or INTELLIGENCE SUMMARY

Army Form C. 2118.

Place	Date	Hour	Summary of Events and Information	Remarks and references to Appendices
SAILLY LABOURSE	Oct 1917	1st	Working parties as usual. The weather still continued to be very sunny and warm but white frosts have started in the early morning. Casualties Capt T.S. SPITTLE wounded – other ranks 1 killed, 3 wounded. These casualties occurred in the CORONS LE RUTOIRE. A shell pitched right in the midst of the gas guard whilst being inspected by Capt SPITTLE.	
		2nd	Working parties as yesterday. Capt SPITTLE died of wounds at No 7. C.C.S NOEUX-LES-MINES about mid-day.	
		3rd	Commanding Officer inspected Resting Platoons at 10 am, after which the Lewis Gun section of 'B' Coy platoon fell in in fighting order with Lewis Gun, and did a battoon exercise. Capt T.S. SPITTLE buried at 2.30 pm in NOEUX-LES-MINES Cemetery. Battalion beat Div MR team in Divisional League by 3 goals to nil.	
		4th	Working parties as yesterday. An extremely strong wind blew all day. Casualties 3 other ranks killed - 4 wounded of D Company.	
		5th	Working parties as usual. Commanding Officer and Adjutant revisited works of A and D Coys after dark. Rain fell very heavily during the morning.	
		6th	Working parties as usual. Heavy rain again fell until mid-day, and then ceased. The 25th Division relieved the 2nd Division in the CAMBRIN sector yesterday. This leaves the I Corps with the following Divisions in the line from left to right 6th, 46th and 25th Divisions.	
		7th	SUNDAY. Church Parade Services for all denominations of Resting Platoons. Rain fell very heavily from 11 am onwards, and the inspection of resting platoons by the Commanding Officer was cancelled.	

WAR DIARY
or
INTELLIGENCE SUMMARY
(Erase heading not required.)

Army Form C. 2118.

Place	Date	Hour	Summary of Events and Information	Remarks and references to Appendices
SAILLY LABORSE	Oct 1917	7am	Working parties as usual. Draft 2 other ranks arrived from Base as reinforcements.	
		8am	Rain fell heavily again from mid-day onwards. Working parties as yesterday. Draft 2 other ranks arrived from the Base as reinforcements. 30 men reported for duty with the Battalion from the Divisional Depot. Battalion Football team beat 5th LEICESTERS in Our League by 2 goals to NIL.	
		9am	Working parties as yesterday. Draft 2 other ranks arrived from Base as reinforcements.	
		10am	Intense rain fell until mid-day. This in addition to the heavy rain of the last few days had caused all trenches to get into a very bad state. The Commanding Officer inspected Reserve Line on HILL 70 with C.R.E. and Brigade Major 139th Bde in the morning. A small Pioneer Battalion composed of details for the 187th Brigade at the Depot Battalion, has been temporarily formed and is being known as the 46th Divisional Provisional Pioneer Battalion. This Battalion is being used for work on the Divisional Front. Capts E.J.JENKINS, E.G. STC. TISDALL, Lieuts J.A. PHILIPS and R.D. EDMISTON have been sent to this Battalion to act as Company Commanders. Draft of 2 other ranks have arrived at the Depot Battalion as reinforcements from Base.	
		11am	Weather beautifully fine. Commanding Officers Inspected Resting Platoons at 10 am. Working parties found as yesterday. Battalion played the 139th Brigade H.Q. in the Divisional League and won 13 goals - 1.	

Army Form C. 2118.

WAR DIARY
or
INTELLIGENCE SUMMARY
(Erase heading not required.)

Instructions regarding War Diaries and Intelligence Summaries are contained in F. S. Regs., Part II. and the Staff Manual respectively. Title Pages will be prepared in manuscript.

Place	Date	Hour	Summary of Events and Information	Remarks and references to Appendices
SAILLY LABORSE	Oct 12th 1915	11.0 am	The following Officers reported as reinforcements and have been posted to Companies as follows:-	
			CAPT G.E.EDWARDS D Company	
			LIEUT J.S.C.BARRIE A "	
			" W.B.WADE B "	
			2/LIEUT W.H.WINN-JONES C "	
			LIEUT A.E.A.M.ATKINS C "	
			" G.E.BUCK A "	
		12th	Working parties as usual for A and D Coys. B and C Coys commenced work on dug-outs in VILLAGE LINE and TENTH AVENUE which C Company are to occupy as soon as the accommodation is ready. Draft 1 other rank reported at Depot Battalion from Base, as reinforcement.	
		13th	Working parties as yesterday. As today is the record anniversary of the attack on the HOHENZOLLERN REDOUBT by this Battalion, a dinner and smoking concert was arranged for the available survivors. The actual numbers now with the Battalion who were serving with the Battalion 2 years ago are 8 Officers and 200 men. Many of these men were wounded and have been returned. All details in Sailly Camp and 5 per Company from forward billets of the survivors attended and about 130 men not blown to dinner at 7pm. At 8.15 pm the Officers went to the Copse, which was commenced after a toast to "Those who fell on 13th October 1915" proposed by the Colonel, was drunk by all present	

2449 Wt. W14957/M90 750,000 1/16 J.B.C. & A. Forms/C.2118/12.

WAR DIARY or INTELLIGENCE SUMMARY

Army Form C. 2118.

Place	Date	Hour	Summary of Events and Information	Remarks and references to Appendices
	Oct. 1917	13th cont'd.	No. 225,987 Cpl WILKINS E. "D" Company has been awarded the MILITARY MEDAL by the Corps Commander for an act of Gallantry in the field on October 11th	
		14th	SUNDAY Resting Platoons paraded for Divine Service at 11 o'clock this morning. The Weather after being very wet for some days has cleared today, being warm and sunny. Working parties were found as yesterday.	
		15th	Working parties as usual. Commanding Officer inspected work of 'A' Coy. and the inspection of Resting Platoons was taken by Major LEWIS. Before the inspection the Commanding Officer presented the Ribbon of the "Military Medal" to Cpl WILKINS.	
		16th	Working parties as yesterday. Commanding Officer visited our Training Battalion and inspected Drafts of this Unit training there. In the afternoon a Private soldier from the Canadians gave a demonstration at 10 am with the TUMP LINE and the method of carrying stores with this line. Weather very fine and warm.	
		17th	Working parties as yesterday. A draft of 5 n.c.o. reinforcements reported at Depot Battalion from Base.	
		18th	Work as yesterday. Commanding Officer inspected works on HILL 70 area. A draft of 50 O.R. arrived from the Divisional Training Battalion.	
		19th	Work as yesterday. "C" Coy moved billets from CORONS LE RUTOIRE to VILLAGE LINE. Commanding Officer inspected Resting Platoons at 10 am	

Army Form C. 2118.

WAR DIARY
or
INTELLIGENCE SUMMARY
(Erase heading not required.)

Instructions regarding War Diaries and Intelligence Summaries are contained in F.S. Regs., Part II. and the Staff Manual respectively. Title Pages will be prepared in manuscript.

Place	Date	Hour	Summary of Events and Information	Remarks and references to Appendices
SAILLY LABORSE	Oct 1917	19th cont'd	One platoon of B. Coy, 28 strong, has had to be isolated owing to two cases of mumps. This platoon has been withdrawn to SAILLY and is billeted in a separate billet outside the Camp.	
		20th	A and B Coys worked as yesterday. C Coy commenced working in RAILWAY ALLEY C.T. which has to be deepened and revetted. D Coy as from today is working under the orders of the 31st Army Troops Coy R.E. on a Railway track in CITE ST. PIERRE. 2/Lt. S.G. BLOW has been awarded the 'Military Cross' by the Commander-in-Chief for an act of gallantry on October 11th, on HILL 70, when in charge of a working party. Capt. C.T. VACHELL of this Battalion attached R.F.C. has also been awarded the 'Military Cross' in the London Gazette dated 18th inst. 5 other ranks joined Depot Battalion as reinforcements. Battalion played 1/2 N.M. Field Ambulance in the Divisional League. The match was drawn 1-1.	
		21st	Working parties as yesterday. Church parade services for Roting Platoons held during the morning.	
		22nd	Working parties as usual. Draft 6 other ranks reported at Depot Battalion as reinforcements from Base. Casualties. 1 Other rank wounded. This was caused by a bomb from a hostile aeroplane falling on the Field Ambulance at FOUQUIERES and wounding a sick man from this Battalion who was in Hospital.	
		23rd	Working parties as yesterday. Platoons at rest moved up to the line and Platoons	

2449 Wt. W14957/M90 750,000 1/16 J.B.C. & A. Forms/C.2118/12.

Army Form C. 2118.

WAR DIARY
or
INTELLIGENCE SUMMARY
(Erase heading not required.)

Place	Date	Hour	Summary of Events and Information	Remarks and references to Appendices
SAILLY LABORSE	Oct 1917			
	23rd cont:		from forward billets moved to SAILLY Camp to rest. Owing to very rainy weather the Commanding Officer's inspection of outgoing platoons was cancelled. Draft: 2 other ranks reported at Depot Battalion from Base as reinforcements.	
	24th		Working parties as usual.	
	25th		Working parties as yesterday. Draft: 2 other ranks reported at Depot Battalion as reinforcements.	
	26th		Working parties as yesterday. Draft: 12 other ranks reported at Depot Battalion from Base. Rain fell heavily nearly all day.	
	27th		Commanding Officer inspected Resting Platoons at 10 a.m. after which B Coy platoon paraded in Fighting Order and did a small tactical scheme. Working parties as yesterday. Battalion played 6th S.W.B's at Rugby football and lost 11 points to nil. Casualties: 1 O.R. killed, 1 O.R. wounded of Light Railway Detachment PHILOSOPHE, caused by one of our own anti-aircraft shells falling and bursting on percussion.	
	28th		SUNDAY. Working parties as usual. Church Parades held for all Denominations during the morning. Weather very overcast but fine. There was a sharp frost last night.	
	29th		Working parties as yesterday. Draft: 6 other ranks joined Depot as reinforcements from Base, also 1 Off: on 28th instant.	

Army Form C. 2118.

WAR DIARY
or
INTELLIGENCE SUMMARY
(Erase heading not required.)

Place	Date	Hour	Summary of Events and Information	Remarks and references to Appendices
SAILLY LABOURSE	Oct 1917	30th	No event of special interest occurred. Battalion played 230th Brigade R.F.A in the Divisional League and lost 2-0	
		31st	Working parties as yesterday. Commanding Officer inspected resting platoons at 10 am Strength of Battalion:- 41 Officers 1025 other ranks	

C.S.M.
Lieut. Colonel
Comd'g 1st Batt The Monmouthshire Regt T.F.

SECRET AND CONFIDENTIAL.

Army Form C. 2118.

Vol 30

WAR DIARY
or
INTELLIGENCE SUMMARY.
(Erase heading not required.)

1st BATTALION THE MONMOUTHSHIRE REGIMENT T.F.

NOVEMBER 1st 1917 TO NOVEMBER 30th 1917.

Army Form C. 2118.

WAR DIARY
or
INTELLIGENCE SUMMARY.
(Erase heading not required.)

Instructions regarding War Diaries and Intelligence Summaries are contained in F. S. Regs., Part II. and the Staff Manual respectively. Title pages will be prepared in manuscript.

Place	Date	Hour	Summary of Events and Information	Remarks and references to Appendices
SAILLY-LABORSE	Nov 1917 1st		Working parties as yesterday. Draft of 3 other ranks reported at Depot as reinforcements	
	2nd		Working parties as usual	
	3rd		Working parties as usual. No event of any importance occurred - Draft 4 OR.	
	4		SUNDAY. Working parties as yesterday. Divine Service held for all denominations during the morning. Owing to Church parades the Commanding Officer's inspection of Resting Platoons was cancelled. LIEUT-COLONEL C.A. EVILL proceeded on 14 days leave and handed over command to CAPT. R.C.L. THOMAS CAPT. W.M.B. BURNYEAT will act as Second in Command to the above and LIEUT. R.D. EDMISTON as Adjutant.	
	5th		Working parties as yesterday with exception of 'C' Company who commenced work to-night repairing Light Railway between CRUCIFIX DUMP in LOOS and TOSH ALLEY (France 36c NW - G.29.d.6.2. and G.30.d.4.6. - 1 OR wounded (unamug ar duty) Draft of 5 O.R. reported at Depot as reinforcements. Visibility low, cold & raw.	
	6th		Working parties today as yesterday A Draft of 3 N.C.O's and 28 O.R. arrived from Our Depot Battn. Rain fell intermittently throughout the day.	
	7th		Working parties as yesterday. The Commanding Officer inspected the new draft of 31 O.R. The Battalion football team played the 8th SHERWOOD FORESTERS in our League match and won by 3 goals to 0. Weather dull and a good deal of rain. Casualties 1. OR wounded.	
	8th		Working parties as usual with exception of D Company who have been switched	

WAR DIARY or INTELLIGENCE SUMMARY

Army Form C. 2118.

Place	Date 1917	Hour	Summary of Events and Information	Remarks and references to Appendices
SAILLY-LABOURSE	Nov 8th cont		into repairing light Railway at LOOS along with 'C' Coy as this line is in a very bad state. 8. O.R joined the Div Depot Batt" today as reinforcements. Weather dull and showery.	
		9th	Working parties were found as usual. Weather dull and a good deal of rain fell.	
		10th	Working parties found as usual. CAPT G. DOBELL reported as reinforcement.	
		11th	Working parties found as usual. B. Coy supplied a working party of 30 men to H6th Div Signal Coy to relay a length of cable situated at junction of HURDLE TRENCH and HYTHE ALLEY H. 31. c. 9. 4. (36.C.N.W). Weather dull but dry. Riding Platoons paraded at 10.30 am for C.E. Service at which the G.O.C attended.	
		12th	Working parties were found today as usual. The Commanding Officer inspected Riding Platoons at 10 am. 5 O.R joined the Div Depot Batt" today as reinforcements. Weather dry and much clearer - some frost during night of 11/12th. The Battalion soccer team played the H5th LINCOLNS in league match and won by 3 goals to 1. 1 O.R wounded (remained at duty)	
		13th	Working parties found as yesterday. Riding Platoons were at disposal of Platoon Commanders for kit inspection and cleaning up. Weather dull & misty	
		14th	Working parties were found today as usual. Casualties: 1. O.R wounded	
		15th	Working parties found as usual. The measles platoon of B.Coy were taken out of isolation. Weather fine and clear overhead. A draft of 9 men reported from Div Depot Batt" as reinforcements	
		16th	Working parties as usual. The Commanding Officer inspected recruits	

Army Form C. 2118.

WAR DIARY
or
INTELLIGENCE SUMMARY.
(Erase heading not required.)

Instructions regarding War Diaries and Intelligence Summaries are contained in F. S. Regs., Part II. and the Staff Manual respectively. Title pages will be prepared in manuscript.

Place	Date	Hour	Summary of Events and Information	Remarks and references to Appendices
SAILLY-LABORSE	Nov 16 cont'd		Platoons also new draft at 10.a.m. The Battalion soccer team played the 1st North Midland Field Ambulance in league match. Result 1 goal each. Weather dull and colder.	
	17th		Working parties found as usual. 1 O.R. wounded by Machine Gun bullet slight. Weather dull.	
	18th		B Coy commenced new work on NEW CUT Communication Trench 34.A.8.8. (Map Sheet 36C.N.W.3) Other working parties found as usual. Resting platoons paraded for C.E. service at 10.15 am in the Cinema SAILLY LABORSE. In the afternoon the Battalion soccer team played Corps H.Q. at home result 2 goals each. Weather very dull but dry.	
	19th		Working parties found as yesterday. The Resting Platoons carried on with musketry and close order drill. 1 O.R. reported as reinforcement from Div. Depot Batt. Weather dull and some rain. Draft +7. O.R. reported at 46th Div. Depot Batt as reinforcements. Casualties. 3. O.Rs. Wounded. 2. O.Rs wounded remained at duty.	
	20th		Working parties found as yesterday. The Commanding Officer inspected Resting Platoons at 10 am. The platoons as usual carried out competition in musketry. LIEUT. COLONEL C.A.F.VILL returned from leave. Weather dull.	
	21st		Working parties found as yesterday. The Commanding Officer inspected Transport Lines and billets. Weather dull and heavy showers of rain	

Army Form C. 2118.

WAR DIARY
or
INTELLIGENCE SUMMARY.
(Erase heading not required.)

Instructions regarding War Diaries and Intelligence Summaries are contained in F. S. Regs., Part II. and the Staff Manual respectively. Title pages will be prepared in manuscript.

Place	Date	Hour	Summary of Events and Information	Remarks and references to Appendices
SAILLY LABORSE	Nov 1917	22nd	Working parties as usual. The Commanding Officer inspected all works in progress. Draft of 5 O.Rs arrived at Depot Battn from Base. Casualties 1 O.R. wounded (remained at duty)	
		23rd	Work carried on as yesterday except that D Coy started on a new sector of the Right Railway to the south of 600S. 26 other ranks reported for duty with the Battalion from the Depot Battn. The Battalion beat the Div Train A.S.C. in the soccer League by 9 goals to nil.	
		24th	Working parties as usual. 'A' Coy completed the section of the reserve line known as HURDLE TRENCH. N.I.b.80.99 and commenced work on the pipe line trench at NETLEY TRENCH. N.I.b.80.99 and commenced work on pipe line trenches in the HILL 70 sector. The dispositions of the Battalion working parties is at present as follows:- A Coy working on pipe lines on HILL 70 B Coy NEW CUT Communication Trench C Coy } Ballasting D Coy }	
		25th	The Commanding Officer inspected Lewis Platoons and the draft that arrived from the Depot yesterday at 10 am. A very strong gale blew all day. Working parties as yesterday. Orders received that the HILL 70 sector will be handed over to the 11th Division and that the H6th Division will take over the CAMBRIN sector on the north of present front so far as A.27.b.5.4. on 27th inst. Casualties 1 other rank killed.	

Army Form C. 2118.

WAR DIARY
or
INTELLIGENCE SUMMARY.
(Erase heading not required.)

Instructions regarding War Diaries and Intelligence Summaries are contained in F. S. Regs., Part II. and the Staff Manual respectively. Title pages will be prepared in manuscript.

Place	Date	Hour	Summary of Events and Information	Remarks and references to Appendices
SAILLY LABORSE	Nov 1917	26th	A, C and D Coys worked on a special job of deepening a cable trench on HILL 70. B Coy worked as usual on NEW CUT G.T. which trench was completed tonight. Casualties: 1 Other rank wounded, 1 Other rank wounded (at duty)	
		27th	B. Coy worked on NEW CUT, C Coy worked on hillets. At 6 pm D. Coy moved billets to allears in CORONS LE RUTOIRE PHILOSOPHE and A Coy moved from GUN TRENCH to the billets vacated by D Coy in the village line. The arrangements as to work are that A and C Coys will work on the water system on the LE RUTOIRE PLAIN laying pipes and digging them in, and that D Coy will work on the right Railway System in the Divisional Sector. Draft 11 Other ranks reported at Div Depot Bath as reinforcements from the Base	
		28th	A and C Coys worked on burying a water pipe line to a depth of 3'6" to prevent it freezing, the section of pipe being by POSEN ALLEY (HULLUCH SECTOR) B Coy worked as yesterday on CHALK PIT ALLEY D Coy spent the day on cleaning up billets. Battalion orders with the H 6th Div Signal Coy in soccer league 1-1 Commanding Officer inspected Reserve Platoons at 10 am. To comply with the wish of the G.O.C. 46th Division, the position of the stencilled dragon worn as a badge on the back of the steel helmet, has been altered from the back to the left side of the helmet	

Army Form C. 2118.

WAR DIARY
or
INTELLIGENCE SUMMARY.
(Erase heading not required.)

Instructions regarding War Diaries and Intelligence Summaries are contained in F. S. Regs., Part II. and the Staff Manual respectively. Title pages will be prepared in manuscript.

Place	Date	Hour	Summary of Events and Information	Remarks and references to Appendices
SAILLY LABORSE	Nov 1917	29th	'A' B and C Companies worked as yesterday. D Coy commenced work on Light Railways on the RUTOIRE PLAIN. Casualties 5 O.R. wounded, caused by enemy shelling billets occupied by A B and C Coys, in the Village Line.	
		30th	Companies worked as yesterday. Considerable shelling of back areas by the enemy both today and yesterday. Casualties. 2. O.R. wounded Strength of Battalion; 41 Officers 1064 Other ranks	

C.S.Bell
Lieut. Colonel
Comdg 1st Batt The Monmouthshire Regt. T.F.

Army Form C. 2118.

WAR DIARY
or
INTELLIGENCE SUMMARY.
(Erase heading not required.)

SECRET & CONFIDENTIAL

Vol 31

1st Batt The Monmouthshire Regt. T.F.

December 1st To December 31st 1917.

Army Form C. 2118.

WAR DIARY
or
INTELLIGENCE SUMMARY.
(Erase heading not required.)

Instructions regarding War Diaries and Intelligence Summaries are contained in F. S. Regs., Part II. and the Staff Manual respectively. Title pages will be prepared in manuscript.

Place	Date	Hour	Summary of Events and Information	Remarks and references to Appendices
SAILLY LABOURSE	Dec 1st		Working parties found as yesterday. Orders received that one Company will move to the CAMBRIN SECTOR on 3rd inst. Very high wind all day. Draft turned to man in the evening. Draft 1 other rank arrived from Base as a reinforcement.	
	2nd		SUNDAY. Owing to Church Parade the Commanding Officer's Inspection of Platoons was cancelled. A, C & D Coys worked as yesterday. B Coy stood by in billets in preparation for to-morrow's move. Major (Acting Lieut. Col.) F.J. TRUMP. D.S.O. attached 1/6 SOUTH STAFFORD REGT was killed at 8 am this morning in NOYELLES, by a shell. Battalion played 6 SOUTH STAFFS in the soccer league, a draw 1 all.	
	3rd		B Coy moved from VILLAGE LINE to billets in ANNEQUIN at F.29.b.5.7. This Company will work on the Reserve Line on the CAMBRIN SECTOR commencing on OLD BOOTS trench from the northern end. LIEUT. COLONEL F.J. TRUMP buried in SAILLY-LABOURSE Cemetery at 2:30 pm with full Military Honours. A detachment of 60 men under Lieut A.N. GOLDSWORTHY was sent to form part of the escort and the Bugle Band attended to sound the Last Post. Weather intensely cold, while frost at night. Draft 3 other ranks reported at Depot as reinforcements from Base.	
	4th		C Coy moved billets from dug-outs in the Village Line in the vicinity of RAILWAY ALLEY (HILL 70 SECTOR) to the dug-outs on the Village Line, in the neighbourhood of NORTHERN SAP REDOUBT vacated yesterday by D Coy. The work for this Company remains unchanged, ie working on Water Pipe Line on the LE RUTOIRE PLAIN. A Coy having finished their Pipe Line work commenced work on CHALK PIT ALLEY. B Coy completed work on OLD BOOTS TRENCH. D Coy worked as yesterday on H9Y Light Railway Branch Track	

Army Form C. 2118.

WAR DIARY
or
INTELLIGENCE SUMMARY.
(Erase heading not required.)

Instructions regarding War Diaries and Intelligence Summaries are contained in F. S. Regs., Part II. and the Staff Manual respectively. Title pages will be prepared in manuscript.

Place	Date	Hour	Summary of Events and Information	Remarks and references to Appendices
SAILLY LABOURSE.	Dec 1917 5th		A, B + C Coys worked as yesterday. D Coy moved one platoon to billets in CAMBRIN. This platoon is to work on the Light Railways in that sector. Weather still very mild and frosty. — Draft 2. other ranks reported at Depot Batt from Base.	
	6th		A, B and C Coys worked as yesterday. The platoon of D Coy remaining at CORONS LE RUTOIRE moved to NOYELLES also D Coy Headquarters - This platoon will now move over to CAMBRIN as soon as accommodation can be arranged. The present dispositions of the Battalion are: Headquarters, Transport, Q.M. Stores and Resting Platoons - SAILLY - LABOURSE. B Company at ANNEQUIN. A Company VILLAGE LINE. C Company - 2 platoons VILLAGE LINE in neighbourhood of NORTHERN SAP REDOUBT. 1 platoon R.T.O. VERMELLES. D Company - 1 platoon R.T.O. PHILOSOPHE. 1 platoon NOYELLES. 1 platoon CAMBRIN.	
	7th		A, B, y C Coys worked as usual. D Coy commenced work on the Light Railways in the CAMBRIN SECTOR. Draft 2 other ranks reported at Depot as Reinforcements.	
	8th		Working parties found as usual.	
	9th		SUNDAY Working parties found as yesterday. Church Parades held for all denominations for Resting Platoons during morning. Draft 2 other ranks reported at Depot as Reinforcements.	
	10th		Working parties as yesterday. The one platoon of D Company billeted at CAMBRIN moved to NOYELLES owing to the CAMBRIN billets having to be handed over to the 42nd Divr.	

Army Form C. 2118.

WAR DIARY
or
INTELLIGENCE SUMMARY.
(Erase heading not required.)

Place	Date	Hour	Summary of Events and Information	Remarks and references to Appendices
SAILLY LABOURSE	Dec 1917	10th cont	Draft Major F.G. PHILLIPS reported for duty with the Battalion as a reinforcement. 20 other ranks reported at Depot. Commanding Officer inspected Lewis Gun Platoon at 10.0.a.m.	
		11th	Working parties as usual except that 'C' Coy not being required for the brake pipe line worked on NORTHERN SAP REDOUBT, repairing the Fire Bays.	
		12th	Works as yesterday. B Company moved one Platoon from ANNEQUIN to dug-outs in the VILLAGE LINE, FACTORY TRENCH. Capt W.P. ABBOTT, 3rd Bn MON REGT reported as a reinforcement. Draft of 5 other ranks reported at Depot Batt from Base.	
		13th	A, B & C Coys worked as yesterday. D. Coy under orders from 46th Division was lent to the 138th Brigade to show tunnels in the CAMBRIN SECTOR and in particular SAVILLE ROW which has been completely blocked by enemy shell fire.	
		14th	All Companies worked as yesterday with the exception that work was commenced on 3 machine Gun emplacements by 2 platoons of 'A' Coy and one of 'C' Coy under Lieut W.B. WADE and C.S. Major D. HUGHES. (Methods in appendix 1)	
		15th	A & C Companies worked as yesterday. B Coy in addition to D Coy has now been lent to the 138th Brigade. These two Companies dug a new trench from BARTS ALLEY C.T. to SAVILLE ROW. (In detail see appendix 1)	
		16th	SUNDAY. Church parade held for all Resting Platoons. B Coy to day moved the 8 platoons billeted in ANNEQUIN to FACTORY TRENCH (VILLAGE LINE, CAMBRIN SECTOR) Working parties found as yesterday. The disposition of the Battalion	

Army Form C. 2118.

WAR DIARY
or
INTELLIGENCE SUMMARY.
(Erase heading not required.)

Instructions regarding War Diaries and Intelligence Summaries are contained in F. S. Regs., Part II. and the Staff Manual respectively. Title pages will be prepared in manuscript.

Place	Date	Hour	Summary of Events and Information	Remarks and references to Appendices
SAILLY LABOURSE	1917 June	16 cont.d	Now are: Headquarters and Rushing Platoons - SAILLY-LABOURSE. A Company - 3 platoons - VILLAGE LINE, HULLUCH SECTOR C " - 2 " - do C " - 1 " - VERMELLES WITH R.T.O. B Company 3 " - FACTORY TRENCH B " 2 " - NOYELLES D " 1 " - PHILOSOPHE WITH R.T.O.	
		17.	Working parties as yesterday. Shelter trenches dug by B & D Companies in the CAMBRIN SECTOR were deepened by these Companies.	
		18.	Draft of other ranks arrived at Depot Battalion from Base. A hard frost has set in after a fall of snow yesterday. A & C Companies worked as yesterday. B. Coy dug a new trench from SAVILLE ROW to the NEW CUT. They dug 3 nights ago. D. Coy dug a fire trench to the South of SAVILLE ROW. All the recent digging operations in the CAMBRIN SECTOR have been rendered necessary owing to enemy shelling of communication trenches and the necessity of having alternate routes. Major F. G. PHILLIPS inspected Rioting Platoons at 10 am.	
		19.	A, C & D worked as yesterday. D Coy has now been relieved from work in the CAMBRIN SECTOR and today resumed work on the Railway from CAMBRIN running up the line.	
		20.	All working parties found as usual. A very hard frost again last night. Draft of 2 other ranks reported at Depot Battalion.	

Army Form C. 2118.

WAR DIARY
or
INTELLIGENCE SUMMARY.
(Erase heading not required.)

Instructions regarding War Diaries and Intelligence Summaries are contained in F. S. Regs., Part II. and the Staff Manual respectively. Title pages will be prepared in manuscript.

Place	Date	Hour	Summary of Events and Information	Remarks and references to Appendices
SAILLY LABOURSE	Dec 1917			
	21st		All working parties as usual. 51 other ranks arrived and reported for duty with the Battalion from the Depot. Good shoot very hard. Capt E.G.S.C. H.S.D.PHILL returning from leave brought with him silver plated Bugles a gift to the Battalion by the Hon Colonel LORD TREDEGAR. One silver one was got to arrive. These Bugles are being formally handed to the Battalion on Christmas morning by the G.O.C. 46th Division. Commanding Officer inspected kennels of transport at 11.30 am	
	22nd		The inspection of working Platoons was made by Major F.G. PHILLIPS at 10am. Working parties found as usual.	
	23rd		Working parties as usual. After a severe frost lasting roughly a week a thaw set in. The working Platoons of A.B. + C. Coys had their Christmas Dinner at 1 p.m. The arrangements to the new one, that as from yesterday, the working Platoons only remain at SAILLY for 2 days, with the exception of D Coy until all have had their Xmas Dinner. D Coy will have its Xmas dinner on 26th of NOYELLES.	
	24		Working parties as usual. The thaw continued and rain fell during the afternoon.	
	25		CHRISTMAS DAY. D company and working Platoons of A,B,+ C Coys paraded at 10.15 am on the Battalion parade ground. BRIG-GENERAL H.M. CAMPBELL C.B. C.M.G. R.A. G.O.C of the 46th Division, in the absence of MAJ-GENERAL THWAITES, on leave, attended and presented the silver Bugles on behalf of the HON-COLONEL LORD TREDEGAR	

Army Form C. 2118.

WAR DIARY
or
INTELLIGENCE SUMMARY.
(Erase heading not required.)

Place	Date	Hour	Summary of Events and Information	Remarks and references to Appendices
SAILLY LABOURSE	Oct 1917	2.5 cont.	BRIG-GENERAL CAMPBELL in addressing the parade, said, it gave him much pleasure to present the Silver Bugles to the Battalion on behalf of its HONORARY-COLONEL. The Battalion had done well in the attacks and also in the works which it was called upon to do in its present capacity as a Pioneer Battalion. He was very pleased that LORD TREDEGAR was showing his esteem for the Battalion by presenting the set of Silver Bugles. The Buglers then filed past the G.O.C. who handed each a Bugle. The parade then moved off to church saluting the G.O.C. as passing. The Silver Bugles consist of a set of one solid Silver and 24 other plated bugles, made by Boosey & Co London. Each is engraved with the Battalion Crest with the Battle Honours of South Africa 1900-1902 underneath. On the lip of the Bell is also engraved. Presented by the Honorary Colonel LORD TREDEGAR, OCTOBER 1917. All men in SAILLY CAMP together with D Coy at NOYELLES and the detachments with the R.T.O. at VERMELLES and PHILOSOPHE all had their xmas Dinner middle day. The Dinner consisted of Roast Pork, potatoes & carrots, Plum Pudding, apples, nuts, oranges and cigarettes and Beer. Cake was also provided for tea. Most of the above was obtainable through the generosity of the High Sheriff of Monmouthshire, J.W. BEYNON ESQ. who gave £150 to buy the dinner. In addition to this gift, 800 francs was given by the H.Q. Divisional canteen from accumulated profits and roughly £30 by other Monmouthshire friends. The Commanding Officer accompanied by the Officers, visited the Dinners	

Army Form C. 2118.

WAR DIARY
or
INTELLIGENCE SUMMARY.
(Erase heading not required.)

Instructions regarding War Diaries and Intelligence Summaries are contained in F. S. Regs., Part II. and the Staff Manual respectively. Title pages will be prepared in manuscript.

Place	Date	Hour	Summary of Events and Information	Remarks and references to Appendices
SAILLY LABOURSE	Dec 1917	25 cont'd	Heavy snow fell during the afternoon. The Sergeants held their Dinner at 5 pm in the Sergeants Mess. This was also waited by the Commanding Officer. A Smoking Concert was held from 6-8 pm in Camp for the men, when more beer and Hot Rum Punch was provided. 9 other ranks reported at Depot Battalion as reinforcements from Base.	
		26th	No working parties found to day. Very severe frost, more snow fell last night. 2/Lieuts BLACKALL and ARCHER reported for duty with the Battalion as reinforcements from England.	
		27th	Working parties as usual. Three platoons, one each from A, B & C Coys had their Xmas Dinner middle day. A Draft of 28 men reported for duty with the Battalion from the Depot Battalion, all but 4 have served with this unit before.	
		28th	Working parties as yesterday. Draft 6 other ranks reported at Depot Battalion as reinforcements from Base. The following have been mentioned in Despatches dated 1st Dec. 1917 "Honours and Awards"	

CAPT. W.M.B. BURNYEAT.
LIEUT. A.W. GOLDSWORTHY
CAPT. G. MARTYN (R.F.C.)
CAPT. J.D. GRIFFITHS (A.D.C. to G.O.C. 3RD CANADIAN DIVISION
22.5571 SERGT. J. CUFF.
325681 C.Q.M.S. A.C. HARDING
325578 SERGT. W.S. PITMAN.

Army Form C. 2118.

WAR DIARY
or
INTELLIGENCE SUMMARY.
(Erase heading not required.)

Instructions regarding War Diaries and Intelligence Summaries are contained in F. S. Regs., Part II. and the Staff Manual respectively. Title pages will be prepared in manuscript.

Place	Date	Hour	Summary of Events and Information	Remarks and references to Appendices
SAILLY LABOURSE	Dec 1917	29th	Working parties as yesterday. Weather colder than ever. A particularly heavy frost last night. The Commanding Officer inspected the Draft which reported from the Depot Battalion on 27th inst. The remaining 3 platoons of A, B & C Companies had their Xmas Dinner, which completed the Xmas dinners of the Battalion.	
		30	Working parties as yesterday. The Adjutant Capt R.C.L. THOMAS and Capt W.L. ROBERTS having been granted 4 days rest in the interests of the service, proceeded to PARIS. Roster Platoons carried on with Syllabus of training. The u/m Officers reported for duty with the Battalion as reinforcements from England. LIEUT. J.G. FRAMPTON " H.J.C. HAINES " S.W. FRY.	
		31st	Weather still frosty and cold. On the night of 30/31st 'C' Company sustained 8 casualties from shell fire while issuing NORTHERN SAP REDOUBT in VILLAGE LINE. 3 of the above were seriously but not fatally wounded. 2 of the above remained at duty. Working parties found as usual. Strength of Battalion : 44 Officers 1068 Other ranks.	

A Sill
Lieut. Colonel
Comd'g 1st Bn Monmouthshire Regt. T.F.

APPENDIX 1

Army Form C. 2118.

WAR DIARY or INTELLIGENCE SUMMARY.

(Erase heading not required.)

Place	Date	Hour	Summary of Events and Information	Remarks and references to Appendices

Details of new works commenced on Dec 14th/17, in connection with the construction of 3 Machine Gun Emplacements are as follows :- Three M.G. positions are situated as follows
Nº 1. H.25.c.5.7.   Nº 2. G.30.b.25.05.   Nº 3. G.30.b.4.4.
Nº 1 M.G. Nest is in front of MEATH TRENCH about 36 yards and is approached by a safe from MEATH.
Nº 2. M.G. Nest is 90 yards in front of CHALK PIT ALLEY
Nº 3 M.G. Nest is in the SPINNEY off and behind RESERVE TRENCH, and is reached by a sap 45 yards long.
The Gallery to M.G. NEST has, in each case, 50 ft cover and off each Gallery Run is a chamber 16ft × 9ft. to accommodate the M.G. team. At the end of the Gallery the Nest is reached by a stairway branching off at right angles.
Nº 1 and Nº 2 are now completed except the chamber and sundry details such as fittings.
Nº 3 has 55 ft of Gallery completed.
The work of digging a new Communication trench from BARTS ALLEY to SAVILLE ROW commenced on 14/12/17. has been rendered necessary owing to the shelling of Hare Tea C.T.s by the enemy. The trench runs from :- approximately (36.C.N.W) G.4.d.45.30 (SAVILLE ROW) to G.4.d.11.40 (BARTS ALLEY), and is known as CURRIN TRENCH.
A New trench has also been dug off CURRIN TRENCH to SAVILLE ROW. G.4.d.30.10 - G.4.d.30.50. In addition VIGO STREET has been opened up as a fire trench.
G.4.d.50.35 - G.4.d.60.20 - This work now makes the above trenches run as follows :-

SKETCH MAP
CAMBRIN SECTOR

[Sketch: BARTS ALLEY, NEW FIRE TRENCH, CURRIN TR., SAVILLE ROW, VIGO STREET]

Ca Sul
Lieut Colonel
Comd 1/4 Bn Monmouthshire Regt T.F.

SECRET
CONFIDENTIAL

Army Form C. 2118.

WAR DIARY
~~INTELLIGENCE SUMMARY~~
(Erase heading not required.)

VK 32

1st BATT THE MONMOUTHSHIRE REGT. T.F.

JANUARY 1ST 1918 to JANUARY 31ST 1918

WAR DIARY or INTELLIGENCE SUMMARY

Army Form C. 2118.

Place	Date	Hour	Summary of Events and Information	Remarks and references to Appendices
SAILLY LABOURSE	Jan 1st 1918		All working parties found as usual. During the morning the Commanding Officer inspected Rotary Platoons in Camp. Weather cold and iron hard.	
	2nd		All working parties found as usual. At 8.30 am this morning an enemy shell pitched at the back of a 3ft brick wall 5 yards immediately behind the Orderly Room with the result that the walls and roof of the Orderly Room quarters were blown up. Most of the records and correspondence were quickly scattered, the most important being recovered. The Orderly Room is a wood building 30ft by 10ft with corrugated iron roof and is situated in two rooms namely the Commanding Officer's Room, the clerks and finally the room occupied by H.Q. Orderlies and Runners. The shell pitched whilst the Orderly Room Staff were finishing breakfast in the room nearest the wall. There were no casualties. The men in the room nearest nothing more serious than a few scratches and a thorough shaking. The accompanying sketch shows plan of building, the part struck being completely demolished.	

```
┌─────────────┬──────────────────┐
│             │   H.Q. ORDERLIES │
│  CLERKS     │       AND        │
│   ROOM      │     RUNNERS      │
│             ├──────────────────┤
│             │                  │
│             │    C.O's ROOM    │
│             │                  │
└─────────────┴──────────────────┘
```

Army Form C. 2118.

WAR DIARY
or
INTELLIGENCE SUMMARY

(Erase heading not required.)

Instructions regarding War Diaries and Intelligence Summaries are contained in F. S. Regs., Part II. and the Staff Manual respectively. Title Pages will be prepared in manuscript.

Place	Date	Hour	Summary of Events and Information	Remarks and references to Appendices
SAILLY LABOURSE	Jan 2nd	12^N	This shell was the only one fired towards the village during the day. Working parties found as usual. A Company has almost completed new wiring of CHAPEL KEEP in VILLAGE LINE. Weather continued frosty and very cold.	
	3rd		Working parties found as usual. Bathing platoons carried on with class series drills & musketry. All working parties as usual. Commanding Officers inspected reserve platoons at 10 a.m.	
	4th			
	5th		2 N.C.O.s & other ranks reported at Depôt Battalion as reinforcements. Extract from London Gazette dated 14/1/18:— The King has been pleased to award decorations as under for distinguished services in the field:—	
			MILITARY CROSS — Quartermaster & Hon Capt R.H. MARTIN MON REGT DISTINGUISHED CONDUCT MEDAL 226198 Rifleman E JACOBSON MON REGT	
	6th		Working parties as usual. The heavy frost continues and the ground is like iron. 13 other ranks at the Highest were received by the Battalion. Warning order received that the Division will be relieved by the 11th Division commencing on the 16 instant.	
	7th		A quiet day with no firing in the evening.	
	8th		Working parties on spectators. Thaw continued all day. Heavy hoar again last night. Snow fell heavily during the morning. A and B Coys were as usual. C and D Coy fatigues only are failed for a while finish the CAMBRIN trenches, which runs from Right Battalion Headquarters to Headquarters near the junction of BARTS ALLEY and SUSSEX TRENCH	
	9th		A the filling in of the cable trench was completed by C and D Coys last evening, D Coy resumed its normal work on the Light Railway on the CAMBRIN sector. A Coy recommenced work on CHALK PIT ALLEY using the men who have been employed in wiring the VILLAGE LINE for the purpose. B Coy worked as yesterday on OLD BOOTS TRENCH. C Coy with all men not employed on the M.G. emplacements commenced wiring the VILLAGE LINE for the C.R.E.	

WAR DIARY or INTELLIGENCE SUMMARY

Army Form C. 2118.

Place	Date	Hour	Summary of Events and Information	Remarks and references to Appendices
SAILLY LABOURSSE	Jan 9th 1916	9.10	Trips troops from NORTHERN SAP REDOUBT to HOBSONS POST. Snow fell again fairly heavily. Casualties 1 other ranks wounded.	
		10ᵉ	Working parties as yesterday. A thaw commenced last night and continued throughout the day. The trenches after the recent frost and in consequence of the thaw, are getting very muddy and in a bad state. Casualties 1 other ranks wounded.	
		11ᵉ	Working parties as yesterday. Thaw continued, all roads and trenches are now getting into a very bad state. 1 Officer and 12 men of the 6th/8th EAST YORKS REGT. 11th Division, are attached to this Battalion as from today. They have been sent in advance to reconnoitre the VILLAGE LINE and act as guides in the event of it having to be manned.	
		12ᵉ	Working parties as yesterday. A strong drying wind blew all day - this has done much to dry up the country after the recent thaw. Work on the 5 M.G. emplacements has been practically stopped and all men on reliefs are to work on CHALK PIT ALLEY, turning and buttressing that trench.	
		13ᵉ	SUNDAY. Rioting Platoons attended Church Service in the morning. The Commanding Officer inspected resting Platoons at 11.45 a.m. in Billet Order. Weather warm and sunny although there was a slight frost again last night. Working parties found as yesterday. Orders received that the Battalion will be relieved by the 11th Division and move to WESTIN-LES-MINES on the morning of the 18th inst. Draft 5 other ranks reported at Depot Battalion from the Base.	
		14ᵉ	Working parties as yesterday. Snow fell fairly heavily again last night.	
		15ᵉ	Working parties as yesterday. Very heavy rain fell all day. Draft 6 other ranks reported at Depot Battalion from Base.	
		16ᵉ	Working parties as yesterday. Heavy rain fell during the morning. The trenches are in a very bad state and the unrevetted parts are falling in badly. Draft 8 other ranks reported at Depot Battalion from the Base.	

Army Form C. 2118.

WAR DIARY
or
INTELLIGENCE SUMMARY
(Erase heading not required.)

Instructions regarding War Diaries and Intelligence Summaries are contained in F.S. Regs., Part II. and the Staff Manual respectively. Title Pages will be prepared in manuscript.

Place	Date	Hour	Summary of Events and Information	Remarks and references to Appendices
SAILLY LA BOURSE	Jan	17	A Company worked on clearing CHALK PIT ALLEY and C Company on clearing POSEN ALLEY in the HULLUCH Sector for the 137th Brigade. D and B Companies cleared RAILWAY ALLEY in the CAMBRIN Sector for the 139th Brigade. The alteration of work has been made necessary by the heavy rains which is causing the trenches to collapse after the frost. Several men fell again owing to the newly being performed resting platoons. Changes as usual after the been inspected but no commanding officers inspection was held.	
		18	Working parties found as yesterday. A drying wind blew all day which helped to dry up roads. The trenches however are still very wet and full of mud.	
		19	Working parties as yesterday. The rest of the Division being relieved by the 41st Division commenced today and is being carried out by a Brigade at a time. This Battalion is to move out on 23rd and on being relieved by the 6th B EAST YORKS will entrain at VERMELLES for [?] and Major F. G. PHILLIPS took over command of Battalion.	
		20	Working parties as yesterday. Orders received that the Battalion on relief on the 23rd inst will march to BETHUNE for the night and on to BELLERIVE on the 24th instant.	
		21	Training parties as usual. Have obtained reduced [?] from 13 to 11 a day as for the 23rd instant.	
		22	Advance parties of 6th EAST YORKS arrived from Battalion Headquarters and Companies. All ranks to both at SAILLY CAMP and in advanced Billets were handed over.	
		23	Working parties found as usual up to 3 p.m. but after that time parties were withdrawn owing to Companies move. That 3 other ranks reported at Depot from base. Battalion paraded for D Company in marching platoons of A and [?] Coys and transport at 10 a.m. when the Battalion moved off to BETHUNE via BEUVRY. The platoons of A and C Coys from HULLUCH Billets via the VILLAGE LINE, HULLUCH Centre marched out at 8 a.m. and reported at BETHUNE between 8 and 9 p.m. The Battalion (less B Coy) billeted for the night at BETHUNE in a Tobacco Factory on the main road to BEUVRY. Map reference E.11.d.3.2	

Army Form C. 2118.

WAR DIARY
or
INTELLIGENCE SUMMARY
(Erase heading not required.)

Instructions regarding War Diaries and Intelligence Summaries are contained in F. S. Regs., Part II. and the Staff Manual respectively. Title Pages will be prepared in manuscript.

Place	Date	Hour	Summary of Events and Information	Remarks and references to Appendices
BETHUNE	Jan.	23rd & 24th	Battalion Headquarters in 119 RUE DE LILLE, immediately opposite the Tobacco Factory. The remaining platoons of B Coy moved from the VILLAGE LINE on the CAMBRIN Sector to NOYELLES. This company is now entirely billeted in that village including the company transport wagons for Pioneer Pool.	
		24th	Battalion moved to BELLERIVE. Owing to troops moving through BETHUNE, having to maintain a distance of 100 yards between platoons, companies paraded independently. The orders being that companies would face the stars roads at E.11.C.8.5 in the following order; C.A.D Coys maintaining an interval as above. The first platoon of C. Coy to pass the above point at 11.5am. BELLERIVE was reached at 1 pm. when guides met the Battalion and guided companies to billets. No one fell out. On arrival in this area the Battalion is attached to the 138th Brigade for training purposes. The billets are all in barns but are fairly good.
Draft. 9 other ranks joined Depot as reinforcement.	
BELLERIVE		25th	Day devoted to cleaning up and settling down in billets. Owing to the area being very wet, and nearly all the fields ploughed, no suitable parade ground seems available. Commanding Officer reported at 138th Brigade Headquarters in afternoon to get instructions as to training. Draft. 2 Lieut E M THOMAS reported as a reinforcement. 21 other ranks reported at Battalion from the Depot. 5 other ranks reported at Depot Battalion from Base.	
		26th	Day again devoted to cleaning up. Lieut Colonel CAEVILL returned from ROUEN and re-assumed command of the Battalion. Commanding Officer inspected draft that arrived yesterday at 10 am. 17 other ranks reported for duty with the Battalion from the Depot.	
		27th	SUNDAY. No training parades held. Church parades for Non-conformists and Roman Catholics held during the morning. Battalion parade for C of E Service at 3 pm.	

WAR DIARY or INTELLIGENCE SUMMARY

Army Form C. 2118.

Place	Date	Hour	Summary of Events and Information	Remarks and references to Appendices
BELLERIVE	June 1916	27	The weather seems the 24 Bart has been beautifully warm and sunny. Weather again warm and sunny. Battalion paraded out at 6.30 am to a training area south of CHOQUES and marched to Billets at 5 pm. The programme of training drawn up by the 118 Brigade is a programme now lasts 6 weeks. Today's parades consisted of bayonet drill, bayonet fighting, platoon and section drill. Compulsory men required from G.O.C. 118 Divis'n through the C.R.E. 118 Division (appendix) B Company sent one platoon – this platoon is to find a daily working party of 25 men for the 118 Field Coy R.E. The platoon is attached to the Field Coy for billet Quft. 2 others were allotted to 1st East Battalion Army Base – Companies paraded at 8 to 9 Am. & 2 – 3 pm for bayonet training, bayonet fighting, section and arm drill. D company went to cut brushway fascines on a 30 yard range at MOUNT BERNANCHON. The whole Battalion worked at intervals throughout the day at CHOQUES. A war savings campaign was inaugurated by the I.C. yes, to induce men to invest their war savings of their pay a/c in war savings certificates has been rates. This mainly was decided by the Battalion Company when Jan. 6.K.11.– The result was as follows:–	
			Total of all ranks investing during the above period 1018	
			Total number of subscriptions 625	
			Total value of subscriptions 6,139/-	
			Total amount subscribed £2,922-5-0	
			Amount subscribed of L £2.17.5¾	

Army Form C. 2118.

WAR DIARY
or
INTELLIGENCE SUMMARY
(Erase heading not required.)

Instructions regarding War Diaries and Intelligence Summaries are contained in F. S. Regs., Part II and the Staff Manual respectively. Title Pages will be prepared in manuscript.

Place	Date	Hour	Summary of Events and Information	Remarks and references to Appendices
BELLERIVE	Jan 1918	30	Training Parades held as follows:— A Coy carried out musketry on the long range N° 8 near LABEUVIERE. C Coy fired on short range at MOUNT BERNACHON. D Coy carried out general training on roads near Company billets. Weather fine and warm.	
		31st	C Company carried on with musketry on the short range. Exonerated (except 2 who refused) who had not been done within 12 months, a total of about 75. This company is carrying on training with any available men, but all those amounted to as incurred duty for 48 hours. D Company carried out training parades as yesterday. C.Os. dans received to move to HINGES to-morrow. Strength of Battalion:— 44 Officers 1092 Other Ranks	

(C. Eur)
Lieut Colonel,
Commanding 1st Bn The Monmouthshire Regt. T.F.

APPENDIX 1.

Army Form C. 2118.

WAR DIARY
or
INTELLIGENCE SUMMARY
(Erase heading not required.)

Place	Date	Hour	Summary of Events and Information	Remarks and references to Appendices
			Complimentary memo received from G.O.C, H6 S Division through the C.R.E.	
			H6 S Division. C.R.E. 46th Division (NM).
			E.348
			I wish to bring to notice of G.O.C. the good work done by the 1st Monmouthshire Regt. in the making of the 3 tunnelled M.G. emplacements off MEATH TRENCH @ CHALK PIT ALLEY and RESERVE LINE Ⓐ + Ⓑ.
			Nº 1 was tunnelled for 112 feet
			Nº 2 " " 138 feet
			Nº 3 " " 174 feet
			at an average depth of 20 feet
			The emplacements were commenced on the 14 & Dec. 1 and 2 being finished on the 12 Jan. and 3 on the 16. There were several difficulties to contend with, and the work put in was good.
			The OC. 1st Monmouths reports that great credit was due to Lieut WADE and C.S.M. HUGHES who superintended the work.
		22/1/18.	
			(Sd) C.WINGFIELD STOPFORD. B.G. C.R.E, H6 S Division.
			46th Div. Gen Staff Nº 3083/75/G
		C.R.E.	
			Tell O/c MONMOUTHS that I have not only to commend the work referred to, but have especially to express my very great satisfaction of the whole hearted manner in which the 1/1st Monmouths have carried out all their work during the 6 months the Division has been in the Line. Please convey to O.C. 1st Monmouths my best congratulations with regard to the high standard which generally his

WAR DIARY
or
INTELLIGENCE SUMMARY

(Erase heading not required.)

Army Form C. 2118.

Place	Date	Hour	Summary of Events and Information	Remarks and references to Appendices
Battalion.				
	25/1/1918		(Sd) WM THWAITES MAJOR GENERAL COMMANDING 46TH DIVISION	
O/C 1st MONMOUTHSHIRE REGT.				
			The attached correspondence is forwarded for your information	
			(Sd) C. WINGFIELD SHATFORD. B.G C.R.E. 46th Division	
	26/1/18			

Army Form C. 2118.

SECRET
CONFIDENTIAL

WAR DIARY
INTELLIGENCE SUMMARY.
(Erase heading not required.)

1st BATTALION
THE MONMOUTHSHIRE
REGIMENT.

1ST Batt THE MONMOUTHSHIRE REGIMENT T.F.

FEBRUARY 1st 1918 to FEBRUARY 28th 1918

Army Form C. 2118.

WAR DIARY
or
INTELLIGENCE SUMMARY.
(Erase heading not required.)

Instructions regarding War Diaries and Intelligence Summaries are contained in F. S. Regs., Part II. and the Staff Manual respectively. Title pages will be prepared in manuscript.

Place	Date	Hour	Summary of Events and Information	Remarks and references to Appendices
HINGES	Feb 1918	1st	Battalion Headquarters and C and D Companies moved to HINGES. Owing to the short distance the move was made independently. Headquarters moving at 11am and the 2 Companies at 2pm. The billets are very good, the villages being until a few days ago Corps Headquarters of XI Corps. Battalion Headquarters are in HINGES Chateau. A Coy remained at BELLERIVE owing to nearly all men having been inoculated yesterday. They will join the Battalion in a day or so. B Coy remains unchanged with 3 platoons at NOYELLES and 1 at BETHUNE.	
			The leave allotment of the Battalion for the month is 4 per day. In accordance with orders received from 46th Division all steel helmets were sent to the D.A.D.O.S. on January 25th last to be painted service grey and to have a black dragon stencilled on the left side. This is now adopted instead of the sandbag cover with a fleece dragon stencilled on the left side which was adopted in April 1917.	
		2nd	C Coy finished its preliminary course of musketry on the short range. The platoons of C Coy not firing, and D Coy, paraded in the grounds of HINGES Chateau for general training of platoons. There is a large grass park in front of the Chateau - this and the gravel drives make an excellent parade ground. No parades held in the afternoon, various inter-Company football matches were played.	
		3rd	SUNDAY. Services for non-conformists and Roman Catholics held in the morning. Battalion Parade at 3pm for C of E Service.	
		4th	D Coy carried out its preliminary musketry course on the short range. A and C Coys paraded from 9am to 12.15 pm and 2pm to 3 pm for general Company training. After approximately one weeks training the Battalion has smartened up very considerably, the men are getting very steady in the ranks and the drill is good. His Majesty the King of the Belgians has awarded the Belgian CROIX DE GUERRE to the	

Army Form C. 2118.

WAR DIARY
or
INTELLIGENCE SUMMARY.
(Erase heading not required.)

Place	Date	Hour	Summary of Events and Information	Remarks and references to Appendices
HINGES	Feb	4th and	following men of this unit:- 225793 Rfn A. GUNTER. D Coy. 305372 " W.H. PERIAM. B Coy. Both of the above are stretcher bearers and have done excellent work ever since the Battalion first came to this Country.	
		5th	Draft of one other ranks reported at Depot Battalion dated 29-1-18 (this has not previously been shown.) Company parades 9am to 12.15 pm in Chateau Grounds for general training. The Battalion paraded in mass at 12 noon, when the Commanding Officer read the memo from the G.O.C. 46 Div. twenty reviews and down in appendice 1 of last month. The Commanding Officer then presented the Silver Bugle which was given to the Battalion by the Hon Colonel LORD TREDEGAR, for the use of the Commanding Officer, to 225194 Bugler W. PICKWICK, who won the competition this morning. The Rev'd J.P. HALES. D.S.O. Senior Chaplain to the 46th Division, who has acted as Chaplain to this Battalion made a farewell speech to the Battalion at the conclusion of the parade, on leaving the Division to take up the appointment of D.A.C.G. VIII Corps. No parades held during the afternoon.	
		6th	Training was carried out today as follows:- A Coy on range C. and D Coys D Coy from 9am to 12.15 pm and from 2pm to 3. pm for Company training A draft of 2 other ranks reported to the 46 Genl Depot Battalion dated 2/2/18. The weather continues mild.	
		7th	A Company moved today from HINGES to ANNEQUIN for work under C.E. I Corps. C. and D Coys paraded in Chateau grounds from 9am to 10am for Physical Training and Bayonet Fighting. The remainder of the day was occupied in bathing.	

WAR DIARY
or
INTELLIGENCE SUMMARY.
(Erase heading not required.)

Army Form C. 2118.

Place	Date	Hour	Summary of Events and Information	Remarks and references to Appendices
HINGES	Feb 1918	8	Training was carried out today as follows:- C Coy - on 300 yards range D Coy - Company training in CHATEAU grounds from 9am to 3pm. B Coy carried on with work as yesterday. A Coy working under C.E. I. Coys burying cable at VERMELLES and LA ROUTOIRE. This Company also commenced work on Brigade Headquarters under the Forge at PHILOSOPHE. Weather continues frosty and a good deal of sunshine during the day. Draft 5 other ranks joined Depot Battalion today as reinforcements	
		9th	The Battalion less A and B Coys paraded at 9.30 am and marched to new billets in LABEUVRIERE, reaching the above village at 12 noon. The Headquarters of the 55th Division moved into the CHATEAU HINGES at 10 am. A and B Coys carried out work as yesterday. Weather as yesterday.	
LABEUVRIERE		10th	There was no Church service today, a padre not being available. C and D Coys spent the day in recreational training football etc. A and B Coys worked on new Brigade Headquarters and burying cable as yesterday. Draft 1 other rank joined this Depot Battalion today as reinforcement.	
		11th	Owing to difficulty in obtaining training grounds C and D Coys carried out a route march marching off from LABEUVRIERE at 9 am passing through CHOCQUES along BETHUNE ROAD ANNEZIN and FOUQUEREUIL and so back to billets. The distance marched being about 9 miles. A and B Coys on work as yesterday. Weather fine. Bugler PICKWICK was sent off. 16 on parade being killed for the Army Commanders to sound the General Salute. The I Corps sent a car for PICKWICK at 10. am	
		12th	C and D Coys carried out training on N°5 Training Ground, where there is quite a good Bayonet fighting course. A and B Coys worked as yesterday. Instructions received from	

Army Form C. 2118.

WAR DIARY
or
INTELLIGENCE SUMMARY.
(Erase heading not required.)

Instructions regarding War Diaries and Intelligence Summaries are contained in F. S. Regs., Part II. and the Staff Manual respectively. Title pages will be prepared in manuscript.

Place	Date 1918	Hour	Summary of Events and Information	Remarks and references to Appendices
LABEUVRIERE	Feb.	12th and 13th	# I Corps to move to Billets in BETHUNE on 14th inst. C and D Coys carried out Physical Training from 9am to 10am and all details of these Companies took on miniature range up till mid-day. The Companies bathed today at CHOCQUES. A and B Coys on work as yesterday. Weather fine but cold. Draft 5 other ranks joins the 11th Depot Battalion today as reinforcements.	
		14th	The Battalion less H and B Coys paraded at 10am and moved off independently to new billets in BETHUNE. C Coy marched off at 10.15am followed by D Coy at 10.30am. The transport moved off independently and had to make two journeys as lorries could not be obtained to carry blankets. Route through ANNEZIN. C and D Coys are billeted in the Tobacco Factory at E.17.b.9.9 (BETHUNE Combined sheet 36) Headquarters E.17.C.8.9 in RUE MICHELET. A and B Coys work as yesterday.	
BETHUNE		15th	C and D Coys paraded at 8am and proceeded to the Ranges No 7 and 8 close to LABEUVRIERE to continue with Divisional Musketry course. B Coy have finished most of the rough excavation of Brigade dug-outs. A Coy continued work on burying cable and dug-outs at PHILOSOPHE. Draft 43 other ranks reported from Divnl Training Batt'n as reinforcements.	
		16th	C and D Coys paraded at 8am and moved off to ranges No 7 & 8 near LABEUVRIERE and carried on with Divisional Musketry course. The Commanding Officer inspected the draft which arrived yesterday. The turn out generally and especially the fitting of equipment was not up to usual high standard. A and B Coys carried on with work as yesterday. Today has been clear and dry, but cold.	

Army Form C. 2118.

WAR DIARY
or
INTELLIGENCE SUMMARY.
(Erase heading not required.)

Instructions regarding War Diaries and Intelligence Summaries are contained in F. S. Regs., Part II. and the Staff Manual respectively. Title pages will be prepared in manuscript.

Place	Date	Hour	Summary of Events and Information	Remarks and references to Appendices
BETHUNE	Feb 1918	17th	There were no parades during the morning. Divine Service C of E was held at 2 pm in the ECOLE DE JEUNE FILLE' RUE MARCELIN near the Place. C and D Coys paraded and marched off independently to the place of worship. A Coy carried on with the work of hanging cable and have now 1 platoon detached at GORRE under 2/LIEUT W.E. WILLIAMS, reinforcing Elephant dug-outs with concrete at F.3.6. sheet 36. B Coy carried on with work on Brigade Headquarters.	
		18th	C and D Company carried out Company training today from 9am to 3pm. D Company were inoculated today and consequently are excused duty for 48 hours. A and B Coys carried on with work as usual in Brigade Headquarters. The weather continues fine but cold.	
		19th	C Coy carried out Company training on ground near billets from 9am to 3pm. D Company did not parade today due to having been inoculated. A and B Coys carried on with work as yesterday. Lieut. Colonel C.A. EVILL. D.S.O. proceeded on 14 days leave and handed over Command of Battalion to MAJOR. F.G. PHILLIPS. Weather continues fine with sharp frost in the morning.	
		20th	C and D Coys carried out Company training from 9am to 3pm in Section & Command drill, Platoon drill, Company Drill & Physical Drill, Training & Bayonet fighting. All the Company Lewis Gunners paraded at 8 am and proceeded to MINT range where the entire day was spent in general handling and firing of the Lewis Gun under LIEUT S.W. FRY. A and B Coys carried on with work as yesterday. Casualties 8. other ranks wounded in billets at NOYELLES through shell fire, 7 of B Coy and 1 of A Coy. One of the above, P/r SEDDON of B Coy died of wounds during the day. Instructions have been received that in accordance with G.H.Q. instructions, that all	

Army Form C. 2118.

WAR DIARY
or
INTELLIGENCE SUMMARY.
(Erase heading not required.)

Place	Date	Hour	Summary of Events and Information	Remarks and references to Appendices
BETHUNE	Feb 1918			
	20th Cont'd		Pioneer Battalions will be re-organised on a three company basis. The conversion to new establishment to be proceeded with forthwith. Staff 7 other ranks joined Depot Battalion today as reinforcements. Lieut. G.J. CLERY rejoins Battalion today.	
	21st		D Coy carried on with company training from 9 am to 3 pm. C Coy provided a party of 1 Officer and 32 other ranks for work in carrying and erection of foot bridges over the River LAWE at E.6.a.2.8, about 2 kilometres N.E. of BETHUNE. Commandant Corps Bridging school. All available Officers and other ranks of C Coy were inoculated to-day. A and B Coys worked as yesterday. The following were to-day handed over to the 42nd Div. 7 light draught horses, 2 pack animals and 2 G.S. wagons together with harness complete. 5 other ranks reported today as reinforcements from Divn'l Depot Battalion.	
	22nd		D Coy paraded at 8 am and proceeded to the range at MINX to complete Gun'l Musketry Course. C Coy did not parade today owing to inoculation. A and B Coys carried on with work as yesterday. The Adjutant Capt R.C.L. THOMAS M.C. returned from 14 days leave. Weather dull and some rain.	
	23rd		C Coy did not parade owing to inoculation. D Coy found 2 parties for Bridging details as on the 21st inst.	
	24		SUNDAY. Church parades held for C. of E and N.C. at 11 am for Companies in BETHUNE. Under orders from I. Corps, D Coy will relieve B Coy by the 25th inst - The relief to taking place over 2 days in order not to interfere with the work. One platoon of the above Companies carried out a relief this afternoon.	
	25		C Coy carried out Training parades from 9 am to 12.15 pm and 2 pm to 3 pm	

Army Form C. 2118.

WAR DIARY
or
INTELLIGENCE SUMMARY.
(Erase heading not required.)

Instructions regarding War Diaries and Intelligence Summaries are contained in F. S. Regs., Part II. and the Staff Manual respectively. Title pages will be prepared in manuscript.

Place	Date	Hour 1918	Summary of Events and Information	Remarks and references to Appendices
BETHUNE	Feb	25	The remaining 3 platoons of B and D Companies were sent out this afternoon with further reference to the reduction made of the Battalion to 3 Companies made in the diary of 21st and made instructions emanating from G.H.Q. No drafts will be sent to this Battalion to carry out the above reduction but the decrease of personnel will be arrived at by not awarding any further drafts to this Battalion, which will be allowed to fall by a process of attrition to the new establishment of 23 Officers and about 734 other ranks. When this state has been reached reinforcements will be sent to maintain it. Lines in arrangements with No 6 Division so this Battalion is at present so strong that 3 Companies would be impractical. The organisation of 4 Coys is being retained and the strength has decreased to about 900.	
		26th	Battalion Headquarters, Transport and B and C Coys paraded at 10 a.m. and marched to LAPUGNOY which was reached about 12 noon - The billets are fairly good but rather scattered.	
LAPUGNOY		27th	C Coy carried out Company training. B Coy completed Part 1 of the musketry course. Weather still very mild and warm.	
		28	Draft of 2 other ranks reported at Depot Battalion as reinforcements. B Coy was placed at disposal of O/C B Coy all day for the purpose of cleaning up. The present dispositions of the Battalion are:- Headquarters, B and C Companies - LAPUGNOY. D Company - NOYELLES A do 3 platoons NOYELLES 1 do GORRE (nr NOYELLES)	

WAR DIARY
or
INTELLIGENCE SUMMARY.

Army Form C. 2118.

Place	Date	Hour	Summary of Events and Information	Remarks and references to Appendices
LAPUGNOY	Feb	28th cont	The work which B Coy has been engaged on in the forward area has been the construction of mined dug-outs under ANNEQUIN FOSSE to be used as Brigade Headquarters. A detailed report as given in Appendix 1. The dug-outs which were completed on 19.2.18, except for fittings, were inspected by the Army and Corps Commanders who were both extremely pleased with the good work done. The latter gave instructions that the dug-outs were to be named MONMOUTH CASTLE and that a detailed report as in Appendix 1 was to be forwarded to him. This he said he intended having printed and circulated. A Company which moved up again to Forward Billets on 7th inst. has employed 3 platoons on constructing similar dug-outs to those made by B Coy at PHILOSOPHE. These are not yet completed. The 4th platoon situated at GORRE is making Elephant dug-outs reinforced with concrete at that place. B Coy in addition to completing the dug-outs known as MONMOUTH CASTLE, started another at of the same pattern under the S.W edge of ANNEQUIN FOSSE - This work was taken over by D Coy on relief on 25th instant. Under instructions from I Corps one bugler (Bugler W. PICKWICK A Coy) was sent to Corps Headquarters this morning to act as bugler of the guard mounted for a visit of the C-in-C. SIR DOUGLAS HAIG. Strength of Battalion :- 44 Officers 1108	

Hyson Mulville Major

Comdg 1st Batt The MONMOUTHSHIRE REGT. T.F.

APPENDIX I.

Army Form C. 2118.

WAR DIARY
or
INTELLIGENCE SUMMARY.
(Erase heading not required.)

Detailed statement of Dug-outs known as "MONMOUTH CASTLE" constructed under ANNEQUIN FOSSE by B Company during period 1/2/18 - 19/2/18, a copy of which was sent to Corps Commander I Corps by O/C B Company on 23/2/18, at the request of the former:—

The position of this Headquarters was marked out on 31st Jan 1918 and the work commenced on February 1st.

The 10 ft square excavations for Elephant Porches were sunk to a depth of 15 ft and the Elephants put into place by the 3rd and both drives down started on the same day. They were completed on the 5th Feb and the drive on this straight started. These were finished on the 8th. (a distance of 26 ft in each case). The communicating gallery was commenced at each end on the 9th and this (a total length of 80 ft) was completed by midday on the 10th. The scout distance driven in 1 shift of 6 hours was 37 ft. working from both ends.

The chambers 10 in number averaging in size 15'0" × 8'0" × 6'0" were commenced on the 11th and were finished and complete with all timbering at 5 am on the 20th February. The number of men on each shift averaged 20. These being Hshifts for 24 hours two men working on each face at the same time all apart being removed in sandbags. The nature of the soil was half chalk and half sandy clay, the roof being flaney.

The earth removed from galleries and chambers was 940 tons. Timber used 217 mining setts 6'6" × 2'6", 112 - 6'0" × 6'0" and 35 rolled steel joists. In these quantities there is not included timber for finishing off such as lagging and material for bunks.

Secret & Confidential

£46.

Vol 34

Army Form C. 2118.

WAR DIARY
—or—
INTELLIGENCE SUMMARY.
(*Erase heading not required.*)

1st Batt The Monmouthshire Regt. T.F.

March 1st 1918 to March 31st 1918

WAR DIARY
or
INTELLIGENCE SUMMARY.

Army Form C. 2118.

Place	Date	Hour	Summary of Events and Information	Remarks and references to Appendices
LAPUGNOY	March 1918 1st		Band & C Coys paraded from 9am to 12.15pm and 2pm to 3pm for general Company training. Weather very cold with some hail storms at intervals. Casualty - 1 other rank wounded, remained at duty.	
	2nd		Parades held only during the morning from 9am to 12 noon. C Coy carried out a route march. B Coy carried out general Company training. Weather very cold, snow fell slightly during the afternoon which interfered with football matches which had been arranged. The Commanding Officer inspected all available personnel and wagons of the 1st Line Transport at 11am. The turn-out was very good. Orders received that the 46th Division will move up to the line, taking over the CAMBRIN Sector from the 11th Division and the GUINCHY Sector from the 55 Division on the 5th and 6th inst. respectively. Headquarters and Band & C Coys of their Battalion move to SAILLY-LABOURSE on the 6th inst. Draft 7 other ranks reported at Depot Battalion as reinforcements.	
	3rd		SUNDAY No parade services were held owing to lack of accomodation. Voluntary services for all denominations were available. No training parades held.	
	4th		B Coy carried out musketry on long range. C Coy carried out general Company training. At 2 pm the Commanding Officer addressed 18 signallers who have been received surplus to establishment by the new organization of 3 Coys for a Pioneer Battalion, and who are being transferred to the Divisional Signal Coy R.E., to help form an extra section for the Divisional Machine Gun Battalion. Weather very cold and misty.	
	5th		Band & C Coys paraded from 9.30am to 12 noon for general Company training. No afternoon parades held owing to to-morrows move to BEUVRY. Weather again cold but fine.	
	6th		Battalion Headquarters Band C Coys and Transport paraded at 9.15am and marched to BEUVRY arriving about 11.45am where billets were allotted. Weather very fine and warm	

WAR DIARY or INTELLIGENCE SUMMARY

Army Form C. 2118.

Place	Date	Hour	Summary of Events and Information	Remarks and references to Appendices
BEUVRY	March 7th		B and C Coys paraded 9am to 12 noon and 2pm to 3.30 pm for general Company training. The Commanding Officer and C.R.E during morning to arrange details of work. Lieut-Colonel C.A. EVILL D.S.O returned from leave and re-assumed command of the Battalion. Draft. 4 other ranks reported at Depot Battalion from Base as reinforcements.	
	8th		Training parades held as yesterday for B and C Coys. No definite details of work for these Coys have yet been received. Owing to the congested area no billets are available for this Battalion in the forward area which makes the arranging of work very difficult. Bethune still fire warning.	
	9th		C Coy moved one platoon to CAMBRIN. This platoon will clear out village for the remainder of the Company to join in. Draft of 35 other ranks arrived from the Depot Battalion.	
	10th SUNDAY		D Coy moved from NOYELLES to SAILLY-LABOURSE and D Coy from BEUVRY to NOYELLES, to take over billets evacuated by D Coy. The remainder of C Coy (less 1 resting Platoon) moved to CAMBRIN. The dispositions of the Battalion now are:- Headquarters, Q.M. Stores Transport and 1 Resting Platoon from B and C Coys - BEUVRY. C Company - CAMBRIN. D do - SAILLY-LABOURSE. B do - NOYELLES Church parades arranged for all denominations hoped for details in BEUVRY. The Commanding Officer inspected the draft that arrived yesterday at 9am.	
	11th		A and B Coys moved from NOYELLES to SAILLY-LABOURSE and took over billets at SAILLY Subfire No. 6 EAST YOUNG. A Coy as from midnight tonight will continue to carry on work they were doing previously dug-outs at PHILOSOPHE but will discontinue work on the cable trenches at VERMELLES. D Coy to-day finished the second set of Brigade H.Q. dug-outs under ANNEQUIN FOSSE - these are exactly the same as MONMOUTH CASTLE completed by B Coy last month. A request has been made to Division to have these Headquarters called TREDEGAR HOUSE. B and D Coys as from to-morrow will commence work on the Village Line	

WAR DIARY
or
INTELLIGENCE SUMMARY.

Army Form C. 2118.

Place	Date	Hour	Summary of Events and Information	Remarks and references to Appendices
BEUVRY	March 11th cont		The Commanding Officer at 1.30 pm addressed a party of 26 men of this Battalion who have volunteered and have been accepted for transfer to the Machine Gun Battalion. The party left at 2 pm to report to the M.G. Corps for duty. The Commanding Officer likes a conference of O/C Coys at 5 pm to discuss work. One other rank wounded by M.G. fire in BEUVRY.	
	12th		Battalion Headquarters and details in the huts — Transport lines remained at BEUVRY. BEUVRY moved to SAILLY-LABOURSE and were billeted in The present disposition of the Battalion are:- Headquarters, A, B and D Coys — SAILLY-LABOURSE Huts. C Company — CAMBRIN. A Coy worked as usual, remainder of Companies did not work owing to change of billets. Casualties. 1 other rank wounded and 1 other rank wounded remained at duty.	
SAILLY LABOURSE	13th		C Coy worked on improvement of billets at CAMBRIN. A Coy is continuing work on the Brigade H.Q dug outs at PHILOSOPHE. B Coy is working on the Village Line North of JUNCTION KEEP and D Coy in the same line North of FACTORY COTTAGES, generally repairing the trench and constructing fire-bays. The enemy now shells SAILLY-LABOURSE more or less regularly every day in bursts of about 12 shells. Three times a day, from a long range gun. As from 8 pm tonight this Battalion (less C Coy) is in Brigade Reserve to the 138th Brigade, and is under orders to move at half an hours notice for the purpose of counter-attacking any ground captured by the enemy. With no definite information of an enemy attack as available, great dispositions have been made along the La Bassée Canal Front. The Division holds a very small Front with 3 Brigades from the LA BASSEE CANAL to CLIFFORD STREET just South of the HOHENZOLLERN REDOUBT, and the following Divisions	

Army Form C. 2118.

WAR DIARY
or
INTELLIGENCE SUMMARY.
(Erase heading not required.)

Place	Date	Hour	Summary of Events and Information	Remarks and references to Appendices
SAILLY LABOURSE	March 14/15 1917		One man in the line in the I Corps front - 55th and 11th Divisions with the 1/3rd Division billeted in the neighbourhood of BETHUNE in reserve. Draft of 3 other ranks reported at Depot Battalion from Base. Casualty - 1 other rank wounded, remained at duty.	
	15th		Went as yesterday. Today is the first day out for Lewis Platoons. No return of 1 platoon per Company resting at SAILLY CAMP for 4 days, after working for 12 days in the forward area. Has again been instituted. The Commanding Officer and Adjutant reconnoitred the ground and known lecture billets and forward areas which the Battalion would have to move over in the event of being ordered up to counter-attack any part of the 138th Brigade's front. Weather continued very fine and warm by day but wild white frosts each night. Casualty. 1 other rank wounded.	
	16th		Working parties as usual.	
	17th		SUNDAY Working parties as usual. Church parades held for all recruitments of Lewis Platoons except B Coy Platoon which carried out musketry on the long range at BEUVRY	
	18th		Working parties as yesterday. At 5.30 pm SAILLY CAMP was shelled with light shells out of a long range gun. About 50 shells fell altogether. No damage was done and there were no casualties. Weather still warm and sunny.	
			An Appendix 1 is inserted copy of correspondence received re the dug-outs wooden ANNEQUIN Sous Confused by B Coy last month.	
	19th		Working parties as usual. Weather changed, it is now cold and rainy. SAILLY CAMP SHELLED about 5 pm with about 25 light shells. Draft of 6 other ranks reported at Depot Battalion from Base.	
	20th		Working parties as yesterday. Weather fine but cold. Draft 2 other ranks reported at No. 16 Div Training Batt from Base	

WAR DIARY
or
INTELLIGENCE SUMMARY.
(Erase heading not required.)

Army Form C. 2118.

Place	Date	Hour	Summary of Events and Information	Remarks and references to Appendices
SAILLY-LABOURSÉ	March 1918	2.1ᵃ 12.15 am	Troops as yesterday. Covering parties as yesterday. At 12.15 am the enemy commenced a heavy bombardment of the Divisional front and raised the trenches held by the 138th and 139th Brigades from the HOHENZOLLERN REDOUBT to about the Railway a few hundred yards to the North. Orders received at 12.50 am to Stand to in billets and await orders. This was done, everything working very smoothly and according to a prearranged plan. At 2 am orders received to Stand down.	
			Working parties found as usual. Working parties as yesterday.	
		23ʳᵈ 2ⁿᵈ	SUNDAY. Usual instructions from Division re working parties were issued today. Church parade held for all denominations. Battalion parade for C of E service held at Mens'en CHATEAU-DES-PRÉS grounds. H.Q. of 138ᵗʰ Brigade. After this parade the Battalion was formed up in SAILLY CAMP and addressed by the Commanding Officer, who told the men that in the present serious situation the Battalion must be prepared to fight as it had done in May 1915, and to hold any ground given it to hold to the last man. That an offensive by the enemy is expected to-morrow in the neighbourhood of the LA BASSEE CANAL. The Battalion turned in at night ready for an immediate Stand to. The Commanding Officer and Adjutant attended a conference at 138ᵗʰ Brigade H.Q. at 2.30 pm on the dispositions of the Brigade in the event of an enemy attack. The Company Officers, Adjutant, all O.C. Coys, Quartermaster and Transport Officer reconnoitred the ground up to and the trenches of the NOELLES-GRENAY Line at 5 pm.	
			A draft of 114 other ranks reported for duty with Battalion from Depot Battalion. Lieut. R.K. WELLSTEED reported as a reinforcement.	
		25ᵗʰ	At 3 am to 6 am a barrage was placed on the enemy front line trenches along the Divisional front to break up any massing by the enemy. At 7.45 am 138ᵗʰ Brigade rang up to say that	

WAR DIARY or INTELLIGENCE SUMMARY

Army Form C. 2118.

Place	Date	Hour	Summary of Events and Information	Remarks and references to Appendices
SAILLY-LABOURSE	March 1918 25th cont		Work could be carried on as usual to-day, and this was arranged. Operation orders required. Not for to-night. The new Divisions would be taken as last night, but at 5 p.m. 138 Brigade rang up to say that their orders were cancelled, and that parties would be sent out to work by night. From them it was assumed that if no hostile attack was expected to-night. At 6.30 p.m. 4 shells fell on the Transport Lines at BEUVRY demolishing one hut and a billet and destroying the hut and a rifles of 20 men who were billeted on it. No casualties were sustained. 3 mules were wounded.	
	26th		Morning very misty. Waited at 9.15 a.m. to the effect that if the hostile situation on the Battle front developed in any way to the Division would be required on the line or the high ground behind it to-night. No working parties went out and the Battalion also lay by for a rest. All officers kits were sent down to 55 Coo and the surplus toys they will be sent this Battalion stores were cut to transport lines at BEUVRY where they will be dumped on the event of a sudden move being south. At 4 p.m. orders received to carry on until 7 p.m. and as usual to-night, and also to-morrow.	
	27th		No orders received yesterday were sent to the effect that the Battalion would march as usual to-day and and normal parties sent would go out 8 a.m. at 8.30 a.m. G.S.O.1. Division came to say that SAILLY Camp was required as a Staging out Place for a Battalion moving out of the Line and that this Battalion would move to NOEUX-LES-MINES, to be clear of SAILLY-LABOURSE by 6 p.m. Working parties went out as usual. Battalion moved to Billets in NOEUX-LES-MINES huts at 2.30 p.m. Companies marching by the road at 100 yards intervals. Weather very cold and windy. The HQ Division on being relieved in the Line by the 55th & 1st Divisions on which are side-slipping to the South and North respectively. The H.Q. Division on	

Army Form C2118/14.

WAR DIARY or INTELLIGENCE SUMMARY

Army Form C. 2118.

Place	Date	Hour	Summary of Events and Information	Remarks and references to Appendices
NOEUX LES MINES	March 27 1916		relief not notified to 4th Canadian Division which holds the HILL 70 and LENS sector, as far south as the SOUCHEZ RIVER.	
	28		Company trained panoplie field from 9:30 am to 12 noon and bathing parades arranged for C and D Coys in the afternoon. Weather went cold and windy with heavy rain in the evening. O.C. Commanding Officer saw the C.R.E. 4th Canadian Division in the morning with reference to work on new area and C.R.E. 4th Division in afternoon with regards to dispositions. Wire received at 9 p.m. that the whole Battalion and Drafts would move to BULLY-GRENAY tomorrow. Draft 5 other ranks reported at Depot Battalion from Base.	
	29 GOOD FRIDAY		Battalion moved to BULLY-GRENAY at 1:30 pm and were billeted. Headquarters situated in White Chateau, near the Church.	
BULLY-GRENAY	30		Commanding Officer and Company Commanders reconnoitred work with C.R.E. during the morning. A Coy moved to CITÉ ST PIERRE after dark, where it is to be billeted. This Company has been moved up principally for defensive purposes, but also in order to be nearer the work. Heavy heavy rain fell during the afternoon and evening therefore working parties were cancelled. 32 other ranks joined Battalion for duty from the Depot Battalion.	
	31 EASTER SUNDAY		During to working parties being cancelled last night, work was carried on as usual to-night by A, C and D Coys. A Company is working on OLYMPIC Strong Point. C and D Coys are working on the LENS Road Switch, which forms part of the rear defences. The trench has already	

Army Form C. 2118.

WAR DIARY
of
INTELLIGENCE SUMMARY.
(Erase heading not required.)

Instructions regarding War Diaries and Intelligence Summaries are contained in F. S. Regs., Part II. and the Staff Manual respectively. Title pages will be prepared in manuscript.

Place	Date	Hour	Summary of Events and Information	Remarks and references to Appendices
BULLY GRENAY	March 1918	31st	Been moved and now has to be disposed down's and battalion. Strength of Battalion:— H.Q. Officers 1071 Other ranks	

C. Gull / Lieut Colonel.
Comdg 1st Batt The Monmouthshire Regt. T.F.

APPENDIX - I

Army Form C. 2118.

WAR DIARY
or
INTELLIGENCE SUMMARY.
(Erase heading not required.)

Place	Date	Hour	Summary of Events and Information	Remarks and references to Appendices
			Correspondence received re the dug-outs under ANNEQUIN FOSSE constructed by B Coy. last month	
Headquarters 1 Corps			C.E. 1 Corps No 2881	
			I would like to place on record the good work done by Hd Qrs Field Coy R.E. O/C Major Zeller R.E. and the two companies of 1st Monmouth Pioneer Battalion especially B.C. O/C Capt Bunyeat, during the month which they have been employed with me. As regards Major Zeller, this Officer has shown great keenness and has organised all the work of my Co. efficiently. I attach a report on the construction of Brigade headquarters ANNEQUIN with a plan of work done. I think that this work ought to go now to establishing a record on dug out construction, and Captain Bunyeat and his Company can just be proud of their achievement.	
			(Sd) H. W. Gordon, Brig General	
			Chief Engineer 1 Corps	
	26-2-18		I have inspected this work and would like all ranks congratulated on having performed a very fine bit of work in what is I believe record time. The way this work has been tackled shows me the fine spirit de corps which prevails in the 466 Field Company R.E. and the 1st Monmouth Pioneers and the soldierly qualities which animate the men of the above units.	
	28-2-18		(Sd) A. Holland, Lt-General	
			Commanding 1 Corps	

WAR DIARY
or
INTELLIGENCE SUMMARY.

(Erase heading not required.)

Army Form C.

Instructions regarding War Diaries and Intelligence Summaries are contained in F.S. Regs., Part II. and the Staff Manual respectively. Title pages will be prepared in manuscript.

Place	Date	Hour	Summary of Events and Information	Remarks and references to Appendices
			C.R.E. 46th Division. G.252 O/C 1st Monmouths (through C.R.E.) Forwarded for information and communication to all concerned. The Divisional Commander considering the work highly commendable and desires all ranks to be congratulated on its behalf. (Sd) F.H. Dorling. Lt. Col Gen. Staff, 46th Division 2.3.18. O.C. 466th Field Coy R.E. O/c 1st Monmouths The above is forwarded for your information and communication. (Sd) G. Wingfield Stratford, Brig-Gen. C.R.E., 46th Division 5/3/18	

46th Divisional Pioneers

1st BATTALION

MONMOUTHSHIRE REGIMENT (Pioneers)

APRIL 1918.

Secret and Confidential.

27

Army Form C. 2118.

Pte 4

Vol 35

WAR DIARY
or
INTELLIGENCE SUMMARY.

(Erase heading not required.)

1st Batt The Monmouthshire Regt. T.F

April 1st 1918 to April 30th 1918

Army Form C. 2118.

WAR DIARY
or
INTELLIGENCE SUMMARY.
(Erase heading not required.)

Instructions regarding War Diaries and Intelligence Summaries are contained in F. S. Regs., Part II. and the Staff Manual respectively. Title pages will be prepared in manuscript.

Place	Date	Hour	Summary of Events and Information	Remarks and references to Appendices
MAROC	April 1918	8 pm	From 10 pm last night until 4 am this morning the enemy heavily gas shelled the FOSSE 7 area, north of MAROC and an area east of LES BREBIS. Owing to the wind being north west the gas blew clear of MAROC. A Coy in CITÉ ST PIERE were also heavily gas shelled. Owing to the withdrawal of B Coy for rest the following redistribution of work has been made:- A Coy - ST PIERRE - OLYMPIC POST C Coy - MAROC - LENS ROAD SWITCH D Coy - MAROC - having finished the northern end of LENS ROAD SWITCH, commenced new work today as follows:- 1. Construction of M.G. dugout in TOSH ALLEY known as the CRAP Battery position. 2. Construction of fire bays in the "RED" Line of defence in the 138th Brigade sector. This line runs from NETLEY TRENCH down to SCOTS ALLEY just to the East of LOOS.	
		9	Morning working parties proceeded as usual but at 11 am Burmoon rang up to say no more working parties would proceed until further orders as the enemy had launched a heavy attack north of the LA BASSEE CANAL. The enemy very heavily gas shelled all the back area of the Division particularly the batteries at FOSSE 7, near PHILOSOPHE and the HILL 70 sector. The gas blew across to MAROC but was not thick enough for box respirators to be worn. Lieut G.P. PEACHELL reported from Draft. 5 other ranks reported at Depot. Battalion from Base sent as reinforcements also 30 other ranks.	
		10	No working parties sent out until 3 pm when Burmoon rang up to say that the new night work for a short while this evening as the situation had cleared a little north of the Canal. At 9 pm a warning order was received that the 4th Division would be relieved by the 3rd Canadian Division to-morrow, if the tactical situation permits. Honours and awards. No 227364 Sergt R. OLDLAND, B Coy awarded Military Medal by Corps commander for an act of gallantry on 2 inst. When under shell fire in MAROC he carried in a wounded General of the 3rd Division.	
		11	At 3 am orders received that Battalion would be relieved by Pioneer Battalion of 3rd Canadian Division on night of 12/13 inst. Working parties sent out to work a short day and carry on from home lines in Brigades. A Coy moved from CITÉ ST PIERRE to BULLY-GRENAY as	

Army Form C. 2118.

WAR DIARY
or
INTELLIGENCE SUMMARY.
(Erase heading not required.)

Instructions regarding War Diaries and Intelligence Summaries are contained in F. S. Regs., Part II. and the Staff Manual respectively. Title pages will be prepared in manuscript.

Place	Date	Hour	Summary of Events and Information	Remarks and references to Appendices
MAROC	April 1918	1ˢᵗ	At 6.30 pm Battalion Headquarters, B, C and D Coys moved to MAROC. The billets are all in cellars. Battalion H.Q. situated at M.R.C. 6.3. The dispositions of the Battalion are now as follows:— Headquarters, B, C and D Coys - MAROC. A Coy pres't - CITÉ ST PIERRE Resting Platoons of all Coys - BULLY GRENAY Transport and C.M. Store	
		2²⁰	After completion of move D and C Coys worked as usual, also A Coy. Working parties as yesterday. B Coy commenced on the new VILLAGE LINE, where it crossed LENS-BETHUNE ROAD, generally repairing it. Billets slightly shelled for one hour at 5 pm, no casualties but a Hospitalier Scout L. WEBB-BOWEN of K.8ᵗʰ Bde, ate. 3rd Divisions etc was reconnoitering tunnels near MAROC and was wounded in the leg by a splinter. While being dressed at the Regimental Aid Post he expressed his thanks for the speedy means by which men of this Battalion had come under heavy shell fire and carried him to cover. Casualties 6 O.R. wounded. Draft of 3 other ranks reported at Depot Battalion from Base. Casualties 1 O.R. wounded (at duty). Working parties as yesterday. Weather various and showery.	
		3ˢᵗ	Working parties as yesterday. Draft of 8 other ranks reported at Depot Battalion from Base	
		4ᵗʰ	Working parties as yesterday. Casualties 1 O.R. wounded	
		5ᵗʰ	Working parties as yesterday.	
		6ᵗʰ	As from today the system of Resting Platoons is being temporarily suspended and the system of the Company resting and training for one week substituted. The Resting Platoons now at BULLY GRENAY accordingly rejoined their Coys and B Coy marched out of MAROC to BULLY GRENAY to rest and train for one week. Weather fine and sunny but heavy rain fell by night.	
		7ᵗʰ	SUNDAY No working parties found owing to landing now being a day off work for the Battalion. A Coy, however, worked their night parties on OLYMPIC POST as Rose were kept in billets last evening owing to this reason. Voluntary services held for all denominations. Draft 5 other ranks reported at Depot Battalion from Base.	

A9193. Wt.W128.9/M1291. 750,000. 1/17. D. D & L., Ltd. Forms/C2118/14.

Army Form C. 2118.

WAR DIARY
or
INTELLIGENCE SUMMARY.
(Erase heading not required.)

Instructions regarding War Diaries and Intelligence Summaries are contained in F. S. Regs., Part II. and the Staff Manual respectively. Title pages will be prepared in manuscript.

Place	Date	Hour	Summary of Events and Information	Remarks and references to Appendices
MAROC	April 1917	11th cont'd	The 139th Brigade is being relieved to-night. Advance party of Relieving Battalion, the 125th Canadian Battalion (Royal Grenadiers) arrived at 3 p.m. and commenced taking over.	
		12th	Orders received at 11 a.m. that Battalion will move to HERSIN on relief. The relief by the 125th Canadian was completed by 2 p.m. and Companies and Headquarters moved out of MAROC in small parties. The Battalion rendezvous was the Cemetery at SAINS-EN-GOHELLE where A and B Coys from BULLY-GRENAY had previously moved. Battalion was billeted in HERSIN by 5.30 p.m. Casualties 1 OR wounded (Gas).	
HERSIN		13th	Battalion paraded 9.30 a.m. and marched to BRUAY where Battalion was billeted with Headquarters in No 76 RUE DE PERNES. The whole of the roads were full of refugees from BULLY-GRENAY, MAZINGARBE, NOEUX-LES-MINES re Army orders practically all civilians have been evacuated. On arrival in BRUAY district the 46 Division came into First Army reserve. Casualties 1 OR wounded. Capt. N.C. BATTEN (3rd Mon Regt) reported for duty.	
BRUAY		14 SUNDAY	Weather very cold and windy. Training parades were held during the morning to practice extended order drill and Artillery formations. All officers paraded at 2.30 p.m. and did a Tactical Scheme (without troops) under the Commanding Officer. Draft of 4 other ranks reported at the Depot Battalion as reinforcement from Base.	
		15th	Battalion bathed during the morning. Training Parades were held from 9 a.m. to 12 noon, when Companies were not bathing. Officers, C.S. Majors and Platoon Sergeants paraded at 2.30 p.m for a Tactical Scheme under the Commanding Officer. Weather still cold and windy.	
		16th	Company Training parades held from 9 a.m. to 12 noon. A boy carried out musketry on 200 yds range. A party of 15 Officers and 220 men visited No 40 Squadron R.F.C. in the afternoon and were shown round the Aerodrome. Commanding Officer held conference of Company Commanders at 5 p.m. on programme of training.	
		17th	Coy training parades held from 9 a.m. to 12.30 p.m. The parade was finished with ½ hour Battalion exercise in Artillery formations. About 90 men have lost their voices as the result of the recent gas shelling in the forward area. These have all been sent to an isolation hut to be kept under control. B Coy carried out musketry practices on the range.	

A7092. Wt. W128/g/M1297 750,000. 1/17. D, D & L., Ltd. Forms/C2118/14.

Army Form C. 2118.

WAR DIARY
or
INTELLIGENCE SUMMARY.
(Erase heading not required.)

Instructions regarding War Diaries and Intelligence Summaries are contained in F.S. Regs., Part II. and the Staff Manual respectively. Title pages will be prepared in manuscript.

Place	Date	Hour	Summary of Events and Information	Remarks and references to Appendices
BRUAY	April 1918	18th	At 2.40.a.m. a wire was received from Division ordering the Battalion to be ready to move at 1 hours notice as an attack was expected on the I Corps front today. In consequence of this order all ranks were confined to billets and Training paraded with the exception of one for Physical training, were cancelled. Blankets were rolled and collected. At 9 a.m. orders were received, that from that time, the Battalion would be ready to move at 4 hours notice. Normal conditions were therefore resumed. An enemy attack was launched at dawn against positions north of the LA BASSEE CANAL, but it was repulsed without the reserves being ordered forward. A draft of 5 other ranks reported at Depot Battalion as reinforcements from Base.	
		19th	All Coys put through an inspection and test of gas helmets by Gas Officer of Division. 2 platoons of 'C' Coy fired on range. Remainder of Battalion carried out General Training. A and D Coys carried out an Advance Guard Scheme during the morning. A draft of 31 other ranks reported from Depot Battalion for duty with the Battalion.	
		20th	Weather much finer and warmer. Commanding Officer inspected draft that arrived yesterday, at 9.15 am. C Coy fired on range. A Coy carried out general Company training. B and D Coys carried out a Field of Fire Scheme. The G.O.C. 46th Division inspected training of the Battalion this morning. No training paraded during the afternoon. The party of about 90 men sent for isolation as the result of the recent gas shelling rejoined the Battalion today. In addition to these men about 90 more who also reported sick with the same symptoms, but these were treated Regimentally. Gas specialists who examined the men affected, state that the men will be normal again in a very few days. The enemy put about 30 9" shells into BRUAY wounding 1 man of this unit who was unaware of duty and are prisoners of the AOC. and are going F.O.N°2 on the Battalion Guard Room. It has reported now as wounded (Gas) by Field Ambulance. From gas shelling other Battalion were in MAROC. Draft of 3 other ranks reported at Depot Battalion from the Base, as reinforcements.	2/Lieut A.L.MEREDITH " H.R.ROWLAND (Brecknock Bn.S.W.B.) Corps as reinforcements

A7092] Wt. W12819/M1297 750,000. 1/17. D. D & L., Ltd. Forms/C2118/14.

WAR DIARY or INTELLIGENCE SUMMARY

Army Form C. 2118.

Place	Date 1918	Hour	Summary of Events and Information	Remarks and references to Appendices
BRUAY	April	21st	SUNDAY. No training parades held, but Officers carried out an Outpost scheme, without troops, in the afternoon. Battalion parade held for C. of E. service at BRUAY THEATRE at 11.30 a.m. After service and while marching back through the RUE DE MAIRIE, one of the large shells with which the Germans have been shelling BRUAY, struck a house immediately above the heads of the leading platoon of C Company, completely demolishing the house and (Casualties) wounding Capt N.T.C.LLEWELLYN, Lieut P.T. WELLSTEED and 14 other ranks. From intelligence reports, it appears the shells falling in BRUAY are fired from a 38 centimetre gun from the neighbourhood of MEURCHIN.	
		22nd	At 1 a.m. orders received that the Battalion would be held ready to move at 2 hours notice. All Coys and details bathed during the morning. B and D Coys carried out Training Parades from 2:30 pm to 3:30 pm. C and A Coys carried out a tactical scheme in the afternoon which was witnessed by all Officers. At 12 noon orders received altering the 2 hours notice of a move, to 4 hours. Draft of 6 other ranks reported as reinforcements from Base. Casualties 1 OR wounded	
		23rd	Company training parades held from 9 am to 12.30 pm. No afternoon parades held, as Division has been ordered up to the line tomorrow and the Battalion will probably move tomorrow as well.	
		24th	Battalion paraded at 2.15 pm and marched to BETHUNE where it was billeted Battalion Headquarters at No 21 RUE MICHELET. The 46th Division. The relief will be completed by the night 25th/26th inst. one Brigade of the 3rd Division. The relief will be completed by the night 25th/26th inst. The Divisional boundaries are X.8.C.4.1 on the North & X.30.a.5.0 on the South. The civilians were Owing to the danger of looting all men are being confined to billets. The civilians were evacuated from BETHUNE at very short notice. Kein Losses and possessions being left behind as the civilians packed out of the villages of FOQUIERES. Casualties 2 ORs rank wounded. 1 OR wounded (remained at duty) to billets for work.	
BETHUNE		25	Tactical Training parades held during the morning. Officers reconnoitred the ground of the N and N.E outskirts of BETHUNE over which ground the Battalion would probably have to reinforce in the event of an attack. Lieut G.H.T. COCHRANE accepted as a reinforcement. This Officer who was Signalling Officer of the	

Army Form C. 2118.

WAR DIARY
or
INTELLIGENCE SUMMARY.

(Erase heading not required.)

Instructions regarding War Diaries and Intelligence Summaries are contained in F.S. Regs., Part II. and the Staff Manual respectively. Title pages will be prepared in manuscript.

Place	Date	Hour	Summary of Events and Information	Remarks and references to Appendices
BETHUNE	April	25	2/Lt Mon Regt has assumed the duties of assistant signalling officer, as Lieut C.T.A WATERS is again leaving the Battalion to act as O/C Signalling School.	
		26	Orders for work received which is to commence to-morrow night, after being reconnoitred to-day by Coy Comdrs. The general nature of the work is the construction of a rear line of defence from LA MOTTE FARM at X.26.C to the LA BASSÉE CANAL at F.2.d.	
		27	The work commenced last night & was continued to-day by B.C. and D. Coys. Owing to the wet nature of the ground the trench is being constructed as a breastwork, only 2 feet depth is being excavated the remainder of the spoil for making the parapet and parados as being obtained from borrow pits. A Coy is erecting barbed wire in front of the trench. Transport Lines and R.M. Stores moved from FOUQUIÈRES to N.E of BRUAY (map reference J.4.b) are the former place is being badly shelled.	
		28	Working parties as yesterday. Staff & other ranks reported at Depot Battalion from Base. This Battalion, in the event of an attack in force by the enemy, has been ordered to hold the BETHUNE and DOCK localities, and the dispositions are roughly as follows:—	
			One Company : Covering road, Canal ie at W.30 and E.6	
			One Company : Covering Bridgehead at F.1 and F.7	
			One Company : Covering BETHUNE - BEUVRY Road at F.13.	
			One Company : In reserve in billets in BETHUNE	
		29	Working parties as yesterday. All work is by night and the dark nights at present greatly restrict the completion of the trench. The supply of barbed wire is also very poor. (2nd Lt W. wounded (severely))	
		30	Coys worked as yesterday, on completion of the trench running from LA MOTTE FARM to the Canal the Commanding Officer reconnoitred future work on the western front of the LAWE CANAL and sites and wiped out the lines for the trench.	

Strength of Battalion : 44 Officers
1065 Other ranks

C.A. Sell
Lieut Colonel
Commdg 1st Batt. The Monmouthshire Regt. T.F.

Army Form C. 2118.

Secret and Confidential.

WAR DIARY
or
INTELLIGENCE SUMMARY.
(Erase heading not required.)

Vol 36

1st Batt The Monmouthshire Regt. T.F.
May 1st 1918 to May 31st 1918

Army Form C. 2118.

WAR DIARY
or
INTELLIGENCE SUMMARY.
(Erase heading not required.)

Instructions regarding War Diaries and Intelligence Summaries are contained in F. S. Regs., Part II. and the Staff Manual respectively. Title pages will be prepared in manuscript.

Place	Date	Hour	Summary of Events and Information	Remarks and references to Appendices
BETHUNE.	May 1918	1st	A Coy carried on with wiring the line by LA MOTTE Farm. B, C and D Coys commenced to dig a new line on the Eastern bank of the LAWE CANAL from W.30.a.2.4 to W.30.6.40.95. This line is to act as a flank defence for the 46th Division, in the event of a break through by the enemy on the north of the above canal. Draft 14 other ranks joined the Depot Battalion from the Base.	
		2nd	B, C and D Coys worked on new line as yesterday. A Coy moved out to billets at BZUAY for one weeks rest and training. Division Line concerned the arrangement of a resting Company. During the early morning C Coys billets at the Institute St Vaast and neighbourhood were bombarded with 8 inch gas shells; 12 direct hits were obtained on the billet. Casualties: Wounded 3 O.R. gas, 62 o/ranks - wounded remained at duty 1 other ranks. Owing to the heavy Gas of this Battalion being increased to 62, the Division in Line memo G.H.Q.95/1 dated 26/4/18 authorises the following tools to be returned to Ordnance, per Company, to make room for the carriage of the extra 6 guns; Hammers, carts 40, Bowls, felt 6, Bars, boring H.H., Crowbars 3/6"-4, Bars, boring 2'6"-8, Road levels 10"-1, Road levels 10"-4, Mineas Ramers boring -15.	
		3rd	Draft. 1. other ranks reported at Depot Batt from Base. B Coy carried on with the wiring of the french in front of LA MOTTE FARM recently worked on by A Coy. C Coy carried on with the french on the eastern bank of the LAWE CANAL. D Coy sent a small party by day to the new french by LA MOTTE FARM, and other parties to M.G. dugouts &c as reqd. 10.a/m 3 other ranks reported at Depot Battalion as reinforcements	
		4th	D Coy commenced work on the construction of a light Railway which is to run from LE QUESNOY to ESSARS. B and C Coys worked on LAWE CANAL trenches. 30 other ranks reported for duty with "Battalion from Training Battalion.	

Army Form C. 2118.

WAR DIARY
or
INTELLIGENCE SUMMARY.
(Erase heading not required.)

Instructions regarding War Diaries and Intelligence Summaries are contained in F. S. Regs., Part II. and the Staff Manual respectively. Title pages will be prepared in manuscript.

Place	Date	Hour	Summary of Events and Information	Remarks and references to Appendices
BETHUNE	May 1918	5ᵗʰ	Working parties as yesterday. The Commanding Officer inspected the Draft that arrived yesterday at 10 am. At 4pm Lieut Colonel C A EVILL. DSO. left in a motor car for hospital, suffering from congestion of the lungs. He called at Div. H.Q as passing to say good-bye to the G.O.C, but had no time to say good-bye to the Battalion. Orders received from Division in the evening that Capt & Adjt. R.C.L.THOMAS. M.C. is to assume command of the Battalion and that he is authorised to wear the rank of Lieut-Colonel.	
		6ᵖᵐ	D Coy worked as usual. B Coy carried on with work on trench by LA MOTTE FARM. 'C' Company who now only parade 50 strong for work, owing to the effects of gas shelling received on 2ⁿᵈ inst, worked specially for the R.E's in filling in the craters on the road at X.21.a. 15.35. Battalion ordered to commence work to-morrow night on the construction of a Reserve Line for the Right Brigade from F.5.a.4.3 to F.5.b.4.9. The C.O and O/C B and C Coys met the G.O.C. 139ᵗʰ Brigade at 6.pm at GORE when the G.O.C. pointed out on the ground the general line of the new reserve line, which is to be about 7- 30 yard lengths of curved and traversed trench with intervals of 80 yards between each length. This line was then taped out by the C.O.	
		7ᵗʰ	D Coy worked as usual. B and C Coys commenced the new Reserve line marked out yesterday pm while the trench was not finished the excavating and parapet were finished and the trench made lockable in an emergency. The G.O.C. Division indicated that the work was most urgent. Draft 3 other ranks reported as reinforcements from Base to Depot Battalion. Casualties 1. Other Rank Killed, 1 other Rank wounded, 1 other rank wounded, remained at duty. The G.O.C Division had agreed to the urgency of the work this Battalion having today off instead of last Sunday, but owing to the urgency of the work this was cancelled. D Coy worked as yesterday. B Coy constructed a line of barbed wire along the trench dug last night for 500 yards. 'C' Coy improved the same trench. Orders received that A Coy would embus at BRUAY at 7.30 pm for BETHUNE. On arrival at the	
		8ᵗʰ	The Third Anniversary of the Second Battle of YPRES.	

Army Form C. 2118.

WAR DIARY
or
INTELLIGENCE SUMMARY.
(Erase heading not required.)

Instructions regarding War Diaries and Intelligence Summaries are contained in F.S. Regs., Part II. and the Staff Manual respectively. Title pages will be prepared in manuscript.

Place	Date	Hour	Summary of Events and Information	Remarks and references to Appendices
BETHUNE	May 1918	8th cont.	Latter place, they would report to the 139th Brigade for a nights work on a part of the Reserve Line after which they are to return to BETHUNE to billets. All these arrangements worked satisfactorily. In order to celebrate the Anniversary of the Second Battle of YPRES, a voluntary C of E. Service was held in the Tobacco Factory at 11.30 am, followed by a Communion Service. About 25 Officers and 250 other ranks attended the Voluntary Service. An issue of beer was made to the men at their dinner and a mess dinner for all available Officers was held at the M.O. Mess at 8 p.m.	
		9th	Orders received that I Corps expects an enemy attack tomorrow morning, and all Divisional Reserves are to take up positions allotted in Defence Schemes by 10 p.m. tonight. A conference of all O/C Coys, L.G.O, Q.M, T.O, M.O, and Signalling Officers was held in the M.O. Mess at 12 noon to discuss dispositions re: after which orders were issued that D Coy would hold the Left Sector and B Coy the Right Sector of the BETHUNE DOCK LOCALITY, which extends from the Bridgehead in E.6.a., along a trench line to F.7.b.3.3. and that A and C Coys would be held in Battalion Reserve in the Tobacco Factory BETHUNE (E.17.6.8.9.). At 6 p.m. however, O/C C Coy reported that the M.O had inspected the remaining men of his Company and had marked them all unfit for duty, as the result of the gas shelling on the 2nd inst. Division was informed, who instructed that this Coy will be moved back to BRUAY tomorrow as they are no use in their present state for fighting purposes. B and C Coys moved out of BETHUNE at 8.30 p.m. and reported all correct with trenches manned at 10 p.m. Beyond general artillery activity no event occurred of any importance. T/Major (Acting Lieut-Colonel) JOHN JENKINS M.C., 20th K.R.R.C. has been appointed by First Army to Command this Battalion — this Officer arrived today but owing to the present situation Division directed that he will not assume Command of the Battalion until tomorrow. The additional 6 Lewis Guns arrived this morning — this now makes the number of Lewis Guns with the Battalion up to 12. 2 other ranks left the Battalion as volunteers for the M.G. Battalion.	
		10th	At 5.30 am orders received from Division to withdraw Companies from the DOCK LOCALITY, which was done	

WAR DIARY
or
INTELLIGENCE SUMMARY.
(Erase heading not required.)

Army Form C. 2118.

Place	Date	Hour	Summary of Events and Information	Remarks and references to Appendices
BETHUNE	May 1918	10th cont'd	At 10 am. Lieut Colonel J. JENKINS. M.C, assumed Command of the Battalion and Capt R.C.L. THOMAS. M.C. resumed the duties of Adjutant. At 2.30 pm "A" Coy were moved to BQUAY to rest, in motor lorries, as owing to the effects of the gas shelling only 6 men are fit for duty. A draft of 60 other ranks reported for duty with the Battalion from the Divl Training Batt'n. The DOCK LOCALITY was not manned to-night but all Coys were held ready to move out at short notice.	
		11th	The C.O. inspected the draft that arrived yesterday, at 10.30am, after addressing all available Officers at 10. am. Work to a limited extent was carried out to-night. D Coy worked on the Right Railway and moved off with Lewis Guns and was prepared to man the Left Sector of the DOCK LOCALITY if needed. A Coy carried on with the new Reserve line in F.5, a & b. linking up the short lengths of trench already dug with C.T's. B Coy was held ready in billets to man the Right Sector of the above locality at a moments notice. The night passed quietly, however, and all Coys out returned to billets without casualties.	
		12th	Work continued under the same arrangements as yesterday for D Coy. B Coy worked on the Reserve Line, Right Brigade, in continuing connecting it up throughout the entire length. This was done as far as digging the trench was concerned, but the parapet has yet to be made bullet proof. A Coy held back in reserve in BETHUNE. All ranks in BETHUNE again slept in boots and were prepared to move at a moments notice.	
		13th	D Coy worked as yesterday. A Coy worked on the Reserve line erecting wire and thickening the parapet. B Coy held back in BETHUNE in reserve. The Battalion is now under 2 hours notice to move from 9am–12 midnight and from then to 9am at 1 hour notice. In view of these orders men were allowed to return their blankets and packs and to sleep without boots. Casualties: 2 other ranks wounded.	
		14th	D Coy worked as yesterday. B Coy carried on erecting a second belt of wire in front of the	

Army Form C. 2118.

WAR DIARY
or
INTELLIGENCE SUMMARY.
(Erase heading not required.)

Instructions regarding War Diaries and Intelligence Summaries are contained in F. S. Regs., Part II. and the Staff Manual respectively. Title pages will be prepared in manuscript.

Place	Date	Hour	Summary of Events and Information	Remarks and references to Appendices
BETHUNE	May 1918	14th cont'd	Right Brigade Reserve Line and also in widening the existing trench of the TUNING FORK LINE. The G.O.C. Division called midday and instructed that the Reserve Company, which is A Coy, will dig a new line of trenches to protect the BRIDGEHEAD at E.6.a. The general line of the trenches is W.30.C.1.1. thence in an easterly direction across the road to E.6.a.5.9. This line was taped out by the C.O. in the afternoon and work was commenced on it after dark by A Coy. Draft 6 other ranks joined Div. Training Battalion from the Base.	
		15th	All Coys worked as last night. At 7 p.m. the enemy shelled the Batteries in rear of Battalion Headquarters. Some shells fell with one Dud hit the Orderly Room and 3 shells which exploded fell in the yard of the Headquarters Mess. Casualties 1 other rank wounded.	
		16th	Coys worked as yesterday. Weather very warm and sunny.	
		17th	Coys worked as yesterday. B Coy on the Reserve Line in the GORRE SECTOR were unable to work owing to heavy shelling. Casualties: 1 other rank killed - 7 other ranks wounded.	
		18th	Draft 2 other ranks joined the Div. Training Battalion from Base. Owing to the shelling (B Coy was subjected to last night) it was decided not to work on that trench. A and B Coys, therefore, worked on digging a position of the HINGES-ROBECQ LINE from W.30.a.0.4 to W.30.C.6.1. A trench about 3' x 3' was dug by the above Coys between the above points. D Coy worked on the Railway as usual. Casualties: 3 other ranks Wounded - Shell Gas	
		19th	WHIT SUNDAY No working parties found by order of the G.O.C. At 2 p.m. orders received to find 100 men to help put out a fire which is burning fiercely in BETHUNE SQUARE. This was done and B Coy finding the parties which worked in relief. Owing to some shelling near Headquarters in the morning all voluntary services which had been arranged were cancelled. Draft 2 other ranks joined Training Battalion from the Base. Casualties: 1 other rank wounded shell gas.	

Army Form C. 2118.

WAR DIARY
or
INTELLIGENCE SUMMARY.
(Erase heading not required.)

Instructions regarding War Diaries and Intelligence Summaries are contained in F.S. Regs., Part II. and the Staff Manual respectively. Title pages will be prepared in manuscript.

Place	Date	Hour	Summary of Events and Information	Remarks and references to Appendices
BETHUNE	May 1918	20th	A Coy was relieved by D Coy at the work of helping put out the fire, early this morning. B & D Coys continued at this work in relief throughout the day. The party is under the direction of the 170th Tunnelling Coy R.E. also are demolishing houses to try and localise the fire which has now gutted the GRAND PLACE and the main street. A Coy worked on the HINGES - ROBECQ LINE thickening the parapet of the trench dug on the night of 18th inst. From 8 am to 2 pm the enemy shelled the batteries in the neighbourhood of the Tobacco Factory, many shells falling short fell close to the Factory. There being several direct hits on the Orderly Room and the Factory itself. At 10 pm the enemy gas shelled the area he shelled this morning. Our gas blankets were at once lowered and except for the close atmosphere no inconvenience was caused. Casualties, 2 other ranks killed - 2 other ranks wounded.	
		21st	B and D Coys continued working on the fire in BETHUNE, which is now being kept under control and confined to the streets already on fire. A Coy worked on the Reserve Line in the GORRE SECTOR erecting the third belt of wire and constructing Fire Bays. The enemy very heavily bombarded all the GORRE SECTOR with "yellow cross Gas" and H.E. shells causing a large number of casualties to the 137th Brigade. A Coy had about 40 men affected, eleven of which have gone to hospital, the remainder have had their eyes affected. Tobacco Factory again shelled in the morning and several direct hits made on that building and the Orderly Room itself.	
		22nd	A and B Coys worked on the TUNING FORK RESERVE LINE constructing Fire Bays and finishing the third belt of wire. D Coy carried on with the Railway. The night was very quiet and no casualties were sustained.	
		23rd	A Coy was sent to a Field Ambulance at HESDIGNEUL to have their clothes disinfected after the recent gas shelling and therefore did not work as usual. D Coy worked as usual on the Tramline. Lieut Colonel E.J.WALTHEW. M.C. C.R.E. 46th Division and his Adjutant Capt. C.H.HINTON. M.C. R.E. were	

A5092). Wt. w 1285/M1191. 750,000. 1/17. D.D & L., Ltd. Forms/C2118/14.

WAR DIARY
or
INTELLIGENCE SUMMARY.

(Erase heading not required.)

Army Form C. 2118.

Place	Date	Hour	Summary of Events and Information	Remarks and references to Appendices
BETHUNE	May	23rd cont'd	Killed yesterday by a shell and buried with full military honours at FOUQUIERES. This Battalion provided one Coy (B Coy) as escort and also 25 buglers to sound the last post. Draft of 70 other ranks reported to the Battalion as reinforcements from the training Batt. Weather very windy and dusty. Lieut AWGROSWORTHY reported sick after tour of duty in England. Orders received that owing to the reduced strength of the 137th Brigade, two companies of this Battalion will be attached to this Brigade for trench duty when the Brigade goes into the line to-morrow. The C.O. and Adjutant called at 137th Brigade H.Q. and arranged details. B Coy with a strength of 4 Officers and 155 men will be attached to the 6th SOUTH STAFFORDS and D Coy with a strength of 4 Officers and 166 men will be attached to the 5th SOUTH STAFFORDS. A Coy worked on the Reserve line in the GORRE SECTOR as usual. B and D Coys did not work.	
		24th	Draft 3 other ranks reported at Depot Battalion from the Base. HONOURS AND AWARDS. The Corps Commander has awarded "THE MILITARY MEDAL" to:- 19557 Sergt J. CUFF. 225375 Rfn W. PERIAM both of B Coy, for an act of gallantry in the Field on 17th inst. (cont'd at bottom of sheet) A Coy worked as last night. Battalion H.Q." moved at 12 noon to 12 AVENUE ROUGET D'ISLE (E.10.6.A.9). At 3 p.m. at a parade of B Coy the C.O. presented the Ribbon of the "MILITARY MEDAL" to Sergt J. CUFF and Rfn W. PERIAM. About 9 p.m. B and D Coys moved off to meet the STAFFORD Battalions to which they will be attached. On joining them the Battalion will march up to the line. Only fighting Orders were carried. Packs and greatcoats being left in BETHUNE. B and D Coys are being rationed by the Battalions to which they are attached. Weather very cold for most of the day.	(E.10.6.A.9)
		24th cont	A and B Coys being to-day moved to billets in houses by the Public Gardens BETHUNE and will move there to-morrow.	

E.10.6.2.8. Battalion H.Q.

WAR DIARY
OR
INTELLIGENCE SUMMARY.

(Erase heading not required.)

Army Form C. 2118.

Place	Date	Hour	Summary of Events and Information	Remarks and references to Appendices
BETHUNE	May 1918	26th	SUNDAY. No work for A Coy. A voluntary service was held in the afternoon for details in BETHUNE. 51 men of A Coy suffering from the delayed action of the gas shelling on night of 21st inst were sent to Field Ambulance. Owing to the Field Ambulance being full the men were sent on to BRUAY and attached to C Coy by orders of Divisions. As a result of a voluntary collection made throughout the Battalion on 8th inst at the memorial service a sum of £52 was collected which has been forwarded to the MONMOUTHSHIRE REGT Prisoners of War Fund. Draft 2 Other ranks reported at Training Battalion as reinforcements.	
		27th	Weather cold and rather unsettled. A Coy worked as usual on the Reserve Line in the GORRE SECTOR.	

		28th	A Coy worked as yesterday. HONOURS AND AWARDS. No 246822 Rfn KELLEHER. W. late C Coy now attached 46th Div Traffic Control awarded MILITARY MEDAL by Corps Commander. The following of this Battalion have been mentioned in Diobatches dated 25/5/18 for gallant and distinguished conduct and devotion to duty in the Field;
			
			    Capt N.T.C LLEWELLIN C Coy
			    225403 Serjt W.J.DAVIES D Coy.	

		29th	A Coy from to-night worked on thickening the parapet of the recently dug trench of the HINGES - ROBECQ LINE. The C O inspected C Coy and the 51 men of A Coy suffering from Gas Poisoning at BRUAY. C Coy is now very much better and will soon be fit for duty. The A Coy men are getting on as well as can be expected. A small brass band which has been formed from the buglers who can play a band instrument has been formed recently and made its first public appearance tonight.	

Army Form C. 2118.

WAR DIARY
or
INTELLIGENCE SUMMARY.
(Erase heading not required.)

Instructions regarding War Diaries and Intelligence Summaries are contained in F.S. Regs., Part II. and the Staff Manual respectively. Title pages will be prepared in manuscript.

Place	Date	Hour	Summary of Events and Information	Remarks and references to Appendices
BETHUNE	May 1918	29th cont.	when it played for 1½ hours in the Public Gardens, BETHUNE. Casualties 1 other rank wounded	
		30th	A Coy carried on with the wiring of the Reserve Line in the GORRE SECTOR.	
		31st	A Coy worked as yesterday. Another 16 men of A Coy were sent to Field Ambulance as a result of the gas shelling on 21st inst. These were sent on to BRUAY to join the 51 men of A Coy already there. Casualties 93 Other ranks classified Wounded Shell Gas dated 22/5/18 1 Other rank wounded remained at duty. Strength of Battalion 45 Officers 938 Other Ranks	

J. Jenkins
Lieut. Colonel
Comdg 1st Batt. The Monmouthshire Regt. T.F.

Secret & Confidential.

Army Form C. 2118.

WAR DIARY
INTELLIGENCE SUMMARY.
(Erase heading not required.)

Vol 37

1st Batt The Monmouthshire Regt T.F
June 1st 1915 to June 30th 1915.

Army Form C. 2118.

WAR DIARY
or
INTELLIGENCE SUMMARY.
(Erase heading not required.)

Instructions regarding War Diaries and Intelligence Summaries are contained in F. S. Regs., Part II. and the Staff Manual respectively. Title pages will be prepared in manuscript.

Place	Date	Hour	Summary of Events and Information	Remarks and references to Appendices
BETHUNE	June 1st		'A' Coy worked as usual on the Tuning Fork Line and commenced digging a new length of trench to connect up that line with the LOISNE LINE	
	2nd		SUNDAY. No working parties found. 'C' Coy moved to BETHUNE from BRUAY. This Coy has now recovered from the effects of the gas shelling it was subjected to early in May. Draft: 5 O.R. reported at Depot Battalion from Base.	
	3rd		'C' Coy worked on the HINGES - ROBECQ LINE from the LAWE CANAL South for 250 yards thickening the parapet. About midnight this Coy was shelled with 4·2 and gas shells with the result that the following casualties were sustained; 2/Lieut A.L. MEREDITH badly wounded. 2 others sent to Killed, 5 other ranks wounded, & 2 other ranks wounded remained at duty. The work was in consequence much hindered. A. Coy worked on the Tuning Fork Line and completed the wiring. There are now 3 belts of wire all the length of the trench. B and D Coys repaired the Battalion Lake at night on the relief of the 137th Brigade by the 138th Brigade. These Coys have had a quiet tour of duty on the line, but the G.O.C. 137th Brigade (Brig. Gen T.V.CAMPBELL V.C. C.M.G, D.S.O.) stated to the Commanding Officer that all ranks had shown great keenness and had carried out their duties in a highly satisfactory manner. Band D Coys will	
	4th		A and C Coys worked as last night. These Coys will	97

WAR DIARY
or
INTELLIGENCE SUMMARY.

(Erase heading not required.)

Army Form C. 2118.

Place	Date	Hour	Summary of Events and Information	Remarks and references to Appendices
BETHUNE.	June	4th contd	not worked until the 6th instant. Casualties: 2/Lieut A.L.MEREDITH and 1 other rank wounded yesterday died to-day and will be buried at PERNES Cemetery to-morrow. Staff: 2 other ranks reported at Depot Battalion from Base as reinforcements.	
	5th		The Battalion was today re-organised on a 3 Company Basis in accordance with orders now in force for Pioneer Battalions. D Coy paraded at Headquarters at 10.am when the Coy was addressed by the Commanding Officer. The Coy was then broken up and sent to Coys as follows:-	
			To A Coy: Capt W.B.T.REES, Capt G.EDWARDS (both supernumerary) Lieut S.MURRAY MC, Lieut H.E.SHARPE, Lieut S.G.BLOW MC and 69 N.C.O's & men	
			B Coy: Lieut J.A.PHILLIPS, Lieut J.R.EVANS and 54 N.C.O's and men.	
			C Coy: Lieut H.J.C.HAINES and 137 N.C.O's and men.	
			The orders for the above transfers were made some days in advance. All Officers and NCO's down to the rank of paid Lance Corporal were posted by name to their new Company according to the vacancies in the Company Establishment.	
	6th		'A' Coy worked on the NEWCASTLE LINE erecting barbed wire, as a supply of 80 coils has been allotted to this unit today. B Coy commenced work with 2 platoons on the new left Brigade Headquarters which are being constructed. The H.Q. consist of cellars of houses linked up	99

Army Form C. 2118.

WAR DIARY
or
INTELLIGENCE SUMMARY.
(Erase heading not required.)

Place	Date	Hour	Summary of Events and Information	Remarks and references to Appendices
BETHUNE	June 1918	6 (cont)	with Elephant Shelters and have partially huts completed by the R.E.'s. The remaining platoon is working on the making of huts and horse standings on the LE QUESNOY and GORRE areas. C Coy with a small party completed the parapet of the ROBECQ-HINGES-LINE and with the remainder of the Coy commenced digging a line of Posts from the LANE CANAL at E.6.a.15.95 to a point E.5.a.6.4. One platoon per company moved out to BRUAY to rest and train. Capt W.B.T. REES to being placed in charge of these platoons. Draft 2.O.R. reported at Depot Battalion from Base & 8 O.R. rejoined Battalion from Depot Battalion. Casualties: 1 O.R. wounded remained at duty.	
"	"	7th	'A' Coy carried on with the new trench from the TUNING FORK LINE to the LOISNE LINE which was completed. B and C Coys worked as yesterday. Draft: 11. O.Rs. joined Battalion from Depot Battalion. Casualties: 1 O.R. wounded.	
"	"	8th	B and C Coys worked as yesterday. A Coy commenced work on the Canal Bridgehead at GORRE, F.3.C to F.9.b. Draft: 12 O.Rs. reported at Depot Battalion from Base as reinforcements. Casualties: 1. O.R. Wounded. 1. O.R. wounded remained at duty.	

Army Form C. 2118.

WAR DIARY
or
INTELLIGENCE SUMMARY.
(Erase heading not required.)

Place	Date	Hour	Summary of Events and Information	Remarks and references to Appendices
BETHUNE	June 1918	9th	SUNDAY. No working parties found. 1 platoon of "C" Coy, however, worked to-night and will rest to-morrow. This platoon works on the GORRE Bridgehead Line, which line is to be constructed round the bridge over the Canal at GORRE, on the north side. Voluntary Service held in the afternoon. At 12.30 pm the G.O.C. called at Battalion H.Q. and gave instructions that the Lewis Platoons at BRUAY are to move to FOUQUIERES to-day. This move was therefore carried out at 6 pm and the platoons billeted on the old I Corps Rest Station, map reference (BETHUNE combined sheet) E.15.d.2.3. Casualties: 1 O.R. wounded remained at duty.	
		10th	A Coy carried on clearing the Posts along the Canal as on Saturday, from F.3.c. to F.9.b. B Coy worked as usual and C Coy carried on with 1 platoon with the Flank defence posts near the Cemetery by the LANE CANAL, and with 1 platoon carried on with GORRE Bridgehead Line. At 11.15 am the G.O.C. Division inspected the Battalion First Line Transport. The inspection was very satisfactory, the G.O.C. saying that the turn-out was the best he had seen the Transport do + that it was a vast improvement on previous inspections and that it reflected very great credit on everyone connected with the Transport. Casualties: 1 other rank wounded remained at duty.	

Army Form C. 2118.

WAR DIARY
or
INTELLIGENCE SUMMARY.
(Erase heading not required.)

Instructions regarding War Diaries and Intelligence Summaries are contained in F. S. Regs., Part II. and the Staff Manual respectively. Title pages will be prepared in manuscript.

Place	Date	Hour	Summary of Events and Information	Remarks and references to Appendices
BETHUNE	June 1918	11th	"C" Coy and B Coy worked as yesterday. A Coy carried on with making a parados on the Bridgehead defence line in E.6.a	
	"	12th	Draft H.D.R. reported to Battalion from the Base. All Coys worked as yesterday. Draft, 1 Oth. reported at Depot Battalion as reinforcement.	
	"	13th	All Coys worked as yesterday. Casualties: 1 O.R. wounded and afterwards died of wounds.	
	"	14th	All Coys worked as yesterday except that A Coy dug a new line of Posts along the south bank of the LAWE CANAL from the Bridgehead in E.6.a. to a point about E.6.c.10.95. These were completed.	
	"	15th	"C" Coy carried on as yesterday. A Coy commenced to work on the NEWCASTLE LINE which runs from the BETHUNE – LA BASSEE CANAL at F.2.d.95.50 in a northerly direction to the BETHUNE–ESSARS Road, joining Keil road at about X.30.c.2.3. This line is to be the main Divisional Reserve Line and has to be rewetted throughout with 'A' Frames, and small elephant shelters erected at frequent intervals. A Coy is commencing work on the south of the above line. B Coy carried on as usual with the Brigade H.Q. dug outs and salvage work. At Coy to-night the area is to be defended by this Battalion in the event of an attack, is alloted to the LAWE LOCALITY from the BETHUNE DOCK LOCALITY	
	"	16th	SUNDAY. No working parties found.	

WAR DIARY
or
INTELLIGENCE SUMMARY.
(Erase heading not required.)

Army Form C. 2118.

Place	Date	Hour	Summary of Events and Information	Remarks and references to Appendices
BETHUNE	June 1918	16th Cont	The locality consists of a series of trenches and breastworks around the Bridgehead in E.6.a. - The boundary runs approximately from the LAWE CANAL at W.29.d.4.8 to W.30.c.40.95. E.6.a.8.2 - E.5.d.4.1 - E.5.a.4.5. then north up the LAWE CANAL to W.29.d.4.8. In the event of necessity it is intended to hold this locality with 2 Coys in the line and one in Reserve in BETHUNE. Relieving platoons changed over during the afternoon. A bombing competition was held during the afternoon to pick out likely men for the Battalion teams at the Divisional Horse Show. 'A' Coy team won and 'C' Coy was second. A concert was given in the evening by the concert parts of the 20th K.R.R.C. Capt W.L.ROBERTS M.C. left for England for duty with the R.A.F. and 'A' Coy was taken over by Capt E.J.JENKINS. Lieut J.A PHILIPS B Coy has been posted to A Coy as 2nd in command.	
	17th		All coys worked as on Saturday last. The 62 men of A Coy who were gassed on May 22nd are now fit for duty, except 5 men, and rejoined their coy today.	
	18th		Coys worked as yesterday. The GORRE Bridgehead line, on which 'C' Coy have been working is now to be known as the NEWCASTLE LINE which will run from a point on CANAL about 200x east of STAFFORD BRIDGE hence in a northerly direction through F.3.d.5.6. Hence in a westerly direction joining up with the old NEWCASTLE LINE at about F.2.6.8.0.	

Army Form C. 2118.

WAR DIARY
or
INTELLIGENCE SUMMARY.
(Erase heading not required.)

Place	Date	Hour	Summary of Events and Information	Remarks and references to Appendices
BETHUNE	June 18th	Contd.	Capt R.C.L.THOMAS. M.C. having been applied for by G.H.Q. Division to be attached to them as learners has today been handing over the duties of Adjutant to Capt W.M.JAMES who will take over as from 9 am tomorrow. The C.R.E. has applied to us for one Officer to be attached for duty to 465 Field Coy R.E., one Officer to be attached for duty with 466 Field Coy R.E., one Officer to be attached to C.R.E, 46th Division for special R.A. work. The commanding Officers decided that Officers should be sent as follows:- Lieut R.K.WELLSTEED - 465 Field Coy R.E. Lieut J.S.C.BARRIE - 466 Field Coy R.E. Lieut H.E.SHARPE - Attached to C.R.E. Division. These Officers left the Battalion today and joined their respective Coys &c with the exception of Lieut BARRIE who on account of having special work tonight will join the 466th Field Coy tomorrow.	
"	19th		Coys worked as yesterday. Capt W.M.JAMES commenced duties as Act/Adjutant of g[?] this morning. Capt R.C.L.THOMAS M.C. leaving the Battalion in a car sent for him by Division at 10.30 am.	
"	20th		Coys worked as yesterday concentrating on the erection of small shelters on the NEWCASTLE LINE	

Army Form C. 2118.

WAR DIARY
or
INTELLIGENCE SUMMARY.
(Erase heading not required.)

Instructions regarding War Diaries and Intelligence Summaries are contained in F. S. Regs., Part II. and the Staff Manual respectively. Title pages will be prepared in manuscript.

Place	Date	Hour	Summary of Events and Information	Remarks and references to Appendices
BETHUNE	June 20.6.18		Draft of 14 O. Rks joined the Battalion today from the "Dent Reception Camp". Coys worked as yesterday. "C" Coy were troubled with gas shelling during the night which somewhat hindered the work. Honours & Awards: Extract from London Gazette dated 17.6.18; The King has been pleased to approve of the award of the "MERITORIOUS SERVICE MEDAL" to the following in recognition of valuable services rendered with the Forces in France during the present war: MON REGT – 227944 Sergt MURPHY. J. 225689 Rfn MORGAN. W.A.	
"	21.2		The Commanding Officer inspected the draft which arrived yesterday. Rest of the men were of "C" Coy and had been gassed on or about May 2nd 1918. Companies worked as yesterday. Casualties: 1. O.Rk wounded "C" Coy. Honours & Awards – Extract from London Gazette supplement of 17-6-18; The King has been pleased to approve the award of the "MERITORIOUS SERVICE MEDAL" to: MON REGT. 225571 Sergt CUFF. J. The Commanding Officer inspected the Resting Platoons at 11 a.m after which the parade was formed up and he presented Rfn W.A.MORGAN with his MERITORIOUS SERVICE MEDAL	96

Army Form C. 2118.

WAR DIARY
or
INTELLIGENCE SUMMARY.
(Erase heading not required.)

Place	Date	Hour	Summary of Events and Information	Remarks and references to Appendices
BETHUNE	June 22nd		Capt W.B.T. REES Ken put the 3 platoons through a few movements of Coy Drill after which the parade was dismissed.	
		23.30	Draft: 1 Offr joined Divl Reception Camp as a reinforcement	
			Being Sunday no work was carried out except in the case of the prisoners, who were put at the disposal of O/C "E" Coy who employed them on the NEWCASTLE LINE. A Battalion Cross Country Race was run in the afternoon with a view to picking a team of five to represent the unit in the Divisional Sports. The course was about 4 miles and entailed the crossing of FOUQUIERES CHATEAU and some again alongside the stream running through E.15.b. Rfn Lamb J.F. A Coy succeeded in obtaining first place reaching home in 22 mins, 2nd Rfn Watkins J.H. 3rd Rfn Williams C.E. 4th Rfn White J.H. 5th Rfn March J. Prizes were given out of the Battalion Funds; 1st - 20 francs, 2nd - 10 francs + 3rd - 8 francs 4th - 5 - 3 francs. After the race the Band performed in the Public Gardens	
	24th		Coys worked as on Saturday last except that B Coy Salvage Party is now to be employed on collecting wood suitable for making "A" frames and loading it on to the 6th Div Train G.S. Wagons which will convey it to H.Q. 463 Field Coy where an "A" frame factory is to be started.	JF

Army Form C. 2118.

WAR DIARY
or
INTELLIGENCE SUMMARY.
(Erase heading not required.)

Place	Date	Hour	Summary of Events and Information	Remarks and references to Appendices
BETHUNE	June 1918	25th	Coys worked as yesterday. About 27 men of B Coy have commenced to work on NEWCASTLE LINE between A and C Coys.	
		26th	Coys worked as yesterday. Lieut ARCHER taped out work which will be done by B Coy as soon as Left Brigade Headquarters is completed at E.18.b.6.4. This work will consist of converting the DURHAM LINE into a C.T. The work will be commenced at junction of Light Railway and Trench at X.26.a.3.8.	
		27th	Coys worked as yesterday. 1 N.C.O and 6 O.R's have been applied for by the C.R.E. to be attached to 230th Brigade R.F.A, 'B' Battery at LABOURSE for work on ferro-concrete dug-outs. They will report to C.R.E at 9 am to-morrow.	
		28th	Coys worked as yesterday. At 6 am this morning the XI Corps made an attack. As we had heard nothing of this the boys were warned to be ready, but on phoning to Division we were informed that it was an operation by XI Corps. At 12 noon to-day from 46th Division so transferred from I to XII Corps. At 11.20 pm a wire was received from Division ordering the Battalion to find the Fire Picquet for BETHUNE. Strength of this picquet is to be 1 Officer, 1 Sergeant, 2 Corporals and 25 other ranks, and they are to take over from the 170th Tunnelling Coy at 8 am to-morrow.	off

Army Form C. 2118.

WAR DIARY
or
INTELLIGENCE SUMMARY.
(Erase heading not required.)

Place	Date	Hour	Summary of Events and Information	Remarks and references to Appendices
BETHUNE	June 29th	1918	Troops worked as yesterday. The Zone Piquet mentioned yesterday is being found by "D" Coy.	
	30th		Being Sunday no working parties were found except the pioneers who worked for "A" Coy. Voluntary services were held in the Palladium at 2.15 p.m. & 3 p.m. The Band played in the Public Gardens during the evening.	
			Strength of Battalion	
			43 Officers	
			939 Other Ranks	

J. Jenkins Lieut Colonel
Commanding 1st Batt The Monmouthshire Regt. T.F.

Secret & Confidential.

Army Form C. 2118.

WAR DIARY

~~INTELLIGENCE SUMMARY.~~

(Erase heading not required.)

Vol 38

1st Batt. The Monmouthshire Regt. T.F.

July 1st 1918. to July 31st 1918.

Army Form C. 2118.

WAR DIARY
INTELLIGENCE SUMMARY

(Erase heading not required.)

Place	Date	Hour	Summary of Events and Information	Remarks and references to Appendices
BETHUNE	July 1st 1918		'A' and 'C' Coys worked as usual on the NEWCASTLE LINE. 'B' Coy, only having 16 men working on the Left Brigade Headquarters providing more head cover, were able to commence work on DURHAM LINE which is to be converted into a communication trench from NEWCASTLE LINE in X.26.a.3.8 to Front Line. The work on this line was somewhat hindered by shell fire.	
"	2nd		Companies worked as yesterday. 'C' Coy's work was hindered by shell fire. Casualties 2 other ranks wounded and 2 O.R. wounded, remained at duty.	
"	3rd		Companies worked as usual. 'C' Coy were again hindered at intervals throughout the night by hostile shelling of GORRE. 'B' Coy have a few men working with O.C. 468 Field Coy assisting in the making of 'A' Frames at Montmorency Barracks. Casualties 3. O.R's wounded, remained at duty.	
"	4th		Companies worked as usual. The Commanding Officer went round work with C.R.E. Two more D.A.C. wagons have been detailed to help carrying timber back to O.C. 465 Field Coy R.E. at FOUQUIERES.	
"	5th		Companies worked last night as usual. The Commanding Officer gave a lecture in the Palladium at 5.30 p.m. to all Officers and N.C.O's in BETHUNE on	

WAR DIARY
of
INTELLIGENCE SUMMARY
(Erase heading not required.)

Army Form C. 2118.

Place	Date	Hour	Summary of Events and Information	Remarks and references to Appendices
BETHUNE	July 6th	1918	Companies worked as usual. Casualties 1 O.R. wounded, remained at duty. The Commanding Officer went on 6 days leave today and Major F.G. Phillips takes over command of the Battalion. Lt. L.J.A. Waters was married this afternoon at PERNES. XIII Corps Schools Bombing & Lewis Gun, commences tomorrow. Lt J.R. Evans and Lt F.L. Moore leave by lorry to-day. Capt. E.J. Jenkins left for Rouen with Sgt. Howes and L/Sgt Scammells for Pioneer Course commencing tomorrow.	
"	7th		Being Sunday no working parties were found with the exception of one by the Prisoners, who filled shell holes on tracks in [E.18.B.6.1] and [F.14.B.1.6.] There was a Battalion Cross Country Run at 5:30 p.m. Rfn Bowdler gained first place. Lt. J.A. Philips takes command of "A" Coy vice Capt. E.J. Jenkins to ROUEN on course. Casualties 5 ORs 'A' Coy wounded, 1 remained at duty, and one, 226929 Rfn BENNETT. S.L. died of wounds, in 11th N.M. Field Ambulance this morning. Capt. W.M.B.BURNYEAT. M.C. admitted to Field Ambulance.	

Army Form C. 2118.

WAR DIARY
or
INTELLIGENCE SUMMARY.
(Erase heading not required.)

Instructions regarding War Diaries and Intelligence Summaries are contained in F. S. Regs., Part II. and the Staff Manual respectively. Title pages will be prepared in manuscript.

Place	Date	Hour	Summary of Events and Information	Remarks and references to Appendices
BETHUNE	July 1918 8th.		Companies worked as on Saturday last. "A" and "C" Companies each had 125 men of Divisional Wing to work on the NEWCASTLE LINE. These men come up by train to KANTARA dump and after doing a 4 hours shift, return by train leaving their picks and shovels at KANTARA. This party is to be furnished every Monday and Thursday night. Rfn BENNETT. S.L. was buried at FOUQUIERES at 2.15 p.m. The bugles were present to sound the "Last Post". Honours and Rewards:- Sgt Cuff. J.M. and Rfn Morgan W.A. were presented with The Meritorious Service Medal Ribbon by the Corps Commander.	
"	" 9th.		Companies worked as usual. It has again been decided to alter the trace of the NEWCASTLE LINE. Traverses have now to be 24' across the back. A shelter have to be put in every traverse and no more "islands" have to be constructed.	
"	" 10th.		Companies worked as usual. B. Coy. is employing a small party on clearing the posts along the CANAL BRIDGEHEAD LINE. This work should be finished in about two days.	
"	" 11th.		Companies worked as yesterday. The party of 250 from the Divisional Reception Camp. worked on NEWCASTLE LINE. The posts along the CANAL —	off

WAR DIARY

INTELLIGENCE SUMMARY.

(Erase heading not required.)

Army Form C. 2118.

Place	Date 1918	Hour	Summary of Events and Information	Remarks and references to Appendices
BETHUNE	July 11th (Cont'd)		BRIDGEHEAD have now to be sandbagged. Orders have to-day been received from Division that the G.O.C. has decided that only one Platoon shall be resting at FOUQUIERES at a time. The order will come into effect as from Sunday 14th inst. Junior Officers course at Divisional Depot commences. 2/Lts W.E. WILLIAMS and H.R. ROWLAND attend.	
"	12th		Companies worked as yesterday. On orders from E.R.E. 7 men and 1 N.C.O are to be attached to R.E's at KANTARA dump for Salvage work. This party will commence work as from to-morrow. Lt. Col. J. JENKINS, M.C. arrived back from "Leave in France" this afternoon.	
"	13th		Companies worked as usual. The Prisoners are now working with "B" Coy on DURHAM LINE which has to be dug through from a point in LIVERPOOL LINE about X.21.c.8.6. The Commanding Officer inspected resting Platoon at 11 a.m. and visited the work (NEWCASTLE LINE) in the evening. Casualties 1 O.R. "L" Coy wounded, remained at duty.	
"	14th		Being Sunday no work was carried out other than that done on DURHAM LINE by the prisoners. From to-day only one resting Platoon is to be allowed.	

WAR DIARY
INTELLIGENCE SUMMARY
(Erase heading not required.)

Army Form C. 2118.

Place	Date	Hour	Summary of Events and Information	Remarks and references to Appendices
BETHUNE	July 14th 1918 (cont'd)		"C" Company is finding this next week, a class of 2 N.C.O's per Company is commencing to-morrow under Lt. L.W. Fry. The duration of the course will be a fortnight – its object being to train Junior N.C.O's as Section Commanders to Lewis Gun Sections. One man per Coy is to report to C.R.E at 8-45 a.m. to-morrow morning to proceed to BURBURE for the purpose of making "A" Frames for XIII Corps.	
"	15th "		Companies worked as on Saturday last. 250 Infantry from Divisional Depot worked on NEWCASTLE LINE. The Commanding Officer visited "B" Coy; work on DURHAM LINE during the night. Capt. E.G.S.C. TISDALL rejoined Battalion from P.O.W. Cage. Lt. takes command of "B" Coy.	
"	16th "		Companies worked as usual. Casualties. 1. O.R. "C" Coy wounded remained at duty.	
"	17th "		Companies worked as usual. The Commanding Officer visited the NEWCASTLE LINE with C.R.E in the morning and reconnoitred a new line which may be dug from NEWCASTLE LINE about F.3.d.6.5. to TUNING FORK SWITCH. Casualties 1. O.R. wounded. 1. O.R. wounded, remained at duty.	
"	18th "		Companies worked as usual, and 250 men from Divisional Depot worked on NEWCASTLE LINE	

Army Form C. 2118.

WAR DIARY
of
INTELLIGENCE SUMMARY.
(Erase heading not required.)

Instructions regarding War Diaries and Intelligence Summaries are contained in F. S. Regs., Part II. and the Staff Manual respectively. Title pages will be prepared in manuscript.

Place	Date	Hour	Summary of Events and Information	Remarks and references to Appendices
BETHUNE	July 19th 1918		Companies worked as usual. From to-night and until Sat: 27th inst. a party of 200 from Divisional Depôt are to work each night on NEWCASTLE LINE. They will not work on Sunday.	
"	20th		Companies worked as usual. The Commanding Officer inspected Rioting Platoon of "C" Coy at 11 am this morning. Casualties. 1. O.R. "B" Coy wounded, remained at duty	
"	21st		Being Sunday no working parties were found except that by the prisoners and a small number of men of "B" Coy, who were required to fill in shell holes on road in BEUVRY. The party working on dumps under the C.R.E. has now to be increased to 12. O.R. "B" Coy are supplying the extra men who have to report to C.R.E. at 9 am this morning. The band played in the Public Gardens from 6 p.m to 8 pm. A musical evening was given by a concert party in the Palladium for the benefit of the T.M. Battery, but the battalion was also invited	
"	22nd		Companies worked as usual. Casualties 1. O.R. C Coy wounded, remained at duty. Draft. 2 O.Rs. R.Q.M.S TOWNSEND W.J and Cpl DRUCE.	

Army Form C. 2118.

WAR DIARY
~~INTELLIGENCE SUMMARY.~~
(Erase heading not required.)

Instructions regarding War Diaries and Intelligence Summaries are contained in F. S. Regs., Part II. and the Staff Manual respectively. Title pages will be prepared in manuscript.

Place	Date	Hour	Summary of Events and Information	Remarks and references to Appendices
BETHUNE	July 23rd 1918		Companies worked as usual. Orders have been received from Corps to the effect that three belts of wire have to be erected, 70, 55 and 40 yards respectively in front of NEWCASTLE LINE starting from existing wire at F.2.d.7.9. and joining up with wire of TUNING FORK LINE at F.4.b central. For this work a party of 300 men from the Battle details of 137th, 138th and 139th Brigades, are to be provided daily. They will work in reliefs of 100 men, at 3am, 9am, and 3pm. and O.s.t "C" "B" and "A" Coys are responsible for finding an officer and the necessary guides for the work. This order will take effect as from to-morrow. Six men have been ordered to-night to report to R.E.s for work on NORTH MIDLAND dump as from to-morrow morning. They are being found by O.C."A" Coy, and they will be rationed and billeted by the R.E.s.	
"	24th		Companies worked as usual. The wiring of NEWCASTLE LINE was carried on, but all three parties were troubled by hostile shelling throughout the day. Casualties, 2. O.R. "C" Coy, wounded, remained at duty.	
"	25th		Companies worked as usual. The wiring parties were not troubled by shelling throughout the day.	

WAR DIARY

~~INTELLIGENCE~~ SUMMARY

(Erase heading not required.)

Army Form C. 2118.

Place	Date	Hour	Summary of Events and Information	Remarks and references to Appendices
BETHUNE	July 1918	26th	In spite of the very wet night Companies worked as usual. The wiring of the new portion of NEWCASTLE LINE has to be completed if possible by to-morrow night as no infantry parties will be available after 27th inst. for this work.	
"		27th	Companies worked as usual. Capt. N.C. BATTEN has to day been admitted to hospital and Lt. A.W. GOLDSWORTHY takes over command of "C" Coy. The wiring of the new portion of the NEWCASTLE LINE as far as F.4.b.2.6. is now complete except for the placing of top Notice Boards and concertinas etc., at roads and gaps.	
"		28th	Being Sunday no working parties were found, excepting Prisoners. During the evening the Band played in the Public Gardens. About 8.45 p.m. billets in the vicinity of Headquarters Mess and Orderly Room were shelled.	
"		29th	At about 3 A.M. billets in the vicinity of Headquarters Mess and Orderly Room were shelled. Casualties 2 O.R's wounded and 1 O.R wounded remained at duty. Sgt Joshua B. who has been Orderly Room Sergeant since May 1915 was wounded and has gone to Hospital. It is a great loss to the Battalion. Companies worked as on Saturday. Both "A" and "C" Coy are now working by day. Officers and guides for the supervision of the 200 men from the	

Army Form C. 2118.

WAR DIARY
or
INTELLIGENCE SUMMARY.
(Erase heading not required.)

Place	Date	Hour	Summary of Events and Information	Remarks and references to Appendices
BETHUNE	July 29th 1918 (cont⁴)		Divisional Depot Battalion were supplied by O⁵C 'A' and 'C' Coy. during the night. 250 men are working for us on Wednesday and Thursday nights this week. The preliminary heats for the 46th Divisional Sports took place this afternoon. Both our Officers' and Mens' Tug-of-War teams were successful against the teams of the A.S.C. who in both cases were by far the heavier sides.	
"	" 30th		Companies worked as usual. The Commanding Officer visited the work with the A/C.R.E. It has been decided that work on the new portion of the NEWCASTLE LINE from F.3.d.8.6. to F.4.b.2.5. shall be concentrated on three Posts. About F.4.c.05.45., F.4.c.50.60, F.4.a.95.30., respectively. The Breast work is to be erected first and finally the posts will be connected up to form a continuous line.	
"	" 31st		Companies worked as usual. Draft 39 O.R. joined Divisional Depot as reinforcements. Strength of Battalion. Off. 41 O.R. 946.	

Jenkins Lieut. Colonel
Commanding 1st Batt The Monmouthshire Reg⁴. T.F.

Secret & Confidential

Army Form C. 2118.

Vol 39

WAR DIARY
or
INTELLIGENCE SUMMARY.
(Erase heading not required.)

1st Batt The Monmouthshire Regt. T.F.

August 1st 1918 to August 31st 1918

Army Form C. 2118.

WAR DIARY
~~INTELLIGENCE SUMMARY~~
(Erase heading not required.)

Place	Date	Hour	Summary of Events and Information	Remarks and references to Appendices
BETHUNE	Aug 1918	1st	Companies worked as usual. The new LINE of RETENTION between LA MOTTE FARM and LIVERPOOL LINE has to be wired first. This work will commence on Saturday night. Stores are being distributed at 4 different dumps along the line. Lt. G.P. PEACHELL and 26 men of B.Coy will work on this to-night and to-morrow.	
"	"	2nd	No working parties were found to-day except about 26 men of B.Coy. who have to complete the carrying up of stores for wiring new LINE of RETENTION. Divisional Sports were held. Unfortunately it rained very heavily which rather put a damper on everything. However the sports were run with remarkable success and those who were present spent a very enjoyable day. Four lorries were obtained to convey personnel to the show. The Band played there from 11.a.m. till after lunch. The Tug of War teams of the battalion met with marked success. The mens' team under the coaching of the R.S.M. and the officers under the coaching of the Colonel. In the finals the mens' team pulled the 231 Bde R.F.A. over without much difficulty. The officers'	

WAR DIARY
INTELLIGENCE SUMMARY
(Erase heading not required.)

Army Form C. 2118.

Place	Date	Hour	Summary of Events and Information	Remarks and references to Appendices
BETHUNE	AUG	2nd continued	team however met with some considerable opposition by the team representing Divisional H.Q. At one time five of our side were pulled over the line. After doing the turn however we soon regained our lost ground and pulled Division over. The Battalion Transport turnout gained 3rd prize.	
"		3rd	Companies worked as usual. The new LINE of RETENTION between LA MOTTE FARM and LIVERPOOL LINE was taped out by the C.O. this morning. This line is to be wired first and for this purpose four officers have been placed in charge of 4 sectors; they have taped the line of their wire so as to be ready for the 210 Infantry of Brigade Battle Details who arrive at KANTARA DUMP at 3-30 am to-morrow morning. This work has to be completed in 3 days time i.e. three belts of double apron in front of line of trench. Lt S. MURRAY. M.C. and 2nd Lieut T.I. SIMPSON have today left the Battalion for transfer to the R.A.F. They are struck off strength.	
"		4th	Sunday. Companies worked as usual today as the weekly holiday was given on Friday August 2nd in view of the DIVISIONAL SHOW.	

Army Form C. 2118.

WAR DIARY
~~INTELLIGENCE SUMMARY~~

(Erase heading not required.)

Instructions regarding War Diaries and Intelligence Summaries are contained in F. S. Regs., Part II. and the Staff Manual respectively. Title pages will be prepared in manuscript.

Place	Date	Hour	Summary of Events and Information	Remarks and references to Appendices
BETHUNE	Aug 1918	4th continued	The wiring of the new LINE of RETENTION was commenced early this morning. A Platoon of "A" Coy have to work on Northern portion of NEWCASTLE LINE in X.19.a. where the trench has to be continued as far as the LAWE Canal. This portion has to be wired first and for this reason, material is being sent up from ESSARS Dump. To-day being the 4th Anniversary of declaration of War, a united Church of England and Non-Conformist Service was held at 6 p.m. in the Palladium. A large number attended.	
"	"	5th	Companies worked as usual. The 250 Infantry from the Divisional Depot Batt. worked under "C" Coy on erecting Breastwork at posts in X.4.c.0.6., X.4.c.5.8., X.4.a.9.3. This party is now working by day from 8.30 am to 4 p.m. Work on Left Brigade H.Q. is now complete so far as it concerns us	
"	"	6th	Companies worked as usual. Three belts of Wire are now completed in front of the new portion of the LINE of RETENTION	
"	"	7th	Companies worked as usual.	
"	"	8th	Companies worked as usual. Casualties 3 O.R. C Coy wounded, Remained at Duty.	#

Army Form C. 2118.

WAR DIARY
or
INTELLIGENCE SUMMARY.
(Erase heading not required.)

Place	Date	Hour	Summary of Events and Information	Remarks and references to Appendices
BETHUNE	AUG 1918	9th	"B" Company find 30 men for work on repairing forward roads under O.C. 465 Field Company R.E. This party report at ESSARS Stone dump at 8.30pm. A further twenty men of "B" Coy are being employed under 465 Field Coy R.E. in erecting Concrete Shelters. Half this party reports to CHAMBOARD Barracks at 7-30 p.m. The remainder reporting at 8.30 am from to-morrow onwards for day work. In view of the likelihood of the Enemy withdrawing his line, orders have been issued to the effect that this Battalion has to provide one Company to form part of The Reserve Brigade which in case of a withdrawal of over 1500 yards, would be used as an advanced guard of all arms. "A" Company has been detailed for this and has to be ready to move at 3 hours notice	
"	"	10th	Companies worked as usual. "B" Coy work was hindered for 1 hour owing to heavy shelling (H.E. & Gas) Bombing E.A were very active and about 50 Bombs were dropped on BETHUNE between 9pm and 10pm. BETHUNE was shelled by H.V Gun between 4 am & 5 am 11th inst. Casualties 1. O.R. "B" Coy Wounded, remained at duty. Draft 13. O.R.	

WAR DIARY
INTELLIGENCE SUMMARY

Army Form C. 2118.

Place	Date	Hour 1918	Summary of Events and Information	Remarks and references to Appendices
BETHUNE	AUG	11th	Twenty five men of "B" and "C" Coys each are working today so that they may be able to attend the XIII Corps Horse Show to-morrow. Being Sunday the remainder of the Battalion did not work. The Band played in the Public Gardens. Capt. W.M.B. BURNYEAT. M.C. rejoined the Batt. from Hospital.	
"	"	12th	Companies worked as usual. Five hundred Infantry from Brigade in Reserve worked on New Portion of NEWCASTLE LINE from 4 am — 11 am this morning. They will also work to-morrow. This line is being dug throughout to a depth of 2', and when material becomes available the necessary breastwork will be erected at selected posts. The XIII Corps Horse Show was held to-day at FERFAY. The Battalion won the Pioneer Battalion Transport Turnout. The Tug of War team was pulled over by the Gordon Highlanders.	
"	"	13th	Companies worked as usual. The 500 Infantry have today completed the new portion of NEWCASTLE LINE digging a 2' trench throughout. Casualties 2 OR "C" Coy Wounded.	

Army Form C. 2118.

WAR DIARY
or
INTELLIGENCE SUMMARY.
(Erase heading not required.)

Place	Date	Hour 1918	Summary of Events and Information	Remarks and references to Appendices
BETHUNE	AUG	14th	Companies worked as usual. Another party of 500 Infantry will work as under on 16th, 17th & 18th instant. "A" & "C" Coys will employ men tomorrow on erecting Breastwork revetment at selected posts in the new LINE of RETENTION.	
"	"	15th	Companies worked as usual. The 250 Infantry party worked for "C" Coy as is usual on Thursdays.	
"	"	16th	Companies worked as usual. 500 Infantry worked on the new portion of LINE of RETENTION. Work on this line is being concentrated on certain Posts which finally will be joined up to form a continuous line. Casualties 1 OR "B" Coy Wounded, remained at Duty. Draft. 1. OR.	
"	"	17th	Companies worked as usual. "B" Coy party working on HAMEL ALLEY were shelled returning from Work. Casualties:- 2 OR Killed in Action. 2 OR Wounded. 2 OR Wounded, still at Duty. d/18-8-18.	
"	"	18th	Being Sunday, Companies found no working parties. The 500 Infantry worked on the LINE of RETENTION. At 7 p.m. a concert was given with considerable success. The Palladium was full.	
"	"	19th	Companies worked as usual. A few men of "B" Coy have commenced a Battalion Battle Headquarters, about E.5 c 7.2.	

Army Form C. 2118.

WAR DIARY
or
INTELLIGENCE SUMMARY
(Erase heading not required.)

Place	Date	Hour	Summary of Events and Information	Remarks and references to Appendices
BETHUNE	Aug 1918	20th	Companies worked as usual. Casualties 1.OR "C" Coy Wounded, remained at Duty. Reinforcements 9. OR.	
"		21st	Companies worked as usual except that "B" Coy have to find 40 men to-night to work on Roads in the forward area under 465 Fld Coy. R.E. The enemy is rapidly withdrawing his line. The withdrawal is apparently pivoting on CAILLOUX Post and according to the latest intelligence the line today runs as follows:- CAILLOUX KEEP - RUE d L'EPINETTE to S 19 b 2.0. - X 24 a 0.7. X18 c 3.4. along RUE DE BOIS to X16 b 5.0. - X 10 d 3.2 - X3 c 2.5. where patrols are pushing forward up Canal. It is probable that the enemy will make every endeavour to delay our advance until his final withdrawal to The AUBERS Ridge which if it comes about will probably be rapidly carried out.	
"		22nd	Companies worked as usual today. The 500 Infantry parties worked on LINE of RETENTION and will do so on 23rd and 24th inst. 250 Infantry from Div Depôt worked on "A" "B" & "C" Posts. Orders have today been received to the effect that Road work is Priority at the moment.	

WAR DIARY
or
INTELLIGENCE SUMMARY.

Army Form C. 2118.

Place	Date	Hour	Summary of Events and Information	Remarks and references to Appendices
BETHUNE	AUG 22nd Continued		Tomorrow 250 men of the Battalion are working on forward Roads. Half will work on LOISNE – LE TOURET Road, which has to be made fit for Lorry Traffic. The other half will work on road between TUNING FORK and ROUTE "A" KEEP. This has to be made fit for Regimental Transport. Orders have been received that the Resting Platoon be moved from the hutments at FOUQUIERES into billets there. At 12 noon today our front line runs as follows, the general line is unchanged since yesterday. S.19 d 7.1., S.19 d 4.5., X 24 a 5.0., X 24 a 4.6., X 17 d 8.5., X 17 b 3.3., X 17 a 9.6., X.17 a 45.30., X.16 b 90.75., X.10 d 08.15., X.10 c 60.95., X.10 a 20.08., X 9 b 20.50., X 9 a 98.95., X 3 c 50.80., X 3 a 35.30.,	
"	23rd		Approximately 100 men of the Battalion worked on LOISNE – LE TOURET road this morning and 150 men on TUNING FORK – ROUTE "A" Keep Road. 500 Infantry were employed as yesterday on the LINE of RETENTION. Orders have to-day been received to the effect that the Battalion will do no further work on NEWCASTLE LINE after the Infantry Party has worked to-morrow. To-morrow the Battalion is to be employed on forward road	

WAR DIARY
or
INTELLIGENCE SUMMARY.

(Erase heading not required.)

Army Form C. 2118.

Place	Date	Hour	Summary of Events and Information	Remarks and references to Appendices
BETHUNE	Aug 1918	23rd Continued	repairs. "A" Coy will find approximately 100 men for work on LOISNE - LE TOURET Road. "C" Coy will find approximately 180 men for work on TUNING FORK - ROUTE "A" KEEP Road. "B" Coy will find 100 men (approx) for work on Roads under O.C. 465 Field Coy R.E.	
"	"	24th	Companies worked as detailed yesterday. The general line of our Front line is the same to-day as it was at noon yesterday except for a slight improvement on Right Brigade Front.	
"	"	25th	Being Sunday no working parties were found by us to-day. A United Service (C of E & N.C.) was held in Palladium at 6 p.m. At 7-15 p.m. a most successful Sing-Song was held under arrangements made by Lt G. P. PEACHELL.	
"	"	26th	Companies worked as on Saturday last. No appreciable change in the situation.	
"	"	27th	Companies worked as yesterday. Reinforcements:- Major R. B. Pughe-Morgan "C" Coy. 2nd Lt E. A. S. Hixon "A" Coy. 2nd Lt A. T. Williams "A" Coy and 1 O.R.	

WAR DIARY
INTELLIGENCE SUMMARY

Army Form C. 2118.

Place	Date 1918	Hour	Summary of Events and Information	Remarks and references to Appendices
BETHUNE	AUG 28th		Companies worked on roads as usual. "B" Coy provided 40 men to work on clearing SUGAR DRAIN, working from LAWE CANAL at X.13.d.3.0.	
"	" 29th		Companies worked on roads as usual.	
"	" 30th		Companies worked to-day as yesterday. This evening orders were received from C.R.E. to the effect that work must be concentrated on EMPERORS Rd from X.16.d.2.9. North and on RUE de BOIS from X.16.d.05.90 East. In order to carry this into effect "B" Coy except Drainage Party on SUGAR Drain will work on EMPERORS Road and "C" Coy on RUE de BOIS forward. 50 men of "A" Coy work daily from to-morrow on extension of LOISNE Light Railway. "C" Company is to move forward to billets in ESSARS. Owing to shortage of accommodation only 2 Platoons will move up tomorrow. The remainder of the Company will move forward on Monday Sept 2nd.	
"	" 31st		Companies worked as yesterday. Two Platoons of "C" Coy have moved up into billets in ESSARS. Casualties "A" Coy. 2 OR Wounded "C" 2 OR wounded. Strength of Battalion OFF 40 O.R. 946.	

A. Jenkins Lieut-Col.
Commanding 1/1st Batt. The Monmouthshire Regt-T.F.

WR 40
P/46

P/46

WAR DIARY.

1/1st Batt. The Monmouthshire Regt. T.F.

1st September 1918 to 30th September 1918

Secret
&
Confidential

WAR DIARY
or
INTELLIGENCE SUMMARY.
(Erase heading not required.)

Army Form C. 2118.

Place	Date	Hour	Summary of Events and Information	Remarks and references to Appendices
BETHUNE	Sept 1st 1918		Companies worked as yesterday although it is Sunday. This was ordered owing to the urgency of the work. A Roman Catholic and United C of E & N.C. Services were held at 5 p.m. and 5.30 p.m. respectively. At 7.30 a Battalion concert was given arranged by Lieut Prachill. It was a great success. Orders have to-day been received to the effect that "A" Coy will in future provide 100 Men and 2 Officers daily for work on the LOISNE – LE TOURET Light Railway. "B" & "C" Coy have to concentrate their energies on the RUE DE BOIS. East of the point X 16 d O.8. They start work there to-morrow. A Light Railway Push track is to be laid along the Right hand side of this road.	
"	2nd		A party of 100 from "A" Coy worked on the LOISNE Light Railway. Repairing existing line and laying extension, supervised by No 8 Forward Coy. Remainder of "A" Company carried on with repair of X roads at TUNING FORK SWITCH. "B" and "C" Companies concentrated on repairing RUE de BOIS. This road is in fairly good condition west of LE TOURET.	

Army Form C. 2118.

WAR DIARY
or
INTELLIGENCE SUMMARY.
(Erase heading not required.)

Instructions regarding War Diaries and Intelligence Summaries are contained in F. S. Regs., Part II. and the Staff Manual respectively. Title pages will be prepared in manuscript.

Place	Date	Hour	Summary of Events and Information	Remarks and references to Appendices
BETHUNE	Sept 1918	3rd	"A", "B", & "C" Companies carried out work as yesterday. Major General W. THWAITES C.B. Commanding 46th Division is leaving the Division to take up post at WAR OFFICE as Director of Intelligence. The following Special Order of the Day was published "To all Ranks of the 46th DIVISION. I desire in all sincerity to express my utmost regret at leaving my Division to take up an appointment at Home, to which I have been ordered at a moment when the great cause for which we are fighting seems to be within reasonable distance of attainment. Apart from this, the association of over two years with the Division leaves memories which cannot be effaced. We have had our bad times and our good times but have pulled through together solid and determined during the former and with their fine spirit and good comradeship during the latter. I cannot thank all ranks sufficiently for the loyal support they have rendered me during the period of my command. I leave the Division in full confidence that the spirit which pervades it will carry it through to the end of the war to great achievements. Do not forget what I have so often expressed "Remember the Honor of the 46th Division."	JJ

Army Form C. 2118.

WAR DIARY
INTELLIGENCE SUMMARY.
(Erase heading not required.)

Place	Date	Hour	Summary of Events and Information	Remarks and references to Appendices
BETHUNE	Sept 3rd 1918 (continued)		I wish the Division the very best of luck in all it may be called upon today and may God be with it. (Signed) W. THWAITES, Major General, Commanding 46th Division. 2nd Sept. 1918. Reinforcements 3 O.R.	
"	4th		"A" Coy worked as yesterday on Light Railway + Tuning Fork X Roads. "B" Coy worked on the RUE de BOIS, forward of LOISNE STREAM and also had a party of 20 men on drainage clearing SUGAR drain. "C" Coy commenced laying Light Railway along the RUE de BOIS from LE TOURET Rd forward. The remainder of the Company repaired RUE de BOIS forward to the LOISNE STREAM. Shelling of this road took place during to the 46th DIVISION in conjunction with 19th DIVISION on left pushing forward their line. Casualties 1 OR. "C" Coy. Wounded. Reinforcements 1 OR.	
"	5		"A" Company found working parties as yesterday. "B" Coy worked on drainage as yesterday, the remainder and also "C" Coy worked on forward portion of the RUE de BOIS to a point about HAYSTACK POST S.14.b. The C.R.E. 46th DIVISION handed over all R.E. and Pioneer work to C.R.E. 19th Division. Lieut J.G. FRAMPTON rejoined from Hospital.	

Army Form C. 2118.

WAR DIARY
or
INTELLIGENCE SUMMARY.
(Erase heading not required.)

Instructions regarding War Diaries and Intelligence Summaries are contained in F.S. Regs., Part II. and the Staff Manual respectively. Title pages will be prepared in manuscript.

Place	Date	Hour	Summary of Events and Information	Remarks and references to Appendices
BETHUNE	Sept 1918	6th	No working parties were found to-day. "A" & "B" Coys were at disposal of O.C. Coys for cleaning up and kit inspection. "C" Coy moved billets from ESSARS to BETHUNE. The move was completed by 12 noon. O.C. "C" Coy reported the loss of rear half limber which the Company had been using for carting road metal and man-handling same. The limber was eventually found at HEN'S POST S.3.d.0.3 by Rfn RALPH A.C. Headquarters Runner. The wagon had been dropped into a shell hole on side of the road and carefully camouflaged.	
"	"	7th	All three Companies carried out training to-day from 9 a.m. to 12-30 in separate fields adjoining billets. The Battalion weekly concert was held in the PALLADIUM to-day instead of Sunday as formerly.	
"	"	8th	No training was carried out to-day being Sunday. Owing to inclement weather the United Service of C.E. and N.C. which was to have been held in the Gardens was held in the Palladium close to Billets. Weather unsettled and showery. Lt. C.T.A. WATERS proceeded to United Kingdom for a course of signalling.	
"	"	9th	"A" Coy carried out firing on Range all day at range at LABEUVRIERE. "B" & "C" Companies carried out training on grounds adjoining billets. Weather very unsettled and a	

Army Form C. 2118.

WAR DIARY
or
INTELLIGENCE SUMMARY.
(Erase heading not required.)

Place	Date	Hour	Summary of Events and Information	Remarks and references to Appendices
BETHUNE	Sept 9th 1918 (Cont.)		good deal of rain falling throughout the day	
"	10th		All Companies carried out training on Coy parade grounds. H.Q. Details paraded in the forenoon for instruction under L.G. Officer. Divisional operation Orders were received in the evening for move of the 46th Division. The Battalion will move billets to LAPUGNOY to-morrow. New billets will not be available until 7 P.M. The Battalion will thin entrain at CALONNE RICOUART at 6.28 a.m. for unknown destination.	
"	11		Training by all Companies was carried out to day from 9 A.M. to 11 A.M. The Battalion paraded on the BETHUNE - ANNEZIN Rd. close to billets at 4.30 P.M. in following order. A - B - Buglers - C Coys. followed by H.Q Details under Lt. S.W. ERT. The transport was picked up at ANNEZIN close to the transport lines. The march to LAPUGNOY was via ANNEZIN - FOUQUEREUIL - LABEUVRIERE. The Battalion marched into LAPUGNOY at about 6.30 p.m and moved straight into billets vacated by the 45th SHERWOOD FORESTERS. Lt A.W. GOLDSWORTHY and 1 N.C.O per Coy and one N.C.O from Transport and Q.M Stores preceded from CALONNE-RICOUART at 6.28 p.m by train in advance as billeting party. The weather is very unsettled and promises more rain. Reinforcements: 2 O.R.	

Army Form C. 2118.

WAR DIARY
of
INTELLIGENCE SUMMARY.
(Erase heading not required.)

Instructions regarding War Diaries and Intelligence
Summaries are contained in F. S. Regs., Part II.
and the Staff Manual respectively. Title pages
will be prepared in manuscript.

Place	Date	Hour	Summary of Events and Information	Remarks and references to Appendices
LAPUGNOY	Sept. 12th	1918	The transport moved off at 2 a.m. to march to CALONNE-RICOUART station to be at station three hours before departure of train. The Battalion paraded at 2.45 a.m. in a very dark and wet morning and reached CALONNE-RICOUART station at 5 a.m. to find that entraining of transport had not commenced. The train being reported four hours late. The rain was still coming down very heavily and by this time everyone was wet through, however tea was provided for everyone from the Company cookers. The train moved into the station at 8 a.m. and by 10.30 a.m. all transport was loaded up and we moved off immediately. CORBIE was reached at 8 p.m. where provision was made for tea for the Battalion. The Battalion then marched to LA HOUSSOYE about 5 miles N.W. of CORBIE where billets had been fixed up. The billets were fairly good on the whole, although most of the officers billets were far from rain proof.	
LA HOUSSOYE	13th "		Companies were placed at disposal of O.C. Companys during the forenoon for cleaning up generally and for repair to billets. In the afternoon boys carried out training from 2 to 4 p.m. The training ground allotted to the Battalion is an excellent one extending from LAHOUSSOYE to a point on the road 1000 yds. N.W. of FRANVILLERS	

Army Form C. 2118.

WAR DIARY
or
INTELLIGENCE SUMMARY.
(Erase heading not required.)

Instructions regarding War Diaries and Intelligence Summaries are contained in F. S. Regs., Part II. and the Staff Manual respectively. Title pages will be prepared in manuscript.

Place	Date	Hour	Summary of Events and Information	Remarks and references to Appendices
LAHOUSSOYE	Sept 14th 1918		Companies paraded at 9 am and carried out training until 12.30 pm paying particular attention to Platoon training in attack, artillery formation and attacked order drill. In the afternoon no training was carried out. In view of inspection by G.O.C. boys cleaned up generally.	
"	15th		The Battalion including transport paraded at 9.30 am LAHOUSSOYE and marched past the G.O.C. on the main ALBERT— PONT-NOYELLES Rd at a point C.28.d.8.0. on the following order. Pioneers & Signallers followed by "A" Coy — Bugles — "B" & "C" Coys then transport, 100 yards between Coys and 50 yards between every 12 vehicles. The state of Battalion on march was as follows. 26 Officers 690 O.R. Transport 16 vehicles and 63 animals. Dress, Fighting Order. The G.O.C. informed Col. JENKINS that he considered the whole turn out excellent and desired the C.O. to inform his men how very pleased he was with the discipline on march and general good turn-out. The Battalion finished with a short route march by HENU-BONNAY and thence back to billets. No training was carried out in the afternoon The C.O. 4/34th and Coy Commanders went out in the afternoon to reconnoitre ground between MERICOURT & BONNAY eastwards in view of the likelihood of the	

Army Form C. 2118.

WAR DIARY
or
INTELLIGENCE SUMMARY.
(Erase heading not required.)

Place	Date	Hour	Summary of Events and Information	Remarks and references to Appendices
LAHOUSSOYE	Sept	15th 19/8 (cont)	Battalion being used in Brigade scheme on the 16th. The weather continues fine.	
"		16th	Programme of training was carried out today as follows. During the morning "B" & "C" Coys on range practiced attack by platoons in lines of sections as follows. Commencing 300 yards from targets double for 100 yards fire two rounds p/man, then advance another 100 yards at double and fire one round & doubly advance 50 yards and fire two rounds standing. This method of attack was carried out in accordance with G.O.C's special orders. In the afternoon all Companies carried out practice in attack by platoons.	
"		17th	"A" & "D" carried out training on the range and "B" Coy was bathing during the forenoon. All Coys. carried out an outpost scheme during the afternoon.	
"		18th	Training was carried out as follows "B" & "C" Coy Platoon, attack on range, Platoon drill etc. from 9am to 12.30. In the afternoon recreational training "C" Coy were attached to 137th Brigade on Brigade scheme. In the afternoon orders from Division were received, placing the Battalion at 2 hours notice to move. At 7.30 pm orders were received for the Battalion to parade at HEILLY at 8.15pm to embus with the 139th Brigade for an unknown destination. The Transport	⟨signature⟩

Army Form C. 2118.

WAR DIARY
or
INTELLIGENCE SUMMARY.
(Erase heading not required.)

Place	Date	Hour	Summary of Events and Information	Remarks and references to Appendices
LAHOUSSOYE	Sept 1918	18th (cont')	joined the 139th Brigade Transport column at 10.45 p.m. The 139th Brigade Bn. column of about 150 buses moved off at 10 p.m. and at 2 p.m. debussed on the main road between MONS-EN-CHAUSSÉE and VERMAND at Q.27.c. sheet FRANCE 62c and bivouaced on side of road until dawn. Shelters were constructed by the Battalion in wood at Q.33.c. and this consisted of digging in and covering over with corrugated sheets. The Battalion spent the remainder of the day in making shelters. The weather fortunately continued fine. Owing to very heavy bombing of this wood by enemy aircraft all men had to get below ground level. On the night previous to arrival of Battalion the enemy dropped 150 bombs in the wood causing about 15 casualties to Labour Battalion billeted there.	
Sheet FRANCE 62c Q.33d	"	19th	The Battalion transport arrived at about 3-30 a.m. and transport lines were found on north side of the wood close to billets. All companies carried out training during the morning. In the afternoon improvements to billets were carried on with	
"	"	20th	Platoon training was carried out during the morning. In the afternoon work	

WAR DIARY
or
INTELLIGENCE SUMMARY.
(Erase heading not required.)

Army Form C. 2118.

Place	Date	Hour	Summary of Events and Information	Remarks and references to Appendices
[Q.33.c] Sheet FAVREUIL 62c	Sept 1918	20th (contd)	on billets was carried on with Instructions were received from C.R.E. that the Battalion would take over work from the 4th AUSTRALIAN PIONEERS and take over their billets in vicinity of VENDELLES. The Adjutant Capt W.M.JAMES returned from 14 days leave.	
"	"	21st	O.C. boys but representatives of the 4th AUSTRALIAN PIONEERS at VENDELLES at 1 a.m. and took over the following work consisting of repair of roads as follows:- "A" Coy on road between VERMAND & VADENCOURT and forward to R.G.C. "B" Coy on road between VENDELLES & LE VERGUIER and thence forward through L.28. "C" Coy on road between VENDELLES & JEANCOURT then forward through L.26 and L.21. H.& C. also on the JEANCOURT – HESBECOURT Rd Companies paraded at 7 a.m. and marched independently to VENDELLES. The 4th AUSTRALIAN PIONEERS having received orders during the night everything then was "A.B.&C. Companies had to find other billets, and these were found as follows:- "A" Coy in old trench at R.2.d. "B" Coy in trench R.2.c.2.9. "C" Coy R.2.c.3.2. Battalion H.Q. and details marched to VENDELLES and took up billets vacated by 4th AUSTRALIANS who had orders to move out about noon Headquarters are situated in the Quarry at	Y

WAR DIARY
or
INTELLIGENCE SUMMARY

Army Form C. 2118.

(Erase heading not required.)

Place	Date 1918	Hour	Summary of Events and Information	Remarks and references to Appendices
[Q33c] FRANCE 62!	Sept 21st (Continued)		North side of railway. Reinforcement 1. O.R.	
VENDELLES	" 22nd		Companies worked on Roads as taken over by O/C Coys from 4th AUSTRALIAN PIONEERS yesterday. Casualties 1. O.R. killed (Rfn MORSE) S.B. and 2. O.R. wounded A.Coy	
"	" 23rd		Companies worked as usual	
"	" 24th		Companies worked as usual	
"	" 25th		Companies worked as yesterday. The C.R.E. Lt Col. Moorshedd D.S.O. was wounded this afternoon. Orders have been received late this evening ordering A and C Coys to work on road running North East from LE VERGUIER from L.34.a.6.3 to L.29.c.3.8. to-morrow. 20 men of B Coy will have to work on advanced Divisional H.Q. to-morrow. Capt W.H. TALFOURD-JONES R.A.M.C. (Medical Officer) admitted to Hospital today accidentally injured	
"	" 26		Companies worked as detailed yesterday. Casualties B.Coy – 1.O.R. killed, 6. O.R" wounded Lieut G.P. PEACHELL & 2. O.R" wounded remained at duty. A. Coy 2. O.R" wounded Reinforcements 6 O.R" reported to Battalion from the Base	

Army Form C. 2118.

WAR DIARY
or
INTELLIGENCE SUMMARY.
(Erase heading not required.)

Instructions regarding War Diaries and Intelligence Summaries are contained in F. S. Regs., Part II. and the Staff Manual respectively. Title pages will be prepared in manuscript.

Place	Date	Hour	Summary of Events and Information	Remarks and references to Appendices
VENDELLES	Sept. 27th	1918	During the day Coys worked as usual on roads. At about 4 p.m. wire was received from Division ordering whole Battalion to work on carrying T.M. ammunition from SOMERVILLE WOOD about G.32.c.4.0. to front line. In spite of working full hours during the day the Battalion moved off again at 7 p.m. to carry out above task. During the afternoon Operation Order No. 67 was received from C.R.E. and in consequence the Commanding Officer held a Coy Commanders Conference at 5 p.m. Casualties 2.O6th wounded 3.O6th wounded awarded to duty	
	28th		It is assumed H.O.I. today is Z day and Commanding Officer holds a conference of all Officers at 12 noon. Battalion Operation Orders Nos 2/34/2 and 2/34/3 are issued by Lieut-Col J. Jenkins M.C. At 7.30 p.m. notification is received to the effect that tomorrow will be Z day and Zero will be 5.50 a.m. After damping packs Band Instruments etc the Battalion moved off and presently about 9.30 p.m. At midnight September 28th/29th the Battalion Headquarters took up its position at G.32.d.45.80. Capt. R. McALPINE RAMC reported for duty as MO from H.Q. Bn M.G. Coy. Casualties 2.O6th B Coy wounded, 1.O6th C Coy wounded.	

WAR DIARY
or
INTELLIGENCE SUMMARY.

Army Form C. 2118.

Place	Date	Hour	Summary of Events and Information	Remarks and references to Appendices
G.32.d.u.5.60	Sept 29th	1918	A & B Coys were employed carrying cork Pier Bridges and Super-structures up to a position immediately behind the assaulting Brigade (137th). These were to be used on the crossing of the ST QUENTIN CANAL and were to be erected immediately the 137th Infantry Brigade had crossed. This material was all brought forward by 5 am to VICTORIA CROSS ROADS. At ZERO our Barrage opened with all its fury, and with it the fog which had shown signs of increasing, suddenly thickened so that it shortly became impossible to see more than a few yards ahead. At ZERO + 15 minutes A and B Coys moved forward and commenced carrying their material to the Canal. In spite of the very dense fog both Coys reached the Canal quickly and plenty of the Bridging material was hauled up. At ZERO + 20 minutes C Coy moved forward and commenced work on road WATLING STREET and to Canal via tracks running South-East through G.28.c, G.34.a and b. Casualties during morning Capt E.G. ST.C. TISDALL, wounded M.G. fire and Capt W.M.B. BURNYEAT wounded slight. Battalion H.Q. were established at G.33.b.05.80 at from 6.30am. After a short rest for lunch boys again set out to work and this time crossed	

Army Form C. 2118.

WAR DIARY
or
INTELLIGENCE SUMMARY.
(Erase heading not required.)

Place	Date	Hour	Summary of Events and Information	Remarks and references to Appendices
G.33.b.05.80.	Sept 1918	29th contd	The Canal and worked on BELLENGLISE-JONCOURT Road as far as Road Junction	
		6.30 to 7.9.	Coys worked in following order from South to North; 'C' Coy, 'B' Coy, 'A' Coy During the morning operations 'A' Coy succeeded in capturing several prisoners about 22 in number, 'B' Coy took about 7 and 'C' about 15 - These last came to light after the fog had cleared away and while 'C' Coy were working on tracks near the Canal.	
			Casualties Officers wounded - 2	
			Other ranks - Wounded - 19, wounded Gas 5. O.R. Killed 1. O.R. wounded remained at duty 5. O.R.	
			Capt S.R. MARTYN reported to Battalion for duty from 17th Bn Northumberland Fusiliers Having worked continuously for nearly 48 hours Coys only worked 4 hours today. Works was carried out as allotted for 2nd Phase in Battalion Operation Orders viz. 'C' Coy G.35.a.55 to G.29.d.25.30 and 'A' Coy G.29.d.25.30.16 G.30.b.3.8. 'B' Coy	
		6.30.6.38	through MAGNY LA FOSSE. Casualties 1 O.R wounded	
		30th	Battalion H.Q. move to G.27.d.1.6.	

J.H. Reed Lieut.Colonel
Comdg 1/1st Bn. The Monmouthshire Regt. T.F.

ACCOUNT OF THE PART TAKEN BY THE I/Ist Batt MONMOUTHSHIRE REGIMENT,
In the Battles of
BELLENGLISE, RAMICOURT, & SEQUEHART.

ATTACK ON CANAL & BELLENGLISE. At about 6.0 pm. on the 27th Sept. after the Companies had returned from their days work, orders were received from Division ordering the whole Battalion to work on carrying Trench Mortar Ammunition from Somerville Wood to the front line that night. In spite of having worked all day the Battalion moved off at 7.0 pm. & after completing their task returned to billets about 2.0 am.

At 9.30 pm. on the 28th Sept. the Battalion moved off from its billets near VENDELLES in order to carry up bridging material as near to our front line as possible. This task was finished about I hour before zero, and the Battalion took up its position immediately behind the 137th Inf. Bde.

At Zero plus 15 minutes 'A' & 'B' Companies under Captain E.G.St.C.TISDALL. & Captain W.M.B.BURNYEAT,M.C. respectively, moved off forward and commenced carrying the Cork Pier Bridges to the Canal. In spite of the dense fog both companies reached the Canal quickly with large quantities of bridging material and immediately returned for more until it was all brought forward. This work was carried out under heavy shell and machine gun fire.

Meanwhile 'C' Company under Lieut A.W.GOLDSWORTHY had moved off at Zero plus 20 minutes, and commenced work on WATLING STREET, and on a track running S.E. to the Canal through G 28 c to G 34 a & b.

During the morning 'A' Company succeeded in taking several prisoners, about 22 in number, 'B' Company took 7, and 'C' about 15. These last were taken when the fog cleared away and when 'C' Company were working near the Canal.

After a short period of rest the Companies again set out for work and crossing the Canal, worked on the BELLENGLISE - JONCOURT Road until dark when they returned to our Old Front Line for the night.

During the day Captain E.G.St.C.TISDALL and Captain W.M.B.BURNYEAT,M.C. were wounded and besides these the Battalion had 30 O.R's casualties. During the following 3 days the Battalion worked on forward roads as far as the village of JONCOURT inclusive. During which time Lt. H.E.SHARPE was wounded and 16 O.Rs became casualties.

ATTACK ON RAMICOURT. At II.15 pm on the 2nd October 1918, Lieut.Col. J.JENKINS,M.C. received orders for the Battalion to move forward to SPRINGBOK VALLEY in readiness for a Divisional attack on RAMICOURT and MONTBREHAIN, which was to take place on the morning of the 3rd October. The Battalion was to be in reserve and attached to the 138th Inf. Bde.

The Battalion moved off at 2.30 am in order to take up its position, and at 4.0 am was reported in position.

At II.15 am orders were received for the Battalion to move forward into the Railway Cutting, S.E. of JONCOURT and take over from the I/5th LINCOLN REGIMENT, and to hold themselves in readiness to help repel any counter-attacks the enemy might make.

At 3.0pm 'B' & 'C' Companies received orders to move up and repel a counter attack which the enemy was making in force from the direction of MONTBREHAIN.

'A' Company, under Captain S.R.MARTYN, who had assumed command vice Captain E.G.ST.C.TISDALL, was held in reserve in the Railway Cutting, which the enemy subjected a fairly heavy bombardment Gas and H.E. shells.

At this time, bodies of cavalry and light Tanks moved across the Railway Cutting to co-operate in resisting the attack. The enemy apparently saw this movement as his bombardment became more intense.

'C' Company advanced in extended order across the open ground between the Railway Cutting and RAMICOURT.

This advance took place under a heavy bombardment of Gas and H.E.Shells and was ably conducted by Lieut A.W.GOLDSWORTHY in command.

'B' Company took up a position in reserve in the sunken road S.W. of the village, where they dug in, this relieved the 8th SHERWOOD FORESTERS' who were exhausted after the struggle of the day.

At approximately 1.0 am, 'A' Company who had suffered considerably from Gas concentration in the Railway Cutting at JONCOURT, received orders to move up on S.W. side of JONCOURT and if possible link up with 'C' Company, who were reported to be holding the line in front of RAMICOURT? and the 137th Inf. Bde. on the right.

In pitch darkness the Companies moved up and succeeded in digging itself in on a frontage of about 200 yards in a sunken road on S.W. of village and by means of patrols, established contact with the 5th N.STAFFS on the right flank and 'C' Company 180 yards on the left.

At Zero, 4th Oct. 'C' Company were ordered to send a strong fighting patrol into MONTBREHAIN under cover of barrage and if possible establish a post there. Cavalry patrols were also detailed to co-operate

It was found that MONTBREHAIN was held in strength and the patrol suffered heavily, only two men returning unwounded from this patrol. During the daytime the enemy shelled RAMICOURT very heavily and at one time, viz; 9.0am appeared to be massing for a counter attack in the region of DOON HILL. O.C. 'A' Company got a message back to Headquarters, who got the artillery on. This concentration very effectively broke up any attempt at offensive action on the part of the enemy.

During the day we inflicted considerable losses to the enemy with our Lewis Guns and snipers and took 9 prisoners.

At 4.0pm instructions were received that the 1st Australian Divisional Pioneers would be relieving the Battalion at dusk, with a view to carrying out an attack on MONTBREHAIN the following morning.

The relief was effected satisfactorily at about 10.0 pm and Companies marched back to trenches in the neighbourhood of NAUROY. This was accomplished in spite of spasmodic harassing fire.

The Battalion during this period had a very arduous time, for not only were Companies compelled to dig in on various occasions, but there was also a great deal of marching to be done. This owing to the great prevalence of gas proved most exhausting work.

A considerable number of casualties were sustained, chiefly by 'C' Company, who lost three officers :- Lieut J.G.FRAMPTON, Died of Wounds, Lieut H.J.C.HAINES, Wounded, and 2/Lieut E.M.THOMAS, Severely Wounded. O.Rs, Killed 13, (Including R.S.M.HUMPHRIES,A.J.). 65 Wounded.

The Battalion rested in the vicinity of ASCENSION VALLEY during the 5th, and 6th inst.

On 7th Oct. the Battalion received orders to relieve the 8th SHERWOOD FORESTERS' at SEQUEHART and come under the orders of the G.O.C. 139th Inf. Bde.

The general scheme was that the line should be held whilst a converging attack was made at dawn by the 6th English, and the 126th French Divisions : this Battalion being thereby cut out.

The Battalion received orders to capture two machine guns located on SEQUHART - MERICOURT Road. This operation had to be carried out by two platoons at Zero plus 10 minutes.

'A' Company were to dig in on the right of 'B' Company and effect contact with the French who were reported to be in CHARBON VERT. This was successfully accomplished during the night and a post in charge of 2/Lieut C.T.BLACKALL pushed forward 500 yards to be in liason with a French detachment.

At Zero a heavy bombardment was opened by us which was promptly replied to by the enemy who laid a heavy barrage on SEQUHART Village and its Eastern outskirts.

'B' Company then made a very gallant attempt to capture the machine guns, which were about 150 yards to their front and under cover of a Trench Mortar bombardment advanced to the attack.

Two platoons under Captain W.P.ABBOTT, and Lieut J.R.EVANS were practically annihilated in the first attempt made, and then Lt-Col J.JENKINS, M.C. and the Adjutant who had come up to superintend the attack decided to make another effort with the remaining two Platoons and call up two platoons of 'C' Company who were lying in reserve behind the village to reinforce.

This attack met with the same result as the first, and Captain W.M.JAMES, who so gallantly led it was killed when within 5 yards of the nearest gun. In addition, heavy casualties resulted, among them being Lt Col J.JENKINS,M.C. Mortally wounded, 2/Lieut H.C.ARCHER, Killed and a total of 72 O.Rs either killed or wounded.

It was then decided to abandon the attack as the machine guns were still active and appeared to be in large numbers. As the day wore on the 6th Division finally enveloped this position which proved to be an organized trench, manned by at least 250 Germans, with 20 machine guns and two Trench Mortars.

Major F.G.PHILLIPS assumed Command of the Battalion and received orders to hold on the positions until further instructions were issued.

Army Form C. 2118.

WAR DIARY
INTELLIGENCE SUMMARY.
(Erase heading not required.)

Secret & Confidential

War Diary

1/1st Batt. The Monmouthshire Regt. T.F.

1st October 1918 to 31st October 1918

Army Form C. 2118.

WAR DIARY
INTELLIGENCE SUMMARY
(Erase heading not required.)

Instructions regarding War Diaries and Intelligence Summaries are contained in F.S. Regs., Part II. and the Staff Manual respectively. Title pages will be prepared in manuscript.

Place	Date	Hour	Summary of Events and Information	Remarks and references to Appendices
G.27.d.1.6.	Oct. 1918	1st	A wire was received last night from Intelligence stating that prisoners taken by the 46th Division amount to over 3000 & still more coming in; guns not counted. "A" Company concentrated their efforts to-day on main road JONCOURT - BELLENGLISE from road junction leading to MAGNY la FOSSE. "B" Company worked thro' MAGNY la FOSSE & North to JONCOURT. "C" Company worked in old sector near LA BARAQUE & North to RIQUEVAL	
G.27.d.1.6.	"	2	At 11.15pm the Battalion received orders to take up position in SPRINGBOK VALLEY by 5 a.m. 3rd inst. in readiness for a Divisional attack on RAMICOURT & MONTBREHAIN. The Battalion to be in reserve & attached to the 138th Inf. Brigade. Casualties Lieut. H.E. SHARPE wounded. 5 O.R. wounded. 6 O.R. wounded (gas).	
G.27.d.1.6.	"	3	At 1.0am. a Company Commanders' conference was called re the move etc., At 2.30 am. the Battalion moved off to take up its new position. Companies moving independently. At 4.0am. the Battalion in position H.Q. in an old Bosch pill box at G.30.b.40.75. At 11.15 a.m. the Battalion received orders to move to G.16.C. in the railway cutting to take over from the 1/5th Lincolns	

WAR DIARY
INTELLIGENCE SUMMARY

Army Form C. 2118.

Place	Date	Hour	Summary of Events and Information	Remarks and references to Appendices
G.27.d.1.6	Oct 3 (Continued)	1918	At 2.0pm the Battalion was reported in position. At 3.0pm "B" & "C" Coy received orders to move up and repel an enemy counter attack. "A" Coy in support. At 6.0pm the Coys reported in position. "C" Coy established at H.11.d in the Sunken Rd with "B" Coy on their right, slightly to their rear. At 7.0pm "C" Coy advanced to H.6.c & H.12.a, while "B" Coy advanced to H.11.d. At 8.0pm orders were received to take over the Line from the 139th Inf. Brigade. "C" Company from RAMICOURT Stn. exclusive to H.12.b. "A" Coy from H.12.b to H.12.b.8.6 with "B" Coy in support in the sunken road H.17.b.8.5 to H.11.d.8.5. Battalion H.Q. remained in the Railway Cutting. At 10pm Companies were in position. Casualties: Wounded Lt J.G Frampton & 2/Lt E. M. Thomas. 1.O.R. Wounded (Gas) Killed 3 O.R. 1.O.R. Wounded remained at Duty Wounded 21 O.R.	
G.16.c Railway Cutting	4th	3.30 am.	Orders received for "C" Coy to despatch a strong patrol (1 platoon) at 6.30 a.m. as far as into MONTBREHAIN as possible, under cover of our bombardment. Patrol moved off at 6.30 am but was driven back.	

Army Form C. 2118.

WAR DIARY
INTELLIGENCE SUMMARY.
(Erase heading not required.)

Place	Date 1918	Hour	Summary of Events and Information	Remarks and references to Appendices
Railway Cutting G.16.c.	Oct 4th (continued)	6.30am	Enemy concentrated M.G. fire from front and both flanks. Only 3 returned unwounded. The remainder of the day was comparatively quiet with the exception of enemy shelling & M.G. fire which was replied to by energetic sniping by our Lewis guns and rifles with good effect.	
"	"	4.30pm	Warning order received for relief by 1st Australian Division	
"	"	6.30pm	The Commanding Officer 1st Australian Pioneer Battalion arrived at Batt H.Qrs to arrange for the relief of the Battalion. Relief complete 11-30pm Casualties Lt H.J.C.HAINES Wounded. R.S.M. Humphries H.J Died of Wounds. 9 OR Killed 22 OR Wounded 10 OR Wounded (Gas) Lt J.G. FRAMPTON Died of Wounds in C.C.S.	
NAUROY	5th	2.0am	The Battalion concentrated at G.17. South of NAUROY.	
G.17.	"	3.15pm	Orders received to move to the neighbourhood of ASCENSION VALLEY G.26.	
"	"	5.30"	Battalion moved off Companies moving independently.	
"	"	7.0..	Battalion established in the Boach Old front line trench at G.20. Battalion HQrs at G.20 b.6.5.	
G.20 b 6.5	6th		The Battalion rested	

WAR DIARY

INTELLIGENCE SUMMARY

Army Form C. 2118.

Instructions regarding War Diaries and Intelligence Summaries are contained in F. S. Regs., Part II. and the Staff Manual respectively. Title pages will be prepared in manuscript.

(Erase heading not required.)

Place	Date 1918	Hour	Summary of Events and Information	Remarks and references to Appendices
G.20 b.6.5	Oct. 6th (Continued)	7.0pm	Warning order received for the Battalion to relieve one Battalion of the 139th Inf. Bde on the 7th inst. Casualties 1. O.R. wounded remained at duty.	
"	7th	4.30pm	The Battalion moved off to relieve the 8th SHERWOOD FORESTERS with orders to capture two enemy M.Gs at H.30 d.7.5 before zero on the morning of the 8th.	
"	"	10.0pm	Relief complete. "A" Coy in sunken road in H.36.a. "B" Coy in the Eastern outskirts of the village of SEQUEHART at H.30.d. "C" Coy in support at H.35.a. Battalion H.Qrs. at H.33.d.3.7. Orders received for 2 platoons of "B" Coy. to capture the two Bosche M.Gs under cover of the barrage at Zero + 10 minutes	
H.33 d 3.7.	8th	3.30am	The Commanding Officer & Adjutant left Battalion H.Qrs. to superintend the attack on the Machine Guns.	
"	"	5.10am	First attack made under Captain W.P. ABBOT & repulsed with very heavy casualties.	
"	"	6.0am	Second attack carried out by the remaining 2 platoons of "B" Coy under	

WAR DIARY
-of-
INTELLIGENCE SUMMARY

(Erase heading not required.)

Army Form C. 2118.

Place	Date 1918	Hour	Summary of Events and Information	Remarks and references to Appendices
H.33.d.3.7	Oct 8th		the Adjutant. Two platoons of "C" Coy moved up to replace casualties of "B" Coy. Attack failed with heavy casualties & the death of the Adjutant.	
"	"	6.30 am	Orders received by the C.O. to cease attacks on the M.Gs	
"	"	6.35 "	Commanding Officer severely wounded.	
"	"	12 noon	Major F.G. Phillips arrived from Transport Lines & assumed command of the Battalion. Companies were unable to move up to 1.30 pm owing to heavy enemy shelling & M.G. fire. Enemy artillery fire continued up to 8.0 pm.	
"	"	1.30 pm	Enemy M.G nest captured by the 1st West Yorks with 250 prisoners (approx) and many M.Gs (approx 20) The Battalion remained in position for the remainder of the day.	

Casualties:- Killed:- Capt. W.M. JAMES (Adjt.) Lt. J.R. EVANS. 2/Lt. H.C. ARCHER.
" " 30 O.R.
" Wounded:- Lieut-Col. J. JENKINS M.C. Capt. W.P. ABBOTT.
" " 40 O.R.
" " 2. O.R. Wounded remained at duty
Reinforcements:- 3. O.R.

Army Form C. 2118.

WAR DIARY
INTELLIGENCE SUMMARY.
(Erase heading not required.)

Instructions regarding War Diaries and Intelligence Summaries are contained in F. S. Regs., Part II. and the Staff Manual respectively. Title pages will be prepared in manuscript.

Place	Date 1918	Hour	Summary of Events and Information	Remarks and references to Appendices
H 33 d 3.7.	Oct 9th		Quiet day owing to enemy retreat. The Battalion remained resting in the same position.	
"	"	4.0 pm	Some of the casualties buried.	
			Reinforcements 2/Lt. D.S. ROWLANDS. 2/Lt. G.M. TUCKER. 2/Lt. S. JARRETT. Lieut. Col. J. JENKINS. M.C. Died of Wounds.	
"	10th	10.30 am	Orders received for the Battalion to move forward to MERICOURT, for work on road running from MERICOURT to BOHAIN via FRESNOY le GRAND under orders from the C.R.E.	
"	"	2.30 pm	Battalion arrived in MERICOURT and Coy's commenced work "A" Coy I 23 a. "B" Coy "C" Coy I.18 d.	
		8.30 pm (approx.)	Companies returned to billets in MERICOURT	
MERICOURT	11th	-	Companies paraded at 7 am and worked on roads between MERICOURT & BOHAIN, clearing roads and filling in craters. The road between MERICOURT and FRESNOY was blown up in two places, forming craters 30 ft in diameter and 10 ft deep. Weather dull & misty.	
"	12th	-	Working parties were found today as yesterday. "A" and "B" Coy's repairing roads, filling in shell holes and clearing streets in and around FRESNOY. "C" Company worked on filling craters and clearing streets in BOHAIN. Instructions have been received from the C.R.E. to move to billets in FRESNOY today. Owing to Companies being still out on work, this move was postponed until to-morrow morning. Guides were sent forward to secure billets. One N.C.O. and 2 O.R. from each Coy and 1 Officer from "C" Coy under Lt. F.L. MOORE O/C billeting party. The billeting party remained over night in new billets. Weather dull & showery. Casualties 2nd Lt. S. JARRETT. Wounded 1 OR. C. Coy. Killed.	

Army Form C. 2118.

WAR DIARY
or
INTELLIGENCE SUMMARY.
(Erase heading not required.)

Instructions regarding War Diaries and Intelligence Summaries are contained in F.S. Regs., Part II. and the Staff Manual respectively. Title pages will be prepared in manuscript.

Place	Date 1918	Hour	Summary of Events and Information	Remarks and references to Appendices
VERICOURT	Oct	13th	The Battalion moved off independently by Coys at 9.30 am. The Transport moving at 9.30 am. Good billets were secured in streets in the vicinity of the square, for both Headquarters and Companies at I 18 d 3.4 Sheet 62.c. Transport Lines and Quartermaster Stores at I 18 b 3.3. Battalion bathed in the afternoon under Company arrangements.	
FRESNOY le GRAND.	"	14th	All Coys worked during the morning in clearing streets in S.E portion of the town, working 4 hours only in view of strenuous times in the near future. In the afternoon, kit inspection and bathing was carried out by Coy arrangements. Reinforcements:- A draft of 38 OR joined the Battalion from the Divisional Reception Camp. Weather bright and dry.	
"	"	15th	Working parties found as yesterday. The Commanding Officer inspected the new draft of 38 OR. These men are a likely looking men and appear intelligent and are mostly from the land. Weather dull but dry.	
"	"	16th	Working parties were found to day as follows :- 1 Officer + 40 OR from "A" Coy. 2 Officers + 35 OR from "B" Coy for work under the 466th Field Coy R.E. This party was employed in constructing advanced Headquarters for the 139th Infantry Brigade, at D 11 & 6.2. Sheet 62.8. The remaining working parties worked on streets in and around FRESNOY. Weather bright and dry.	

WAR DIARY
or
INTELLIGENCE SUMMARY.
(Erase heading not required.)

Army Form C. 2118.

Place	Date 1918	Hour	Summary of Events and Information	Remarks and references to Appendices
FRESNOY le GRAND	Oct	17th	The 46th Division attacked the BOIS de RIQUEVAL from a N.W direction; jumping off from the BOHAIN-VAUX ANDIGNY Rd. Zero Hour 5.20 am. This was carried out as a part of a major operation; the French being on our right and the 6th Division on our left. Instructions were received from C.R.E. to have a working party 380 strong ready to move off at 7.0 am and go forward to clear the BOHAIN-REGNICOURT Rd as far forward as ANDIGNY les FERMES as soon as the attack had succeeded in crossing this road. "A" and "B" Coy. moved off at 8.0 am to an assembly place in the Railway cutting just south of BOHAIN. At 10.0am these Coys moved forward from assembly place; and working on late into the afternoon succeeded in clearing the road as far forward as ANDIGNY LES FERMES. Weather dull but dry.	
"		18th	All three Coys worked on roads in and around FRESNOY during the forenoon. In the afternoon "B" & "C" Coys worked on clearing roads of mud between REGNICOURT and ANDIGNY les FERMES, as owing to enemy shelling these roads had been covered with soil thrown up from shells pitching close to roads. 52 O.Rs having reported at 46th Divisional Depot are taken on the strength. Capt E.J. JENKINS assumed command of "A" Company vice Lt A.W. GOLDSWORTHY. Lt. A.F.A.M. ATKINS assumed command of "B" Company. Lt A.W GOLDSWORTHY transferred to "B" Coy as second in command. Weather still continues dry but cold.	
"		19th	All Coys worked on roads and streets in the town. The C.O. inspected draft of 52 O.Rs of these men are a particularly good looking lot. Recreational training was carried out in the afternoon.	

Army Form C. 2118.

WAR DIARY
or
INTELLIGENCE SUMMARY.
(Erase heading not required.)

Place	Date 1918	Hour	Summary of Events and Information	Remarks and references to Appendices
FRESNOY les GRAND	Oct.	20th	A Divisional Parade C. of E. Service was held today at FRESNOY les GRAND at 10.15 a.m at which all units in the Division were represented. Each Infantry Batt. parading 200 OR. with complement of officers. R.E's 6 Officers and 150 OR. The Battalion also paraded 6 Officers and 150 OR. Rain commenced early in the morning and capes had to be worn. During the afternoon Coys bathed under Coy arrangements after the arrival of all dubbin, washing kit &c &c from B.G.Ds. Btde Dump.	
"		21st	"A" Coy supplied 1 Officer & 50 OR for work for French Mission. Remainder of Battalion carried out training from 9 a.m. to 1 p.m. The afternoon was devoted to recreational training. The Commanding Officer had to congratulate the undermentioned on receiving the following awards:- Bar to Military Medal 225987 Sgt WILKINS E. (M.M.) "A" Coy. Military Medal 227744 Sgt MURPHY J. "C" " Military Medal 227975 Rfn PURNELL J. "A" " Lt G.P. PEACHELL returned from short leave.	
"		22nd	One Officer and 50 OR of "B" Coy carried out work for French Mission clearing streets and repairing civilian houses. "A" and "C" Coys and remainder of "B" Coy carried out training during the forenoon. Weather showery and dull.	
"		23rd	"C" Coy provided 1 Officer and 50 OR for work for French Mission. "A" & B Coy and remainder of "C" Coy carried out training during the forenoon. During the afternoon recreational training was carried out by all Coys. Captain W.M.B. BURNYEAT M.C. rejoined the Battalion from Hospital. The following officers joined the Battalion from the Base and are posted to Coys as follows :—	

Army Form C. 2118.

WAR DIARY
INTELLIGENCE SUMMARY.
(Erase heading not required.)

1st BATTALION,
THE MONMOUTHSHIRE
REGIMENT.

Place	Date 1918	Hour	Summary of Events and Information	Remarks and references to Appendices
FRESNOY les GRAND	Oct. 23 (Continued)		Lt J.C. THOMAS "A" Coy 2/Lt W.E. PRITCHARD "C" " 2/Lt J.W. WALTERS "C" " 2/Lt K.H WILLIAMS "C" "	
"	24th		Working parties for French Mission were found to day by "A" Coy. "B" & "C" Coys and remainder of "A" Coy carried out programme of training during the forenoon. The afternoon was devoted to Recreational training.	
"	25th		Working parties for French Mission found by "B" Coy for work on roads and repair of civilians houses. The remainder of the Battalion carried out training as usual.	
"	26th		Working parties for French mission were found by "C" Coy, the remainder of the Battalion carried out training during the forenoon and recreational training in the afternoon. Weather dry but cold.	
"	27th		Bathing parades for whole Battalion were held to-day from 8 am to 1 p.m., at Divisional Baths in the convent at FRESNOY les GRAND. Voluntary services were held as follows – C.E – Whys Bang Hall. N.C.– Y.M.C.A. Hut. R.C.– Parish Church.	
"	28th		"A" Coy found working parties for French Mission. Remainder of Battalion carried out training during the forenoon. Recreational training was carried out in the afternoon. A draft of 31 O.R. reported from Divisional Depot was taken on strength of the Battalion. These recruits	

Army Form C. 2118.

WAR DIARY
INTELLIGENCE SUMMARY.
(Erase heading not required.)

Place	Date	Hour	Summary of Events and Information	Remarks and references to Appendices
FRESNOY les GRAND	Oct 1918 29th		"B" Coy provided working party for French Mission. Remainder of Battalion carried out training in Platoon and Section Drill, Gas drill etc. The afternoon was devoted to recreation. The C.O. inspected the new draft of 31 OR.	
"	30th		"C" Coy supplied working party for French Mission and the remainder of the Battalion carried out training as usual, and recreational training in the afternoon. Instructions have been received for the Batt. to move to BOHAIN tomorrow. Weather continues dry.	
"	31st		The Battalion including transport and Q.M Stores moved from FRESNOY to BOHAIN. The Battalion paraded at 1315 o'clock and marched off by Coys at 100 yds distance between Coys in the following order:- HQrs, B Coy "C" & "A" Coy. BOHAIN was reached at 1430 hours when the billets of 16th Battalion (H.L.I.) 32nd Division were taken over. All billets are good and the town is very little damaged by shell fire. H.Qrs are situated on main street on S. side of the square near the church. Weather, Rain commenced soon after getting into billets. Strength of Battalion Officers - 35 OR's - 791	

Hiram Phillips Major
Commanding 1/1st Batt The Monmouthshire Regt TF

Secret and Confidential

Army Form C. 2118.

WAR DIARY
of
INTELLIGENCE SUMMARY.
(Erase heading not required.)

1/1st Batt The Monmouthshire Regt. T.F.

Nov 1st 1918 to Nov 30th 1918

Army Form C. 2118.

WAR DIARY
or
INTELLIGENCE SUMMARY.
(Erase heading not required.)

Instructions regarding War Diaries and Intelligence Summaries are contained in F. S. Regs., Part II. and the Staff Manual respectively. Title pages will be prepared in manuscript.

Place	Date	Hour	Summary of Events and Information	Remarks and references to Appendices
BOHAIN.	Nov. 1918	1st	Capt. R.C.L. THOMAS M.C. returned to the Battalion from "B" Branch 46th Division and took over duties of Adjutant from LIEUT. R.D. EDMISTON A/Adjutant. Training grounds have been allotted to the Battalion on S.E. outskirts of BOHAIN. All Coys carried out training from 09.30 hours to 13.00 hours in Platoon and Section drill and Company drill. A class for the training of young N.C.O.'s was taken by R.S.M. HOUSDEN. Deakin, Romney.	
		2nd	One Officer and 30 O.R. are attached to the 465 Field Coy. R.E. for work on advanced Inf. Bde. H.Q.'s for coming operations. This detachment marched off at 09.30 hours to proceed to L'ARBRE DE GUISE at W.6.b.y.5 MAP WASSIGNY 57.A S.7.B 62.A 62.B. The remainder of the Battalion carried out training as yesterday during the greater part of the day.	
		3rd	During the forenoon the Battalion battled between 09.00 hours and 12.00 hours. The Battalion Transport and Q.M. stores paraded at 11.00 hours and marched via VAUX ANDIGNY, including TRANSPORT RIVIERE to a point 200 yards S.W. of L'ARBRE DE GUISE where bivouaced NOHAIN (ST.MARTIN RIVIERE). The transport and Q.M. stores dropped out of line 5th march at ST. MARTIN RIVIERE where billets had been secured in advance. Ran commenced just before we quarters were reached. The enemy were at present holding a line W. of LANDRECIES 62.0 & 62 S.26 a. along the eastern bank of the canal except at CHATILLON where the enemy have the greater part of the town on the west bank, but November H.Q. Zero the 32nd Division will attack on a front from west of LANDRECIES 62.0 to CHATILLON MEZIER RD inclusive. The 1st Division will deliver from the CHATILLON MEZIER RD exclusive to S.15.d 1000 yds N.S. OISY. The French are on our right S.P. 1st Division and XIII Corps on left S.P. 32 nd Division. The first objective is about 1000 yards East of the canal. 2nd Objective 2500 East and 3rd Objective on a N & S line includes LANDRECIES and OISY. The above is part of extensive operations on a 25 to 30 mile front.	

Notification received of following awards:-

226274 Pte. MAHONEY.T. } "B" Coy.
225280 " HERBERT. F.H. }
226721 L/Cpl TAYLOR. E } MILITARY
226536 " RALPH. E } "C" Coy. MEDAL.

Army Form C. 2118.

WAR DIARY
or
INTELLIGENCE SUMMARY.
(Erase heading not required.)

Instructions regarding War Diaries and Intelligence Summaries are contained in F.S. Regs., Part II. and the Staff Manual respectively. Title pages will be prepared in manuscript.

Place	Date	Hour	Summary of Events and Information	Remarks and references to Appendices
L'ARBRE DE GUISE	Nov 4th 1918		The Battalion as from 5.45A.M. was held in readiness to move at 5 minutes notice at 11.30 hours. A and B Coys moved off with H66 and H65 Field Coys R.E. respectively to build Pontoon Bridges at M32 d 3.5 at 5.1 a 3.9 and 5.1 d 3.8. These bridges were successfully placed. B Coy containing 2 casualties. C Coy at 12 noon moved off to a detail above Coys H.Q. making approaches to the bridges, however they were not required. Battalion H.Q.rs moved to X 10 a at 13.00 hours where it was joined by Coys after work. The Battalion bivouacked here for the night.	
	Nov 5th		A and B Coys paraded at 04.30 hours and worked on road as follows. A Coy employed filling shell holes and clearing the road generally from MEZIERS to CROSS ROAD "LA GROIS'S CROSS ROAD" at M9 M.C.0.0. A mine having been sprung at MEZIER - LA GROIS'S Cross road was made good for single way traffic. B Company repaired road between BOIS DE L'ABBAYE M32 C and CROSS ROAD 2 N of FESMY 5 a 6. C Coy made good the main CATILLON PRISCHES RD. between M19 b and M22 a filling shell holes and removing obstructions such as fallen trees. Two platoons of this Coy assisted R.E's to repair the Canal bridge in CATILLON.	
LA GROISE	Nov 6th		The Battalion moved from bivouacs at SSF REJET DE BEAULIEU to billets in LA GROISE. Working parties moved off to work at 06.30 hours and marched into "new billets" on completion of work. Battalion H.Q.rs and Transport moved off at noon. About one hour after expiration of new billets, orders were received from C.R.E. to move forward to PRISCHES that night. Arrangements were finally made to move next day as the men had long marches to work and long hours and were wet through. Weather continued wet throughout the day.	
PRISCHES	Nov 7th		The Battalion HQrs with Transport moved billets from LA GROISE to PRISCHES moving off at 10.00 hours. Coys started off to work at 04.00 hours. C Coy worked on Cross road B at 19 b 3.6 about 2000 yds N of LE SAR. These Cross roads were mined with delayed action shells at 12 different points. 3 of these mines were Spring making craters 30 ft diameter by 10 ft deep. A and B Coys concentrated on	

WAR DIARY or INTELLIGENCE SUMMARY.

Army Form C. 2118.

(Erase heading not required.)

Place	Date	Hour	Summary of Events and Information	Remarks and references to Appendices
PRISCHES	Nov 7th (cont)		Road making between PRISCHES and CARTIGNY which has been continually cut by mines for a distance of 50 ft by 15 ft deep. That part of the road was repairable for single traffic by 1700 hours.	
			Reinforcements:- 24 O.R's 10 inch Battalion from R.E Base.	
	8th		Working parties today were formed at Polemps:- A Coy worked on the Southern Road between CARTIGNIES and BOULOGNE at 0154 at the same hour which 6 men have been forming Craters 3-Pl arrived by 1530. B Coy at 20 Am. E Coy on Landslides. Craters about 200 yards left of B Coy at SP. MARBAIX. A Coy moved to billets in BOULOGNE consolidating with their work R 10 Lef R Sp Marbaix. A Coy moved to billets in BOULOGNE dropping their working parties on the way. The Battalion including Transport moved to billets on Eastern outskirts of CARTIGNY arriving in billets at about 1500 hours. One platoon of B Coy worked on the demolition of craters laid by Enemy. Bank C Coy's worked on three 10 temporary bridges across river in CARTIGNY.	
CARTIGNY	9th		Working parties were formed today as follows. One platoon of B Coy worked on cradles to revetting and making side track round demolition. B and C Coy worked on the bridges across river in CARTIGNY. A Coy Reserve.	
	10th		Working parties formed at Polemps. A Coy 0530 hours Bank C Coy 0800 hours all employed to work on the AVESNES—SANS DU NORD ROAD where mines on the road have been forming at numerous places. B and C Coy's worked on craters on Southern outskirts of AVESNES. A Coy moved to work completed with transport halted at 1100 hours and found billets in SANS DU NORD. Battalion HQrs and Transport arrived at 1100 hours and moved from CARTIGNIES to billets on the AVESNES — SANS DU NORD ROAD at Q.3.a.2.4. Bank C Coy were billeted in turns on main road close to HQrs.	
			CASUALTY. MAJOR PUGH MORGAN. Accidentally injured through the head by an axe flying off and cutting his jaw.	

WAR DIARY or INTELLIGENCE SUMMARY

Army Form C. 2118.

Place	Date	Hour	Summary of Events and Information	Remarks and references to Appendices
AVESNES	Nov	11th	Working Parties paraded at 0800 hours and worked on craters as yesterday. The filling in of the 8 craters entails a great deal of work as anything from 150 to 200 lorry loads of soil and road metal is blown up, which make it necessary to go to both ends of material for filling. The craters are kept that size either owing to the road are filled and sent into suitable lengths and dropped into the crater which is finally made up of broken earth & road metal. At 0900 a wire was received that an armistice would commence at 1100 hours today. The continued marching & working parties of the best of any kind considerably patched alluring. Owing to the broken nature of the billets and the scarcity of shelter supplies it was not possible in any way to celebrate the armistice.	
		12th	CASUALTIES. 1 O.R. Wounded. Working parties were found today as yesterday. All craters in hand have now been filled & good for single line traffic & P and D, it being necessary to carry on with this work in spite of cessation of hostilities as this throws up lengthy parties for burying up supplies in transit & in the line. No working parties were found today. The Battalion joined the 124th Infy Bde Group and marched to Billets in HVESNES. The Battalion paraded at 1400 hours in field adjoining H.Q.'s and marched to HVESNES taking over the billets vacated by the 8/16th Battalion H.L.I. Previous Battalion to the 32nd Division. Reinforcement	
		13th	12 O.Rs joined Battalion from the Base.	

WAR DIARY
or
INTELLIGENCE SUMMARY.
(Erase heading not required.)

Army Form C. 2118

Place	Date	Hour	Summary of Events and Information	Remarks and references to Appendices
BOUSIES.	Nov	14th	The Battalion with Transport paraded at 0845 hours on the AVESNES road and marched to the bivouac outskirts of AVESNES to form the 137 Bde Column. The Bde moved off at 1000 hours en route for the LANDRECIES area marching via MARBAIX, MAROILLES and LANDRECIES. A halt of 1 hour was made at 1200 hours and dinners were supplied from cookers. LANDRECIES was entered at 1500 hours. The Battalion left the Bde Column here and proceeded to BOUSIES arriving about 1630 hours where good billets were secured. The distance marched today was 26 Kils [kilometres] throughout. When the Battalion reached BOUSIES all went reported for cmd. On arrival in BOUSIES the Battalion was attached to the 138 Bde Group.	
		15th	Companies were placed at disposal of O/C Companies for cleaning up generally and return to billets. Reinforcement. 3 O.Rs Joined Battalion	
		16th	The Battalion paraded at 0930 hours in drill order in streets of the village for an Inspection by the G.O.C 46th Division. The Battalion was drawn up in close column of companies. The B.O.C first inspected the Battalion and afterwards made the following Speech:— Officers, N.C.Os and Men of 1/2 Monmouthshire Regiment. I have taken the present opportunity of inspecting your Battalion while the thoughts of the recent fighting are still clear in everyone's mind. I want to say how splendidly this Battalion has done in the recent action, the work you have had to do in many cases is not glory work but it is work which calls for the highest forms of courage and endurance and without which no operation could take place. Having the recent operations when the Battalion was ordered called upon to hold the line, and to make an attack the keenness with which you carried out the former duty and the commence way the latter is beyond all praise. The G.O.C then concluded by MT Meeting Medal to —	

WAR DIARY
or
INTELLIGENCE SUMMARY.
(Erase heading not required.)

Army Form C. 2118

Instructions regarding War Diaries and Intelligence Summaries are contained in F. S. Regs., Part II. and the Staff Manual respectively. Title pages will be prepared in manuscript.

Place	Date	Hour	Summary of Events and Information	Remarks and references to Appendices
BOUSIES	NOV	16th	(Continued)	
			227444 Sergt. J. MURPHY	
			224995 Rfn. J. TURNBULL	
			225280 " F.H. HERBERT	
			226244 " T.E. MAHONEY	
			The Battalion then marched past the G.O.C. taking the salute.	
			2nd Lieut. D.S ROWLANDS senior S.O. strength having gone sick whilst on leave.	
			Regnt. S.W. FRY struck off strength on being transferred to England sick.	
			The Battalion Weapon consisted by 2 officers and 50 O.Rs from each company paraded at 09.30 hours and marched to LANDRECIES to attend Divisional Cafe Service.	
			This Service was a Thanksgiving Service for the cessation of hostilities and for the Welcome's given to the H.Q. 46th Division during the last 2 months. Voluntary Service of non conform C/F and R.C's in BOUSIES were attended.	
			18th	C. Company paraded at 09.00 hours on Company Training Ground and carried out Arms drill and Platoon Drill finishing up with a Short Route March.	
			Reinforcements: -	
			20 O.Rs joined Battalion from the Base.	
			19th	The XIII Corps to which Corps the 46th Division now belongs to today commenced a Salvage Scheme and a clearing up of the Battlefield. This work is being undertaken by troops of the 1st and 3rd Army. A and B Coys today found salvaging parties to work under 230 and 231 Brigades R.F.A for salvaging material equipment, ammunition etc in Battle area in L11.6 and L4.b in vicinity of BOUSIES. The working hours are from 09.00 to 13.00 hours i.e. 4 hours per day. The men who are employed on Salvage work and remaining over that time, can get general training during the afternoon. C. Coy carried out training in P.T. Arms Drill and Platoon Drill.	

WAR DIARY
or
INTELLIGENCE SUMMARY.
(Erase heading not required.)

Army Form C. 211

Place	Date	Hour	Summary of Events and Information	Remarks and references to Appendices
BOUSIES	NOV	20th	Salvage parties were found by B and C Coys & testing A Coy carried out General Training. The R.S.M. took the Coy training from 1000 to 1100 for instruction in Arms Drill and Platoon Drill. All recent drafts were paraded for one hour in the afternoon for further training in Arms and Platoon drill under the R.S.M. Reinforcements.	
"		21st	Lieut D.W. HUGHES (3rd Battalion Monmouth Regt) 2/Lieut W.J. REPER (Brecknock Battalion SWB.) Salvage parties were found today by A and C Coys. B Coy carried out General Training. The R.S.M. as of yesterday took the Coy in training for instruction in Arms and Platoon drill for 1 hour	
"		22nd	Salvage parties were found by A and B Coys. C Coy carried out training today. The Battalion Rugby team played the 9th Battalion Tank Corps and won by 11 points to Nil.	
"		23rd	B and C Coys found Salvage parties today. A Coy carried out training. Following Officers reported as Reinforcements:—	

Lieut. J.M. REYNOLDS (3rd Bn Mon Regt)
Lieut. E.P.H. LANE (1st Mon Regt)
2/Lieut. H.H. ROWLAND (Brecknock Bn. S.W.B)
2/Lieut. W.V. JONES (Brecknock Bn S.W.B.)
2/Lieut. E.C. WILLIAMS (Brecknock Bn SWB)
13 O.R.s joined the Battalion from the Base.

WAR DIARY
or
INTELLIGENCE SUMMARY.
(Erase heading not required.)

Army Form C. 2118

Place	Date	Hour	Summary of Events and Information	Remarks and references to Appces
BOUSIES	Nov 24th		(Sunday) Church Parade held for all denominations.	
"	25th		Companies worked as usual. "A" and "C" Coys Salvaging. One platoon "B" Coy repairing roads in the village, the remainder of "B" Coy carried out General Training. All Coy's breffic [brittle?] between the hours of 0800 and 1700 hours. The weather today is cold and raw.	
"	26th		Working parties for Salvaging were found by "A" and "C" Coys. "B" Coy found a party for return of Surplus, the remainder of this Coy carried out training. Reinforcements:— 1 C.S.M. } Reported for duty from the Base. 1 C.Q.M.S. } 11 O.Rs	
"	27th		Salvage and other working parties were found as yesterday. The G.O.C. ordered Transport Vehicles in Transport lines of the Bde. were it at stables afternoon to inspect Coy Cookers and "one billet" to be inspected him[self] by field well with everything he saw. Major F.G. PHILLIPS now commanding the Battalion pro. more acting Lieut-Colonel whilst holding this Command.	
"	28th		Salvage and other working parties were found today as yesterday. 10 Men & one NCO interviewed at LANDRECIES and accepted for "Leaves" Col. & Lieut. Colonel F.G. PHILLIPS having proceeded to PARIS on 3 days leave, Capt. R.C.L. THOMAS assumes Command of the Battalion. 2nd Lieut R.D. ELMSLIE assumes the duties of R.A/Adjutant. Rain fell continuously throughout the day.	

WAR DIARY or INTELLIGENCE SUMMARY

Army Form C. 2118

Place	Date	Hour	Summary of Events and Information	Remarks and references to Appces
BOUSIES	Nov. 29th		No working parties were found owing to todays concentration not arriving until mid-day. All men slept in billets. Under the Demobilization Scheme 35 men were despatched to Bry Grds today from Coys as follows:- "A" Company 12 O.Rs, "B" " 13 O.Rs, "C" " 10 O.Rs	
	30th		The men paraded at 12.0 hours and were marched to RUTHERA at SOLESMES headed by the Battalion Band until clear of the Village. Many men of the Battalion paraded to see the party off. Salvage parties were found today by parts of Companies. "D" Company carried out General training. The present strength parades for one hour in the afternoon for instruction in arms and Platoon drill under R.S.M. The following award for gallantry in the Field have been received.	
			LT. F.L. MOORE "C" Company. MILITARY CROSS	
			2016025 Cpl BEARDMORE E.B. "H.Q." MILITARY MEDAL	
			227953 Rfm. MORRIS "H.Q." "	
			Also awarded in October 1918 but not previously included in the War diary CROIX DE GUERRE awarded by the 126th Sibrian Division to Capt. S.R. MARTYN for gallantry in action during the operations which took place in the early part of October 1918, when this Division was fighting side by side with the 53rd French Division.	
			BAR TO MILITARY MEDAL - 225744 Sergt. F.R. GLMS. M.M. "B" Coy.	
			Reinforcements - 27 O.Rs joined Battalion from H.Q Base.	
			STRENGTH OF BATTALION 34 OFFICERS 743 O.Rs.	

R.C.W. Thomas, Captain
Comdg. 1/5th Monmouthshire Regt. T.F.

Secret & Confidential

Army Form C. 2118.

1st BATTALION,
THE MONMOUTHSHIRE
REGIMENT.

WAR DIARY
or
INTELLIGENCE SUMMARY
(Erase heading not required.)

Instructions regarding War Diaries and Intelligence Summaries are contained in F.S. Regs., Part II. and the Staff Manual respectively. Title pages will be prepared in manuscript.

1/1st Batt The Monmouthshire Regt T.F.

1st December to 31st December 1918.

Place	Date	Hour	Summary of Events and Information	Remarks and references to Appendices

Army Form C. 2118.

WAR DIARY
INTELLIGENCE SUMMARY.
(Erase heading not required.)

Place	Date 1918	Hour	Summary of Events and Information	Remarks and references to Appendices
BOUSIES	Dec 1st		There were no Church parades held this morning owing to the visit of H.M. The KING. All officers and men desirous of seeing the KING, paraded at 12.45 hours and marched to LANDRECIES, joining the head of the 138th Infantry Brigade column on the Eastern outskirts of the village. The main street in LANDRECIES were lined with troops at 14.30 hours. The KING was due to pass through at 15.00 hours, but owing to block in the traffic further east it was 15.30 hours, before the arrival of the KING and the PRINCE of WALES who on dismounting from his car, walked down the full length of the street as far as the canal accompanied by the G.O.C. The Battalion then marched back to BOUSIES arriving in billet about 17.00 hours. The following officers joined the Battalion from the Base as reinforcements: Lieut F. J. WEBB 2/Lieut A. J. PHELPS.	
	2nd		Salvage parties were found to-day by "B" and "C" Companies. "A" Company found working parties for work on Battalion Recreation Room and also parties for repairs to roads in neighbourhood of billets. The 138th Brigade baths were at disposal of the Battalion during the day.	
	3rd		The salvage of general war material in the area having been completed, the Battalion is detailed to carry on with salvage of wire entanglements, this is being carried out in two days out of every three days, the third day is reserved for general training.	

Army Form C. 2118.

WAR DIARY
INTELLIGENCE SUMMARY.
(Erase heading not required.)

Instructions regarding War Diaries and Intelligence Summaries are contained in F.S. Regs., Part II. and the Staff Manual respectively. Title pages will be prepared in manuscript.

Place	Date	Hour	Summary of Events and Information	Remarks and references to Appendices
BOUSIES	Dec 1918 3rd		The Battalion commenced general training today, finishing up with an hours Ceremonial drill. 2nd Lieut H.R. ROWLANDS is struck of strength, being found unfit by Medical Board while on short leave to United Kingdom.	
"	" 4th		Working parties were found to day by all Companies for the salvage of wire. The following N.C.O.s have been struck off the strength on being transferred to Home Establishment on tour of duty:- 225227 Sgt SCAMMELLS W.H. "A" Co 225386 Cpl WARD J.H. "A" Co 226695 Cpl THOMAS C.G. "B" Co	
"	" 5th		Salvage parties were found today as yesterday. Owing to increased Correspondence in connection with Demobilization Scheme Lieut C.H.T. COCHRANE has been appointed Demobilization Officer for the Battalion.	
"	" 6th		Companies carried out general training today from 0900 hours till 1200 hours. Ceremonial drill was carried out from 1200 hours to 1300 hours.	
"	" 7th		Salvage parties were found today for salvage of wire by all Companies. The Battalion found Brigade duties commencing at 1600 hours today. A good deal of work has been done towards fitting out a Battalion Recreation Room which is provided with a wet and dry canteen. The Recreation Room was opened today.	
"	" 8th		Sunday. Church parade Services held for all denominations. Lieut Col. F.G. PHILLIPS returned from PARIS leave and resumed command of the Battalion. Battalion beat 5th LEICESTERS at Rugby Football by 20 points to 5. 50 O.R. draft men reported at Battalion from Divisional Depot.	

Army Form C. 2118.

WAR DIARY
INTELLIGENCE SUMMARY
(Erase heading not required.)

Instructions regarding War Diaries and Intelligence Summaries are contained in F. S. Regs., Part II. and the Staff Manual respectively. Title pages will be prepared in manuscript.

Place	Date	Hour	Summary of Events and Information	Remarks and references to Appendices
BOUSIES	Dec. 1918 9th		Salvage parties found as usual. Battalion bathed during course of day at Village baths.	
"	10th		Commanding Officer inspected draft that arrived yesterday at 10.30 hours. Draft of 12 O.R's reported at Battalion from Div. Depot. Training parade for Company drill etc. 09.00 - 11.00 hours. The Battalion parade arranged for 11.00 - 12.00 hours had to be cancelled owing to heavy rain. A meeting was held at Headquarters Mess at 17.15 hours when it was decided to start a Battalion Mess as soon as possible.	
"	11th		Salvage parties were found as usual, but these were withdrawn at 10.00 hours owing to very heavy rain.	
"	12th		Salvage parties not sent out as rain fell without ceasing all day. A Battalion Officers Mess was started today in house lately used for Headquarters Mess and Orderly Room, the latter being moved yesterday to a house about 200 yards away.	
"	13th		Owing to wet state of fields it was not possible to hold a Battalion drill parade. Companies paraded at 09.00 - 10.00 for Physical Training and Bayonet fighting. The Battalion paraded at 10.30 for a route march. The weather today whilst very dull and overcast was fine. 2 Other Ranks 225061 C.Q.M.S PHILLIPS and 225733 C.Q.M.S DARTNELL left the Battalion for the Base for transfer to ENGLAND as Pivotal men under the Demobilization Scheme. These 2 N.C.O's are the first 2 actually to	

WAR DIARY
INTELLIGENCE SUMMARY

Army Form C. 2118.

Place	Date	Hour	Summary of Events and Information	Remarks and references to Appendices
BOUSIES	Dec 1918	13th Continued	To leave for Demobilization previous men sent as miners have only been transferred to the Army Reserve	
"	"	14th	Salvage parties found as usual at 08.00 hours. 40 NCOs and men who were miners before the war left the Battalion for the Base for transfer to the Army Reserve, so that they may carry on their civilian employment as Coal Miners. The Commanding Officer said "Good bye" to the party which marched away to the Regimental March.	
"	"	15th	Sunday. Church parades held for all denominations. Weather fine but still overcast. Battalion beat 138th Brigade at Rugby Football by 25 points to Nil.	
"	"	16th	Salvage parties found as usual. Battalion bathed. <u>HONOURS & AWARDS</u> 225061 C.Q.M.S PHILLIPS M.S awarded <u>MILITARY MEDAL</u> by Corps Commander for an act of gallantry in the field.	
"	"	17th	Salvage parties were found as usual. Capt. & Adjutant R.C.L. THOMAS M.C. vacated the appointment of Adjutant on being granted the acting rank of Major whilst acting as Second in Command of the Battalion.	
"	"	18th	Owing to very wet weather which lasted throughout the day all training parades arranged were cancelled. Lieut A.E.A.M. ATHINS assumed duties of Acting Adjutant vice Major R.C.L. THOMAS M.C. Lieut L.H. BARNES 1st Mon Regt joined Battalion as reinforcement. Reinforcements 13 Other Ranks.	

Army Form C. 2118.

WAR DIARY
or
INTELLIGENCE SUMMARY.
(Erase heading not required.)

Instructions regarding War Diaries and Intelligence Summaries are contained in F. S. Regs., Part II. and the Staff Manual respectively. Title pages will be prepared in manuscript.

Place	Date	Hour	Summary of Events and Information	Remarks and references to Appendices
BOUSIES	Dec 19th 1918		Salvage parties found as usual. A further draft of 161 miners left the Battalion to be sent to England. These men paraded at 07.45 hours when the Commanding Officer said "Good Bye". The draft marched away to the Regimental March. This practically clears the Battalion of miners, only 9 miners being left, even men who joined this Battalion in the field as recently as October 1918 have been sent home as such.	
"	" 20th		Salvage parties found as usual.	
"	" 21st		Short training parade held 09.00 – 10.00 hours for Physical Training & Bayonet Fighting, followed by a route march of 7 miles.	
"	" 22nd		Sunday. Church parades held for all denominations during the morning.	
"	" 23rd		Salvage parties found as usual. Maj. Gen. G.F. BOYD, C.M.G., D.S.O., D.C.M., G.O.C. 46th Division dined with the officers.	
"	" 24th		Salvage parties found as usual.	
"	" 25th		Xmas Day. Voluntary Services for all denominations, held during the morning. Owing to the non arrival of the pork and other Xmas Stores the mens Xmas dinner could not be held. Beer was served in the evening and a concert and band programme was arranged in the evening from 18.30 – 22.00 hours. While all ranks were very disappointed that the Christmas dinner could not be held the day passed in a very enjoyable way. A Battalion Concert was arranged in the evening.	

Army Form C. 2118.

WAR DIARY
or
INTELLIGENCE SUMMARY.
(Erase heading not required.)

Instructions regarding War Diaries and Intelligence Summaries are contained in F. S. Regs., Part II. and the Staff Manual respectively. Title pages will be prepared in manuscript.

Place	Date	Hour	Summary of Events and Information	Remarks and references to Appendices
BOUSIES	Dec 1918. 26th		Boxing Day. One hours Physical Training & Bayonet Fighting was carried out in the morning. At 2 p.m. the Battalion had it Xmas dinner by Companies, owing to the arrangements made by the E.F.C. for the supply of pork failing through lorries breaking down, only a small proportion of the pork ordered was available for the Xmas pudding arrived alright, but all the extras, such as oranges, nuts, etc, did not arrive. The Commanding Officer visited Companies while at dinner and wished the men a Happy Xmas and New Year.	
"	27th		Salvage parties found as usual.	
"	28th		Salvage parties found as usual. An advance party of 4 Officers and 32 O.R's left at 09.60 hours for WASSIGNY, to which place the Battalion has been ordered to move on the 2nd prox. Weather still very wet.	
"	29th		Sunday. Church parades held for all denominations. Weather dry but cold and damp.	
"	30th		Orders received that the move ordered for January 2nd is postponed and will probably not take place.	
"	31st		Company training parades held from 09.00 - 10.30 hours for Physical Training & Bayonet fighting & arms drill. Battalion parade 10.30 hours for route march. The advance party sent to WASSIGNY rejoined Battalion this afternoon. Strength of Battalion Officers 37. O.R. 626.	

Army Form C. 2118.

WAR DIARY
or
INTELLIGENCE SUMMARY.
(Erase heading not required.)

Place	Date	Hour	Summary of Events and Information	Remarks and references to Appendices
			General Review of situation of the Battalion on 31/12/18	

The thoughts uppermost in the minds of all ranks at present is demobilization and everything done or ordered at present has some bearing on that point. Owing to about 250 miners being sent home, the Battalion is now largely composed of men who have only served a very short time in this country, the total strength being about 600. Recent orders indicate that general demobilization in a limited form will commence early next month and it can only be a few months before the Battalion is finally demobilized. A cadre of 4 officers and 41 ORs has had to be earmarked, but it is not known whether this cadre will eventually proceed to England or be disposed of in this country.

Everything possible is being done to keep the men amused, the Divisional Cinema gives a performance twice a night, and the 138th Brigade Concert Party once a night.

Company whist drives are held each week for each Company

Army Form C. 2118.

WAR DIARY
or
INTELLIGENCE SUMMARY.
(Erase heading not required.)

Instructions regarding War Diaries and Intelligence Summaries are contained in F. S. Regs., Part II. and the Staff Manual respectively. Title pages will be prepared in manuscript.

Place	Date	Hour	Summary of Events and Information	Remarks and references to Appendices
	5/1/19		Company in the Battalion Recreation Room, which are very popular. The Band plays after the Whist Drive for the men to Dance. These amusements combined with Boxing, Football etc, in the afternoon and Salvage parties in the morning fill up the day as far as it is possible to do so.	

Hunn Quinfs Lieut Colonel
Commanding 1/1st Batt The Monmouthshire Regt T.F.

Army Form C. 2118.

WAR DIARY
or
INTELLIGENCE SUMMARY.
(Erase heading not required.)

Instructions regarding War Diaries and Intelligence Summaries are contained in F.S. Regs., Part II and the Staff Manual respectively. Title pages will be prepared in manuscript.

Place	Date	Hour	Summary of Events and Information	Remarks and references to Appendices
BOUSIES	Jan 1st 1919		Salvage parties found as usual. The following have been mentioned in despatches dated 1/1/1919. Capt. W.B.T. REES. Lieut. F.L. MOORE - M.C. 228024 Sergt. G. HOWES.	
	2nd		Company parades held for T.O.J. & B.Z. and Ammo Drill 09.00 - 10.30 hrs. Battalion Parade for Route March 10.30 hrs. Weather fine but still cold and damp.	
	3rd		Salvage parties as usual.	
	4th		Salvage parties as usual.	
	5th		Church Parade for all denominations were held during the morning. 4 Other Ranks left the battalion to be demobilized.	
	6th		Training parade were carried out by companys in the morning consisting of T.O.J., Arms Drill and short route march. Batt. had 6th Division 2/5 inf. to N.co.m Rugby. Bouvines Boxing finals held at Bousies. Capt. E.J. Simkins went on special leave and will probably be demobilized in England. 5 Other Ranks left batt. to be demobilized.	
	7th		Salvage parties as usual. A grand concert was given in the Batt. recreation room by the Batt. concert party under Lieut. E.D. Stratchell. the room was packed and the concert was thoroughly enjoyed by all.	

Army Form C. 2118.

WAR DIARY
or
INTELLIGENCE SUMMARY.
(Erase heading not required.)

Instructions regarding War Diaries and Intelligence Summaries are contained in F. S. Regs., Part II. and the Staff Manual respectively. Title pages will be prepared in manuscript.

Place	Date	Hour	Summary of Events and Information	Remarks and references to Appendices
BOUSIES.	Jan 7th contd.		First really fine day we have had for about a month.	
	8		Salvage parties as usual. Another concert given by the B at Concert Party under Lt Peachell. Weather fine	
	9th		Training parade carried out by companies from 09.00 hrs to 12.00 hrs comprising P.J. Arms Drill and short march. 2nd Lt Garrett departed from hospital for duty and is posted to A Coy.	
	10th		Salvage parties as usual	
	11th		Salvage parties as usual.	
	12th		Church parade all Denominations.	
	13th		Training parade carried out by companies. Batt bathed at Brigade Baths.	
	14th		Salvage parties as usual. Brig Gen Whitcomby (commdg 148th Division) inspected the Education Scheme and B boys billets. M.C.	
	15th		Capt. W M B BURNYEAT left the battalion to be demobilized. Salvage parties as usual. Battalion played the 5th Sherwoods (Soccer) in first round of Corps Knock Out Competition, and won by 3 goals to 2. A concert was given in the battalion recreation room by the Beloncourt Party under 2nd Lt R. Peachell.	
	16th		Company training parade 09.00 hrs - 12.00 hrs.	
	17th		Salvage parties as usual.	
	18th		Salvage parties as usual. Major R.C.L.THOMAS M.C. left the battalion to be demobilized. Battalion bathed at Brigade Baths. Boxing Tournament held at the Kings Arms (to-night).	
	19th		Church parade all denominations. Brig Gen Pawley G.O.C. 2.30 attended the Church of England parade in the Lyceum BOUSIES at 11.00 hrs	

Army Form C. 2118.

WAR DIARY
or
INTELLIGENCE SUMMARY.
(Erase heading not required.)

Place	Date	Hour	Summary of Events and Information	Remarks and references to Appendices
BOUSIES	1918 Dec. 19th		Lt G.P. PEACHELL left the battalion to be demobilized. Batt" played 46th Div 17 to a 2nd round of Corps Soccer KnockOut Competition but lost by 3 goals to Nil.	
	20th		Training parades carried out by companies from 0900 hrs to 1200 hrs. A Coy commenced work on BOUSIES-FONTAINE Road, which consists of repairing a culvert which had been blown up during the Boche retreat and filled in solidly thus causing an immense flood on the left side of the road as you go towards FONTAINE.	
	21st		Salvage parties as usual. Lt SG BLOW MC left the battalion to be demobilized.	
	22nd		Salvage parties as usual. A lecture was given at the Coliseum BOUGIES by Capt E.S. Moore on Demobilization. 4 Officers and 50 other ranks of the battalion attended the lecture.	
	23rd		Training parades carried out by companies from 0900 hrs - 1200 hrs. 46th D.Bawn sent a Football team to Paris to play the STADE FRANCAIS &c. 11 C.Os and men of this unit were chosen for the Rugby team and one man for the soccer team. 2/1. L.Coo. Spectators were allowed to go with the team. Rugby team: C.Q.M.S. Stanton, 6pl White, 6pl Evans, L/Cpl Ward, 11/r Booth, 11/r Hathaway. Soccer: 11/r Pike. Systalions Sgt Sweet, Sgt Rudd.	
	24th		Salvage parties as usual.	
	25		Salvage and working parties found as usual.	

Army Form C. 2118.

WAR DIARY
or
INTELLIGENCE SUMMARY.
(Erase heading not required.)

Instructions regarding War Diaries and Intelligence Summaries are contained in F.S. Regs., Part II. and the Staff Manual respectively. Title pages will be prepared in manuscript.

Place	Date	Hour	Summary of Events and Information	Remarks and references to Appendices
BOUSIES	Jan 25th		Major General G.F. Boyd C.B. C.M.G. visited the battalion. 46th Division played the STADE FRANÇAIS. Results:— Soccer Team 46th Div. won 5 goals to Nil. Rugby Team (Drawn) 9 points all.	
"	26th		Church parades for all denominations. It snowed fairly hard. A concert was given in the Recreation Room by the Battalion Concert Party under 2/Lt A. Philipp.	
"	27th		All available men employed on clearing away snow from the vicinity of the billets. Lieut Y.A. PHILIPS left the battalion to be demobilized. Capt D.A. Martyn rejoined the unit from hospital. A battalion dance was held in the Recreation Room.	
"	28th		Salvage parties found as usual.	
"	29th		Salvage parties as usual. A boy completed work on BOUSIES-FONTAINE Road.	
"	30th		Company training parades carried out from 0900 hrs to 1200 hrs. A party from B Coy employed on dismantling a Y.M.C.A. hut near PREUX-AU-BOIS, to be erected in Bousies. 2nd Lieut C.T. BLACKALL struck off strength on being ordered a Medical Board in England whilst on leave.	
"	31st		Salvage parties were found as usual. Strength of Battalion 28 Officers 570 Other Ranks	

Hutton Lumsgy.
Lieut Colonel
Comdg 1/1st Bn. The Monmouthshire Regt. T.F.

1/1 Monmouth Reg¹
Army Form C. 2118.
No 45

WAR DIARY
or
INTELLIGENCE SUMMARY.
(Erase heading not required.)

Place	Date	Hour	Summary of Events and Information	Remarks, and references to Appendices
Bavai.	Feb 1/1919		Salvage parties found as usual.	
	2		No Church of England parades. Voluntary Service in the Brigade Recreation Room at 1100 hours, other denominations as usual.	
	3		Company Training parades from 09.00 hrs - 12.00 hrs. Salvage parties found as usual.	
	4		Battalion was inspected on the march by Major General G.F. BOYD. C.B. CMG. DCM. Dress, Fighting order with Steel helmets, but without box respirators. ROUTE Church Bavai, Square Brigade HQ Mues (Lsa 6'6 Sheet 57B 20000) Road through Transport lines and back to billets along Factory Rad. Saluting Point Lsa 6.6. The battalion was inspected with the 138 Infantry Brigade and followed the 4th Leicestershire Regt. past the Saluting point. Band played Regimental March while battalion marched past.	
	6		Salvage parties found as usual.	
	7		Salvage parties found as usual. Warning order received for Officers and men to be dispatched to Army of Occupation (2 Mon. Regt.) Lieut A.E.A.M. ATKINS appointment as Adjutant and Acting Captain was approved by G.O.C. XIII Corps.	
	8		Salvage parties found as usual.	

Army Form C. 2118.

WAR DIARY
or
INTELLIGENCE SUMMARY.
(Erase heading not required.)

Instructions regarding War Diaries and Intelligence Summaries are contained in F. S. Regs., Part II. and the Staff Manual respectively. Title pages will be prepared in manuscript.

Place	Date	Hour	Summary of Events and Information	Remarks and references to Appendices
Bouais	Feby 1919		Church parade for all denominations	
	10		Salvage parties found as usual.	
	11		Salvage parties found as usual. 15 men dispatched for demobilization. Men for Army of Occupation paraded and were divided into platoons and sections. Lt Col Phillips proceeded on leave, Capt S.R. Martyn took command.	
			The 7/O.E. gave permission for Capt S.R. Martyn to wear badges of rank of Major and Lieut A.W. Reynolds badges of rank of Subaltern during his [absence?]	
	12		The whole of the Battalion was employed in clearing the snow from and preparing the Battalion Football ground for the final of the Corps Football Competition to be held on the 13th inst. 17 men dispatched for demobilization.	
	13		Battalion employed same as yesterday 20 men dispatched for demobilization including R.S.M. Howden D.C.M.	
	14		Salvage parties found as usual. 29 men dispatched for demobilization	
	15		Company training parades 0900 hrs - 1200 hrs. 33 Other Ranks dispatched for demobilization	
	16		Church parade for N.C.s and O.Rs only a voluntary service for O.E.	
			25 dispatched for demobilization	
	17		Companies at the disposal of O.E. companies	
	18		Companies at the disposal of O.E. companies. Battalion having had orders to proceed to Montay of the 20th inst, an advance party under 2/Lt A.J. Cochrane was sent forward to prepare billets.	

WAR DIARY or INTELLIGENCE SUMMARY

Army Form C. 2118.

Place	Date	Hour	Summary of Events and Information	Remarks and references to Appendices
Bonau	Feb 19 1919		Companies at the disposal of O.C. Companies. Battalion moved from Bonau to Montay and left the 138 Infantry Brigade Group.	
"	20		The whole battalion is billeted on the hill at Montay. The Officers Mess in a Chateau both the mill and the chateau have been badly knocked about by shell fire. 25 Other Ranks kept for demobilization.	
Montay	21		All men employed on improving billets. Commanding Officer inspected billets at 11.10 hrs. Lt Col Green D.S.O. & 2/Lt 1 visited the battalion. O.C. visited battalion billets. Draft for 2nd Monmouths cancelled. 16 Other Ranks dispatched for demobilization.	
	22		Men employed on improving billets, building cookhouses, repairing roofs etc. No Church Parades. Voluntary services for all denominations held in the Bataau.	
	23		Men employed on repairing billets.	
	24		Companies at the disposal of O.C. Companies. Men employed on improving roofs of billets, following battalion dining room.	
	25		From today onwards all men in the battalion will be paraded at 09.00 hrs each day except Sundays. Dress khaki. Company fatigues will be told off and the remaining men will parade at 10.15 hrs for a short march. The officers not on duty will be in charge of both these parades. 13th Division played this 25th Division in the final of the Korps Rugby Competition	

Army Form C. 2118.

WAR DIARY
or
INTELLIGENCE SUMMARY.
(Erase heading not required.)

Instructions regarding War Diaries and Intelligence Summaries are contained in F.S. Regs, Part II. and the Staff Manual respectively. Title pages will be prepared in manuscript.

Place	Date	Hour	Summary of Events and Information	Remarks and references to Appendices
Monday	Feb 26	1919.	46th Division. 35th Division. Cpl. Ford, Rfn Booth and Rfn Vincent played for the 46th Division. Each member of the team was presented with a cup.	
	27		Parade carried out the same as yesterday. 1 Corporal and 20 other ranks were sent to the Divisional Reception Camp for temporary duty. 6 Other Ranks were sent to D.A.D.O.S. 46th Division for duty. Notification was received that the following N.C.O. and men had been awarded the Military Medal. 225322 Sgt. GRIFFITHS. G.G.W. 325203 Rfn. RALPH. H.C.	
	28		Parade were carried out as yesterday. The Officers played the Boy Soccer Result B Coy 3 gols - Officers 1 goal	

Marten Phillips Lt. Col Commanding
1/2 Bn Monmouthshire Regt JJ

46th.Div.Packet.

　　　　　　Herewith copy of War Diary for the month of March please.

　　　　　　　　　　　　　　　　　　Hman Phillips Lieut-Colonel,
5-4-19.　　　　　　　　　　Commanding I/Ist Bn The Monmouthshire Regt.T.F.

46

1/1 Monmouth Rgt 46

Army Form C. 2118.

WAR DIARY
or
INTELLIGENCE SUMMARY.
(Erase heading not required.)

Instructions regarding War Diaries and Intelligence Summaries are contained in F. S. Regs., Part II and the Staff Manual respectively. Title pages will be prepared in manuscript.

Place	Date	Hour	Summary of Events and Information	Remarks and references to Appendices
MONTAY.	1/3/19	—	G.O.C. 46th Division visited the Battalion. The Adjutant and 2nd Lieut H.B. Paragrouts(?) received orders to return for demobilization. Bus on arrival at CAUDRY received orders to return — Demobilization being temporally stopped owing to Congestion at Corps demobilization Camp CORBEHEM. The Officers played HQ men Soccer in the afternoon. Result - Draw. One goal each. Summer time came into force at 23.00hrs today. Church parades for all denominations were Voluntary. 18 Other Ranks (men retainable for the Army of Occupation) dispatched for duty with Chief Ordnance Officer. CALAIS. Batt. received orders to move to TROISVILLES on the 5th Inst. Lieut Col. J.G. Phillips returned from leave to the U.K.	
MONTAY.	2/3/19	—		
MONTAY.	3/3/19	—	The usual parades were carried out at 09.00hours and 11.15 hours.	
			A telegram was received from 46th Division ordering 2 Officers and 200 other ranks, Volunteers or Retainable men to be sent to the 24th Batt Royal Welch Fusiliers. DUNKIRK.	
MONTAY.	4/3/19	—	An advanced party consisting of 2 Officers and 20 Other Ranks, under Lieut J.H.T. Cochrane, was sent to TROISVILLES to prepare billets for the Battalion.	
TROISVILLES.	5/3/19	—	Battalion moved billets to TROISVILLES. Very little fighting has been done in TROISVILLES and the Village is in very good repair — Billets are good. We are not as compact as MONTAY. The 137 Infantry Brigade also moved to TROISVILLES today. Lieut W.F. Williams returned from leave to England.	
TROISVILLES.	6/3/19	—	Companies were at the disposal of O.C. Companies. A party under 2/Lieut. R.T. Phelps commenced erecting a Cookhouse.	
TROISVILLES.	7/3/19	—	All men for the Army of Occupation paraded at 11.00hours. Brig.-Gen N.L. Hornby, A.D.C. 137 Infantry Brigade visited the Battalion. The C.O. inspected billets. 10 Other Ranks despatched for Demobilization.	
TROISVILLES.	8/3/19	—	Companies were at the disposal of O.C. Companies for interior economy. Special attention being paid to the Clothing, Boots, and small kit of the men for the Army of Occupation. The C.O. held a Conference of Company Commanders, T.O. and Q.M. at 10.00 hours — re draft. 4 Other Ranks Dispatched for Demobilization. Voluntary Service for Church of England held in No 5 Billet TROISVILLES at 18.00 hours. One Other Rank dispatch for Demobilization.	
TROISVILLES	9/3/19	—	All available N.C.O's. and men paraded on the Road outside. Orderly Room at 09.30 hours, for Short Route march, all Company refusing to fall into Dress, Fighting Order (less Steel Helmets and Box Respirators.) Q.M. commenced taking over Stores. Orders received that all waggons not in use, to be parked near CAUDRY Station on the 13th Inst.	
TROISVILLES	10/3/19	—		
TROISVILLES	11/3/19	—	Route march for all available W.C.Os. and men, the Same as yesterday. The Officers played "A" Coy. Soccer, but were beaten by 4 goals to nil.	
TROISVILLES	12/3/19	—	Route march the same as yesterday. 4 Other Ranks dispatched for Demobilization.	

WAR DIARY
or
INTELLIGENCE SUMMARY.
(Erase heading not required.)

Army Form C. 2118.

Place	Date	Hour	Summary of Events and Information	Remarks and references to Appendices
TROISVILLES.	13/3/19.		Draft paraded at 13.30 hours and being checked with Roll, were sent to the Field Ambulance for scabies inspection. All available men bathed at Le Cateau during the morning. Capt. A.E.R.M. ATKINS proceeded on leave and Lieut D.W. Hughes acted as Adjutant during his absence. Orders received for the draft to proceed to Dunkirk.	
TROISVILLES.	14/3/19		Draft of 2 Officers (Lieut. J.J. WALTERS and 2nd Lieut W.T. REMPER) and 127 Other Ranks paraded at about 13.30 hours and marched to Caudry, where they entrained during the afternoon for L. Batt. Royal Welch Fusiliers at Dunkirk.	
TROISVILLES.	15/3/19		Demobilization having begun for officers as follows: All officers over 37 years of age and 50% of the officers who advanced either for commissioned service from the Ranks in 1914. The following officers proceeded from the Unit: Major S.R. Martyn, Capt. J.M. Reynolds and 2nd Lieut A. Sutton. The Commander-in-Chief (F.M. Sir Douglas Haig) invited all Divisional H.Q. and 2nd Lieut A. Sutton. The Commanding Officers were invited to meet him.	
TROISVILLES.	16/3/19		Voluntary Church of England Services were held morning and Evening. 7 Other Ranks (including Sgt A/R.S.M. Griffiths E.W. M.M.) left the Battalion for Demobilization. Sgt Wilson, the Battalion Orderly Room Sergeant and Sgt Jenkin, the Officers Mess Sergeant left the Battalion for Demobilization.	
TROISVILLES.	17/3/19		The Battalion formed into one Company with Lieut W.F. Williams in command for Administrative purposes. Inter Company transfers will not take place at present. 1 other rank left for Demobilization from 46 Div. Reception Camp. Capt. A.L.C. Mackenzie R.A.M.C. & Major S. Jarret and 2/Lt W.H. Williams returned from short leave with United Kingdom.	
TROISVILLES.	18/3/19		1 other Rank left his Unit for Demobilization. Capt A.L.C. Mackenzie R.A.M.C. attached left Unit to proceed to Boulogne to join 137 Infantry Brigade.	
TROISVILLES.	19/3/19		The Divisional Commander (Major General G.T. Boyd C.B. C.M.G. D.S.O.) on leaving the Division came to the 137 Infantry Brigade H.Q. TROISVILLES. To say goodbye to the Troops. All Officers, N.C.O.'s and men were invited to meet him at 11.00 hours. The Commanding Officer dined with the G.O.C. at Divisional H.Q.	
TROISVILLES.	20/3/19		EXTRACTS FROM BATTALION ORDERS 20-3-19. HONOURS AND AWARDS. The Commanding Officer has much pleasure in notifying and congratulates the recipients:- Military Cross - Capt. E.G. BEC. MEDAL. EXTRACTS FROM LONDON GAZETTE 17/3/19. Major (A/Lt-Col) F.G. PHILLIPS to be Temp Lt-Col. (Dt 29/11/1918). A kit inspection, for all details and belongings will be held tomorrow at 9/c Battalion orders 24/2/19 nature and awards officer has not place above. No 7/c the Recipient "MEDAILLE BARBATTE DE CREDANTA 3rd Class" Rfn. PENROSE. R.F. Voluntary Church of England Services were held during the day.	
TROISVILLES.	22/3/19		2 other Ranks left unit for Re-enlistment in the Regular Army.	
TROISVILLES.	23/3/19		Demobilization opened up to all officers over 35 years of age, and all other officers named below 1st Jan 1916 could be released. The following officers left the Unit for Demobilization. Lieut P.D. Milligan. Lieut E. Mortimer. Lieut G.H.T. Cochrane. Lieut H.F. Williams and Lieut R.A. Baker.	
TROISVILLES.	24/3/19		46th Div. H.Q. moved from TROISVILLES to CAUDRY. Lieut. General S.M. Morland on leaving the XIIIth Corps sent the following farewell message: "On leaving the XIIIth Corps I wish to express to the G.O.C. the Divisional Generals and Staffs, Brigadiers and all Ranks of the Division my hearty thanks for their loyalty and good work during their service in the Corps. I wish them all the best of luck in their future - whether in the Army or Civil life."	
TROISVILLES.	26/3/19		A draft of 40 Other Ranks left this Unit to join the 24th Royal Welsh Fus. at Denain 2/Lt R.W. Williams acted as Draft Conducting Officer. The party entrained at CAUDRY.	
TROISVILLES.	27/3/19		The last of the Riding Horses in the Unit were dispatched for de-mobilisation.	
TROISVILLES.	28/3/19		Battalion Rugger v/ 1/5th North Staffords. Soccer Result Draw. 2 goals each.	
TROISVILLES.	29/3/19		Voluntary M.C. Service was held in the Church Army hut/store at TROISVILLES.	
TROISVILLES.	30/3/19		Auxiliary N.C. ATKINS returned to the Unit from leave, and took up the duties of Adjutant. Lieut. D.W. Hughes left the Unit for Demobilization.	
TROISVILLES.	31/3/19		Capt A.E.R.M. ATKINS returned to the Unit for Demobilization including a for Re-enlistment in Regular Army. Brig Gen L. Hornby Commanding 5 Other Ranks left the Unit for Demobilization. 46th Division Visited the Battalion. Strength of Battalion. EFFECTIVE OFFICERS. 21.5. Officer Ranks 247. Actual OTHER RANKS. 443	

Countersigned. 1/1/ (signed) For the Monmouthshire Regt.
(signed) Lieut-Colonel.

1/1 Monmouth Rgt
Vol 4+7

WAR DIARY.
for
April
1919

1/1st Bn The Monmouthshire regt. T.F.

WAR DIARY
or
INTELLIGENCE SUMMARY

Army Form C. 2118.

1/1st Bn. The Monmouthshire Regt. "T.F."

April 1919

Place	Date	Hour	Summary of Events and Information	Remarks and references to Appendices
TRI/5N/2225	1.4.19		All men with the Battalion are being transferred to "A" Coy. from today. The 46th Division will be called the "46th Divisional Packet" and is commanded by Brig. Gen. M.L. Hornby, C.M.G., D.S.O.	
	2.4.19		Orders received that an Inspection Committee would visit the Battalion and inspect stores, equipment etc. Orders received that an Audit Board of which the President and one other member are to be from another Battalion is to hold an all Battalion Accounts and a Balance Sheet together with a certificate to March 31st 1919 is to be sent to D.A.Q.G. by the 10th inst.	
	3.4.19		Baths at CAUDRY allotted to this Unit. G.R.O. received saying that all Officers who joined before 1st Jan 1917 who were surplus to requirements could be released.	
	4.4.19		In view of the fact that the remaining animals are to be sent away tomorrow all the vehicles at present with the Battalion have been parked with the others near CAUDRY Station.	
	5.4.19		The Inspection Committee consisting of the late D.A.D.O.S. 46th Division and a number of N.C.O's visited the Battalion and inspected all surplus stores. All remaining animals on the Unit entrained at CAUDRY for the 2nd Army COLOGNE.	
	6.4.19		Capt & Qrmaster R.H. Martin M.C. proceeded on leave to the U.K. The N.C. voluntary service arranged for to-day has been cancelled, as the N.C. Padre is proceeding to the Rhine. - 2 N.C. service was held at INCHY at 1000 hrs.	
	7.4.19		Lieut S. Jarrett and one other rank (for re-enlistment) despatched for Demobilization. One man despatched to the 25th Royal Welsh Fusiliers. The Battalion played the R.A.S.C. Soccer. Result - Drawn. No score.	
	8.4.19		Battalion played a Battery of the 18th Division Soccer (whom we beat by 2 goals to nil.	
	9.4.19		The 46th Divisional Packet Reception Camp is being closed to-day and Lieut. Adjutant L.J. Pitt is posted to this Unit for duty, with effect from to-day.	
	10.4.19		G.O.C. 46th Divisional Packet (Brig. General Hornby) visited this Battalion.	

Army Form C. 2118.

WAR DIARY
or
INTELLIGENCE SUMMARY.
(Erase heading not required.)

Instructions regarding War Diaries and Intelligence Summaries are contained in F. S. Regs., Part II. and the Staff Manual respectively. Title pages will be prepared in manuscript.

Place	Date	Hour	Summary of Events and Information	Remarks and references to Appendices
TROUVILLES.	11.4.19		All stores surplus to A.F. G1098. were handed in to the Intermediate Collecting Station. CLOUDY.	
	12.4.19		Major W.V. Jones returned from short leave in the U.K.	
	13.4.19		Voluntary services were held for C of E. and R.C's. The Battalion played Capt. Smith's team (which was picked from the remainder of the Division) Rugby but were beaten by 6 points to 3. Lt-Col F.G. Phillips refereed the match. The game was played at 6TH ENGCMT before a considerable number of spectators. It rained very hard at times during the match.	
	14.4.19		Today is the worst day we have had this month. It is raining quite hard.	
	15.4.19		Weather still very unsettled, cold, and wet.	
	16.4.19		It is proposed to reduce the Cadres, by 25% or 50%. The Unit will reach it 25%	
	17.4.19		Nil.	
	18.4.19		Brig-General M.L. Hornby visited the Battalion.	
	19.4.19		Nil	
	20.4.19		Voluntary Church Parades held for C of E and R.C's. Battalion beat Remainder of Division Rugby - won by 16 pts to 3.	
	21.4.19		Nil.	
	22.4.19		Major J.W.F. Marshall visited the Unit to inspect the Unit Register - A.F. G500.	
	23.4.19		25 Other ranks went to VILLENEUVES in a lorry supplied by Division. G.R.O. published saying that all Officers and other ranks supplies to requirements who had had no leave to the Army of Occupation could be demobilised. Capt. + Q.M. W.H. Marston M.C. returned from leave in the U.K.	
	24.4.19		Nil.	
	25.4.19		Division supplied another lorry for the remaining men to go to VILLENEUVES.	
	26.4.19		Voluntary R. of E services held in CLOUDY. 2nd Lieut H.H. Rowland proceeded on leave to U.K.	
	27.4.19		Nil	
	28.4.19		Nil	
	29.4.19		Nil	
	30.4.19			

Hector Phillips Lieut Colonel
Commanding 1/3th Monmouthshire Regt T.F.

Strength of Battalion:
Officers 10. O. Ranks 34.
Other Ranks 34

46th DIVISIONAL PACKET.

Herewith copy of War Diary for the month of MAY 1919.

4-6-19.

[signature]
Lieut-Colonel.
Commanding 1/1st Bn The Monmouthshire Regt. T.F.

MAY, 1919.

WAR DIARY
or
INTELLIGENCE SUMMARY.

Army Form C. 2118.

1/@ Bn. The Monmouthshire Regt. T.F.

(Erase heading not required.)

Place	Date	Hour	Summary of Events and Information	Remarks and references to Appendices
TROISVILLES	1-5-19	—	4th Divisional Packet supplied a lorry for a party from this Unit to go to 'LILLE'. The lorry broke down about 9 Kilos out of CAMBRAI, so the party got back to CAMBRAI and spent the night there, and proceeded on by another lorry on the following day.	
TROISVILLES	2-5-19	—	A new officers mess cart (two wheeled) was drawn from Ordnance in place of the four wheeled one, which has become unserviceable.	
TROISVILLES	3-5-19	—	The party returned from the trip to LILLE.	
TROISVILLES	4-5-19	—	A Memorial service for the Allied fallen and the British Soldiers buried in CAUDRY Cemetery was held at CAUDRY. Voluntary Church of England Services were held at CAUDRY also.	
TROISVILLES	5-5-19	—	The Unserviceable Officers mess cart was handed in Ordnance CAUDRY. A quantity of Demobilization Stoves were drawn. A S.S/Sergt Hibbert left the Unit for Re-engagement furlough.	
TROISVILLES	6-5-19	—	The Divisional preliminaries to the 13th Corps Group Packet Sports were held at the Aerodrome CAUDRY at 14-30 hours. Orders received that Cadres of Infantry Battalions are to be reduced to 3 Officers and 36 Other Ranks.	
TROISVILLES	7-5-19	—	Lt-Col. F.G. Phillips proceeded on 5 days leave to Paris.	
TROISVILLES	8-5-19	—	The Fourth Anniversary of the Second Battle of Ypres.	
TROISVILLES	9-5-19	—	2nd Lieut Pritchard proceeded on short leave to the United Kingdom.	
TROISVILLES	10-5-19	—	The XIII Corps Group Packet Sports Gala was held at the Aerodrome CAUDRY.	
TROISVILLES	11-5-19	—	The 4th Division played the 122nd French Engineers "Rugby" at BETHENCOURT and won by 6 points to 3 points. 18 Officers and 4 Other Ranks from this Unit played for the Division, and the 2 Tries scored by the Division were scored by Sgt Cartwright and Rfn Hughes of this Unit.	
TROISVILLES	12-5-19	—	"NIL"	
TROISVILLES	13-5-19	—	"NIL"	
TROISVILLES	14-5-19	—	A hockey match was played between the 137th Inf Bde (including 1/1st Mon's Regt) and the 139 Inf Bde at BETHENCOURT. Lt.Col. F.G.Phillips returned from leave in Paris.	
TROISVILLES	15-5-19	—	Orders Received that the Cadre of a Pioneer Battalion would be reduced from 4 Officers and 41 Other Ranks to 3 Officers and 36 Other Ranks.	
TROISVILLES	16-5-19	—	The Battalion played the TROISVILLES Rovers in Soccer and won by 2 goals to nil. 2nd Lieut W.H. Rowlands returned from short leave to the United Kingdom.	
TROISVILLES	17-5-19	—	NIL	

MAY 1919.
WAR DIARY or INTELLIGENCE SUMMARY.
(Erase heading not required.)

1/2 Bn. The Monmouthshire Regt. T.F. Army Form C. 2118.

Place	Date	Hour	Summary of Events and Information	Remarks and references to Appendices
TROISVILLES	18-5-19	—	NIL.	
TROISVILLES	19-5-19	—	NIL.	
TROISVILLES	20-5-19	—	NIL.	
TROISVILLES	21-5-19	—	The 139 Inf Bde (including 1/2 Monmouthshire Regt) played the 139 Inf Bde at TROISVILLES Hockey. The result was: 139 Inf Bde won by 7 goals to 5. 1st. Col. F.G. Phillips and 2nd Lieut K.H. Williams played for the 2/137 Inf Bde.	
TROISVILLES	22-5-19	—	NIL.	
TROISVILLES	23-5-19	—	2nd Lieut H.H. Rowland left this Unit to be demobilized. This Unit played the 6th. N. Staffs Regt in Cricket and won by 19 Runs.	
TROISVILLES	24-5-19	—	NIL.	
TROISVILLES	25-5-19	—	Voluntary Services for Church of England and Non-Conformists were held at CAUDRY. A Memorial Service was held by the French in TROISVILLES to the French and English fallen during the War. A number of Officers and Other Ranks from this Unit attended.	
TROISVILLES	26-5-19	—	A proposal was received to reduce cadres to 2 Officers and 12 Other Ranks.	
TROISVILLES	27-5-19	—	A picnic for all troops in the Corps, was held on the Southern border of the forest de Mormal at HOCHETTE/BADGE. 7 Other Ranks from this Unit went. The Corps provided Tea, Cake, etc.	
TROISVILLES	28-5-19	—	The Battalion played the 1/3rd N.M. Field Ambulance Cricket and Won by 40 Runs.	
TROISVILLES	29-5-19	—	Division supplied a lorry for a party of men to go to VALENCIENNES. 2nd Lieut A. Jones left Unit to be Demobilized (Repatriation to the UNITED STATES).	
TROISVILLES	30-5-19	—	Orders received that the remaining retainable Other Ranks, would be sent to join the 6th South Wales Borderers under Records wire "C.M. 69 dated 28-5-19."	
TROISVILLES	31-5-19	—	7 Other Ranks (retainable) were dispatched to join the 6th S.W.B. (30th Division) at DUNKIRK. The Battalion played the 1/3rd N.M. Field Ambulance Cricket but lost by one Run.	

EFFECTIVE STRENGTH OF BATT.
OFFRS. 9. O.R.S. 34.
31-5-19 CAPTAIN STRENGTH = 6. 24.

Gordon Phillips
Lieut-Colonel.
Commanding 1/1st Bn. The Monmouthshire Regt. T.F.

46th Div Packet.   427

1st BATTALION,
THE MONMOUTHSHIRE
REGIMENT.
No. 4462
Date 21·07·19

Herewith War Diary
to date.

[signature] Capt + Adjt.
OC Equipment Guard
1/1 Mon. Regt.

46th DIVISIONAL PACKET

Herewith War Diary for the month of June 1919.

> 1st BATTALION,
> THE MONMOUTHSHIRE
> REGIMENT.
> No. 4116
> Date 2/7/19.

R.H.Marsh
Capt & QrMr,
O.C. Equipment Guard I/1st Monmouthshire Regt.T.F.

WAR DIARY
INTELLIGENCE SUMMARY

Army Form C. 2118.

1/1 Monmouth

Place	Date	Hour	Summary of Events and Information	Remarks and references to Appendices
TROSVILLES	1/6/19	10.30	A Church of England Parade Service was held for all troops in TROSVILLES in the field adjacent to the 6th South Staffords Officers Mess	
		11.30	The battalion played no. 283 A.T. Coy R.E. cricket and won by 105 runs	
	2/6/19	16.15	Orders received that the Battalion would be reduced to 2 officers and 10 other ranks, to be known as the Equipment Guard. The remaining personnel known as the Cadre are to be sent home as soon as possible. Stores are to be packed in the Depot as Cadre and a decent place over items. The unit is forming Cavalry and 137 Infantry Brigade for the purpose.	
	3/6/19		With the 137 Infantry Brigade the 139 Infantry Brigade and H.M. the King's Birthday was held. Lord Gort which were representatives to celebrate H.M. the King's Birthday.	
			The 1/1 Monmouthshire Regt. held none representatives. The unit was supplied.	
	5/6/19		The following officers left the unit to join the Overseas of men. Boys Lieut N.C. Buckland 96th P.O.W. Coy. Lieut W.P. Hopes 107 P.O.W. Coy. Lieut R.B. Williams 116 P.O.W. Coy and Lieut W.J. Pitt 128 P.O.W. Coy. All these officers are volunteers for the Armies of Occupation.	
	26/6/19		The following Honours and Rewards were made this week on the occasion of H.M. the King's Birthday (June 3)	
			MILITARY CROSS LIEUT J.H. PHILIPS	
			DISTINGUISHED CONDUCT MEDAL	
			225011 C.S.M. Taylor J.	
			7254402 Sgt Rudd W.E.	
			226234 Sgt SPOONER R.H.	

WAR DIARY
or
INTELLIGENCE SUMMARY

Army Form C. 2118.

Place	Date	Hour	Summary of Events and Information	Remarks and references to Appendices
TROISVILLES	6.6.19		Division supplied a lorry to move all stores into the wagons at the wagon park at Oudry.	
	7.6.19		A lorry was again supplied to complete movement of stores. Instructions were received that all stores would be placed in packages and would be labelled to the destination in packages and would be labelled to the destination in	
	8.6.19		ENGLAND. Voluntary Church of England service were held in Nav. Sunday. Oudry.	
	9.6.19		NIL	
	10.6.19		NIL	
	11.6.19		The Battalion played the 46th Divisional Picket Cricket but lost the score being 46th Divisional Pkt. 77 runs for 3 wickets, 1/5 Leic. 49 runs.	
	12.6.19		NIL	
	13.6.19		NIL	
	14.6.19		The Division supplied a lorry for a party from the unit to go to VALENCIENNES.	
	15.6.19		Voluntary Church of England service were held in Oudry.	
	16.6.19		NIL	
	17.6.19		NIL	
	18.6.19		NIL	
	19.6.19		Orders received that the Cadre consisting of L/Cpl Phillips & 2 other rank would proceed to CAMBRAI on the 23rd inst.	

WAR DIARY or INTELLIGENCE SUMMARY

Army Form C. 2118.

Place	Date	Hour	Summary of Events and Information	Remarks and references to Appendices
TROISVILLES	20.6.19		Bn Boys are building a number of Bonfires on the LE CATEAU 1914 Battlefield for the Peace Celebrations — the next lad to find a Team of 1 NCO & 3 men on No 4 Bonfire N. of BERTRY.	
	21.6.19		Nil	
	22.6.19	1145	A Church of England service was held on the field adjoining the Officers Mess of the 6th Staffordshire Rgt.	
	23.6.19		Germany accepted the Allies Peace terms unconditionally. Orders received that the EQUIPMENT GUARD is to move into BOUDRY on the 25th inst.	
	24.6.19		Nil	
	25.6.19	0930	The Battn (Col L.G. Phillips and 20 other ranks) left before for CAMBRAI on route for the United Kingdom. Major General G.F. Glasgow & Officers was received from Major General G.F. Boyd CB CMG DSO saying Good bye Good luck & well done Monmouths.	Col ROSWELLS & Bn R Boyd
BOUDRY	26.6.19		Peace Celebrations were arranged by the Br R Boyd and Hon Bye-Products. The following Peace Celebration — Thanksgiving services C.E. and Non Conformists.	
			1. Routine 10.30am	
			2. Hippodrome —— Football match French v British (Buckley Game) 2.30pm French Military Band. Free tea to all Regts.	
			3. Public 6 to 8 —— Concert 6. Factory Transvaal — Bell Glow at 2am	
			4. Hippodrome —— Concert 8.15 to 10	
			5. Hippodrome —— Fireworks to 10pm	
			6. Bonfires on LE CATEAU Battlefield of 1914 lit at 10.30pm	

Army Form C. 2118.

WAR DIARY
or
INTELLIGENCE SUMMARY.
(Erase heading not required.)

Instructions regarding War Diaries and Intelligence Summaries are contained in F. S. Regs., Part II. and the Staff Manual respectively. Title pages will be prepared in manuscript.

Place	Date	Hour	Summary of Events and Information	Remarks and references to Appendices
CRUDRY	27.6.19		The Equipment Guard moved from ROSULLES to CRUDRY and billeted in 90 & 92 Rue St Quentin. B & 6ays arranged some swimming, but the bath reservoir had to be postponed owing to the bath heater.	
	28.6.19	5.12.	The Germans signed the Peace Treaty at VERSAILLES	
	29.6.19		Voluntary Church of England services were held.	
	30.6.19	10.0.	Orders received that a unit (Serial No 6486) would arrive on No 6 train carrying Booty destination for baggage BULNELL. The first train will probably arrive BULNELL about 7th July. Orderly Room records to are to be transferred to Race H.Q. & baggage lighter through N.T.O. Cambrai. Baggage consigned to Race H.Q.	

EFFECTIVE STRENGTH:

Officers	ORS	Equipment Guard	ORS
3	34		90 10
			2

RATION STRENGTH:
2   9

K. M. M. Kenton
Capt & Adjt
O. Equipment Guard 1/st Monmouthshire Regt. T.F.

Capt & Adjt
1/st Monmouthshire Regt. T.F.

Army Form C. 2118.

WAR DIARY
INTELLIGENCE SUMMARY.
(Erase heading not required.)

1/1 Bn The MONMOUTHSHIRE REGT 77.

Place	Date	Hour	Summary of Events and Information	Remarks and references to Appendices
Caudry	3.7.19		Orders received that Capt & Q.M. R.H. MARTIN. M.C. is to proceed to join 1st Labour Group at ROUEN.	
	6.7.19		Voluntary Church of England Services were held in Caudry.	
	8.7.19		Capt. R.H. MARTIN M.C. proceeded to join the 1st Labour Group ROUEN.	
	13.7.19		Capt. R.E.A.M. PERKINS assumed command of the Equipment Guard and Capt & Major S.J. LLOYD reported for duty from Bury attached to The Tank Corps.	
	14.7.19		France celebrated the Taking of Paris.	
	16.7.19		Capt & Major S.J. LLOYD reported at the Corps Concentration Camp to be disposed.	
	18.7.19		Orders received from 46th Divisional PICKET that the Equipment Guard would entrain at Caudry Station on 22.7.19.	
	19.7.19		Being the day arranged for the Equipment Peace Celebrations XIII Corps arranged a fieté at HACHETTE. FEAST OF NORMAL. The 46th Divisional PICKET H.Q. at 09.30 toured and returned about 21.30. Tea was provided for all ranks.	
	20.7.19		Voluntary Services were held in the Church (Army Room).	
	21.7.19		138 Infantry Brigade H.Q. is attached to this unit from to-day. The following Officers and others ranks were mentioned in Ld. Songs's MARCH 1919.	
			OFFICERS OTHER RANKS	
			Lt Col Ths. PHILLIPS VARD. Col. VOKES. H. L/Cpl SIDNEY. H.E.	
			Lt. C. .... F.H. Ptes PERKINS. H.	
				Acting C.M.S. Capt. Mayr
				1/1 Equipment Monmouthshire 77
	22.7.19			